Data Analytics With R

A hands-on approach

SECOND EDITION

VISWA VISWANATHAN

Infivista Inc.

PUBLISHED BY INFIVISTA INC.

ISBN-10: 1941773028

ISBN-13: 978-1-941773-02-4

August 2015

Contents

List of Figures

List of Tables

Dedicated to three women who have taught me much: my late aunt Anandavalli, my sister Sankari and my wife Shanthi.

Preface

It would hardly surprise me if you are asking the deadly "WABOX" question – "Why another book on X?" (substituting "Data Analytics" for X). Answering that would be a great place for me to start.

I teach an MBA course on data analytics for students from diverse backgrounds. I describe below three representative students (with their names changed).

Joe, a senior executive from a hospital wanted to put the rich data from his hospital to good use. For example, he wanted to find out which of his recently discharged patients had a high likelihood of being readmitted within 30 days. Having been a doctor for many years, Joe's mathematical skills had rusted; he had not used any software beyond Microsoft Office and his hospital management software. Yet, based on things he had heard and read, he seemed sold on the idea that his organization ought to be doing more with data. Ready to get his hands dirty and hoping to learn the ropes, he enrolled in my class.

Brenda, a marketing manager at a luxury car dealership wanted to see how she might use her promotional budget wisely. She had run direct mail campaigns with expensive brochures and invitations to test-drive vehicles. She had tried her best to mail the brochures to households that she felt were squarely in the target group. However, she faced the problems of poor response rates and inappropriate respondents. Several respondents who had no intention of buying a vehicle took up her dealership's valuable time and resources by test driving vehicles just for the fun of it. Brenda felt frustrated and wanted to see if she could use data to do better. She hoped that my course would help her.

Carolyn, an administrator at a university, had access to a lot of data but felt that her school was not making use of this rich resource to make better decisions. She had turned to my course to empower her to make an impact at work.

Joe, Brenda and Carolyn, and most of my other students, lack a solid grounding in mathematics or have rusty mathematical skills. They would have trouble learning to use mathematical software tools on their own. They would have been out of place in a typical analytics course that used standard texts requiring a significant amount of mathematical knowledge.

I had been looking for a suitable text for my course – the kind of text that Joe, Brenda and Carolyn would find useful. I tried a few, but failed to find one that addressed the topic at an appropriate level for my students. Specifically, I was looking for something that preferred intuitive explanations over rigorous mathematics. My students needed not just the concepts, but also extensive guidance in translating the concepts into practice using a free software tool that they would continue to use after completing my course.

No luck. I ended up trying a few inadequate (for our needs) texts and then spending much time on preparing extensive supporting material and guides for hands-on use of the software. I found my students relying almost exclusively on my materials rather than on the prescribed texts. Yet they learned the concepts and ended up with a good working knowledge of the software too.

Based on my experience, I felt that more people would benefit from a drastically different approach to teaching business analytics. These days most people in business and other domains use computers, and frequently use data to accomplish tasks. Yet, quite unnecessarily, the skills for extracting value from data continue to remain the exclusive preserve of a few.

Anyone who has completed high-school mathematics and has sufficient motivation and the skills to use a computer can acquire useful analytics skills. They might not grasp the underlying mathematics fully, nor might they be able to write programming code to perform data analysis. Yet they can learn to do very useful things. Equally importantly, when needed, they will be able to talk intelligently to an analytics expert to get help with some of the more advanced aspects.

Hence this book.

I have written this book to be useful as a one-stop self-study guide for the motivated reader.

If you are already well-versed in analytics or are looking for a mathematically-oriented treatment then this book might not be or you.

If, on the other hand, you want to develop your hands-on analytical skills but do not want to be tied down by the underlying mathematics that typical books on the topic will require, then this book can help. I am confident that the intuitive explanations of the concepts and the step by step guidance on using powerful software to actually apply the concepts will empower you.

Getting Started

In October 2006, Netflix, the current leader in dvd-rentals and video streaming, initiated a public competition with a $1 million award. The task – to improve by 10% the company's current method of predicting customers' ratings of movies that they have not yet seen. A million dollars for a measly 10% improvement?

Netflix did find a winning team and the CEO remarked[1] that, on the average, people liked one out of three movies they watched and that he expected this 10% improvement to boost it to two out of three. This, in turn, would significantly enhance Netflix's ability to retain customers at a time when people have many video streaming and rental options.

[1] D. MacMillan. Netflix, AT&T are real winners of Netflix Prize, September 2009. URL `http://www.businessweek.com/the_thread/techbeat/archives/2009/09/netflix_att_are.html`

Later in the book, we will go into more details about problems like these. For now, we want only to highlight how powerful even a seemingly minuscule 10% improvement can be.

Companies have been using automated transaction processing systems for several decades now to conduct their operations. As a by product of this they end up with huge amounts of valuable data that reveals useful intelligence.

Computer based systems produce large amounts of data as a by product of routine operations.

More recently, web giants like Google, Facebook Amazon and Twitter have been able to find surprising uses for seemingly insignificant information gathered from the hundreds of millions of user interactions they facilitate daily.

Web based applications have the potential to gather stupendous amounts of data as millions of people interact with them each day.

Far too many organizations – despite having sophisticated transaction processing systems that produce huge amounts of useful data as a by-product of operations – fail to exploit the goldmine that data represents.

Today more and more organizations have awoken to the rich promise of analytics. Researchers and practitioners have racked up many success stories. We have at our fingertips many well-tested techniques and incredibly powerful free and commercial software products. The unending march of Moore's Law has also helped to increase our ability to process data. Computer

Advances in computer hardware and software constantly enhance our ability to gather and process huge amounts of data.

scientists have also been continuously enhancing our ability to manipulate huge quantities of data by developing means to process large data sets on thousands of computers simultaneously. All this means that almost all of us have the resources to extract value from whatever data we have access to.

This book will demystify some of the commonly used techniques and help you to master the process of using analytics software to apply these techniques. Given the amount of publicly available data and the easy access to them[2], you might be able to think up some interesting personal projects as well.

[2] P. Warden. *Data source handbook: A guide to public data.* O'Reilly Media, January 2011

To benefit fully from the book, you should be comfortable with high-school level mathematics and possess basic skills in using computers. Even more importantly, you will need lots of curiosity and should be willing to experiment and to get your hands dirty. We learn practical skills only by doing and not by just listening or reading.

This book will give you sufficient background knowledge and guidance to enable you to get on the computer and actually apply the techniques that we cover. It explains every method through simple, but carefully designed illustrative examples. It provides many review questions, lab activities and lab assignments (with suggested answers) for you to learn and practice. I have designed the lab activities in such a way that you will not just mechanically carry out the tasks and see the results; instead you will perform the steps and *understandin* what you did and why. The text in the chapters explains the concepts, and the lab activities and exercises provide you an ideal platform to cement your understanding and take ownership of the concepts and skills. The step-by-step guidance will also serve as a useful reference later on as you apply these ideas at work.

One-stop shop for starting with data-analytics.

Seamless integration of concepts, exercises and software guidance.

When learning new things, we face challenges and frequently get frustrated to some degree as the new learning forces our brains to rewire themselves. To continue the learning process in the face of such challenges we need to experience the joys of small and large successes to offset the inevitable frustrations. The labs and lab assignments play a big role in orchestrating these successes. So, I recommend that you do as much of hands-on practice as you possibly can.

Labs and lab assignments form the backbone of this book.

In this book, we use the free analytics package **R**. Just because it is free, don't come to any negative conclusions about its power or stability – many commercial software packages have **R** at their core. **R** can be used for processing very large

We will use the free, powerful and widely used **R** software package.

data sets. Many large companies routinely use it for their analytics applications. Once you understand the concepts and learn the features of **R** that I cover, you will be well-equipped to quickly learn any other tool, should the need arise.

Installing R and RStudio

While the **R** statistical package comes with its own rudimentary user-interface, most people use the **RStudio** environment to connect to **R**. Accordingly you will need to install both **R** and **RStudio** on your computer to use this book. Instructions for downloading and installing software often change with versions. We therefore keep the most current instructions on the book's web-site. Please visit `http://books.infivista.com/dar2ed.html` and follow the instructions in the file *installing-r-rstudio.pdf*.

Data files for the book

To get the most out of this book, you should definitely work through all of the labs and lab assignments that appear throughout the book. To get the full flavor of the techniques, you need to work with large data sets. You can obtain all the data sets that we use from the book's web site at `http://books.infivista.com/dar2ed.html`

R code for this book

This book uses the **R** statistical computing package to illustrate and to teach all of the techniques. **R** can initially seem daunting to people who have not used older style command based computer user-interfaces. In these, we get a computer program to do what we want by typing in commands.

My experience with teaching data analytics with **R** gives me confidence that even beginners can quickly surmount the learning curve of **R**'s command-line user-interface. Learning **R** can be useful by itself, but can be time-consuming.

To strike a balance between the amount of **R** you have to learn, and the need to quickly become proficient in applying the analytics techniques that the book covers, I provide some useful **R** functions. These functions hide some of the complex details so that you can get your job done with a few commands. You can find the code and installation instructions at `http://books.infivista.com/dar2ed.html`.

Structure of data

In the spirit of a practical, hands-on approach, let us learn about some concrete concepts up front. We will first discuss the structure of data and set the stage for a quick lab and a related assignment.

In this book, we will look only at *tabular* data.

Table 1 shows the structure of the tabular data.

sno	name	region	income	gen	educ	credit	accept
1	Jane Fontana	3	30,000	F	1	3	0
2	Paul Finch	2	45,000	M	3	4	1
3	Jody Auerbach	4	38,000	F	3	3	1
4	Ming Yu	4	43,000	F	2	4	0
5	Kim Sung	5	39,000	M	3	2	1
6	Alex Rodrigues	2	56,000	M	2	5	0
7	Sheba Ahmed	4	73,000	F	3	3	1
8	Nikhil Pandey	2	49,000	M	1	4	0
9	Jason Bourne	1	52,000	M	2	2	0
10	Sabrina Smith	1	32,000	F	2	3	0

Table 1: Example of *tabular* data.

Like typical tables, Table 1 has rows and columns. It shows ten rows from among possibly thousands of rows of some information that a bank might have on its customers. Each row shows the name and some other demographic information for one person and also whether or not the person accepted an earlier loan offer from the bank.

We refer to column names as *attributes* or *fields*. Attribute *gen* (short for gender) has only two possible values "F" and "M," whereas attribute *educ* (short for education) has three possible values – 1, 2 and 3.

Attributes or fields or variables

You might have noted that some of the attributes have numerical values and others have textual values. We refer to attributes that have textual values as *categorical* attributes. Clearly, attributes *name* and *gen* are categorical. Categorical attributes are sometimes also referred to as *nominal attributes*. The **R** program that we will be using refers to them as *factors*.

Categorical attributes – also referred to as factors or nominal attributes

The attribute *income* has numerical values and we will treat it as such – as a *numerical* attribute.

Numerical attributes

Not all attributes with numerical values should necessarily be treated as numerical. For example, the attribute *region* tells us in codified form the region to which a person belongs. For example, 1 could mean *South*, 2 *North East* and so on. Though ostensibly numeric, its value plays no numerical role – we cannot meaningfully perform numerical operations like addition or subtraction on these. The magnitudes of the numbers do not indicate any ordering of regions either. We could very well have decided to code *North East* as 1 and *South* as 0 without changing anything important. The number here merely indicates a category and hence we should treat this attribute as categorical.

Attributes with numeric values sometimes have to be treated as *categorical*.

Look at the attributes *sno*, which represents the serial numbers of the rows in the table. You will find that data files often have such a column or attribute. Although *sno* is numeric, its numeric value has no significance and it cannot be used in any calculations. In fact, we cannot even say that it represents a real attribute of the real-world objects that the data describe. We will not use such attributes at all in any of our analyses, other than possibly for display.

Serial numbers, identifiers and such values do not generally play a role in data analytics.

The attribute *educ* hides more nuance. The value of *educ* encodes the person's highest educational achievement, with 1 representing high school, 2 an undergraduate degree and 3 a graduate degree. At first glance these numbers too seem to just serve as categories. Does *educ* differ from the categorical attributes that we have looked at so far?

It sure does. Apart from being categories, the values for *educ* clearly exhibit an ordering. Higher numbers represent greater levels of educational achievement. Should we then treat *educ* as numerical?

Think about it before reading on.

Before we answer that question, let us compare *educ* with *income*. A person earning $60,000 earns twice as much as a person earning $30,000. Can we say the same about *educ*?

Can we say that a person with a value of 2 is twice as educated as a person with value 1? Clearly not. But we can say that this person is *more* educated. Thus, *educ* displays some numerical characteristics without being fully so. More specifically, the ordering of values for *educ* has significance but we cannot go beyond that to meaningfully perform arithmetic operations. Statisticians call such attributes *ordinal*.

Ordinal attributes

The attribute *credit* represents the length of a person's credit history. The actual values (say, number of months of credit history) have been converted into a 5 point scale with 1 representing "very short" and 5 being " very long." How would you categorize this attribute?

credit is also *ordinal*

You will see that some analytical techniques require all attributes to be numeric. In such cases, we will sometimes treat ordinal attributes as if they were numeric – an approximation for sure, but sometimes better than treating them as just categorical. You will also see later that we do have ways of converting categorical attributes into numbers.

Later, we will see ways of converting the values of categorical and ordinal attributes to numbers and values of numeric attributes into categories.

Conversely, some techniques only work with categorical data. In such cases, we use methods to convert numerical attributes into categories.

You will also encounter situations when we would like some attributes to be numeric and others to be categorical. In such cases, we can convert attributes to make the data suitable for the chosen technique.

Having looked at *attributes*, which represent the columns of a data set, let us turn our attention to the rows. In our example data set, each row represents the offer of a loan to a single person. In a different data set, each row might represent a company or a sale or something else. We refer to each row of a data set as a *case* or *instance*.

Each row of a data set represents a *case*.

Review 1: Structure of data

You can find suggested answers to these questions starting from page 351

Answer the following questions based on the data in Table 2.

Table 2: Data for review question

state	region	urban	income	under18	expense
ME	1	508	3944	325	235
NH	1	564	4578	323	231
VT	1	322	4011	328	270
MA	1	846	5233	305	261
RI	1	871	4780	303	300
CT	1	774	5889	307	317
NY	1	856	5663	301	387
NJ	1	889	5759	310	285
PA	1	715	4894	300	300
OH	2	753	5012	324	221

1. How many attributes does this data set have?
2. How many cases or instances does the data set have?
3. Which attributes seem to be categorical ?

Lab 1: Introduction to ***RStudio***

Pre-requisite(s)

- ✓ If you have not already installed **R** and **RStudio**, go to the web-site mentioned on page 7 and install **R** and **RStudio** for your platform.
- ✓ If you have not already done so, use the instructions on page 7 to download the data files for the book into a suitably named folder on your computer.

Objective

After completing this lab, you will be able to:

- ✓ Open **RStudio**.
- ✓ Set the *working directory*.
- ✓ Enter **R** commands into the **RStudio** environment.
- ✓ List and explain the purpose of each frame of the **RStudio** environment.

Overview

In this lab, you will learn how to start the **RStudio** environment and enter and execute **R** commands. You will also learn about the various frames in the **RStudio** environment and the purpose of each one.

Activity steps

1. **Start RStudio:** Windows users should find a shortcut for **RStudio** on their *desktops*.

   Mac users will find **RStudio** in their *Applications* directory and in the *Launcher*.
2. **RStudio user interface:** Figure 1 indicates the purpose of each region in the **RStudio** user-interface.
3. **Command prompt:** In the very last line of the left hand-pane, you see the command prompt ">". You will enter all your **R** commands at the command prompt. For starters, just type the command *1+1* and press enter. You see that **R** prints the result right away. You will interact with **R** by typing in commands and seeing the results.

Figure 1: **RStudio** user interface

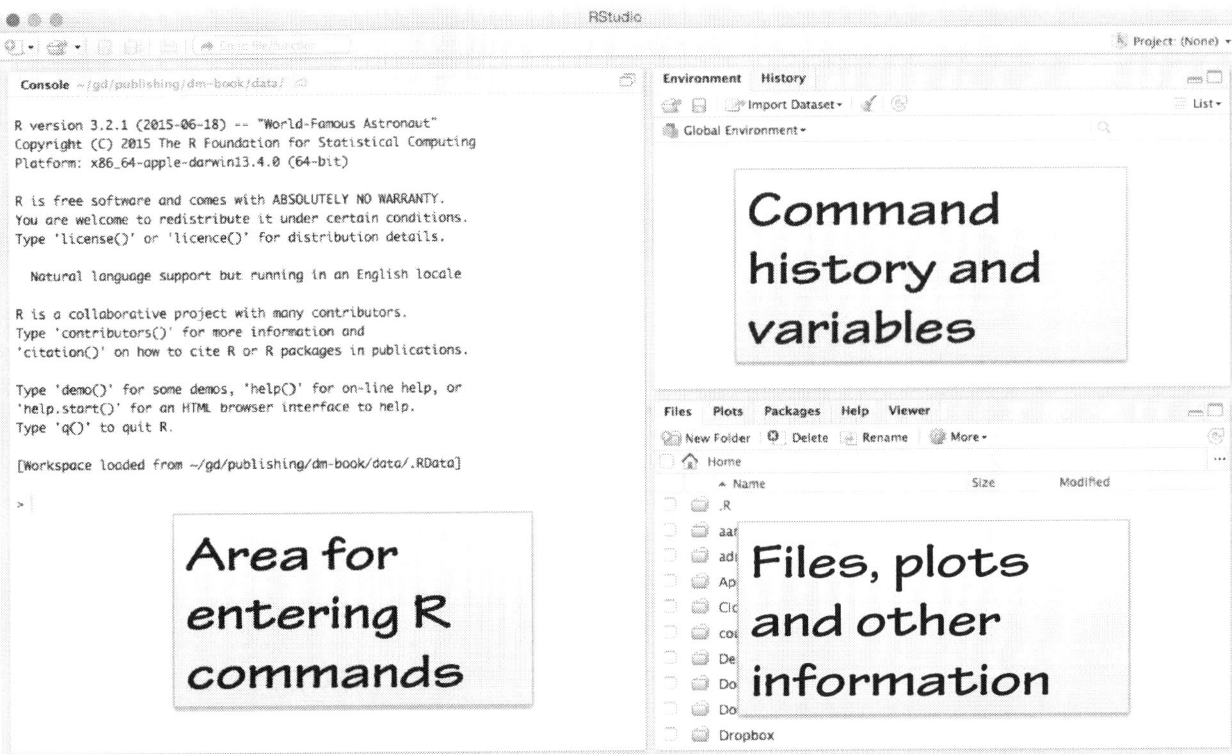

Setting the working directory . . .

4. **Set default working directory:** You need to type in commands to do almost anything in **R**. For example, to read a file into **R**, you will need to type in a command. That command requires you to specify the exact location of the data file on your computer – its complete path, like

   ```
   c:\users\joe\courses\analytics\myfile.csv
   ```

   or some such. These paths can be very long and cumbersome to enter. To avoid having to supply long file paths every time, you can ***set the working directory***.

   The *working directory* is the default directory where **R** will look for files. Once set, you can avoid paths and just mention the filenames alone. To continue the example from above, with the ***working directory*** set to:

   ```
   c:\users\joe\courses\analytics
   ```

   we can simply refer to

   ```
   myfile.csv
   ```

   instead of the complete path as above.

For this book, I suggest that you keep all your data files in one folder or directory, and set that as the ***working directory*** using the instructions shown below. You need to perform this step only once. Before you proceed, be sure that all the data files for this book are in the location which you are about to set as the ***working directory***.

- *Windows users:* Choose the menu option "Tools -> Global options" and click the "Browse" button next to the text box corresponding to "Default working directory" and select the folder where you plan to keep all the files for this book. After this you should exit and reopen **RStudio** for this change to take effect.

  ... on Windows

- *Mac users:* Select the menu option "RStudio -> Preferences" and use the "Browse" button to select the directory where you plan to keep your files. Restart **RStudio** for the change to take effect.

  ... on Macs

You do not have to do this again unless you reinstall **R**. Now, whenever you startup **RStudio**, the working directory will be the one you set above.

5. **Test your working directory:** Enter the following command at the command prompt ">"; don't worry if you do not understand it yet. You should enter the "<-" in the command as a mathematical *less than* sign followed by a hyphen ***with no space in between***. You should not enter the command prompt ">"; just enter what follows it, exactly as it appears. I have shown the command prompt just to indicate that you should enter the command at the command prompt:

```
> perf <- read.csv("college-perf.csv")
```

   We will get into the details later, but if the command worked without an error message, then all is well.

6. **Temporarily changing the working directory:** Sometimes we would like to refer to files that are not in the working directory. In such situations, you do not have to change the default working directory as above. Instead you can temporarily change the working directory. You do not need to do this now, but Figure 2 shows you how you can, if you need to. This setting is valid only for the current **RStudio** session and will not affect the default working directory when you next start

RStudio.

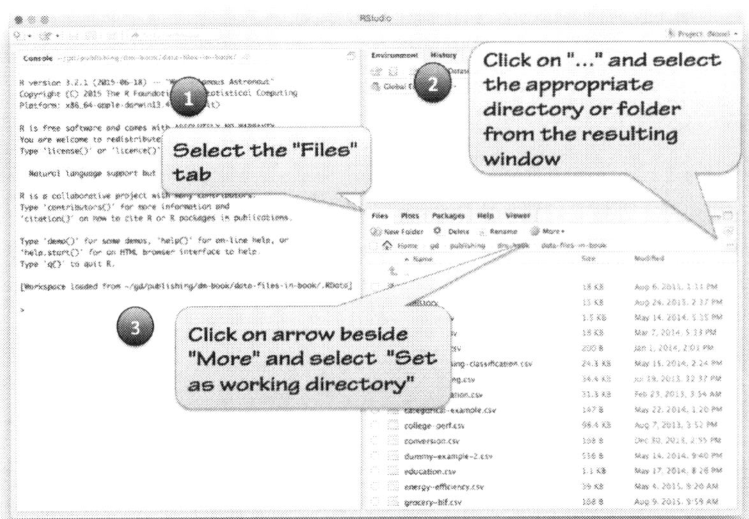

Figure 2: Temporarily changing the working directory

7. **Finding what the working directory is set to:** To find out the current setting of the working directory, enter the following command:

```
> getwd()
```

   There is also an easier way: the title bar of the console window always displays the current working directory (see Figure 3).

8. **Command history:** Go over to the top right pane and select the *History* tab. You will see that it displays both the commands you executed earlier. This serves as an easy reference. You can re-execute commands from the *History* tab easily by double-clicking on a command and pressing *Enter*.

9. **The plot area:** You will be creating many charts as you analyze data. Just to get a feel for where **RStudio** displays plots, enter the following command exactly as it appears. You should already have performed the step *Test your working directory* above for the following command to work. For now, do not try to understand the command – we will get to that shortly.

```
> hist(perf$SAT)
```

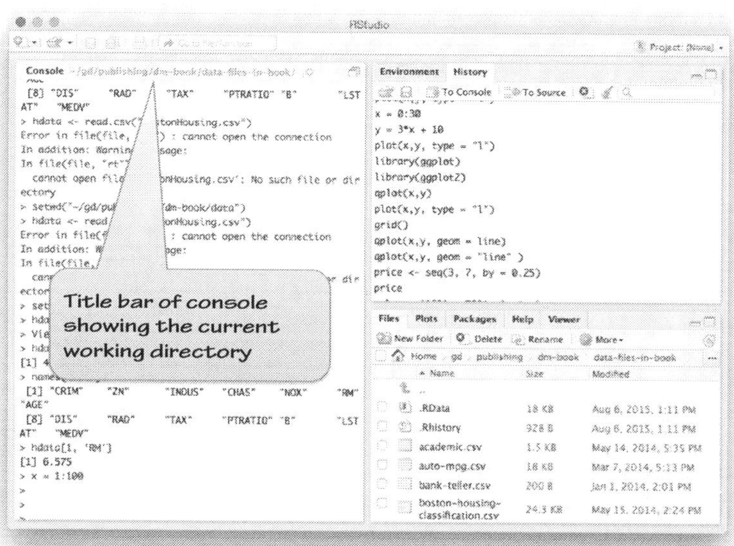

Figure 3: Title bar of console shows the current working directory

You should see the plot on the bottom right pane of **RStudio**, as Figure 4 shows.

10. **The Workspace:** Use the menu option or the window controls to quit **RStudio**. When you do this, you see a dialog that asks you whether you want to save your *workspace*.

    R provides you the capability to save the state of your **R** environment (all variables and their values) and then restore it when you start next without having to issue all the commands. In a work environment, you will use this all the time. **However, for this book, I actually recommend that you do not save and load the workspace each time. Instead, execute all commands each time to gain practice.**

    For completeness, I describe below the process of saving and restoring the **R** workspace.

    If you choose to save, then **R** will save all the objects in the workspace (variables and their values) to a file called ".RData" *in your current working directory*. Note that **R** will save the file in whatever happens to be the *current working directory* – this might not necessarily be the default that you set in step 4 if you subsequently changed it using the *Files* tab in the bottom right pane.

    When you start **RStudio** next, it will automatically

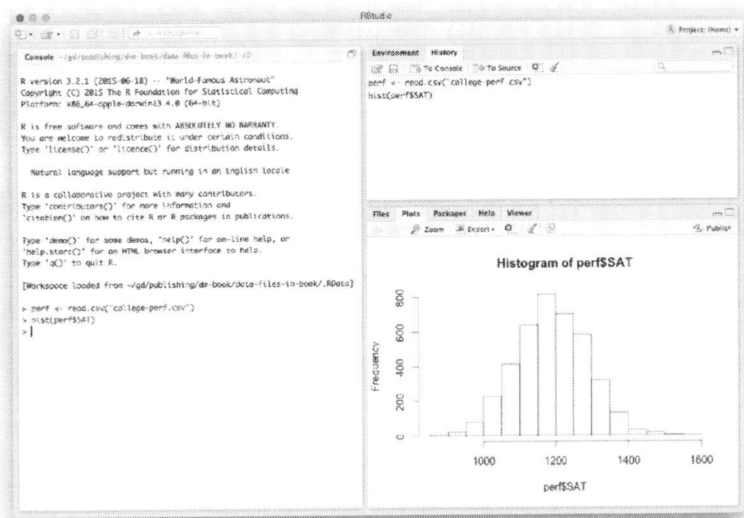

Figure 4: The plot area in **RStudio**

load the saved objects from the file ".RData" from the default working directory that you had set earlier in step 4. The last line of the **R** console will indicate where it loaded the workspace from.

If you had saved the workspace somewhere other than your default working directory, then that ".RData" file will not be accessible to **R** and hence the workspace will not be as you had left it on exiting. If you want everything to be restored then you should set working directory as the location that contains the relevant ".RData" file then execute the following command:

```
> load(".RData")
```

If you also want the command history, you can execute:

```
> loadhistory()
```

11. **Why RStudio?:** You might have heard about more friendly user-interfaces for **R** and could be wondering why this book does not use those. Here is a brief justification for my choice of **RStudio**.

    Some add-ons to **R**, like **R Commander**, allow us to avoid entering commands and to use some features of **R** conveniently from a menu-based user-interface. **R Commander** is an excellent tool for traditional statistical analysis; it does not cover the subject matter of this book.

The **Rattle**[3] tool specifically addresses data analytics tasks and you can check it out at `http://rattle.togaware.com/`. Tools like **Rattle** are specifically designed to enable people without a knowledge of **R** to be able to perform data analytics. However, this book aims to teach data analytics *and* some core aspects of **R**. Learning **R** requires people to use the command-line interface and actually type in commands. While people can surely do this in the base **R** system, I wanted to simplify some of the peripheral details. **RStudio** represents a good *via media*.

[3] Graham J. Williams. *Data Mining with Rattle and R: The art of excavating data for knowledge discovery*. Use R! Springer, 2011. URL `http://www.amazon.com/gp/product/1441998896/ref=as_li_qf_sp_asin_tl?ie=UTF8&tag=togaware-20&linkCode=as2&camp=217145&creative=399373&creativeASIN=1441998896`

Review 2: Introduction to **RStudio**

You can find suggested answers to these questions starting on page 351

1. What do we gain by setting the *Working Directory*?
2. In **RStudio**, how do we set the working directory in such a way that this setting takes effect whenever we start **RStudio**?
3. How can we change the working directory setting *temporarily*?
4. How can we find out what the working directory is currently set to?

Lab 2: Introduction to **R** *Data Frames*

Pre-requisite(s)

- ✓ You should have completed the lab on **RStudio** on page 11.
- ✓ You should have downloaded the data files for the book and set the working directory to point to the location of those files. For download instructions, see page 7.
- ✓ You should have read the section titled *Structure of Data* on page 8 and worked through the corresponding review questions on page 10.

Objective

After completing this lab, you will be able to:

✓ Load data sets from csv files into **R** data frames.

✓ Explore data frames.

✓ Compute simple statistics on data frames.

✓ Create categorical attributes (*factors*) in **R**.

Overview

For this activity, we will be using the Boston Housing data set[4], available for download from the UCI Machine Learning Repository[5]. It contains data on 14 attributes for each of 506 Boston neighborhoods. You will load this data into **R** and manipulate it in various ways. In the process, we will learn important **R** concepts and procedures.

[4] D. Harrison and D.L. Rubinfeld. Hedonic prices and the demand for clean air. *J. Environ. Economics & Management*, pages 81–102, 1978

[5] K. Bache and M. Lichman. UCI machine learning repository, 2013. URL `http://archive.ics.uci.edu/ml`

As you have already seen in the prior lab, **R** and **RStudio** present you with a *command-line user interface*. This means that rather than using the mouse to point and click your way through it, you will need to enter textual commands on a *command-line*. **R** supports a sophisticated programming language that enables users to create new features on top of existing ones. We will mostly be using built-in functionality and need to learn only a small, but useful, subset of the language.

In this book we take a crass, utilitarian approach and teach you just enough **R** as needed. After working through this book, you will have picked up useful **R** skills to get things done and be in a position to enhance your skills by reading books dedicated to teaching more details of the **R** programming language, and to benefit from the numerous web resources.

Activity steps

1. **Look at the data:** You should already have downloaded the data files for the book and stored them in a specific location of your choice on your computer. We will use the file *BostonHousing.csv* in this activity. Almost all the data files which you downloaded from the book's web site have a "csv"file extension – they are in the "comma separated values" format. This means that the data is in plain text format. You can examine the contents

We will mostly use csv files

of *csv* files using *Excel* or *OpenOffice.org*. Open the file *BostonHousing.csv* using a suitable spreadsheet program for now. We will soon be opening it in **RStudio**.

Table 3 provides a brief description of each attribute in the file.

Recall that attributes are the columns in a typical table of data.

Table 3: Boston Housing attribute descriptions

Attribute	Description
CRIM	per capita crime rate by town
ZN	proportion of residential land zoned for lots over 25,000 sq.ft.
INDUS	proportion of non-retail business acres per town.
CHAS	Bounds Charles River or not (1 if tract bounds river; 0 otherwise)
NOX	nitric oxides concentration (parts per 10 million)
RM	average number of rooms per dwelling
AGE	proportion of owner-occupied units built prior to 1940
DIS	weighted distances to five Boston employment centres
RAD	index of accessibility to radial highways
TAX	full-value property-tax rate per $10,000
PTRATIO	pupil-teacher ratio by town
B	$1000(Bk - 0.63)^2$ where Bk is the proportion of blacks by town
LSTAT	% lower status of the population
MEDV	Median value of owner-occupied homes in $1000

Looking at the data and at the attribute descriptions, see if you can identify some of the attributes whose values might influence the median value of homes in a neighborhood – in the very last column. For example, what characteristics seem to be common to neighborhoods with low median home values? High values?

You can gain useful preliminary insights by taking a close look at the data before diving into building models.

2. **Get ready:** Perform the following steps to get ready. See the **RStudio** lab on page 11 if you need assistance with any of these steps:

   - Start **RStudio** using the appropriate method for your platform.
   - If you have not already done so, download the data files for the book to a known location on your computer.
   - Set your working directory to point to the location of the above files.

3. **Read in the data:** We have provided most of the data files for the book as "csv" (comma separated values) data files. **R** can directly read in such files. Enter the following command right next to the ">" on the last line in your **R** console. You must enter the "<-" as a mathematical *less-than* sign followed by a hyphen without any space in between. Press the *Enter* key after entering the

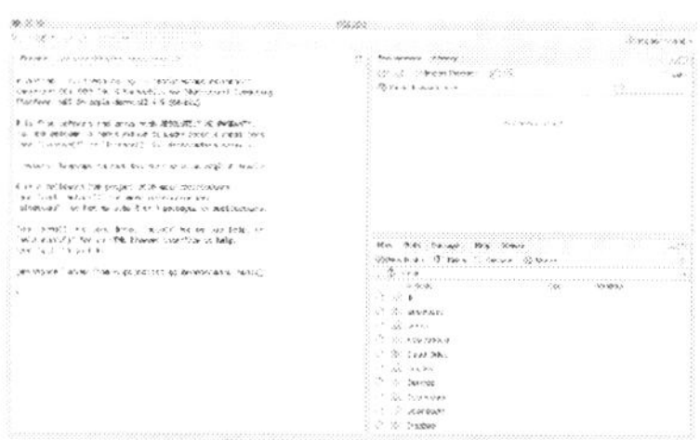

Figure 5: RStudio screen

Reading a csv file

command:

```
> hdata <- read.csv("BostonHousing.csv")
```

When typing the double quotes in **R**, use the double-quote character on the keyboard – do not copy and paste from word processing programs like Microsoft Word, because they automatically convert quote characters into "smart quotes" which **R** does not recognize.

Beware of "smart-quotes" – do not copy and paste double-quotes from other programs into **R**.

The portion of the command to the right of "<-" asks **R** to read a csv file whose name is mentioned within double-quotes inside the parentheses. You enjoyed the luxury of specifying just the filename without including the complete path to the file only because you had already set the working directory and put the file there.

read.csv is a predefined **R** *function* to read *csv* files. The above command simply *called* or *invoked* it to get the job done. While *invoking* the function, we obviously need to tell the function the name of the file we want to read. You therefore supplied the filename as an *argument* within parentheses. Figure 6 explains.

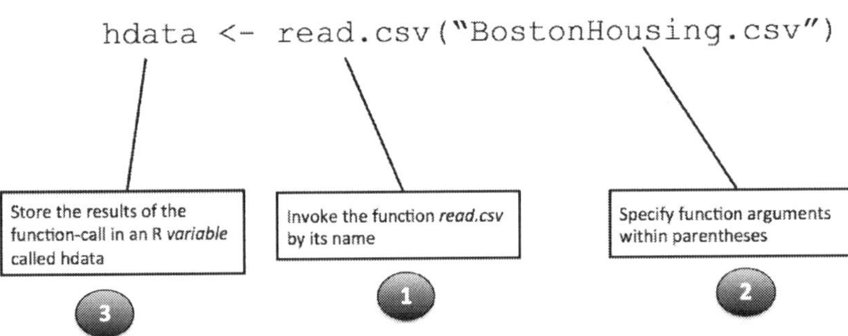

Figure 6: Invoking a function – function name and argument.

As you work through this book, you will encounter other functions. Function invocations, like the above, always have parentheses following the name of the function.

Note the quotes around the argument "BostonHousing.csv". In **R** you need to surround literal text with double-quotes – this will allow **R** to distinguish between variable names – which we do not have to surround with quotes – from literal text. Programming languages often refer to literal text as *strings*. Don't forget the quotes in future exercises and assignments.

Place double-quotes around literal text or *strings*

The above command reads the input data from the

file and stores the result in a *variable* called *hdata* within **R**. The "<-" sign is the *assignment operator* – to store the value on the right hand side into the *variable* on the left hand side. In **R**, we have the freedom to choose our own variable names. We chose the name *hdata* for the variable (because this is housing data). We are free to choose whatever names we want for our **R** variables. Pretty much the only rule is that a variable name cannot contain a space within it.

In **R**, we often store data in *variables* before operating on them. Incidentally, we call *hdata* a *variable* because the value we store in it can *vary* over time. For now we have stored the housing data in this variable. Later we can store something else in it – although we will not do that a lot in this book.

All the information in the file is now in **R** and available to you in a variable called *hdata*, which is a *Data Frame*.

Data frames enable us to store entire tables of data and refer to them by a single variable name

Variables like *hdata* which store entire tables are referred to as *data frames* in **R**. We will soon learn commands that will enable us to display all or part of a *data frame*.

An **R** data frame is one type of variable in which we can store an entire table of data. **R** has a few other variable types that have this ability; we will predominantly use data frames in this book.

4. **Displaying all the data:** Now that all the data is contained in a variable, we can manipulate it in various ways. First let us display all the data. Type in the command:

```
> hdata
```

all by itself and see what happens. **R** displays the complete data – all 506 rows and all columns. Note that, in addition to the actual data, **R** also displays row numbers for convenience.

If your console window was not broad enough, **R** would have displayed all data for some columns (as many as will fit in the width of the console) and then displayed the remaining columns below. By widening the window before issuing the command, you can prevent this kind of splitting when there are many

You can display the value of a variable by typing its name as a command columns. Try running the command with various window widths and observe the results. Of course the files that we will deal with often have too many columns and we sometimes cannot avoid this kind of splitting.

Type the name of a variable to see its value

In general, when you type the name of a variable as a command then **R** prints the value of the variable as the result.

5. **Seeing just the initial set of cases:** After reading in some data, we should check to see that everything came in fine. To do this, it is often not necessary to display the entire data frame – as we did earlier. In the following commands you see some text shown after the "#" sign. In **R**, this sign is a *comment* and **R** ignores anything starting from "#" till the end of the line. These are meant for human consumption only. So you do not have to type anything in the code examples from the "#" till the end of the line. I have added those just for clarity.

is a comment in **R**.

```
> # Lines starting with # are comments
> # Display the initial cases
> head(hdata)

> # Display the last few cases
> tail(hdata)
```

6. **Displaying attribute names** We can use the *names* function for this. Type in:

Use the *names* function to display the names of the attributes in a data frame.

```
> # See the attribute names in a data frame
> names(hdata)
```

Figure 7 shows the output. The numbers on the left help us to easily determine the column positions of the attributes. For example, we can see that *CRIM* is the first attribute and that *RM* is the sixth. We can infer that *INDUS* is the third attribute and that *TAX* is the tenth attribute. You will find this to be useful later in the book.

By supplying the name of a data frame as the argument to the function *names*, you can see the attribute names in that data frame.

So if our data frame was named *sales*, then we would substitute that for *hdata* in the command, and enter the command *names(sales)*. Of course, since we do not have

```
 [1] "CRIM"    "ZN"      "INDUS"   "CHAS"    "NOX"
 [6] "RM"      "AGE"     "DIS"     "RAD"     "TAX"
[11] "PTRATIO" "B"       "LSTAT"   "MEDV"
```

Figure 7: Output from the command *names(hdata)* – the numbers on the left help us to easily determine column numbers of attributes a data frame named *sales*, that command will not work now.

7. **Finding the number of rows:** Use the function *nrow* to get the number of rows in a data frame.

```
> nrow(hdata)
```

Recall that each row of data in a data frame represents one single case or observation. In the current example, each row contains data on a single neighborhood in a Boston suburb.

8. **Displaying the contents of a data frame in RStudio without entering any command:** In **RStudio**, the top right pane generally has two tabs *Environment* and *History*. The *Environment* tab displays a quick overview of the **R** variables we have created during a session. Click on the *Environment* tab on the top right. You should see the variable *hdata* listed there (see Figure 8).

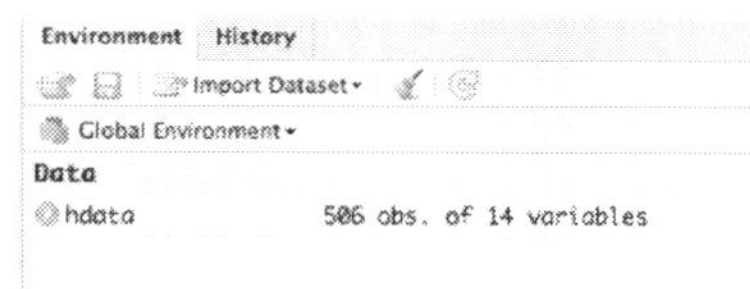

Figure 8: The *Environment* tab

   If you click on the arrow to the left of the variable name, your should see a complete list of the attributes in the *hdata* data frame along with a listing of the initial few values of each attribute (see Figure 9)

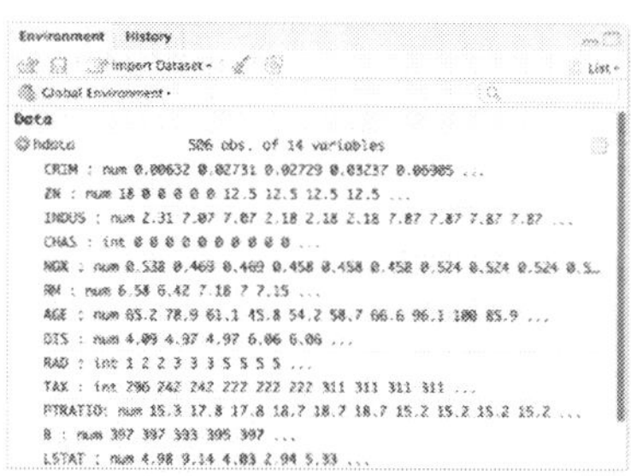

Figure 9: The *Environment* tab with a variable expanded

   Now click on the text *hdata* in the *Environment* tab – as you hover over the text, the cursor changes to a hand. This results in a neat tabular display of the contents of the *hdata* data frame (see Figure 10) in the top left pane.

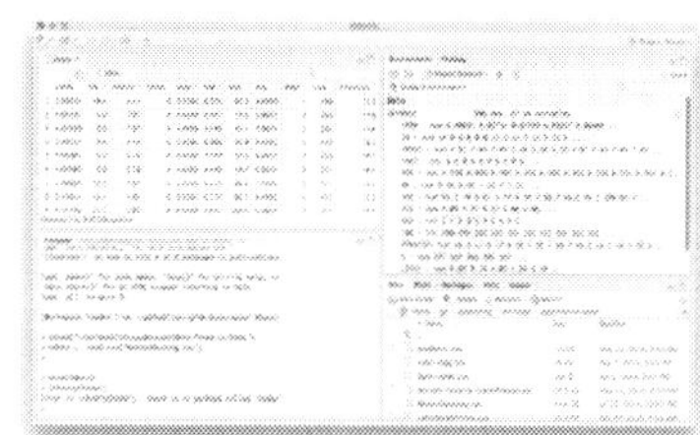

Figure 10: Displaying the contents of a data frame in **RStudio**

9. **Accessing a specific element:** Type in the command below (note the square brackets). A data frame can contain many columns and many rows. We refer to a single item at a [row, column] position as an element.

```
> hdata[1,6]
```

What happened? **R** showed us the value in the sixth column of the first row. You can verify this by comparing **R**'s response with the data file displayed in the top left pane.

   The row number comes first, followed by the column number.

   Although we sometimes access elements of a data frame just to look at their values, most often we access elements in order to perform some computations on them. For example, suppose we wanted to find the median value per room for the neighborhood in the 100th row we could use the following:

```
> hdata[100, 14]/ hdata[100, 6]
```

When retrieving elements of a data frame, we use square brackets. For supplying arguments to functions, we use parentheses. You have to be sensitive to these differences and use them correctly for **R** to process them properly. Otherwise you will see error messages.

Use parentheses after function names; use square brackets when retrieving elements from a data frame

10. **Error messages:** Making mistakes and seeing the resultant error messages is an integral part of learning to use a new software package, especially one where you type in commands. Do not be alarmed when you make mistakes and see error messages.

Error messages do not hinder – they help!

When you do see an error message, try to read it and make sense of it rather than just being frustrated because "something" went wrong. Although initially **R**'s error messages seem undecipherable, you will start getting the hang of these and learn to use them to correct mistakes.

You can enhance your learning by trying to decipher error messages rather than just being puzzled

11. **Using attribute names to address data frame elements:** The items we specify within square brackets when retrieving data from a data frame are called *subscripts* or *indexes*.

When we specified numerical *subscripts* for attributes, we used row numbers and column positions of attributes in our data frames. It might seem more natural to use the attribute names rather than their column positions. For example, why not use "RM" to refer to that attribute rather than the attribute's column position?

For subscripts or indexes, if you prefer to use the names of attributes rather than their column positions, you can also type in commands like:

```
> hdata[1,"RM"]
```

You can access columns by their numeric position or their names – in the latter case you have to enclose the column name in quotes

Note that the attribute name is enclosed in quotes. The above command has the same effect as:

```
> hdata[1,6]
```

because *RM* is the name of the sixth attribute. When using attribute names you have to include the quotes. Without the quotes, **R** will treat it as the name of a variable. We do not have an **R** variable named *RM*. Also,

Incidentally, **an R** is correct because it is the *sound* of the following word, and not its *spelling*, that determines whether we use *a* or *an* when we use attribute names, we have to spell them exactly as they are. **Attribute names are case-sensitive**.

For practice, look at the same data element in your data frame – if you have been following these instructions, the top left frame should be displaying the data now. Choose a specific value (from some row/column of the data). Now enter the command in **R** to retrieve that specific value using both of the above approaches (attribute column position and attribute name). Try this for at least three different values from different rows and columns.

12. **Displaying an entire row:** Type in the command

```
> hdata[1, ]
```

What happened? **R** displayed the entire first row of the data frame – values of all attributes of the first row. When we omit the second index as above, **R** returns the values of all columns. That is just how it works. Note that even though we skipped the second index, we still had to include the comma. If you leave out the comma, something entirely different happens, which we will not go into now.

Now enter the command to get the entire 200th row. What would the command be to get just the *TAX* for the neighborhood on that row?

hdata[200,]
hdata[200, "TAX"] or
hdata[200, 10]

You can also omit the first subscript as in:

```
> hdata[,5]
```

You probably guessed that this will show all the rows for column 5. Because we omitted the first subscript, **R** displays all values for that subscript.

Recalling that the first subscript stands for rows and the second one for columns, leaving the first one out gets us all rows and leaving out the second one gets us all the columns. What would the following command show us?

All the data, because we left out both the subscripts!

```
> hdata[ , ]
```

Of course we would never actually use this because we have the simpler alternative of just using the variable name alone.

13. **Displaying a range of rows or columns:** What if we wanted to see the values of all attributes for rows 10 through 20? Try the command (don't forget the comma)

```
> hdata[10:20, ]
```

We specify a range using a colon. Can you think of two different commands by which we can get the MEDV for rows 100 to 150?

```
> # MEDV is in the 14th column so ...
> hdata[100:150, 14]
> hdata[100:150, "MEDV"]
```

Use a colon to specify contiguous ranges of rows or columns.

You can also specify ranges for columns. Try:

```
> hdata[10:20, 2:3 ]
```

Can you explain the results?

You see the values of the second and third attributes for rows 10 to 20

14. **Specifying non-contiguous ranges:** If the range we want to specify is contiguous (for example, all rows between 10 and 20), then we can get by with the colon. What if we want to see *CRIM, NOX* and *PTRATIO* for rows 50 through 100?

Here we see no problem with the rows since they are contiguous and we can use the colon. The column indexes are not contiguous since *CRIM* is the first column, *NOX* is the fifth column and *PTRATIO* is the eleventh column. Either of the following commands will do the job.

```
> hdata[50:100, c(1, 5, 11)]
> hdata[50:100, c("CRIM", "NOX", "PTRATIO")]
```

To see the data from rows 1, 3, 8 and 10, for the attributes *NOX* and *PTRATIO*, we can use:

```
> hdata[c(1,3,8,10), c("NOX", "PTRATIO")]
```

In the above example, we have used the *c* function to get data for non-contiguous rows and non-contiguous attributes.

Figure 11 explains.

The *c* function combines its arguments to form a collection (a *vector* actually, but we will not go into the

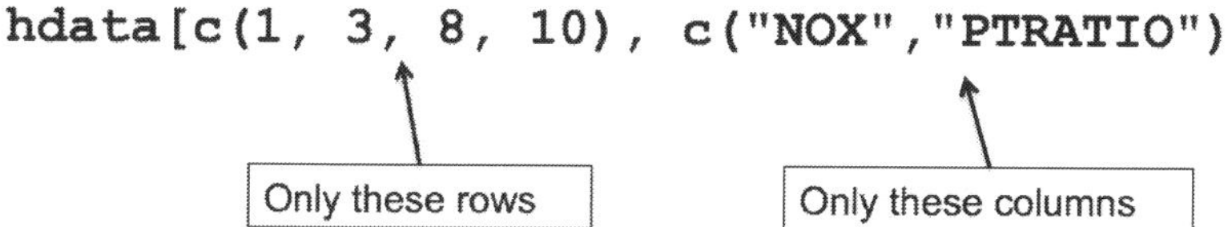

Figure 11: Using the *c* function to specify non-contiguous rows and columns

details now) and we can supply the resulting collection to specify a list of row or column subscripts for data frames. We will use it later for other purposes as well. While using this approach, be sure not to miss the function name *c*.

15. **Difference between [ ] and ( ):** You have probably noted and been a bit confused by the use of both square brackets and parentheses in different places. To make matters worse, the last few examples used both in the same command.

    Use square brackets only for accessing elements of a data frame – not for anything else. Use parentheses to invoke functions. Function arguments appear within the parentheses. We must use parentheses even if we use a function that requires no arguments – you will see examples of this later.

16. **Using the $ operator to refer to data frame attributes:** We often need to refer to all values of a given attribute in a data frame. For example, we might want to display all the values of *PTRATIO*. The $ notation helps with this:

    Using the $ notation to refer to attributes

```
> hdata$PTRATIO
> hdata$PTRATIO[10]
> hdata$PTRATIO[10:15]
> # ... and so on
```

    As you can see, we use the name of the data frame followed by the dollar sign, followed by the attribute name – note that we do not use double quotes when using the $ notation to get attributes.

    Do not use quotes when using the $ notation to access attributes

17. **Vector operations** The dollar notation becomes very useful when we have to perform the same operation on many values. In such cases, it helps us to accomplish much through very few commands. Just for illustration, suppose we want to make the PTRATIO as 0 for each of

the 506 cases:

```
> # Change PTRATIO to 0 for all cases
> hdata$PTRATIO <- 0

> # Display to confirm the change
> hdata$PTRATIO
> # prints all zeros
```

This way of operating on an entire set of values at a time with a single command is called an *Vector Operation* in **R**.

Array operations are powerful!

For another example, let us expand on what we did in step 9 above. Let us compute the median value per room for all the neighborhoods – with a single command:

```
> hdata$MEDV/hdata$RM
```

18. **Specifying *factors*:** Recall that categorical attributes store the name of a category to which a case belongs. **R** calls categorical attributes *factors*.

Recall that we call a row of the data table an *case* or *observation*.

When reading data from a file, **R** generally treats attributes with textual values (like names of people, names of colors and so on) as categorical attributes in the data frame.

By default, **R** stores attributes with numerical values in the data file as numbers in the data frame.

A tricky situation arises when we encounter data files that store the values of categorical attributes as numbers. For example, we might see a data file in which colors are stored as numbers. The underlying interpretation might be: 1 = *Red*, 2 = *Orange*, and so on. However, the file only has the numbers and we are told about the interpretation by other means.

In such situations, when **R** reads in the file, it sees numeric values for this attribute and treats it by default as a numerical attribute.

Analytical methods typically treat numeric and categorical attributes quite differently. In the above example, clearly, it would not make any sense to treat the numbers of colors like actual numbers. For example, doing arithmetic operations like calculating sum and average for these would make no sense. Even though the attribute has numeric values, it really represents a categorical attribute. We can get incorrect results if we misrepresent categorical attributes as numeric. If we happen to know that the numerical values actually represent only categories, we have a way to flag that for **R**.

The file *categorical-example.csv* has the above mentioned attribute (called *group_color*) to indicate the group to which a team belongs. Read the file into an **R** data frame called *catex* and then display the file's contents:

```
> catex <- read.csv("categorical-example.csv")
> catex      # display the data
> class(catex$group_color)   # what type of attribute?
```

As the above code shows, you can use the *class* function to check what kind of values a variable contains. You see from the output that **R** is treating the attribute *group_color* as numeric. We see that from the result of the last command which tells us that the attribute has *integer* values. We should inform **R** that this attribute is categorical. **R** calls categorical attributes *factors* and we can use the *factor* function:

```
> # replace group_color with corresponding factors
> catex$group_color <- factor(catex$group_color)

> # Check to see the type now
> class(catex$group_color)
```

In the above command, we exploited the dollar notation to refer to all the values in the *group_color* attribute. We applied the *factor* function to the values of the *group_color* attribute and then replaced the existing values with the new values. The output from the last command confirms that *group_color* is now a *factor*.

Figure 12 explains.

If we print the data in the data frame, we will not notice any difference from before – we will still see only numbers. However, **R** will now treat this attribute as a *factor* – that is, as a categorical attribute and will not mistakenly perform arithmetic operations on its values.

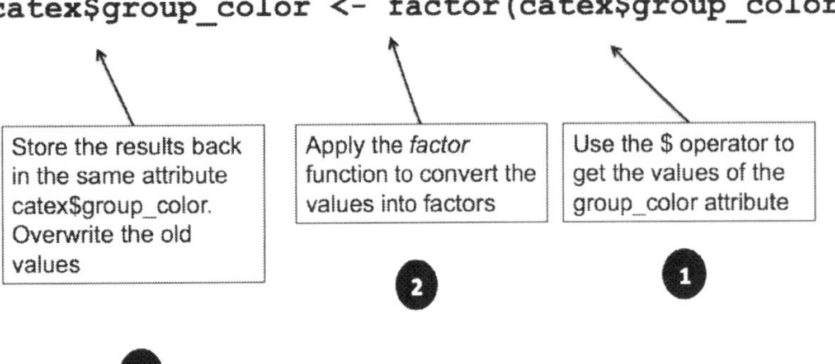
catex$group_color <- factor(catex$group_color)
Store the results back in the same attribute catex$group_color. Overwrite the old values
Apply the factor function to convert the values into factors
Use the $ operator to get the values of the group_color attribute
1
2
3

Figure 12: Using the factor function. Note also the use of the $ operator.

19. **Calculating summary statistics:** Switching back to the Boston Housing data, we can easily compute summary statistics like average, maximum and minimum. For example, we can get the maximum value of *CRIM* with either of the following (note carefully the use of both square brackets and parentheses):

```
> max(hdata[, "CRIM" ])
> max(hdata[, 1 ])
> max(hdata$CRIM)
```

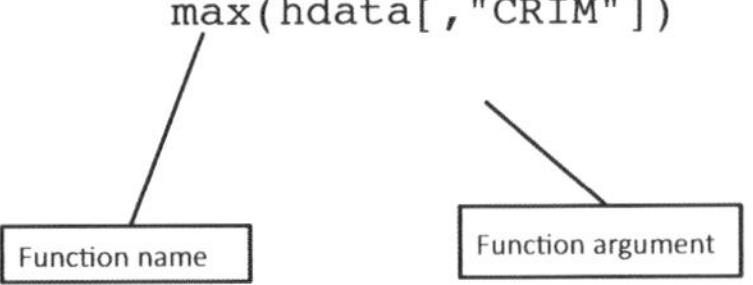
max(hdata[,"CRIM"])
Function name
Function argument

Figure 13: Elements of a function call revisited

We used the *max* predefined function above and supplied *hdata[,"CRIM"]* as an argument. Figure 13 clarifies. Since we left out the first index after the square brackets, **R** will assume that we want to consider all rows and hence we will get the maximum *CRIM* value across all rows.

How would you get the maximum *NOX* value in the rows 50 to 150? Can you think of two different ways of doing this? How might you get the minimum *PTRATIO* value across all rows?

max(hdata[50:150,"NOX"]) or max(hdata[50:150,5])

min(hdata[,"PTRATIO"]) or min(hdata[,11]) or min(hdata$PTRATIO)

20. **Getting summary information:** We can get summary information for all attributes in one shot by using the *summary* function:

```
> # Summary information for Boston Housing data
> summary(hdata)

> # Summary information for categorical example
> summary(catex)
```

In a later chapter we will explain the details of the results, but you should be able to make some sense of it by yourself right now. What difference do you see between the summary information we get for numerical and categorical attributes?

For numerical attributes, the summary shows various computed values like the minimum, maximum, mean and median. For categorical attributes it shows the count of the cases belonging to each category.

21. **More powerful features:** What if we want to extract only those rows that have *AGE* less than 10? **R** actually allows us to use logical conditions within square brackets! Try this:

```
> hdata[hdata$AGE < 10, ]
```

The above command printed out all attributes for all rows where *AGE* is less than 10. We got all attributes because we left the second part (after the comma) blank. If we want to store that output in a variable we could do that too:

```
> new.data <- hdata[hdata$AGE < 10, ]
```

Now the variable *new.data* is a new data frame containing only those rows from *hdata* for which *AGE* is less than 10.

Incidentally, the "." or period in *new.data* has no special significance. Variable names can include periods and we can use them to create meaningful and readable variable names.

22. **Ordinal attributes:** Read the data from the file *ordinal-example.csv* into an **R** variable called *ordex*. The file has an attribute called *salary* which looks numeric but is really ordinal – 1, 2 and 3 stand respectively for "High", "Medium" and "Low". In this sense the actual ordering is 3 < 2 < 1.

If we just convert *salary* to a factor as we did earlier, it will become categorical, but will not encode the implied ordering 3 < 2 < 1. We have to let **R** know about the ordering so that methods that use the ordering information can work correctly.

```
> # First read the data
> ordex <- read.csv("ordinal-example.csv")

> # See the type of the salary attribute
> class(ordex$salary)    # an integer

> # Convert to ordinal and specify the order
> # c(3,2,1) tells R that 3 is the lowest and so on
```

```
> ordex$salary <- ordered(ordex$salary, levels = c(3,2,1))
> class(ordex$salary)    # an ordered factor

> ordex$salary[1]    # this shows the ordering
```

The above approach works even when the attribute is not numeric. The frame *ordex* also has an attribute *skill* with values *High*, *Medium* and *Low*. By default **R** just reads these in as factors and has no idea about the implied ordering *Low* < *Medium* < *High*. The following commands rectify this situation:

```
> class(ordex$skill)    # just a factor
> ordex$skill <- ordered(ordex$skill,
       levels = c("Low", "Medium", "High"))

> class(ordex$skill)
> ordex$skill[1]    # shows the ordering
```

23. **Breaking a command across several lines:** Sometimes a command is long and you might want to enter it in multiple lines. In **RStudio**, if you enter part of a command and press *Enter* then **RStudio** recognizes that the command is incomplete and prompts you on the following line with a "+" sign to continue the command. To test this, enter the following and press *Enter*:

```
> hdata <-
```

You will see that **RStudio** prompts you with a "+" on the next line. You can now continue your command and finish it.

If at this point, you want to abandon the command, just press the 'Escape" key on your keyboard to get back the ">" prompt.

24. **CSV files – variations:** The *CSV* file that we use in this book use commas as field delimiters and have column headers. By default the *read.csv* function assumes these and so everything works well for the files we use in this book.

You will sometimes find *CSV* files that use other delimiters like semi-colon or tab. Also, sometimes *CSV* files do not contain column headers. The *read.csv* function has options to cover all these cases, but we do not go into those in this book. If the need arises, a quick web search will reveal all.

25. **Getting help:** **R** provides on-line help. Although comprehensive, the help system is not very beginner-friendly. While you cannot hope to learn much from the help system, it can help you to learn about the use of specific functions. With its numerous functions and a plethora of options in most functions, navigating **R** without such comprehensive help would be close to impossible.

```
> # start the help system
> # Opens a browser interface to the help system
> help.start()

> # Help on a specific function
> # ?function-name  (no space after ?) or
> # help(function-name)
> ?summary
> help(summary)

> # Example of function usage
> example(summary)
```

26. **The assignment operator:** In the previous example, we used the assignment operator <- to assign the value on the right hand side of an expression to the variable on the left. After the command, the variable on the left contains the value that was assigned to it.

    Technically, we can also use the = sign as the assignment operator. The two forms of the assignment operator differ subtly, but we will not go into that in this book. This book adopts the common **R** practice of using <- as the assignment operator.

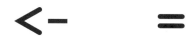

Figure 14: The two assignment operators in **R**; they differ subtly; **R** users generally prefer the one on the left; for the purposes of this book, you can use either.

That's it. You now know almost all the **R** concepts that we will be using in this book. We will, of course, encounter many new *functions* in later chapters.

Remember, we have covered only a minuscule fraction of what **R** and **RStudio** have to offer, but this will suffice for our needs in this book and for you to apply the techniques we will be learning.

*Lab assignment 1: Introduction to **R** data frames*

You can find the answers to this lab assignment on page 352.

From the data files you downloaded, read in *college-perf.csv* into a variable with a name of your choice.

1. How many attributes does the data frame have?
2. How many rows or instances does the data frame have?
3. What are the names of the attributes?
4. Which attributes have numerical values and which one are *factors*?
5. Type the **R** commands for each of the following:
   - i Display all the data.
   - ii Display the values of all attributes for row 256.
   - iii Display the values of all attributes for rows 10 to 20.
   - iv Display the values of only the second, third and fourth attributes for all rows – do this using the column positions of the attributes.
   - v Display the values of only the first and third attributes for all rows – do this using the column positions of the attributes.
   - vi Same as above, except use column names instead of column positions.
   - vii Display the values of the first and third attributes for rows 200 through 230.
   - viii Display the values of the second and fourth attributes by column positions for rows 2, 3, 10, 15 and 20 only.
   - ix Display summary information for all attributes.
   - x Display summary information for *SAT*
   - xi Convert the attribute *Perf* to be ordinal, with the proper ordering.
   - xii Display all the attributes for the cases for which the GPA is 3 or more.
   - xiii Compute the value of SAT plus (GPA*100) for each case.
   - xiv What is the name given to the kind of operation in which we operate on a whole set of values in a single command?
   - xv Set the value of *Income* to 0 for all cases.

What is Data Analytics?

Actionable intelligence from large data

Data analytics extracts actionable intelligence from large volumes of data. Organizations gather huge volumes of data using computer based transaction processing systems. They gather much of such data just to conduct their day-to-day operations rather than with any specific goal of extracting intelligence.

Organizations gather lots of data for supporting their operations . . .

For example, millions of customers use Amazon.com's web-based system to order various products. As a result, Amazon.com's databases contain information about: the millions of orders its customers placed, customers, the date and time of the order, all the items in each order, and so on. The stored data and the web-based front-end that customers use to interact with Amazon.com enables customers to search for products to purchase and to keep track of their orders. It enables the company to capture customers' orders for fulfillment – that is, to ship the correct products on-time to customers. All of this data just enables the company to carry out its routine business activities.

. . . and can extract intelligence from this data.

However, the data that Amazon.com captures to just operate the business holds valuable nuggets of intelligence. Like panning for gold, people at Amazon.com have to devise methods for carefully sifting through mountains of data to find the useful nuggets. For example, by examining customers' demographic information and the kinds of items they buy, Amazon.com can then find patterns in the underlying data. It can then use this intelligence in many ways. For example:

- **Recommend products based on profile:** Identify what profile of people seem to be prone to purchase what kind of products, and display appropriate products prominently when customers visit the site.
- **Recommend products based on which products are often purchased together:** When a customer A purchases a particular product, Amazon.com can, based on patterns it finds

in the data, recommend to customer A products that other customers who bought the same product also purchased.

- **Run targeted retention campaigns:** Based on a customer's purchase patterns and based on historical information, Amazon.com might be able to identify the customers who are most likely to stop being regular purchasers of products on the site. The company can then woo these customers with offers to prevent them from leaving. Note that this targeted approach differs from an across-the-board campaign directed at all customer, or at a random set of customers. With analytics, the company directs its extra expenditures precisely where they might yield the most benefits.

The following represent other possible applications of analytics:

- A university might want to avoid admitting students who end up failing many courses and eventually leaving without graduating. Instead, the university might have been better off admitting students who are able to successfully graduate. Based on historical information on various attributes of past incoming students and whether or not they graduated, the university might be able to identify the likely future performance of candidates. Patterns in historical data could reveal things that might not have been obvious at all.
- Providers of email services receive millions of emails on behalf of their customers. With the proliferation of spam mail, email providers must be able to look at various attributes of an incoming email and automatically determine whether the email is normal or is spam and either put the mail in the recipient's inbox or spam folder.
- Credit card companies process millions of transactions daily. These days they try to instantly determine, based on analytics – whether or not a transaction is likely to be fraudulent. If it seems that a transaction has a high likelihood of being fraudulent, then the company can call the customer to confirm. Of course calling customers too often for legitimate transactions can frustrate them. Failing to call a customer when a fraud has occurred could be even worse. Thus a good method for fraud detection can be a competitive advantage for a credit card company.

The above examples should give you a good feel for the territory. Let us look at a few definitions of the term *data mining* which is closely related to *data analytics*.

- Tan, et al[6] – Process of automatically discovering useful information in large data repositories.
- Shmueli, et al[7] – Statistics at scale and speed ... and simplicity
- Linoff and Berry[8] – Business process for exploring large amounts of data to discover meaningful patterns and rules.
- Gartner group[9] – The process of discovering meaningful correlations, patterns and trends by sifting through large amounts of data stored in repositories. Data mining employs pattern recognition technologies, as well as statistical and mathematical techniques.

[6] P. Tan, M. Steinbach, and V. Kumar. *Introduction to Data Mining, (First Edition)*. Addison-Wesley Longman Publishing Co., Inc., Boston, MA, USA, 2005. ISBN 0321321367

[7] G. Shmueli, N.R. Patel, and P.C. Bruce. *Data Mining for Business Intelligence: Concepts, Techniques, and Applications in Microsoft Office Excel with XLMiner (Second edition)*. John Wiley and Sons., Hoboken, NJ, USA, 2010. ISBN 0470526823

[8] G. Linoff and M. Berry. *Data Mining Techniques: For Marketing, Sales, and Customer Relationship Management*. IT Pro. Wiley, 2011. ISBN 9781118087459

[9] Gartner Group. IT glossary, 2013. URL `http://www.gartner.com/it-glossary/data-mining/`

The examples we have seen so far and a look at these definitions should give you a good picture of the impending adventure.

Can you think of anything that you did today which resulted in data that (possibly coupled with data from actions of other people) could be used for valuable insight?

A few possibilities:

Some suggestive examples of how data analytics might be used

- You might have visited the grocery store and purchased some items. The store could use your purchasing information along with that of many others to gain valuable insight – for example:
  - What products do people with your kind of demographic seem to prefer? The store can use this information for product promotions.
  - Which products seem to be purchased together? The store can use this for cross-selling by recommending products to people based on products that they have already purchased.
- You might have rated a song on iTunes or a movie on Netflix. Apple or Netflix can use your rating and those of numerous others to predict the ratings that various people might assign to certain songs or movies and help those people in their choice process.
- A student might have logged in to the school's course management system. The system administrators could use this information along with the login time preferences of other students to determine the number of servers to keep on-line during various times of the day.
- You might have checked you email and clicked on an advertisement that your mail provider displayed next to your email. Based on your click and those of millions of others, your mail provider can identify who seems to be interested in what kinds of advertisements, and fine tune the advertisements that it displays to mail users so as to increase the response rate.
- You might have logged in to your bank's web site for personal banking and used some of the features of the web site. Based on your usage patterns and those of other customers, the bank might categorize the customers into a three distinct groups. The bank could then

present a different customized user interface for customers in each group, tuned to their usage patterns.

- You used a search engine to search for "red bunny rabbits." The search engine can aggregate your search terms with those of millions of others (including demographic and other information like the locations from where these searches originated) and use this information to suggest search terms as other people type into their search box. For example, if many others, perhaps with identifiable similarities (based on location, demographics, ...) had also searched for "red bunny rabbits" and a matching person starts typing "red" into the search box, then the search engine can suggest "red bunny rabbits" as one of the possible searches. Surely you have noticed how the search suggestions make our web searches easier and more efficient.

People sometimes wonder about the difference between traditional statistical analysis and data analytics. On the surface the two terms might seem synonymous. In fact, many even use them interchangeably. Granted the two activities share lots of similarities. However, they differ in emphasis.

Traditional statistical analysis vs. data analytics

Traditional statistical techniques evolved predominantly during times when acquiring data was costly and time-consuming. As a result, traditional statistical techniques necessarily focused on making reasonable inferences from small amounts of data. They also placed a premium on enabling us to precisely assess the reliability of inferences based on small amounts of data. Furthermore, early statisticians could not employ computers for calculations and hence even if given large quantities of data, they would not have been able to process them easily.

Many assumptions underlying traditional statistical techniques do not apply in several contexts. Thus data analytics has a somewhat different emphasis.

All-round developments in information technology – specifically the ability to gather, store, transmit and process data – have comprehensively transformed the data landscape. In many arenas of operations, organizations possess abundant quantities of data, and massive computational capabilities to process them. The shackles that data-poverty imposed on statistics have come undone. Computer scientists and statisticians have invented analytical methods that more readily embrace a world of abundance of data and of processing power. Enter *Data Analytics*.

The focus has therefore shifted. Data analysts seek to identify patterns from very large data sets and are therefore not as hard-pressed as early statisticians were to establish that the results apply beyond the data that they analyzed. Inferences based on small sets of data leave open the possibility that the results might not apply more generally. When we arrive at inferences based on very large amounts of data, the likelihood that the results can apply more generally increases astronomically.

Relationships

Suppose we told you that we are thinking of two people A and B – about whom we tell you nothing else – and asked you "Does A own a car?" "What about B?" We also inform you that around 15% of the people in the world own at least one car. Knowing nothing specific about A and B, how would you proceed?

If you guess that A owns a car, what chance do you have of being correct?

Pay close attention to the question – we do not ask "Is your answer correct?" but "What *chance* do you have of being correct?" How do these two questions differ?

In reality your answer will either be correct or not – which is what the first question addresses. Without knowing A's actual car ownership status, we can never be sure of the correctness of our answer – it could be correct or it could be incorrect. Given this, is it just a toss-up which answer we give?

In a game of soccer, suppose you find yourself with the ball and only the opposite goalie to beat. Would you think "The goalie will either stop my shot or not and so it does not matter where I shoot?" Hardly. You will surely try and shoot the ball where you estimate that the goalie is, *least likely* to be able to stop it. Likewise, you should try and guess A's car ownership status in such a way that it has the *highest chance of being correct*.

What do we mean by *chance of being correct* in this context?

Let us suppose we were given 100 people instead of just A and B and were asked to guess each person's car ownership status, again without any additional information about each person. Suppose, after careful consideration, we arrive at what seems to us to be a good decision for one of them. The same decision would be our best one for all of them because we have no additional information. Whatever answer we give, we can expect it to be correct for some and wrong for others. An answer that has the highest *chance of being correct* would be the one that yields the greatest proportion of correct answers among the 100 people.

We seek to make predictions that have a high chance of being correct.

Let us say that you plan to guess that A owns a car. If you

were given 100 randomly chosen people (from the whole world) instead of just A, and you made the same guess (*owner*) for each one, then how many can you expect to get correct?

Given that 15% of the people in the world own cars, we can expect that close to 15 of the 100 people will be owners and that close to 85 would be non-owners. Since we are guessing that each one is an owner, we will be correct only for those 15 people who own cars and incorrect for the 85 who don't. Thus the choice has only a 15% chance of being correct. We would have had an 85% chance of being correct if we had guessed *non-owner*.

Suppose now we told you that A resides in the US and that B resides in India, what would your guess be for their car ownership status? We also give you the additional information that according to the World Bank[10], in 2009, US had 815 automobiles per 1,000 people while India had 18. For now, let us simplify and assume that all the automobiles belong to individuals and also that the data for 2009 still apply today, at least approximately. Approximating a little, let us assume therefore that 81% of the US residents and 2% of India residents own cars. Given this information, you would then be better off predicting that A owns a car and that B does not.

[10] World Bank. Motor vehicles (per 1,000 people), July 2013. URL `http://data.worldbank.org/indicator/IS.VEH.NVEH.P3`

Why did your answer change?

Well, you had more information. You were given information on an additional attribute – country of residence – and that enabled you to provide a "better" answer. Of course when we look at specific individuals it can well turn out that A might be a tramp from the streets of LA owning no car, and B might be a top Bollywood film star owning 10 cars.

Intuitively we might feel that our answer (A – owner; B – non-owner) is the best possible one under the circumstances. However, given that it could still be incorrect, how can we justify the intuition?

If we picked a large number of residents of India and the US *randomly*, and predicted that all US residents own a car and that no India residents owns a car, we would be correct on about 81% of the US residents and about 98% of the India residents. Specifically, if we made the predictions for 100 US residents and 100 India residents, then we can expect to get about 19 of the US predictions and about 2 of the India predictions incorrect for a total error rate of 21 over the 200 people, or 10.5%.

Knowing the relationship between attributes helped us to make a better guess.

If on the other hand, if we had to answer without the benefit of knowing each person's country of residence on the above group of 200 people, we would answer that none of them owns a car (after all only 15% of the people in the world own cars). We can expect to be wrong on 81 of the US residents and 2 of the India residents, for a total of 83 errors on 200 – an error rate of 41.5%.

Knowledge of the value of the attribute *country of residence* and of its *relationship* to *car ownership* enabled us to reduce the error rate from 41.5% to 10.5% – nearly a 75% improvement.

Target and predictor attributes

In data analytics we are often interested in making predictions or ascribing a value to an attribute whose value we do not know. In the above example, we wanted to determine a person's *car ownership status*. In analytics we refer to it as a *target attribute*. The other attributes whose values we use for determining the value of the target attribute – like the *country of residence* above – are *predictor attributes*.

Many data analytics techniques seek to uncover such *relationships* between attributes and then use these relationships to make predictions. Of course, we will invariably need to deal with situations much more complex than the toy example above, but the example does serve to illustrate the usefulness of *relationships* between attributes as aids to prediction.

Here are some more examples of *relationships*:

Examples of relationships

- Most colleges clearly consider a student's SAT score to be strongly related to a student's college performance – after all they use it as an important factor in their selection process.
- In the US, a person's educational level is known to be closely related to their income – people with college degrees generally earn more.
- The fuel economy of a car (miles per gallon in the US and kilometers per liter elsewhere) is related to the car's weight; it takes more energy to move a heavier object.

From the above relationships, can we infer that one attribute *caused* the other?

Not all relationships are causal.

For example, does a student's high SAT score *cause* her to do well in college or vice versa? Does having a college degree cause a person to earn more, or does its absence *cause* a person to earn less? Does a car's increased weight *cause* it to consume more fuel?

Not all *relationships* are *causal*. In the above cases, we would most likely agree that a high SAT score does not *cause* a student to do well in college. Perhaps a high SAT score indicates the student's general academic aptitude and this aptitude causes the students to do well in the SAT as well as in college.

We would also perhaps agree that a college degree *causes* people to get higher paying jobs. Employers might perceive that a person with a college degree brings more useful skills to the workplace. If someone had the necessary skills but lacked a college degree, then they might be able to command only a lower salary. Equally, a person with a college degree, but lacking the expected skills might still command a higher salary than someone without a college degree who has the necessary skills.

We might also easily see that increased weight *causes* a car to consume more fuel because the engine has to expend more energy to move a heavier object.

Observe that *causality* goes only in one direction in these two cases. We would not normally say that a high income *causes* people to have college degrees (although this also holds in other contexts – people might invest some of their earnings to go to college and earn degrees). We would definitely not say that a low fuel efficiency causes a car to become heavier!

In data analytics we are usually happy to exploit all *relationships* – causal or otherwise – to arrive at good predictions.

Data analytics places less emphasis on *causality* than traditional statistical analysis does

Researchers who seek to understand natural and social phenomena seldom stop with just establishing relationships and instead seek to establish *causality*. Data analytics, on the other hand, mostly looks to exploit all relationships in large data sets *so long as they help to make good predictions*; causality does not play a critical role in predictive data analytics.

The above examples of relationships should not lead you to believe that we always use only a single predictor attribute that has a relationship to the target attribute; most often we will need to use several.

Consider a holiday resort chain with many locations and advance reservations for the upcoming few months at its locations. Suppose it wants to predict, for each family that has made a reservation for the next month, how much money the family will spend during its stay. The resort chain's financial managers want this information for estimating sales revenues and planning cash flows.

A resort wants to predict sales revenue and cash flow

The resort might have historical data on several attributes for each family that stayed at one or more of its locations. Some possible attributes could be: family income and size, length of stay and the specific resort location and information on their expenditure. This information could enable the resort to develop a method to predict the spending of a family, given the values of all other attributes. Once the resort has built such a method, it can then apply it on future reservations for which it knows the values of all attributes other than the actual spending, and predict how much each family is likely to spend.

Given family size, resort name, length of stay, family income, etc., predict how much the family will spend during its stay.

That is, the resort is looking to develop a method of calculating the predicted spending based on the values of the other attributes.

To state the same thing succinctly, we can say that the resort seeks a function f:

$$spending = f\,(income, location, family\,size, length\,of\,stay)$$

More generally, we are looking for a function f that computes the value for a target attribute based on the values of the predictor attributes:

$$target\_attribute = f\,(predictor_1, \quad predictor_2, \quad predictor_3 ...)$$

For now, we will not look at the actual function and will be satisfied with just saying that we are looking at some method of calculating the a value for the target attribute. Later chapters will delve deeper – without getting into involved mathematics.

Review 3: Relationships

You can find the answers to these questions on page 356

1. To identify fraudulent credit card transactions, credit card companies try to classify each transaction as either normal or as fraudulent. If they record a charge to a credit card and can classify it as potentially fraudulent, then they can immediately alert the card holder by calling to confirm the validity of the charge. What attributes of a transaction might be related to the legitimacy of a transaction – that is, whether the transaction is normal or fraudulent?

2. A potential buyer of a new car at a car dealership offers his current used car as a trade-in. The car dealership needs to assess how much the trade-in car will sell for, and offer a trade-in value based on the estimated price. What attributes of the trade-in car might be related to its possible sale price?

How much is good enough?

People often make the mistake of expecting too much from data analytics. Before we race into learning new techniques, we will be well-served by understanding how well our techniques need to perform in order to be considered useful. Recall that the Netflix CEO was ready to do cartwheels over a mere 10% improvement.

Consider a hypothetical luxury car dealership. Suppose the dealership wants to run a direct mail campaign. It wants to mail an expensive invitation costing $7 each with a chance to test drive their latest vehicles. A person responding to the campaign and test-driving a vehicle without buying one might be considered as a beneficial outcome in general, but for the present let us consider only actual car sales as beneficial outcomes of the campaign.

The dealership has a limited budget that will enable it to mail out only 10,000 brochures. The cost of mailing a brochure exceeds $7 because the dealership also has to deal with those who respond. Salespersons will need to spend the time and they also need to factor in the costs of letting people test-drive the vehicles. The dealership has a 200,000 strong pool of prospective customers and needs to select 10,000 from this pool. It can either select the recipients through data analytics or through other methods that it has used historically.

Let us suppose that the dealership makes $5,000 from the sale of each car and that it costs the dealership $100 for each person who responds to the promotion and shows up at the dealership. Suppose that the dealership has traditionally had a 7% success rate in past direct mail campaigns – which means that they would sell 700 cars if they mailed 10,000 invitations.

Let us suppose that data analytics will enable the dealership to do just 10% better than before. What does this mean? Although the dealership would still mail out only 10,000 invitations, the recipients would be different from what their old approach would have selected and would be more likely to buy. What does this translate into in terms of numbers?

A 10% increase would mean selling 70 more cars and therefore an increase in profit of $350,000 over the earlier approach. Once the data analytics approach – model – has been designed, the dealership would incur negligible costs to run it each time. Even apparently small percentage increases in performance can help a lot!

We have to consider the *incremental* benefit of using data analytics against its *incremental* cost. Often the cost of acquiring the data and developing models do not amount to very much and therefore even small improvements in performance help a lot. Very often companies already gather much of the data in the process of conducting their normal business and store such data in a way that enables them to be easily harnessed for other purposes.

Incremental performance of analytics more important than absolute performance.

We did not mean to indicate in the preceding discussion that data analytics can only produce marginal improvements. In fact, many applications have yielded stellar improvements. However, beginners, excited at learning a new skill expect dramatic results every time and tend to overlook the bottom-line impacts of even seemingly small improvements. I wanted to sensitize you to this phenomenon up-front.

Important Data Analytics Concepts

You now understand the structure of data and can load data into **R** and navigate the resulting data frame. You must be eager to get on with real data analytics. We will get to the first technique as soon as we learn some basic concepts and terms. We will look at general concepts that apply to many of the techniques and will therefore discuss these without reference to any specific analytics technique. In future chapters we will amplify our discussion of some of these general concepts as they apply to specific techniques.

Predictive vs. *Descriptive* data analytics

Predictive Analytics seeks to analyze historical and current facts and make predictions about future or about unknown conditions. Analytics techniques look at two broad types of predictive analytics problems.

- **Classification:** In the email example on page 36, the email provider wants to *predict* whether a given email message is spam or not. This task involves *classifying* an email message into one of two categories This exemplifies *classification*.

- **Regression:** In the iTunes and Netflix examples on page 37 the task involves assigning a specific number to the rating that a user might assign to a song or movie. Unlike *classification* which only requires to put cases into one among a few bins or categories, this task involves computing a specific number. Such tasks exemplify *regression*.

Predictive analytics techniques look at historical data and understand or *learn* how to use some attributes (predictors) to predict the value of an attribute of interest (target). They then apply this knowledge to new data for which we need to make predictions about the value of the target attribute.

Supervised learning

Because the correct values in the data *guide* the learning process, we call predictive analytics techniques as *supervised* techniques.

Unsupervised learning

Descriptive data analytics does not seek to make any predictions, but only to identify patterns that help to understand the data better. We call these *unsupervised* techniques.

sno	name	region	income	gen	educ	credit	accept
1	Jane Fontana	3	30,000	F	1	3	0
2	Paul Finch	2	45,000	M	3	4	1
3	Jody Auerbach	4	38,000	F	3	3	1
4	Ming Yu	4	43,000	F	2	4	0
5	Kim Sung	5	39,000	M	3	2	1
6	Alex Rodrigues	2	56,000	M	2	5	0
7	Sheba Ahmed	4	73,000	F	3	3	1
8	Nikhil Pandey	2	49,000	M	1	4	0
9	Jason Bourne	1	52,000	M	2	2	0
10	Sabrina Smith	1	32,000	F	2	3	0

Table 4: Example of *tabular* data – repeated for convenience.

For convenience, we have repeated in Table 4 the sample table showing the basic structure of a data set. You now know that a data set has one or more attributes. In a predictive data analytics task, we are often interested in one of the attributes from a decision making perspective. For the data in Table 4, the bank might be interested in the value of the attribute *accept*, because that tells us whether or not a person accepted the bank's loan offer. The bank will likely have data on not just ten, but tens of thousands of people for whom it had made loan offers in the past – which is why the information on whether or not they accepted the offer is available.

The bank might now be planning to make loan offers to people to whom it has not lent money before. It might be interested in identifying people who are likely to be receptive to the loan offer and to expend resources on courting them.

The bank might start with a list of well-qualified potential customers about whom it has obtained demographic information from some other source. However, for these people, the bank does not know whether they will accept a loan offer or not. In other words, unlike the data in Table 4, for these people the bank does not have information about the last column, *accept*. The bank now needs to identify from this list those peo-

Use historical data to identify the characteristics of loan acceptors.

ple who are most likely to accept an offer of a loan. Analytics can help the bank to use historical data like that in Table 4 to *learn* the characteristics of loan acceptors.

Specifically, given the values of attributes like *region, income, gen* (gender), *educ* (education level) and *credit* (length of credit history) for a person, the bank might want to classify the person as *acceptor* or *non-acceptor*, and make offers only to those it classifies as *acceptor*. If the bank has a limit on the number of people that it would like to offer loans to – say 1000 – and the analytics procedure classifies 2000 people as *acceptors*, then the bank should make loan offers to the 1000 people who are most likely to accept the offer.

That is, the bank would like to estimate, based on the values of the other attributes (*region, income, gender, education* and *credit*), the probability that someone will accept a loan offer.

We refer to *accept* as the *target attribute* or *dependent attribute* – often also as *target variable* or *dependent variable*.

Target attribute/variable
Dependent attribute/variable

We refer to the other attributes, based on which the bank wants to determine the value of the target attribute as *predictor attributes* or *independent attributes* (Also as *predictor variables*) or *independent variables*.

Predictor attribute/variable
Independent attribute/variable

Can you see the rationale for the terminology for *dependent* and *independent* attributes?

We aim to find some way to calculate the value for *accept*, the *dependent* attribute, based on the other *independent* attributes. The value for *accept* **depends** on the value of the predictor attributes.

In later chapters we will learn a few different techniques that the bank could use to learn such patterns.

In data analytics we refer to the resulting pattern as a *model*. So we can talk about building a *model* to identify loan acceptors.

Model

Once the bank has built such a *model* and has determined that the model is good enough, it can then use the model on new data for which the value of the target attribute *accept* is unknown.

The bank cannot just find any model and start using it for identifying recipients of future loan offers. Obviously the bank would need to test the model on unbiased data to evaluate the model's usefulness before using it for future cases. That is, the bank needs to measure the *quality* of the model before deploying it. What might *quality* mean in this context?

Quality of a model

Clearly the bank should only deploy a model that does a *good* job of classifying people. Let us see how we can get an unbiased measure of the quality of the model.

As we said earlier, suppose the bank has historical data on 10,000 people to whom it made loan offers and for each one it has information like that in Table 4.

What if the analysts *randomly* chose 3,000 of these 10,000 rows and put this data away. Now the analysts are left with 7,000 rows and can build a model based only on these 7,000 rows. Once the model is ready, the analysts have the ability to classify a customer based on the predictor attributes and can use this model to classify each of the 3,000 rows that they initially put away. This smart arrangement enables them to compare the model's prediction with reality for each of the 3,000 rows.

Data partitioning

Figure 15 summarizes the process.

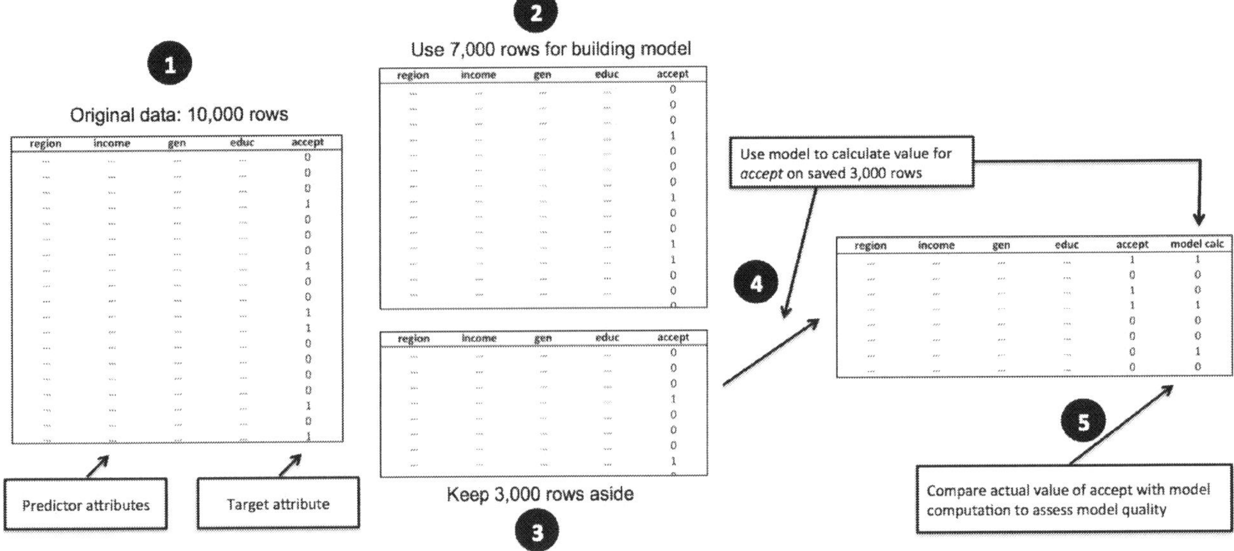

Figure 15: Outline of Bank's analytics process.

Fortunately, the original data also has information on whether or not each person actually accepted or ignored the loan offer. Thus there might be cases among the 3,000 for which the people accepted the loan and the model classified them as *acceptor*. There might also be cases where the people actually accepted the loan, but the model incorrectly classified them as *non-acceptor*. Similarly, there might be cases where the people did not accept the loan and the model classified them correctly as *non-acceptor* and cases where people did not accept the loan

Evaluating the model's performance on data that we put aside earlier and the model classified them incorrectly as *acceptor*. We can summarize the above long – and tiring – explanation with a so-called *classification-confusion matrix* or *error-matrix*. Figure 16 shows a hypothetical classification confusion matrix for our situation.

Classification-confusion matrix or *error-matrix*

		Predicted	
		acceptor	non-acceptor
Actual	acceptor	300	200
	non-acceptor	500	2000

Figure 16: Hypothetical *classification-confusion matrix* or *error-matrix* for bank example showing the actual and model-predicted number of cases for each class.

This clever approach allows the analysts to see how the model might perform on data that they did not use for building the model. They can see how many cases among the 3,000 the model classified correctly – a measure of the model's *quality*. In the *error matrix* in Figure 16 we see that out of the total of 3,000 cases, the method classified 2,300 cases correctly and 700 cases incorrectly. The overall error rate is 700/3,000 or 23.33%.

Data analysts refer to the process of dividing up the historical data into sets like we discussed above as *partitioning*.

We have to be careful to ensure that we use a truly random process for choosing the data for building the model. Otherwise we might not build the model on data that is representative of reality and get a poor model. For instance, if the data used to build the model happened to predominantly represent males, then the model might turn out to be poor when applied to females.

When we use a part of the available data to build a model and the rest to evaluate the model, the process is called *supervised learning*.

Supervised learning relies on data-partitioning

We use some of the data to *train* the model. The analytical technique *learns* from the available data to arrive at a model that can calculate a value for the target attribute.

Many data analytics methods require the data to be divided into *training* and *test* partitions through a random selection process. As we discussed earlier, we must be careful to select the cases for the training partition truly randomly. Being just partitions of the original data, all rows of both partitions have values for the target and predictor attributes.

Training and *test* partitions

In the bank example, the 7,000 rows that the bank used for model-building comprise the *training partition*. The remaining 3,000 rows comprise the *test partition*, or *holdout data*, which the analysts used for an unbiased evaluation of the quality of the model.

Why do we need to partition the data? Why not use all of the 10,000 rows to build and evaluate the model? After all with more data would we not get a better model? If the analysts used all the 10,000 rows and got a model that worked well on the same 10,000 rows, would they be in a position to assume that the model will perform comparably on new data?

An exam prep analogy for data partitioning

Let us consider an analogy to see why the analysts cannot make this optimistic assumption. Suppose a student is studying for a test and uses some practice questions to prepare for the test. Of course when the student answers a practice question incorrectly, she reads up on the concerned topics. After doing this several times, suppose the student is able to score 90% on the same practice questions that she used for preparation. Can we expect this student to score 90% on the real examination?

Obviously that would be a very optimistic assumption, because we cannot use the very same questions that the student practiced on to evaluate how the student would perform on new questions that she will face in the examination. To get a better assessment, we would need to evaluate the student's performance on a fresh set of questions that she did not use in preparing.

We should not evaluate the quality of a model based on how it performs on the data we use to create it – its performance on the training partition

Likewise, we should not evaluate an analytics model based on how well it performs on the very same data we used to train it. We would need to see how the model performs on data that it did not use to build the model.

To round out the analogy, the *training* partition is like the questions that the student used while preparing for the examination. The *test* partition is like a new set of questions on the same examination topic, but those that the student had never seen before. Performance on the new set of questions serves as a much more realistic estimate of where the student really stands.

The bank used the training partition to build the model. Suppose for example, the model classifies 95% of the cases on the training partition correctly. Is this an accurate indication of how well it will perform on new data? Based on our earlier discussion, we should be very wary of assuming this.

The bank has to apply the model to the 3,000 cases in the *test* partition – the holdout data – and see how many of these the model gets correct. We should rely more on the model's performance on the holdout data – the data in the *test* partition – to assess how it might perform on new data.

Table 5 shows a modified version of the bank data that we have been looking at. This version has an additional column – the amount of the loan, which has a non-zero value for those who accepted the loan offer and is zero for those who did not.

Table 5: Bank data with additional attribute.

sno	name	region	income	gen	educ	credit	accept	amount
1	Jane Fontana	3	30,000	F	1	3	0	0
2	Paul Finch	2	45,000	M	3	4	1	10,000
3	Jody Auerbach	4	38,000	F	3	3	1	12,000
4	Ming Yu	4	43,000	F	2	4	0	0
5	Kim Sung	5	39,000	M	3	2	1	20,000
6	Alex Rodrigues	2	56,000	M	2	5	0	0
7	Sheba Ahmed	4	73,000	F	3	3	1	21,000
8	Nikhil Pandey	2	49,000	M	1	4	0	0
9	Jason Bourne	1	52,000	M	2	2	0	0
10	Sabrina Smith	1	32,000	F	2	3	0	0

For the data in Table 5, the target attribute is still *accept*, but we now have an additional attribute, *amount*, that we can potentially use as a *predictor* attribute. Should we use it in our model?

We can expect *amount* to have tremendous predictive power. Note that whenever *amount* is zero, the person did not accept the loan offer and whenever it was non-zero, the person accepted the offer. In fact we can expect it to be so good that we do not even need any other predictor attributes – *amount* alone suffices. How much does *amount* appeal to you as a predictor attribute?

Let us suppose we built a model that included *amount* as one of the predictor attributes. How will we use the model to classify future cases? To classify a new customer as a loan acceptor or not, we would need the values for all the predictor attributes of that customer. Plugging those into the model will yield a value for the target attribute.

For a new customer, will the bank have a value for *amount*?

Obviously not! That attribute was available for historical cases but will not be available for new cases – we can know the loan amount (0 or otherwise) only for cases that were already made loan offers – historical cases. We will not have this value for future cases unless we happen to be clairvoyant! Only attributes whose values will be available at the time we use the model for prediction should even be considered for inclusion as predictor attributes.

Inappropriate predictor attributes

Choose simple models

We usually aim to build the simplest possible model that performs adequately. For example, suppose we can obtain a model with a performance level of 80% using five predictor attributes and another model with 20 attributes that performs at 81%, then we will choose the former because of its relative simplicity and almost identical performance. Very complex models involving numerous attributes are also difficult to explain and justify.

When creating partitions, we generally use approximately 70% of the data for the training partition and the remaining 30% for the test partition.

How many cases in each partition?

Treat this as rough guideline. Feel free to deviate so long as you have sufficient numbers of cases in each partition.

How much data do we need for predictive data analytics? Suppose grocery store A analyzes historical data for 100 customers and arrives at a model for determining whether a future customer is likely to buy a specific product or not. Suppose grocery store B does the same thing, but bases its analysis on historical data for 10,000 customers. Which of the two models would you rely more on?

The first model leaves open a much greater chance that future customers could exhibit very different behavior patterns than those that the model was based on. The model's predictions could thus be off by a lot. The second model is much less likely than the first to have the problem and we can have greater confidence in its predictions.

More generally, we can have confidence in a model that we build using large amounts of training data.

These days, data analysts usually have the luxury of having huge amounts of data. When we do not have this luxury, we need to avoid the mistake of basing our model on too little data. So a key question arises – at the very least how much data do we need?

A common rule of thumb [11]says that we need at least 10 cases per predictor attribute for numerical target attributes and at least $6nx$ cases in the file if we have a categorical target attribute with n different category values and x predictor attributes.

[11] G. Shmueli, N.R. Patel, and P.C. Bruce. *Data Mining for Business Intelligence: Concepts, Techniques, and Applications in Microsoft Office Excel with XLMiner (Second edition).* John Wiley and Sons., Hoboken, NJ, USA, 2010. ISBN 0470526823

Thumb-rule for number of cases needed

For example, if we have a numerical target attribute and use 20 predictor attributes, then we will need at least 200 cases.

Example for number of cases needed for numerical target attribute

If we have a categorical target attribute with two possible categories (e.g., *acceptor* and *non-acceptor*) and 8 predictor attributes, then we will need 96 cases.

Example for number of cases needed for categorical target attribute

Review 4: Important data analytics concepts

You can find answers to these questions starting on page 357

1. For each of the following items, indicate if the problem is one of *classification* or *Regression*:

   i A text analysis application is to be provided text fragments and it is supposed to identify if the fragment came from the *New York Times* or the *Wall Street Journal*.

   ii An amusement park wants to predict the number of visitors on a particular day based on factors like: the expected weather; weekday or not, summer vacation or not, ...

   iii A rice farmer wants to build a model to predict the number of tons of rice his land will produce during a specific year.

   iv Gmail divides the inbox into three tabs *Primary*, *Social* and *Promotions*. For each mail that it will place in a user's inbox, it needs to determine the appropriate tab.

   v A publishing company has two types of books that it publishes – *fiction* and *non-fiction*. The company wants to build a model to predict the sales of each type of publication based historical data on several attributes of its prior publications.

2. A credit card company used its historical data to build a model to classify a credit card transaction as *genuine* or *fraudulent*, based on several attributes that would be available at the time a transaction takes place. Of course, for each row of historical data, the company knew if the corresponding

transaction was genuine or fraudulent. The company plans to use this model on every new credit card transaction.

As described in this text, they used data partitioning. They had 100,000 rows in the training partition and 40,000 rows in the test partition.

Without worrying about how they built the model or what is in the model, explain how you might test the quality of the model.

R Packages

When we first install **R**, the process installs a huge amount of functionality. However, while in an **R** session, you have access only to a subset of the *installed* functionality. When you start **R**, it does not *load* all of its *installed* functionality into memory – because we do not need all of them all the time. Loading all would only serve to tie up our computer's resources, especially its main memory, and affect the performance not just of **R**, but of other programs that we might be using concurrently.

How do we access the additional functionality that has been *installed* but not *loaded*?

The installed functionality of **R** is kept in the form of coherent chunks called *packages*. **R** allows us to *load* and *unload packages* as needed. To access the functionality in a package that is *installed* but not *loaded*, we need to first *load* the relevant package.

Be sure to understand the distinction between *installed* and *loaded* packages

What if we need functionality that is not even installed on our system?

In addition to the packages that came with our **R** installation, thousands more are available for us to easily add-on. Furthermore, people continuously extend **R** by writing more new packages and making most of them available for free. As researchers invent new data analysis techniques, people soon make the corresponding **R** packages available as well.

By default, **R** loads a few packages automatically at startup. These include *base*, *graphics*, *stats* and *datasets*, and a few others. We have to explicitly load any other packages we might need during a session.

Figure 17 illustrates the ideas. As the figure shows, we can either directly install packages from the outside world onto our **R** installation, or download the installation file first and then install it. Most of the time, you will find yourself installing directly from the Web.

To install a package on your **R** system from an external repository, use the command below (replace "<package-name>"

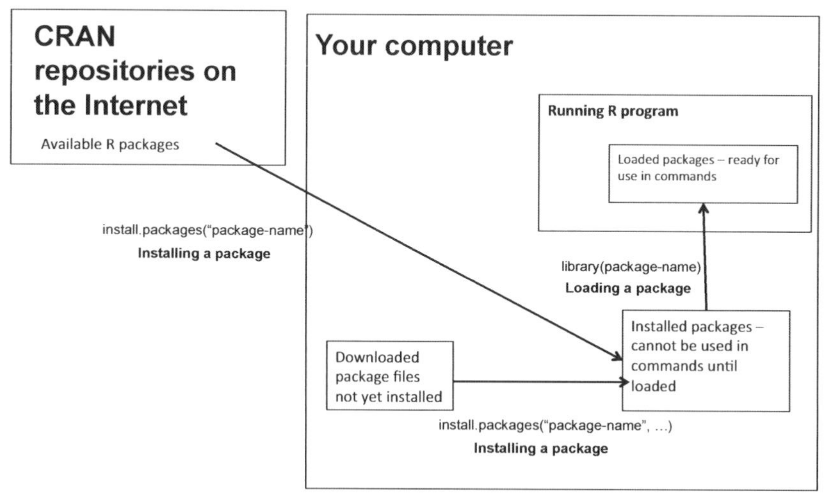

Figure 17: R packages – available, installed and loaded. A package needs to be installed just once on your computer; it can be loaded as needed. We can either directly install a package from an external repository or first download the package file locally and then install it.

with the name of the actual package; quotes are required):

```
> # Installing a package from an external repository
> # install.packages("<package-name>")
> # for example
> install.packages("FNN")
```

You can find packages to install easily through a Web search. We will see this process in the next lab.

*Lab 3: Installing and loading **R** packages*

Pre-requisite(s)

✓ **R** should already be installed on your computer – if not, see the instructions on page 7.

✓ You should have read the text section on **R** packages on page 54.

✓ You should be connected to the Internet.

Objective

After completing this lab, you will be able to:

✓ ***Install*** a package from en external repository.

✓ ***Load*** an installed **R** package.

✓ Recognize **R** error messages related to packages.

Overview

The core **R** system that you installed includes functionality related to the most commonly used mathematical and statistical analyses. **R** loads this core functionality automatically at startup. The designers of **R** made it possible to load (and unload) additional functionality in the form of *packages* as-needed. If there are some packages we use on a regular basis, we can set up **R** so that it loads these at startup as well. We do not address that in this book.

By default, **R** loads a few packages automatically at startup. These include *base*, *graphics*, *stats*, *datasets*, and a few others. We have to explicitly load any other packages we might need during a session.

We will look at two stages in using **R** packages. The first stage involves *installing a package*. To install a package, we can ask **R** to directly download and install the code for the package via the Internet from a CRAN repository – this is what we will generally do. It is also possible to first download a package file and then separately install it – but this is seldom needed and we do not cover this.

Once you install a package, its code becomes available on your **R** system, but is not yet quite ready for use.

We can run the code in an installed **R** package only after we *load* the package. *Installing* and *loading* a package represent two different steps that we need to perform before we can use a package.

Figures 18 and 19 clarify.

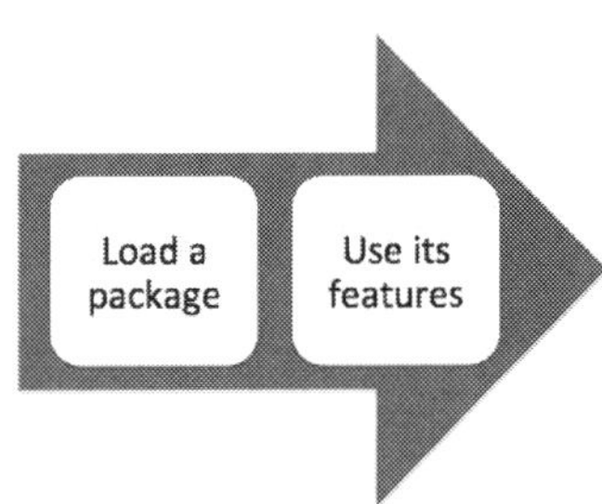

Figure 18: Using an already installed package – once installed, a package can be loaded and used without the need to install it again

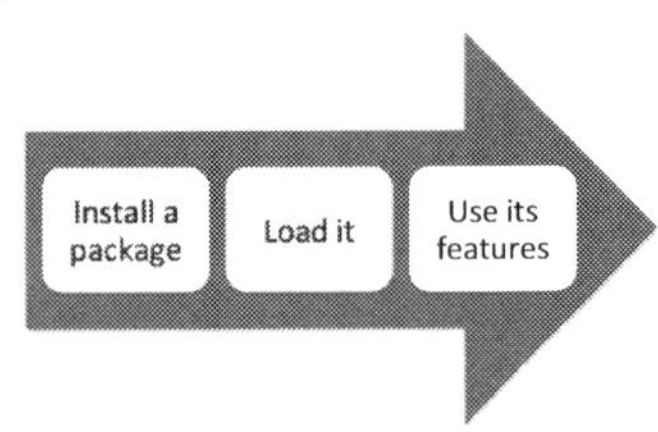

Figure 19: Using a package that is not already installed on your system – a package has to first be installed before we can load and use it

You might be wondering why they designed it such that we need two steps. Why not just make the code automatically available in every **R** session after installing a package? Would that not be more convenient?

Think about your own computer – you have *installed* many programs on it – programs for web browsing, word processing, spreadsheet manipulation, image processing and so on. However, not all the programs start running as soon as you boot up your computer. You open and close – that is *load* and *unload* – programs as needed. For example, you would hardly want your image processing program to be running and consuming your computing resources (like main memory) when you do not intend to use that program during a session. That would only waste resources and possibly slow down your system needlessly.

The same logic applies to **R**. Beyond a set of core packages, we have the choice of selectively loading only the packages we intend to use during a session.

R users typically install many packages, but do not

need access to all of their features all the time – just as we do not need all installed programs on our computer to be running all the time. If all the features of all the installed packages were to be ready to run all the time then **R** would use up a huge amount of system resources and could slow down the computers unnecessarily with useless code. This is why we *load* and *unload* packages as needed.

Activity steps

1. **Seeing the list of available packages on the web:** To get an idea of the add-on packages available for **R**, visit this web site for the CRAN repository:

   `https://cran.r-project.org/web/packages/available_packages_by_name.html`

   This should give you an idea of the sheer volume of free functionality that is out there for the taking.

2. **Listing installed and loaded packages:** In **RStudio**, go to the bottom right pane and select the *Packages* tab. You now see a list of packages that are installed on your system. You see that some are checked.

   RStudio has check-marked those that are already loaded. Incidentally, this list does not show the *base* package.

   The *packages* tab shows us the installed and loaded packages

3. **Finding the name of a package that you need:** Before you install a package, you need to know the name of the package. You can use a web search engine to easily find this. For example, suppose we want to install the package for doing *association rules* analysis in **R** – for now, do not worry about what that means; we will look at it in detail in a later chapter.

   Search the web to find names of packages that might be available to fulfill your needs

   Use a search engine and type a search query like "R package association rules" and you will quickly realize that you need the package called *arules*.

4. **Installing packages from an external repository:** Now that we know the name of the package we want to install – *arules* – we can **use one of the following two ways** to install it. For now, execute the instructions in both steps below because we install different packages in each.

   You can use either the console or the "Install" button in the *Packages* tab to install packages

   a **In the RStudio console:** Type the following command

   ```
   > install.packages("arules")
   ```

In general, if you know the name of a package to install, you can substitute its name in the command above. Do not forget the quotes.

While we are at it, let us also install some other packages that we will need for the techniques that the book covers:

```
> install.packages(c("rpart","rpart.plot", "class"))
```

You should now see the names of these four new packages in the *packages* tab. Since we have only installed, but not loaded them, they are not checked. You might need to refresh the display by pressing the arrow to the *right of Update.*

b **Using the RStudio user interface:** In the packages tab, right below the menu bar, you see "Install"; click on it. In the resulting dialog, enter *FNN dummies e1071 caret lattice ggplot2*, without quotes, and press *Install*. After a brief wait, you will see signs in your console that the installation of these six packages has started. Wait for the process to finish and for the command prompt ">" to come back.

Once again, you see the names of these six new packages in the list – not yet checked.

5. **Loading a package:** Once installed, you need to *load* a package before you can use its functionality. The following command loads the *arules* package that we just installed:

Load a package with the *library* function or just by checking its name in the *Packages* tab

```
> library(arules)
```

Note that we did not use quotes in the above command. Instead of issuing the above command, you can simply check the corresponding box in the listing on the *Packages* tab.

6. **Need to reload on restart:** Once you load a package, its features are available for the *current session.*

However, when you quit and restart **R**, it only loads the basic packages mentioned previously. Any other packages that you might have loaded in an earlier session are not available by default. To use the functionality from any other package, you will have to load it afresh for the present session with the *library* command or through the **RStudio** user interface. If we use a set of packages constantly and want to avoid having to manually load them each time we start **R**, we can automate the process. We will not get into that feature in this book.

7. **Unloading a package:** We will never actually have to do this for what we cover in this book, but let us see how to anyway. To unload the *arules* package that you just loaded, type the **R** command:

   ```
   > detach("package:arules", unload=TRUE)
   ```

   Alternately, you can just uncheck the package name in the *Packages* tab.

8. **Detecting a package-related error:** You already know that just *installing* a package is insufficient to start using its functionality – we also have to *load* it. We sometimes forget to load a package and still try to use functionality that it provides. Suppose you type in a command (let us say the command is "xxx") that is available from a package. If you have not loaded the package, you will get the error *Error: could not find function "xxx"*.

   You must beware though. You will get the same error message even if you have loaded the package, but mistype the function name. So when you get such a message, check and see if you have typed the function name correctly. If you have, then you know that the error is the result of not having loaded the appropriate package.

If you think that you typed a function name correctly but still get an error message to the effect that **R** is unable to find that function, then check to see that you loaded the appropriate package

*Review 5: **R** Packages*

You can find answers to these questions starting on page 358

1. What is the name given to a chunk of **R** functionality that we can load and unload as needed?
2. List two ways by which we can install packages.
3. What two things would you need to do have done before you can use the functionality of a package?
4. What must we already have done before we can load a package?
5. List two ways by which we can load a package.

Lab 4: Data partitioning in R

Pre-requisite(s)

✓ Completed the *Data Frames* lab on page 17.

✓ Read about data partitioning in the section *Important Data Analytics Concepts* on page 45.

✓ Completed the lab on **R** packages on page 55.

Objective

After completing this lab, you will be able to:

✓ Use the *caret* package to create partitions.

✓ Set the seed of the random number generator so as to match your results with those shown in the text.

Overview

You have already seen that predictive data analytics require us to partition our data. In this lab, you will learn how to create data-partitions.

We will use the *createDataPartition* function from the *caret* package.

Activity steps

1. **Read in the data:** We use the Boston Housing data[12] [13] once again. Do you remember the command to read in this file? If not, review page 20.

   ```
   > bh <- read.csv("BostonHousing.csv")
   ```

   In what follows, I assume that you called your data frame "bh" – if not, modify your commands accordingly, replacing "bh" in the commands listed below with whatever name you used. In fact, I suggest that you use a different name so that you avoid mechanically following these instructions without having to think for yourself.

2. **Load the *caret* package:** The *caret* package provides a convenience function called *createDataPartition* for creating partitions. Recall that in the lab on **R** packages (page 55), we installed the *caret* package. However, before we can use the package, we have to first load it.

[12] D. Harrison and D.L. Rubinfeld. Hedonic prices and the demand for clean air. *J. Environ. Economics & Management*, pages 81–102, 1978

[13] K. Bache and M. Lichman. UCI machine learning repository, 2013. URL `http://archive.ics.uci.edu/ml`

Recall from the lab on **R** packages (page 55) that we can either use **RStudio**'s *Packages* tab on the bottom right pane, or enter a command to load a package. You can click on the *Packages* tab in the bottom right pane and check *caret*.

Alternately, you can enter the following command:

```
> library(caret)
```

3. **Identify the *target* attribute:** Partitioning the data well is not just a matter of randomly selecting cases to put in the training partition. Consider the *BostonHousing* data. Here, we might be trying to build a model to predict the median value of homes in a specific neighborhood – the *MEDV* attribute.

   In supervised learning, the attribute that we are building a model to predict is called the *target* attribute.

   In the present case, we would not want most of the cases in the training partition to represent either high or low values of *MEDV*. Ideally we would want the whole range of values of *MEDV* to be represented in both the training and test partitions. In other words, we want *MEDV* to have very similar distributions in the two partitions. The *createDataPartition* function of the *caret* package can take care of this for us, provided we can tell it what the *target attribute* is.

   For our current example, we know that the *target attribute* is *MEDV*. We will use this in the next step. It does not matter if the target attribute is numeric or categorical.

4. **Create the partitions:** We can now create the partitions using the *createDataPartition* function in the *caret* package. Enter the following commands exactly as they are (**R** is case sensitive) – we explain the commands below:

```
> set.seed(2015)
> sample <- createDataPartition(bh$MEDV,
       p = 0.7, list = FALSE)
> sample
> train <- bh[sample, ]
> test <- bh[-sample, ]
```

The first line of code above might seem strange. In this book, we will partition data often. Generally the *random* partitioning results will differ from one trial to the next. Therefore, unless we take special steps, your results will not match those that the book shows. To confirm that you are on the right track, you might want your results to match those in the book. This is what the first line of code above achieves. It ensures that your random sample matches those we used for the book's results.

Mathematical software systems use an internal random number generator for all random sampling operations. By setting the *seed* of this random number generator, we can match up random number sequences that the programs generate. If you also set the seed to 2015 as above, then your results will match those in the book. If you skip that line, then your results will still be *correct*, but will not match those in the book – because your random sample will differ. For your benefit, in all lab activities, this book sets the random number seed as above.

Our choice of 2015 is purely arbitrary; we could have chosen any other number. Of course, using a different number will result in a different sequence.

The second line of code above:

```
> sample <- createDataPartition(bh$MEDV,
      p = 0.7, list = FALSE)
```

generates a random sample of 70% of the row numbers between 1 and 506 (which is the number of rows in *bh*) and stores this in a variable called *sample*. (We will not go into the *list = FALSE* part; just use it as such whenever you create partitions).

We passed *hdata$MEDV* – the target attribute values – to the function so that it could try to give us a set of random rows that are representative of the distribution of values of *MEDV* in the complete data set. We passed $p = 0.7$ to get a training sample of 70% of the rows. You will adopt the same approach even if the target attribute is categorical.

After executing that line of code, the variable *sample* contains approximately 70% of the row numbers between 1 and 506. The following line prints *sample* and Figure 20 shows the first ten values. We see that the random sample picked rows 1 through 7, 12, 13, 14, 16 and so on.

The fourth line:

```
> train <- bh[sample, ]
```

uses the contents of the variable *sample*, to select only those rows from the main data frame and keep them in a new data frame called *train*. We need all the columns and hence left the portion after the comma as blank. The original data frame *bh* still contains all the 506 rows.

The variable *train* now contains the training partition.

The last line does a bit of magic. Having selected the rows in *sample* as the training partition, we now want the *rest* of the rows in the *test* partition. The line:

```
> test <- bh[-sample, ]
```

does this elegantly. By placing a minus sign before *sample*, we tell **R** that we want all the rows from *bh*, *except* those whose indexes are in *sample*. Cool!

The variable *test* has the *test* partition.

```
        Resample1
 [1,]           1
 [2,]           2
 [3,]           3
 [4,]           4
 [5,]           5
 [6,]           7
 [7,]          12
 [8,]          13
 [9,]          14
[10,]          16
```

Figure 20: First ten rows of the random sample generated by *createDataPartition*

5. **Using the partitions:** Now that we have the data partitions, we can use them simply by specifying the variable names we used for them – *train* and *test*. For example, we can see the number of rows in each:

```
> nrow(bh)                      # prints 506
> nrow(train)                   # prints 356
> nrow(test)                    # prints 150
> nrow(train) + nrow(test)      # prints 506
```

We can now use the variables *train* and *test* whenever we need to access these partitions.

Lab assignment 2 Data Partitioning

You can find answers to these questions starting on page 359
Show the **R** commands you will use for the following. If a specific package is needed, you should show the **R** command to load it specifically in the step where it is needed.

1. Read the data from the file *college-perf.csv* into an **R** data frame called *cp*. The target attribute is *Perf*. You will use this data frame for questions 2 to 6.

2. Set the seed for the random number generator to 2015.

3. Generate a set of random row numbers from the data frame amounting to 65% of the rows and store the result in a variable called *sel*.

4. Create a data frame called *training* that contains the rows of *cp* corresponding to the rows sampled above.

5. Create a data frame called *testing* that contains the remaining rows of *cp*.

6. Write the **R** code to see the total number of rows in *cp*. Then write an **R** expression to total the number of rows in *training* and in *testing*. Should the two match?

7. Read the data from the file *auto-mpg.csv* into a data frame called *auto*. Write all the necessary commands (including loading of packages) to create a training partition with 70% of the rows and a test partition with the rest. Call these two partitions *train* and *test*, respectively. You can assign any name to the other variables you use. As a good practice, always use meaningful names. The target attribute is *mpg*.

Affinity Analysis

When you buy an item at an electronics store – say a DVD player – an associate at the store might suggest that you buy something else – say cables. Similarly, if you buy shoes, it would make sense for a shop to try and sell you socks as well, or when you buy a laptop, a prudent sales associate would certainly ask if you might also be interested in an external backup device.

The suggestions seem quite obvious in the above cases. However, in stores that sell thousands or even hundreds of thousands of items – like an on-line retailer or a modern grocery store or a mega store like WalMart or a membership warehouse like Costco – just using common-sense to make such recommendations would be impractical. Furthermore, what about the non-obvious combinations of items that people buy? By examining thousands of customer transactions, data analytics can help us to spot items that are frequently purchased together and to use this information to automate the process of making recommendations.

Figure 21: Example of a recommendation by Amazon.com.

If you have been a reasonably frequent shopper at Amazon.com, you might have noticed that as soon as you add an item to your shopping cart, the site often comes up with something like "People who bought X, also bought ..." (see Figure 21)

Affinity Analysis uses historical data to identify items that occur together *frequently*. People also refer to this technique by other names – *Frequent Itemset Mining* and *Market Basket Analysis*. Many retailers use *Affinity Analysis* to recommend products to customers – cross-selling. They can also use this information for other decisions like store layout, catalog design and customer segmentation.

Affinity Analysis
Frequent Itemset Mining
Market Basket Analysis

On-line stores offer several thousands of products and customers need a lot of assistance in finding their needle in this haystack. Recommendation systems take on added prominence in this context.

While it appears that *Affinity Analysis* can only be applied to sales, it has wider scope for application. If you use Gmail, you might have noticed that when you create a list of recipients for an email message, Gmail sometimes makes suggestions like "Consider adding X, Y and Z as recipients" based on patterns occurring in the recipient lists of your past emails. In a university setting, analyzing the sets of courses students register for can enable the system to also recommend courses to students as they register on-line for classes.

Other examples of the use of affinity analysis

Given its scope for creative uses, you might find it useful to learn the basic concepts of affinity analysis.

Affinity Analysis[14] is one of the two *unsupervised* data mining techniques that we cover. Although it uses historical data, it does not aim to learn any "correct answers" from the data. Instead it simply finds items that occur together and uses this information for making recommendations. Therefore the technique does not use data-partitioning.

[14] Rakesh Agrawal, Tomasz Imieliński, and Arun Swami. Mining association rules between sets of items in large databases. In *Proceedings of the 1993 ACM SIGMOD International Conference on Management of Data*, SIGMOD '93, pages 207–216, New York, NY, USA, 1993. ACM. ISBN 0-89791-592-5. DOI: 10.1145/170035.170072. URL http://doi.acm.org/10.1145/170035.170072

Let us look at a very small example so that we can wrap our brains around important concepts. We will then look at a larger and more realistic example.

Affinity analysis is an example of an *unsupervised data mining technique*

Affinity Analysis example

Look at Table 6 showing fictitious baskets of items purchased by 10 customers. We will use this data to illustrate the important concepts underlying *Affinity Analysis*.

We have taken a small example so that you can easily grasp everything.

Assume that you are the manager of the store in which the 10 transactions of Table 6 occurred. A customer just added a toothbrush to her basket and you want to recommend another item to the customer. Which other item from the table would make most sense?

Which product should you recommend?

Customer no	Items purchased
1	Toothbrush, Toothpaste, Moisturizer
2	Toothpaste, Toothbrush, Pen
3	Toothpaste, Pen
4	Toothpaste, Paper
5	Toothbrush, Toothpaste, Paper
6	Toothbrush, Pen
7	Toothbrush, Toothpaste, Pen, Moisturizer
8	Toothpaste, Paper
9	Soda
10	Toothpaste, Pen

Table 6: Fictitious purchase data.

We refer to a set of items as an *itemset*. Any collection of items, not necessarily only those making up a full basket, can make up an *itemset*. An example of an *itemset* that occurs in at least one of the customer transactions in our data would be: $\{Pen, Moisturizer\}$. An example of an *itemset* that does not occur in any of the customer transactions is $\{Toothpaste, Soda, Paper\}$.

Customers 1, 2, 5 and 7 all purchased both Toothbrush and Toothpaste. It therefore looks like we have a good *rule* which states that people who buy toothbrushes are likely to buy toothpaste as well. We did not really need a computer and data analytics to tell us that. However we were able to arrive at this finding by mechanically looking at data and without using any of our understanding about how the real world works. The following:

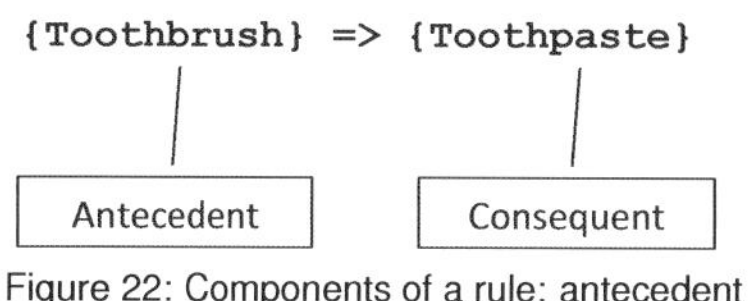

Figure 22: Components of a rule: antecedent and consequent

$$Rule\,1 : \{Toothbrush\} \implies \{Toothpaste\}$$

expresses the crux of our *rule* into mathematical notation. In mathematics, the sign in the middle of the rule stands for *implies*. We call the left hand side of the rule as the *antecedent* and the right hand side as the *consequent* of the rule. Although the *antecedent* and *consequent* of the above rule each had just one item, in general these can be any *itemsets*, even empty.

Rules inherent in item sets

Below is an example of a rule in which the antecedent has more than one item:

$Rule\,2 : \{Toothbrush, Toothpaste\} \implies \{Pen\}$

We will be describing a few important concepts and associated calculations below. You will not have to manually perform any of these calculations for actual analysis. However, to cement your understanding, we implore you to work through these simple calculations as we describe them on the sample data set in Table 6.

Consider the first rule $\{Toothbrush\} \implies \{Toothpaste\}$. In our data set, the antecedent of the above rule, the itemset $\{Toothbrush\}$ occurs in five transactions (1, 2, 5, 6 and 7). Of these five, the consequent $\{Toothpaste\}$ occurs in four (1, 2, 5 and 7). Since the consequent occurs 80% of the time that the antecedent occurs, the rule has an 80% *Confidence* level.

Another way to look at it is, if we pick any transaction that has *Toothbrush* in it, we can be 80% *confident* that it will also have *Toothpaste*.

Confidence of a rule is the proportion of times the consequent also occurs when the antecedent occurs

$$confidence = \frac{No\_of\_transactions\_having\_both\_antecdeent\_and\_consequent}{No\_of\_transactions\_having\_antecedent}$$

Confidence is our first measure of a rule's quality. What is the *confidence* of the second rule above?

$\{Toothbrush, Toothpaste\} \implies \{Pen\}$?

The antecedent $\{Toothbrush, Toothpaste\}$ occurs in four transactions (1, 2, 5 and 7). Of these, the consequent $\{Pen\}$ occurs in two (2 and 7) for a confidence of 50%.

Even with a small number of transactions and only a few items in each one, we have a potentially very large sets of rules. We therefore need to measure the quality of a rule and pick only the good ones for use. Should we judge a rule by its confidence measure?

We need a way to generate only *good* rules

Even a small itemset generates numerous possible rules (not all of them good). Figure 23 shows quite dramatically the number of rules that can result from an itemset of just three items. If we consider all the rules from every transaction in a data set, then we will end up with a huge number of rules.

For example, with data on 20,000 customer transactions, we could easily end up with millions of rules. Just *generating* all of them would be a huge task – and quite pointless. Generating only the *reasonable* ones and picking the best among those might be sensible. So we might generate a set of 500 good rules and pick the best 100 of those. In *affinity analysis* we are trying to find the best x rules, where x depends on how many we can use effectively.

```
{} => {Toothbrush}
{} => {Toothpaste}
{} => {Moisturizer}
{} => {Toothbrush, Toothpaste}
{} => {Toothbrush, Moisturizer}
{} => (Toothpaste, Moisturizer)
{} => {Toothbrush, Toothpaste, Moisturizer}
{Toothbrush} => {Toothpaste}
{Toothbrush} => {Moisturizer}
{Toothpaste} => {Moisturizer}
{Toothpaste} => {Toothbrush}
{Moisturizer} => {Toothbrush}
{Moisturizer} => {Toothpaste}
{Toothbrush, Toothpaste} => {Moisturizer}
{Toothbrush, Moisturizer} => {Toothpaste}
{Toothpaste, Moisturizer} => {Toothbrush}
{Moisturizer} => {Toothbrush, Toothpaste}
{Toothpaste} =>  {Toothbrush, Moisturizer}
{Toothbrush} => {Toothpaste, Moisturizer}
```

Figure 23: Rule explosion: Rules implied by the item set {Toothbrush, Toothpaste, Moisturizer}

To cement your understanding, at this point, you should take a look at the data and write out a few rules from it. Try writing one rule with just one item in the antecedent and the consequent; one with two items in the antecedent and one in the consequent and then a rule with one item in the antecedent and two in the consequent. For each of these rules, calculate the *confidence*.

Returning to our question: Should we judge the quality of a rule by its confidence measure?

To illustrate an important point, we step away for a second from our little example. Suppose a data set has 20,000 customer transactions and we have two rules:

$$Rule\,3 : \{X\} \implies \{Y\}, \text{with confidence 100\%}$$
$$Rule\,4 : \{P\} \implies \{Q\} \text{ with confidence 80\%}$$

Is Rule 3 better than Rule 4? Certainly sounds like a reasonable conclusion.

What if the itemset $\{X\}$ occurs in only 100 out of the 20,000 transactions, whereas itemset $\{P\}$ occurs in 5,000 of the 20,000 transactions?

Since the antecedent for Rule 3 is very rare, we will be able to make use of it for recommendations only very infrequently. Let us suppose that over a certain time-period, this rule comes into play 200 times overall, resulting in 200 recommendations for product Y. Let us assume, optimistically, that each one of these 200 recommendations results in a sale.

High *confidence* alone might not suffice

During the same month Rule 4 might be applied 10,000 times – because its antecedent itemset is much more common. The rule has a confidence factor of 80%, and hence 8,000 of these transactions would also contain the consequent. Even if we pessimistically assume that only 10% of the recommendations using Rule 4 turn into sales, this would mean that this rule would still account for 800 purchases compared to the 200 for the first rule – where we optimistically assume 100% conversion. So even with the odds stacked heavily against Rule 4, it turns out to be much more useful – despite having a much lower *confidence*.

Clearly therefore, we cannot rely on confidence alone to determine the usefulness or quality of a rule; we have to consider how frequently we might be able to use the rule. This analysis leads us to our second criterion to judge a rule: its *support*.

We define *support* for a rule as the proportion of transactions in which all of the items involved in the rule occur together. We repeat the information in Table 7 for convenience.

Table 7: Fictitious purchase data – repeated for convenience.

Customer no	Items purchased
1	Toothbrush, Toothpaste, Moisturizer
2	Toothpaste, Toothbrush, Pen
3	Toothpaste, Pen
4	Toothpaste, Paper
5	Toothbrush, Toothpaste, Paper
6	Toothbrush, Pen
7	Toothbrush, Toothpaste, Pen, Moisturizer
8	Toothpaste, Paper
9	Soda
10	Toothpaste, Pen

$$support = \frac{No\_of\_transactions\_having\_antecdent\_and\_consequent}{No\_of\_transactions}$$

Going back to the example from Table 6, repeated in Table 7, let us compute the *support* for $Rule\,1 : \{Toothbrush\} \implies \{Toothpaste\}$.

The two items Toothbrush and Toothpaste occur together in four out of the ten transactions for a *support* of 40%.

What about the *support* for $Rule\,2 : \{Toothbrush, Toothpaste\} \implies \{Pen\}$?

Toothbrush, Toothpaste and Pen occur together in two out of the ten transactions for a *support* of 20%.

Again, let us step away from our little example to see another important point. In some other situation, suppose we have found the following rule with high *support* and high *confidence*.

$$Rule\,5 : \{Bananas\} \implies \{Razors\}$$

Can we infer from this that these two items have a high affinity – that is, when one of them occurs, the other also occurs disproportionately often – like the frequent co-occurrence of shoes and socks?

To make matters concrete, if we look at many shopping carts in a supermarket, we might find bananas and razors in a good proportion of them. Ignoring for a moment the relationship between bananas and razors, let us just look at the rate of occurrence of each one separately. Suppose 10% of baskets happen to contain bananas and that 5% contain razors.

Suppose that we randomly examine 1000 transactions in which people bought bananas. Because 5% of all baskets contain razors, we would expect that 5% or 50 of these 1000 transactions that have bananas will also contain razors. These two items can occur together just by coincidence rather than because of any special affinity.

However, suppose we examine the 1000 transactions with bananas, and find that 20% (or 200) of these also have razors. Razors occur in only 5% of all baskets, but occur in 20% of the baskets that contain bananas. That is, razors occur four times more frequently than we should expect on the average. This suggests a true affinity, well beyond coincidence. This analysis leads us to the third measure of a rule's quality – *lift*. Rule 5 has a lift of 4.

Lift helps to rule out accidental co-occurrence of items

A rule's *lift* is the ratio of its confidence to the support for its consequent.

Lift

$$lift = \frac{confidence}{support\_for\_consequent}$$

To calculate *lift* ratio for a rule, we first find the proportion of times the consequent occurs in the data set and call this B. We then take only the transactions in which the antecedent occurs and among these find the proportion of times the consequent occurs in this set and call the result A. We divide A by B to get the *lift* ratio for the rule.

What is the *lift* ratio for $Rule1 : \{Toothbrush\} \implies \{Toothpaste\}$ from our data in table 6?

We can use the description above to calculate this. Note that *Toothpaste* occurs in eight of the ten transactions for a support of 0.8 (which is our B). We see that the antecedent *Toothbrush* occurs in five transactions and *Toothpaste* occurs in four of them for a confidence of 0.8 (which is our A). The *lift* ratio for the rule therefore is $0.8/0.8 = 1$. So we see that *Toothpaste* occurs with *Toothbrush* only as frequently as it does otherwise. Thus we could consider their joint occurrences as mere coincidences! In general we would want a rule to have a lift ratio above 1, with larger numbers being better.

What about *lift* for

$$Rule6 : \{Toothbrush\} \implies \{Moisturizer\}$$

We have seen that *Moisturizer* occurs in 2 of the 10 transactions for a *support* of 0.2. In the five transactions where *Toothbrush* appears, *Moisturizer* occurs in 2, for a confidence of 0.4. It therefore has a *lift* of 2.0! That is it occurs twice as frequently with *Toothbrush* than its independent rate of occurrence.

We have looked at three different measures of the quality of a rule – *confidence, support* and *lift*. Unfortunately, techniques do not specify any hard and fast criteria for precisely ranking the rules based on these three measures.

We definitely want rules with a high *lift* ratio – to rule out coincidental co-occurrences, and high confidence – to increase the likelihood of customers acting on our recommendations.

What about *support*? Of course, we would like a high value for sure. But, how high? Consider a typical supermarket that sells approximately 20,000 items. An average customer transaction might include ten of these 20,000 items. Consider the itemset $\{Pen, Pencil\}$. Clearly, given 20,000 items, we cannot reasonably expect this itemset to occur in even 10% of the transactions and so a support of even 10% would be huge. We have to expect far lower values for this measure. Given that even modest data sets can imply millions of rules, we cannot hope to enumerate all the rules. Instead, we set a cutoff value for *support*, like 0.01 and ask the algorithm to generate only rules that have at least this level of support. From among the rules that the system generates, we can then choose those which have high values for all three measures.

Returning to the question that started our example – if someone just added toothpaste to her basket and, based on this choice, you had to recommend one other item from the table based on , what would it be?

Initially, you might have said *toothpaste* because it seems to co-occur with toothbrush a lot. Armed with new concepts, what can we say?

We can look at all applicable rules with $\{Toothbrush\}$ as the antecedent and a single other item as the consequent. Table 8 shows the details:

Antecedent	Consequent	Support for rule	Confidence	Support for consequent	Lift
{Toothbrush}	{Toothpaste}	0.4	0.8	0.8	1.0
{Toothbrush}	{Moisturizer}	0.2	0.4	0.2	2.0
{Toothbrush}	{Paper}	0.1	0.2	0.1	2.0
{Toothbrush}	{Pen}	0.3	0.6	0.5	1.2

Table 8: Analysis to find what we should recommend for someone who has just picked a toothbrush.

From the first row in Table 8, we see that the lift for our initial response to recommend *Toothpaste* is just 1.0. This means that *Toothpaste* does not occur with an increased frequency with *Toothbrush*. *Toothpaste* occurs just as frequently with *Toothbrush* as it generally does. We should look for items that have a high lift and decent support and confidence. Moisturizer might be a good recommendation – although a higher confidence level would be nice.

Review 6: Affinity Analysis

You can find the answers to these questions on page 360

1. Table 9 contains information on a set of emails that a person sent and the recipients for each email. An email system could use a person's past email recipients to suggest recipients for new emails that the person is in the process of constructing by looking at the recipients already included for the email and suggesting new recipients. Gmail does something like this when it comes up with messages like "consider including xxx."

   Answer the following questions based on the data in Table 9. Based on the data, we can see that the antecedent and consequent of rules in this situation will be sets of email recipients.

Table 9: Emails and recipients

Email no	Recipients
1	John, Ma, Chris, Eduardo, Ram
2	Ram, Eduardo
3	John, Emily, Chris, Ma
4	Ma, Chris, Eduardo
5	Chris, Eduardo

a List any two rules that you can infer from the first email's recipients.

b What is the support for item set $\{Ma, Chris\}$?

c What is the support for item set $\{John, Eduardo\}$?

d Which item sets of size 2 have the highest support?

e What is the confidence for rule $\{Chris, Ma\} \Rightarrow \{Eduardo\}$?

f What is the confidence for rule $\{Chris\} \Rightarrow \{Eduardo, Ma\}$?

g Why are the confidence levels different for the above two even though exactly the same items are involved in both?

h What is the lift for rule $\{Chris\} \Rightarrow \{Eduardo\}$?

i What is the lift for rule $\{Ma, Chris\} \Rightarrow \{Eduardo\}$?

j Which rule with $\{Ma\}$ as the consequent and having exactly a single item in its antecedent has the maximum lift?

2. Suppose we have a rule $\{A\} \Rightarrow \{B\}$ that has a confidence of close to 1. This would mean that whenever A occurs, B is also almost certain to occur. Under what conditions might this alone still not be a very good indicator that these two items are closely associated?

3. Under what conditions might a rule with a very high lift still not be a useful?

4. Suppose we have a rule with support of 1.0, what would its confidence be? What about lift?

5. Which of the following statements **are** possible in the context of the three measure of the quality of rules?

a A rule with confidence of 0.8, support of 0.3 and lift of 1.5

b A rule with confidence of 1.5, support of 0.3 and lift of 1.5

c A rule with confidence of 0.8, support of 1.3 and lift of 0.75

d A rule with confidence of 1.2, support of 1.3 and lift of 1.0

Lab 5: *Affinity Analysis using **R***

Pre-requisite(s)

- ✓ You should have completed the labs on *Introduction to **R** Data Frames* on page 17 and *Installing and loading **R** packages* on page 55 before you start this one.
- ✓ You should have downloaded the data files for the book and stored them on your computer.
- ✓ You should also have set up **R** to point to the above location as the working directory.
- ✓ You should have read the section on *Affinity Analysis* on page 66 and answered the corresponding review questions on page 73.

Objective

After completing this lab, you will be able to:

- ✓ Use **R** functions for performing Affinity Analysis.
- ✓ Use appropriate parameters to control the number of rules generated.
- ✓ Interpret the results of affinity analysis.

Overview

In this lab, we will take the data file corresponding to our grocery example from the section on *Affinity Analysis* on page 66 and generate the rules for it. We have reproduced the table here as Table 10 for convenience.

Customer no	Items purchased
1	Toothbrush, Toothpaste, Moisturizer
2	Toothpaste, Toothbrush, Pen
3	Toothpaste, Pen
4	Toothpaste, Paper
5	Toothbrush, Toothpaste, Paper
6	Toothbrush, Pen
7	Toothbrush, Toothpaste, Pen, Moisturizer
8	Toothpaste, Paper
9	Soda
10	Toothpaste, Pen

Table 10: Fictitious purchase data – repeated for convenience.

You will learn to control the number of rules generated and to interpret the output to apply the results.

Activity steps

1. **Read the data file:** Load the data file *grocery.csv* into an **R** variable called *grocery*.

   ```
   > grocery <- read.csv("grocery.csv")
   ```

2. **Look at the data:** In the *Environment* tab on the top right, click on the variable *grocery* to see its contents. What do you see? Compare what you see in the **R** data frame with what is in Table 10. Does it make sense?

   In the table, the first transaction has the items Toothbrush, Toothpaste and Moisturizer. In the file, this information is represented in three rows. The first three rows all have "id" as 1 to indicate that they all pertain to transaction 1 or shopping-basket 1.

   Just to make sure you understand this correctly, identify the rows of the **R** data frame for the sixth transaction.

   Rows 14 and 15 both have id 6 and hence pertain to the sixth transaction. We see that row 14 mentions Toothbrush as the item and row 15 has Pen.

   This is one common representation of data for affinity analysis and is sometimes referred to as the *transaction* representation.

   An alternative is to represent the data as a *Binary incidence matrix*. In this, there is one row for each transaction. The matrix has as many columns as there are items overall. The matrix has a 1 whenever an item occurs in a transaction. Table 11 shows how our data would look if represented in this format.

Toothbrush	Toothpaste	Moisturizer	Pen	Paper	Soda
1	1	1	0	0	0
1	1	0	1	0	0
0	1	0	1	0	0
0	1	0	0	1	0
1	1	0	0	1	0
1	0	0	1	0	0
1	1	1	1	0	0
0	1	0	0	1	0
0	0	0	0	0	1
0	1	0	1	0	0

Table 11: Grocery data in binary incidence matrix format

   If the number of items is large, the binary incidence matrix representation can have too many columns. In this book we will therefore use the *transaction* format.

   So if you want to perform affinity analysis using what we cover in this book, you should first convert your data into the *transaction* representation with the *transaction id* as the first attribute and the *item* as the second. You can give whatever names you want to the two columns.

3. **Load the needed packages:** To perform *Affinity Analysis* in **R**, we need functions from a package called *arules*, which we installed in an earlier lab. **R** does not load the package *arules* by default.

```
> library(arules)
```

4. **Generate the rules:** We are now ready to generate the rules. We will use the *apriori* function from the *arules* package. This function expects the transactions to be supplied in the *binary incidence matrix* representation. In the code below, we first convert the data from the *transaction* representation. We first show the commands and then explain them. Type the following commands:

```
> binary <- as(split(grocery[,2], grocery[,1]), "transactions")
> rules <- apriori(binary, parameter=list(support=0.1, confidence = 0.1))
```

   The first line of code converts the data from the transaction to the binary incidence matrix representation. You do not need to know the details. Whenever you need to use it in the future, just substitute *grocery* with the name of the data frame containing data in *transaction* representation. You do need the *arules* package to be loaded for this step to work.

   The second line generates the rules and stores the results in the variable *rules* – as always, we can name the variable as we please; it does not have to be *rules*.

   The first argument *binary* is just the transaction data in binary incidence format – just as the function requires. The second argument specifies the cutoff values for *confidence* and *lift*. As the text has shown, even a small number of transactions can generate a very large number of rules. It makes sense to generate only rules that have at least some minimum levels of *confidence* and *support*. In the above command, we set these as 0.1. The system will then only generate rules with at least the specified levels of *confidence* and *support*. If we find that this generates too many rules, we could raise one or both of these values.

5. **Examining the rules:** First type the command:

```
> rules
```

From the output you can see that the system generated 41 rules. You can look at the generated rules by typing the command:

```
> inspect(rules)
```

Although we see the 41 rules with the *support*, *confidence* and *lift* for each one, the order of the listing does not help very much in identifying the good rules.

6. **Sorting the rules:** To help us to see the rules in a more helpful sequence, let us sort the display by confidence so that we see the rules with highest confidence on top. This will help us to pick the good ones more easily. Type the command:

Sorting the generated rules

```
> inspect(sort(rules, by="confidence"))
```

7. **Choosing rules:** Data analysts do not lay down any fixed set of criteria to select the rules to use. In general, we want rules with relatively high values for all the three measures. We can approach the process of selecting rules from two angles. We might decide to use a certain number of rules – say 5 or some such. Once we decide on the number, we can then pick the best. Alternately, we can set a cutoff for each measure and pick rules that meet the cutoffs. In the present case, if we want to pick the five best rules, we can easily choose those that have a confidence of 1.0. However, we have more than five of these. We can then narrow down by support and lift. The second and eighth rules in the list are solid – high lift and good support. We can also pick rules 1, 5 and 7 from the sorted list.

   We could also set a cutoff for *support* and *lift* and pick the rules. Suppose we set the cutoff for support at 0.2 and lift at 1.25, we will then be able to select the rules we want to use.

8. **Controlling the number of rules generated:** As we have discussed, even small files can generate a huge number of rules. Even our relatively small file with only 10 transactions generated 41 rules, When files get larger, we will need to actively control the number of rules generated – otherwise we can quickly run out of memory. In the present example, we have 10 transactions. An item set with a support of 0.1 actually occurs in just a single transaction. If we felt that a support of 0.1 is

too low, we could place a cutoff for support and make the system generate only rules that had that minimum level of support. Similarly we can place a cutoff value for confidence as well. By default, the rule generator assumes a cutoff of 0.1 for support and confidence if we do not specify anything.

Let us now generate the rules again with the command

```
> rules <- apriori(binary, parameter=list(support=0.2, confidence = 0.8))
```

In this modified usage of the function, we are passing the cutoff values for *confidence* and *support* (in the second argument, *parameter*). Here we are specifying a cutoff of 0.8 for *confidence* and hence will not get any rules with confidence lower than 0.8. Nor will we get any rule whose item sets have support less than 0.2.

We now get only 8 rules as shown by the command:

```
> inspect(rules)
```

On very large data sets, we cannot hope to have high support values. For example, if a store sells 20,000 different items (as a typical grocery store in the US does) and we are looking at 1,000,000 transactions, then for an item set to have a support of 0.1 it would have to appear in 100,000 transactions. With so many distinct items being sold, that is too much to ask for and we will need to reduce the cutoff value for support. In such cases, you might need to use trial and error to find reasonable cutoff values.

9. **Summary of steps:** Table 12 summarizes the steps that we used in the activity. You can use this as a template for your work with other data. Be sure to replace various elements (like the file name and the data frame name) based on context.

Lab assignment 3: Affinity Analysis

You can find the answers to this assignment on page 363

A school wants to make its on-line course registration system more student-friendly. To do this, the school wants to augment the registration system with course recommendations for students. When a student registers for a particular course, the

Table 12: Summary of steps for *Affinity Analysis*.

Step no	Description	R command	Remarks
1	Read the data	`grocery <-` `read.csv("grocery.csv")`	Our file is in the "transaction" format

2	Generate the rules	`library(arules)`
		`binary <- as(split(grocery[,2],`
		`grocery[,1]),`
		`"transactions")`
		`rules <- apriori(binary,`
		`parameter=list(support=0.1,`
		`confidence = 0.1))`
			Convert the data to binary incidence representation before generating the rules

3	Examine the rules	`rules` `inspect(rules)`	Use the inspect function to actually see the rules and their confidence, support and lift.

4	Sort the rules by various criteria	`inspect(sort(rules, by="confidence")`
		`inspect(sort(rules, by="lift")`
		`inspect(sort(rules, by="support")`	

5	Select the rules to use based on above		

6	Control the number of rules generated	`rules <- apriori(binary,`
		`parameter=list(support=0.2,`
		`confidence = 0.8))`
			Replace the confidence and support values depending on context. With big data files, we cannot expect a very high support.

7	Look at the new rules	`inspect(rules)`	

school wants its system to suggest other courses to the student based on historical information about sets of courses that students took in the past. The data file *student-courses.csv* contains information on courses that students took in the past. The file contains 4247 rows of data with each row containing a student id and a course number. The data represents the sets of courses taken by 1645 distinct students. An extract of the data appears in Table 13.

If a student has taken several courses, then several rows of data occur for that student. For example, student 4 has taken 6 courses whereas student 5 has taken just one course. You can see the similarity of this data with the market basket data that we looked at in the lab. The student id here is like the transaction id earlier and the course number is like the item.

1. Load the data into **R**.

student_id	course_no
4	FI201
4	LA321
4	LA325
4	MG501
4	MK601
4	EC408
5	MK605
6	IT701
7	AC103
7	LA301
7	EC402
8	AC104
8	FI201
8	MG501
8	QA812
8	EC408
...	...

Table 13: Course registration information.

2. Perform an affinity analysis using the settings $support = 0.02$ and $confidence = 0.3$.
3. How many rules did the system generate with the above values for support and confidence?
4. Sort the display by descending order of *lift*.
5. Look at the first rule. What are the values of *support*, *confidence* and *lift* for the rule?
6. Use one or more of the above measures to find out the following without going back to the original data: Of the total of 1645 students, approximately how many took all the courses involved in the first rule displayed?
7. Infer, without actually going back to the data file, how many students took the courses appearing in the antecedent of the first rule displayed.
8. If a student has taken AC104 and you had to recommend just one course for this student, which one would that be? Why?
9. If a student has taken AC104 and FI201 during the current registration session and your system had to recommend just one course to this student, which course would that be? Why?
10. As above, but if you could recommend two courses which two would they be?
11. We see that the lift for even the last rule is 3.84 – very high. What might you do to get even more rules?

Exploratory Data Analysis

Applied data analytics often differs in emphasis from traditional statistical analysis.

In a typical research study, researchers usually want to find answers to specific questions and go about gathering data to answer those specific questions. In this sense, data gathering in research studies occurs with very specific purposes in mind.

Typical research projects gather data for a specific purpose

Many analytics efforts on the other hand, take a very opportunistic approach. Usually organizations gather lots of data to support their operations. For example, chain stores collect data on store purchase transactions – like the specific store at which the transaction occurred, the items purchased, customer loyalty number if available, time of purchase and other such items. At data-collection time there might not be a clear picture of how exactly they will use the data, other than for supporting regular operations.

Data analytics often seeks to exploit existing data creatively

Later on a data analyst could mine this data for interesting patterns and exploit the findings to run the organization more efficiently.

What do you generally do when given a large data file – with or without a specific purpose in mind?

People who learn a few data analytics techniques can generally carry out the mechanics of applying specific techniques if told in advance the technique to apply. In the real-world, data sets do not come with a tag that says "you should use the xyz method on me to build a classification model for identifying fraudulent transactions." Instead, you have to look at the data and develop a basic understanding of some important characteristics and then think of useful patterns the data might possibly yield.

Exploratory data analysis seeks to unearth opportnities

Whereas the subsequent chapters all delve directly into a data analytics technique and show how each one can be applied, in reality you will employ a very opportunistic and exploratory approach by first probing the data to come up with ideas for exploiting it.

Thus, rather than taking a data set and jumping into applying a specific technique, as the later chapters might seem to imply, we have to first understand the data. This chapter shows you some standard things to look for in most data sets.

Basic data summary

A bank wants to improve its customer service. Among other things, they want to decrease the waiting times for customers.

```
> st <- read.csv("bank-teller.csv")
```

From its regular transaction processing system, the bank was able to extract information on the service times – Table 14 shows the data for 50 customers. You can load the data from file *bank-teller.csv* and follow along as we explain the concepts and also perform some of the steps in R. The data has only one attribute, called *svc_time*. In what follows, we assume that the data is stored in an R variable called *st*.

Customer Service Times (mins)				
5.2	1.8	7.5	1.4	4.7
2.3	2.5	0.8	6.4	2.9
4.3	5.5	0.7	3.3	4.9
1.6	3	1.4	1.4	10
5.9	2.6	4.9	9.5	4
3	6.3	12.4	3.9	4.2
12.7	2.4	2.6	0.4	1.5
3.4	9.6	5.5	0.8	1.8
11.7	8	2.6	3.2	6.1
1.3	8.1	3.9	5.9	4

Table 14: Bank teller service times

What can you make out from the raw data? What would be some things that you might look for?

Knowing the maximum, minimum and average service times would certainly be useful. You can find these using the R commands (*mean* is the average):

```
> max(st$svc_time)
> min(st$svc_time)
> mean(st$svc_time)
```

You can see that the above values are 12.7, 0.4 and 4.476 minutes respectively.

An even easier way to get these numbers and a few more is to use the *summary* function.

```
> summary(st)
```

```
   svc_time
Min.   : 0.400
1st Qu.: 2.325
Median : 3.900
Mean   : 4.476
3rd Qu.: 5.900
Max.   :12.700
```

Figure 24: R summary output for the bank teller example

Figure 24 shows the output from R. You can see that this gives the minimum, mean and maximum in addition to a few other values that we will shortly discuss.

Of course, you surely figured out that R calculated the mean by summing up all values (yielding 223.8) and dividing by the number of values (50).

Whereas the 50 different service times might have overwhelmed us – most people would find it difficult to wrap their heads around 50 numbers – the maximum, minimum and mean give us a good idea of the whole set of data. Together they say quite a lot about the data. For example, if these data are representative of overall service times in the bank, then we would think that a service time of 20 minutes would be extremely unlikely. Let us suppose the bank wanted to achieve a certain service level. They might want to plan the number of tellers based on service times and the customer inflow at various times during the day. They could probably do a passable job with just these numbers describing service times during various times of the day.

Measures of central tendency:

You have most certainly calculated the average of sets of numbers many times. In some sense the average represents in a single number something useful about a set of numbers. We often use the average to represent a *typical* member of a group, as when a company announces, "we sold an average of 10,000 units every month."

Useful as it is, the average represents only one of three *measures of central tendency*. Consider this fictitious anecdote "10 people with an average annual income of $78,000 were seated at a Seattle bar. In walked Bill Gates ..."

Incomes of the ten people: 100,000, 90,000, 60,000, 40,000, 50,000, 50,000, 85,000, 75,000, 110,000 and 120,000

What happened to the average annual income after this eleventh person walked in?

If we had begun the story with "11 people with an average annual income of $10 million were seated at a Seattle bar." you would surely have assumed that almost everyone out there was a millionaire many times over and yet the anecdote paints a very different picture.

Averages can be misleading in the face of extreme values – so called *outliers* – in the data. Outliers can skew the average.

Because of this problem, statisticians have looked to other *measure of central tendency*. You might have noticed that economists often cite the *median*. For example, we almost always hear the median household income – rather than the average – of a city or state being reported on. The *median* represents the middle value of a set of numbers. To compute the *median* we order the numbers (either ascending or descending order will work) and take the middle value if we have an odd number of elements. With an even number of elements, we will of course not have a middle value and we take the two middle elements and use their average as the median.

Mean vs. median

Returning to th Seattle bar, the median income of the 10 initial customers is $78,000. If we add Bill Gates to this set (assuming that his annual income is $200 million), the median now becomes $85,000, but the mean jumped to $18 million!

Mean: sensitive to outliers
Median: insensitive to outliers

Even if Bill Gates and Warren Buffet had walked in, the median would still have risen only to $90,000, whereas the mean would have shot up even more dramatically.

Going back to the bank teller example, note that the basic summary that R produced included the median as well.

Clearly, the median is insensitive to outliers. In fact people who aim to mislead us often cite averages instead of median values.

A third, but rarely used measure of central tendency is the *mode* – the most frequently occurring number in a set, irrespective of its magnitude.

Numeric summaries can sometimes mislead

Numeric summaries can be extremely useful and help us to wrap our heads around large data sets. However, whenever possible, we should try to look at graphical displays of our data. Nothing illustrates this better than the famous *Anscombe's quartet*[15]

You can check out the details on Wikipedia. In 1973, Francis Anscombe presented four different data sets. These four sets had almost identical summary statistics. Table 15 shows

[15] Wikipedia. Anscombe's quartet, August 2015. URL `https://en.wikipedia.org/wiki/Anscombe%27s_quartet`

the summaries for the four data sets. You might not be in a position to grasp the significance of all the summary information below right now, because we have not yet looked at all the concepts involved. We will get to all but one in this chapter.

Table 15: Summaries of Anscombe's quartet

Property	Value
Mean of x in each case	9 (exact)
Sample variance of x in each case	11 (exact)
Mean of y in each case	7.50 (to 2 decimal places)
Sample variance of y in each case	4.122 or 4.127 (to 3 decimal places)
Correlation between x and y in each case	0.816 (to 3 decimal places)
Linear regression line in each case	y = 3.00 + 0.500x (to 2 and 3 decimal places, respectively)

Although the four data sets seem identical from the summary measures, Figure 25 shows the plot of each one. Clearly these data sets are vastly different from each other.

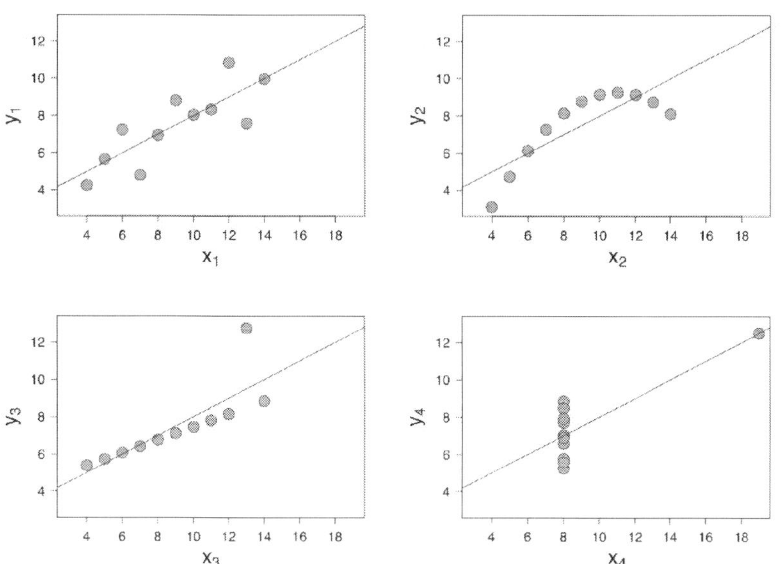

Figure 25: Anscombe's quartet

Anscombe carefully constructed his quartet to make a point. Nevertheless, it underscores the risk of relying solely on summary data. We should make every effort to look at graphs to get a deeper understanding of data. We now turn to various graphical displays of data.

Histograms

A *histogram* greatly aids in comprehending the complete data set very quickly. Let us first generate one for the bank teller example. Enter the **R** command:

```
> hist(st$svc_time)
```

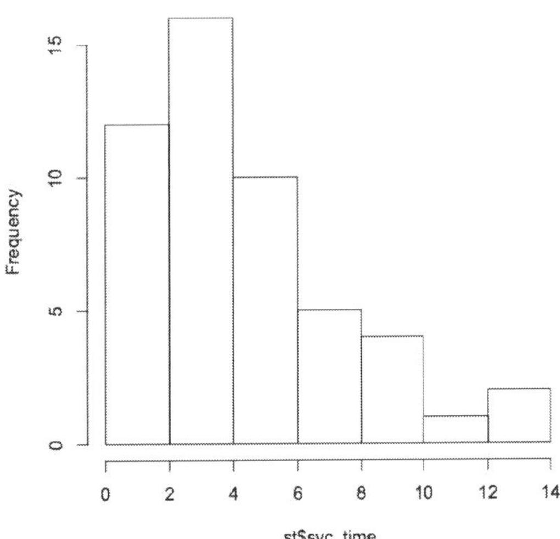

Figure 26: Histogram of bank teller service times.

Figure 26 shows the results.

If you want a more friendly chart with a better title and labels of your choice on the axes, you can use the following. Recall that if you choose to enter this command over multiple lines, then R will prompt you with a "+" sign on each new line to continue the command.

```
> hist(st$svc_time, main="Bank teller service times",
    xlab="Service time",
    ylab="Number of occurrences")
```

Figure 27 shows the result.

You might have inferred that you can use the *main* argument to control the title of the chart and the *xlab* and *ylab* arguments to control the label text on the x and y axes.

A histogram divides the complete range of values into several (usually) equal sized bins. For example, if the values range

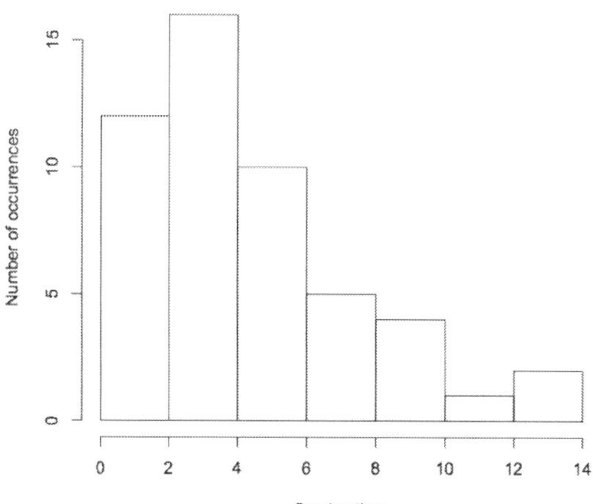

Figure 27: Histogram of bank teller service times with better labels

between 100 and 199, we can divide this into say ten, equal sized bins: 100 to 109, 110 to 119 and so on.

A histogram visually displays the number of values falling in each bin. It shows the bins on the x axis and, for each bin, it shows a bar whose height represents the *frequency* – the number of observations in that bin.

In the present example, R divided the whole range of service times (min to max) into 7 bins (0-2, 2-4, 4-6 and so on), and for each bin, it showed, with a vertical bar, how many data points fell in that bin.

Can you see from the histogram how many service times were between 8 and 10 minutes?

Looking at the vertical bar for the bin 8-10, we can see that its frequency is 4.

The size of each bin – referred to as *bin_size* can affect the results dramatically. Too few bins will generally not give sufficient detail and too many bins can make it difficult to see any useful patterns. **R**'s defaults usually work well.

The histogram that we generated earlier has 7 bins. Suppose we wanted to get a finer histogram with more bins, we could use the following:

```
> hist(st$svc_time, breaks=14,
        main="Teller service times")
```

Fig 28 shows the resultant histogram.

By specifying the *breaks* option, we can control how many bins R generates. With n breaks, we get n-1 bins. You can change the title by setting a value for *main*.

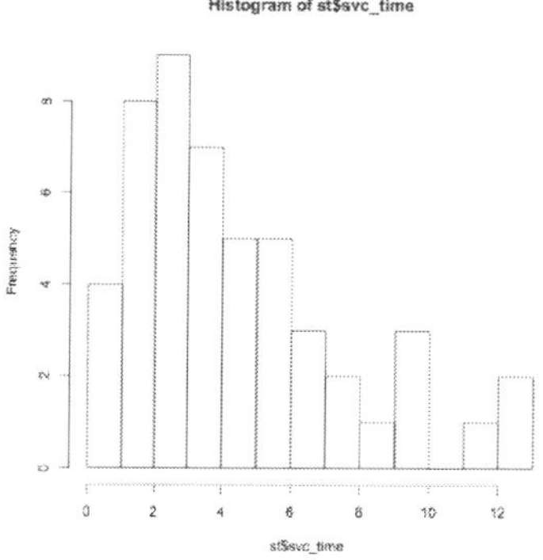

Figure 28: Histogram of bank teller service times – with more bins.

Fig 29 shows a histogram with only three bins for the same data.

R provides numerous options for us to customize a histogram – the color of the bars, the number of bins, the title, where to place the ticks on the axes and on and on.

We can see that the histogram, rather than trying to collapse a data set into a single number, provides us an approximate view of the entire data set. We can see whether the values are more or less uniformly distributed between the minimum and maximum or whether most of the values are somewhere in the middle with fewer values at the extremes. From Figure 27, what do you see?

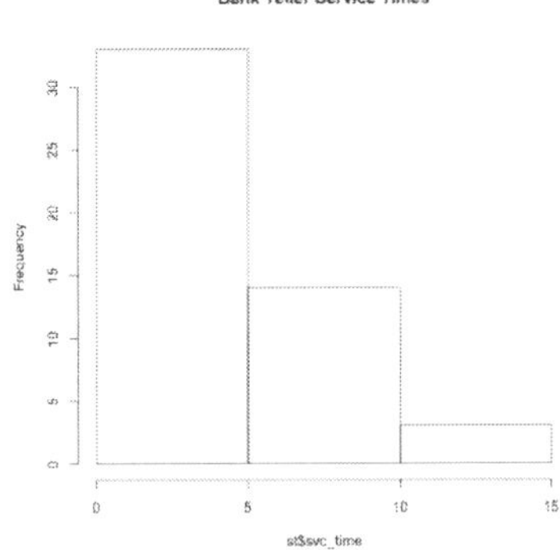

Figure 29: Histogram of bank teller service times – with only three bins.

How many occurrences of 6 minutes or less did we have?

Adding up the frequency counts for each of the bins 0-2, 2-4 and 4-6 from Figure 27, we get 12+16+10 = 38.

So even though the service times range from almost 0 to 14, 76% of the values in fact fall between 0 and 6.

Sometimes we want our histograms to show the relative proportions rather than the actual numbers of observations that fall into each bin.

```
> # Histogram showing proportions rather then frequency
> hist(st$svc_time, freq=FALSE)
```

Because histograms are sensitive to the number of bins, people sometimes use a *kernel density plot* which provides a more smooth representation. We will not go into the details of how R generates the plot, but show the R command you can use:

```
> # Generate a KDE plot
> plot(density(st$svc_time),
     main="Density plot of service times")
```

Clearly then knowing just the measures of central tendency does not suffice – we can also use information about how the values are distributed across the whole range. You might have already guessed that statisticians have invented mathematical measures for this too.

- **Range:** $maximum - minimum$
- **IQR:** $3^{rd} quartile - 1^{st} quartile$
- **Variance:** $variance = \frac{\sum_{i=1}^{n} (x_i - mean)^2}{n}$
- **Standard deviation:** $\sqrt{variance}$
- **Coefficient of variation:** $\frac{std\ deviation}{mean}$

Measures of dispersion or spread

We can have two different sets of values with the same average, but with very different distributions of values.

Figures 30 and 31 show two data sets with the same average of 100. The values in one set are more closely clustered around the average than in the other – the two look very similar, but look carefully at the range of values in each.

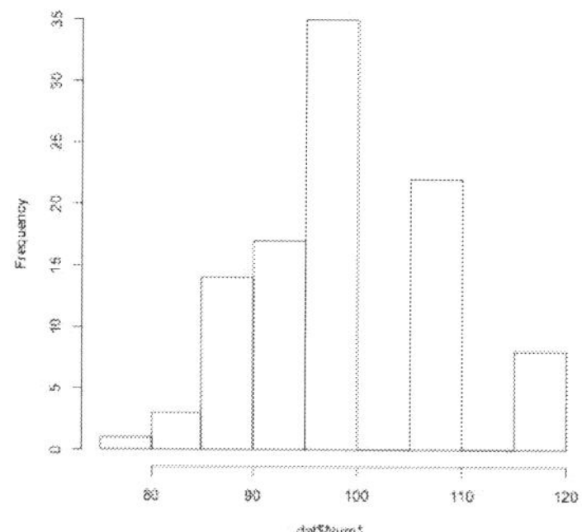

Figure 30: Some data with average=100.

We could have yet a third set of numbers with the same average, but in which many numbers are well below the average, and we have a small set of very high values. Although all three have the same average you will most likely agree that they could have very different implications for decisions.

The simplest measure of dispersion is just the overall *range*. The range for a set of values is the difference between the maximum value and the minimum value. For example, suppose we have a set of items and are looking at their prices. If the most expensive item costs $125 and the least expensive one costs $25, then the range is $125 - $25 = $100.

Often most data points tend to cluster around the middle value (with varying degrees of closeness) and hence the *Inter-Quartile Range or IQR* conveys important information as well. Before we discuss IQR, let us review the concept of *quartiles*.

If we order the data from lowest to highest, then the value at the quarter mark is said to be the 25th percentile or the *first quartile*. The one at the middle is the 50th percentile or the *second quartile* and the one at the three-fourths mark is the 75th percentile or *third quartile*. Usually much of the data will lie between the first and third quartiles and IQR calculates the range between these two values.

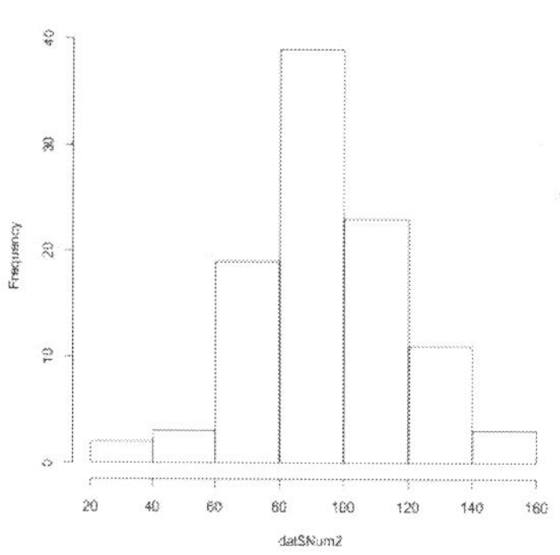

Figure 31: Some other data with average=100.

Incidentally, the median is the same as the second quartile.

Looking back at Figure 24 we see that the *summary* function provides the values of the first and third quartiles as well.

A more comprehensive numerical measure based on all the data values is the *variance*. Suppose we have data on the number of times people visited each of three web sites over a 10 day period. Table 16 shows the data.

Can you rank the three sites by the stability of number of visitors? Which site has had the most amount of variability and which one the least?

Clearly Site 3 has had no variability at all. Between Site 1

Site 1	Site 2	Site 3
1000	800	1000
1100	1200	1000
1050	1300	1000
990	700	1000
890	650	1000
1100	1200	1000
1020	1200	1000
1000	1000	1000
980	700	1000
990	1000	1000

Table 16: Number of web site visits for two web sites.

and Site 2, although both have had fluctuations, we can see that Site 1 has experienced lower variability - its numbers cluster around their average of 1012 much more closely than do Site 2's numbers around their average of 885. The measure *Variance* makes this intuition concrete.

To clarify variance computation, Table 17 shows how we could compute the variance for Site 1.

Site 1	$(value - mean)^2$
1000	144
1100	7744
1050	1444
990	484
890	14884
1100	7744
1020	64
1000	144
980	1024
990	484
Variance (Avg 2nd col.)	3416

Table 17: Variance computation for site 1. The mean of the first column is 1012.

Variance reflects the square of the average amount by which a value differs from the mean.

Variance is the average of squared deviations from the mean

$$variance = \frac{\sum_{i=1}^{n} (x_i - mean)^2}{n}$$

To compute the variance we first compute the mean. Then for each value we find its deviation from the mean as $(value - mean)$ and square this deviation. We then take the average of these squares. Why should we square the values and not just take the average of the deviations?

Statisticians distinguish between *sample* and *population* variance. We will not worry about that in this book.

We square the deviations to prevent positive and negative deviations canceling out and lowering the average.

To calculate the variance for the bank teller data, you can use the *var* function. The corresponding R command is:

```
> var(st$svc_time)
```

What are the units of *variance* in our example?

Variance of service times measured in minutes has units of minutes^2;not particularly easy to interpret

For the bank teller example that would be minutes-squared, because each of the deviations is measured as minutes.

To get an idea of how much the absolute deviation is on the average we can take the square root of the variance to get the *standard deviation*. The *standard deviation* has the same units as the original data – minutes in our bank teller example. The R command *sd* calculates the standard deviation.

standard deviation

```
> sd(st$svc_time)
```

Henceforth we will shorten standard deviation to just *sd*.

We find that the *standard deviation* for the bank teller data (rounded to two decimal places) is 3.13, The average is 4.48. Together these two tell us that the typical value lies in the range 4.48 ± 3.13.

We will use the short form *sd* for standard deviation. When we are talking about the standard deviation of a specific attribute x we will use the notation *sd(x)*. Imagine that we have the end-of-day share prices for two different companies for a year, and want to see which of these two shares has been more volatile (changed more) during the year. From what we know already, we could calculate the variance or standard deviation for each. Can we say that the share with the higher standard deviation has greater variability? What if one of the shares trades in the $100 range and the other in the $200 range? If both shares have a standard deviation around $20 can we say that they show nearly equal variability?

When we compare data sets for variability, standard deviation and variance might not tell the whole story – we need the *coefficient of variation*

In this case we would say that the share that trades at a higher price has lower variability. We use the notion that we have to look at the standard deviation in conjunction with the mean while comparing different data sets. The statistical measure *coefficient of variation* captures this intuition numerically. We use the notation c_v to denote it.

Coefficient of variation

$c_v = \frac{sd}{mean}$

What are the units of c_v?

Since the numerator and denominator have the same units, c_v has no units – great for comparing data sets with completely different units – like for example, the daily closing price of a particular share and daily average temperature!

Boxplots

Boxplots help us to visualize the spread of data. Let us first see one. Enter the R command:

```
> boxplot(st$svc_time)
```

Figure 32 shows the resultant plot. *Boxplots* compress a lot of information in a small space and every element conveys useful information. Figure 33 points out the various informational elements on the bank teller boxplot.

Figure 32: Boxplot of bank teller service times.

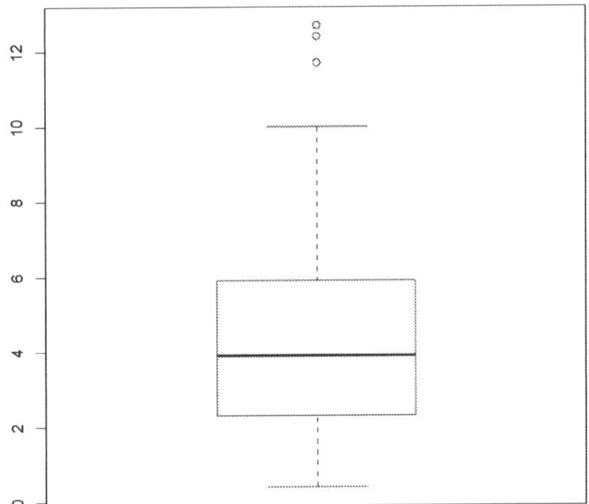

outliers

You surely got everything on Figure 33 except *outliers*. As we saw in the scenario where Bill Gates walked into the Seattle bar, extreme data values – or *outliers* – can distort the calculations of various summary measures.

Boxplots tell us how many outliers we have and, although not shown in our boxplots thus far, can also point out precisely which values in the data represent outliers. Of course when we say "outliers," we simply mean extreme values. What constitutes an extreme value? Statisticians do not have any hard and fast rules to determine this. However, one common approach is to mark any data values that are above the third quartile by 1.5 IQR or below the first quartile by 1.5 IQR as *outliers*, and R boxplots use this approach.

From the figure we see outliers above the maximum value – how is this possible? Should the very highest value not be

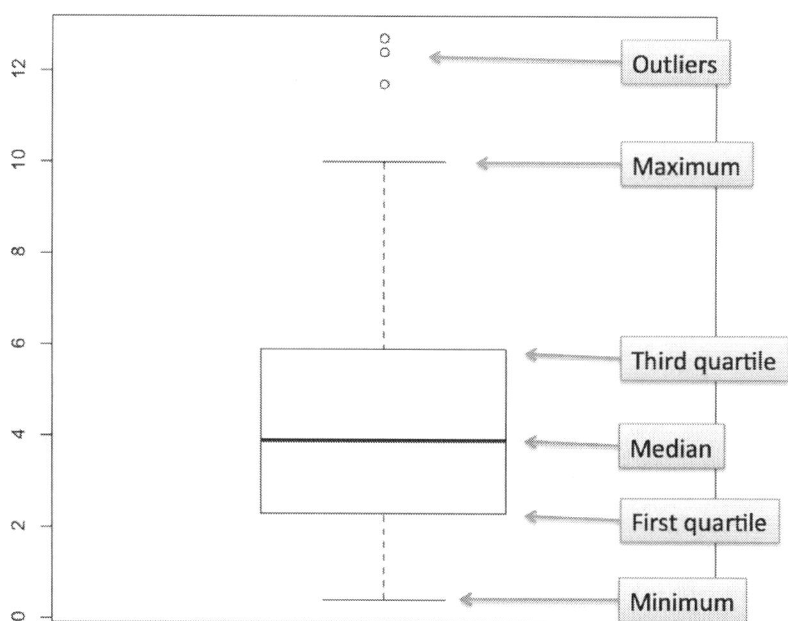

Figure 33: Informational elements on a boxplot.

marked as the maximum? Good question. Boxplot computations exclude outliers from the calculations of maximum and minimum.

While performing data analyses, we might want to weed out outliers up-front and we can use boxplots to see how many we have and precisely which ones they are and decide on the data points to eliminate.

Skewness of data

Look again at the first histogram (Figure 26) and boxplot (Figure 32) of the bank teller data. Considering the whole range of data, we see a clustering of values on the lower side of the spectrum in the histogram. The boxplot shows the main box and the median also on the lower side of the range. In this case, we can expect the mean to be above the median. On the histogram we can imagine the data tailing off to the right and statisticians call this a *right-skewed* distribution of values. If it was the other way, then it would be *left-skewed*. If the data was clustered more or less around the middle, then the mean and median would be very close and such a distribution would be *balanced*.

Scatterplots

In the Section *Relationships*, on page 39, we discussed how data analytics crucially relies on how the values of different attributes *relate* to each other.

Specifically, we saw a simple example where knowing the country where a person lives enables us to make a better guess about whether the person owns a car or not. Of course we cannot be certain about correctness of the answer, but we can improve our chances of being correct by exploiting the relationship.

In many data analytics techniques, we seek to exploit such relationships to estimate a value for an unknown attribute – *target attribute* – based on the known values of *predictor attributes*.

Given the crucial role that *relationships* play in data mining, it should come as no surprise that examining relationships constitutes a crucial step in data exploration.

Let us first consider numerical attributes. You can use *scatterplots* to easily visualize relationships between two numerical attributes.

Consider the data in the file *height-weight.csv*, which shows the heights and weights of several people in the age group 7 to 21. You can load the data into a data frame called *hw* to follow along.

```
> hw <- read.csv("height-weight.csv")
```

The data has attributes *age*, *height*, *weight* and *gender*.

You can check this by using the command: *names(hw)*

Let us first look at how closely *age* and *weight* relate to each other. Look at the raw data to see if you can see any relationship. Of course we already know what to expect – in the age group in question, older people can be expected to be heavier. We have taken a familiar example so that you have something you can readily relate to. We will later look at a more elaborate example. To generate a scatterplot of age and weight, enter the R command:

```
> plot(hw$age, hw$weight)
```

Figure 34 shows the scatterplot of age and weight.

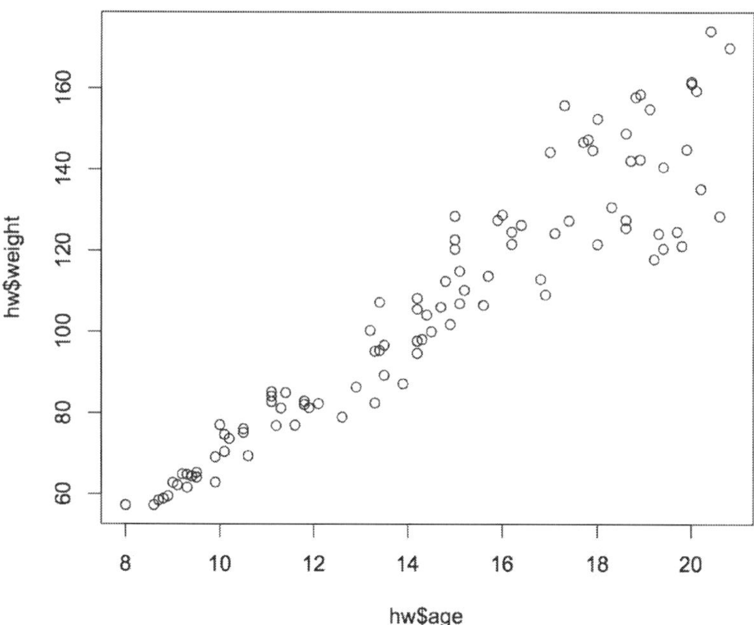

Figure 34: Scatterplot of age and weight for youth

Each row of our data frame has values for *age* and *weight*. The scatterplot of Figure 34 shows one small circle for these two attributes of every row of the data frame.

The scatterplot of Figure 34 could be more user-friendly. At the very least we would like a title for the chart and more "friendly" labels on the axes. As with histograms earlier, you can enter the following command to control these:

```
> plot(hw$age, hw$weight,
       main="Age vs. weight", xlab="Age",
       ylab="Weight (lbs)")
```

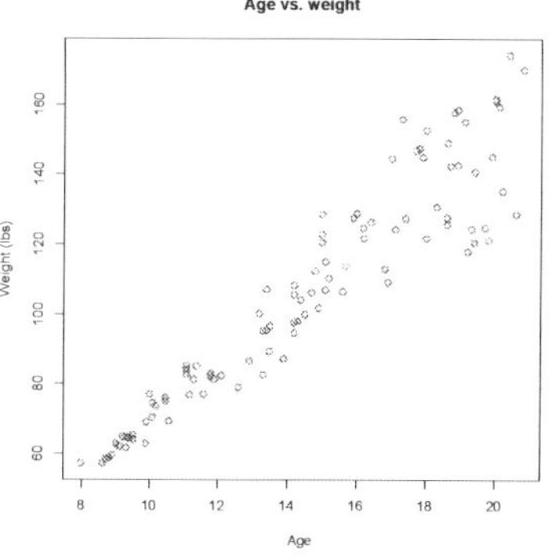

Figure 35: Age vs. weight – friendly version.

Figure 35 shows the result.

Figure 36 clarifies what a point on a scatterplot represents. For every data point, if we drop a line vertically down to meet the horizontal or x axis, the place where it meets the axis represents the *age* corresponding to the point. Similarly, if we draw a horizontal line to the left from a point to the vertical or y axis, the place where the line meets the y axis represents the weight corresponding to this point.

Looking at Figure 35, we can clearly see that points (or cases) with higher age also tend to have higher weight. Why do we say *tend to have*? Why not an unqualified statement like *points with higher age have higher weight*?

We cannot make such an unqualified statement because we can see, especially in the top right region, many points with lower age but higher weights than other points. Even though we cannot make the above unqualified statement, we cannot deny the overwhelming trend that, in general, points with higher age do tend to have higher weight. The points do line up approximately along an imaginary upward-sloping straight line.

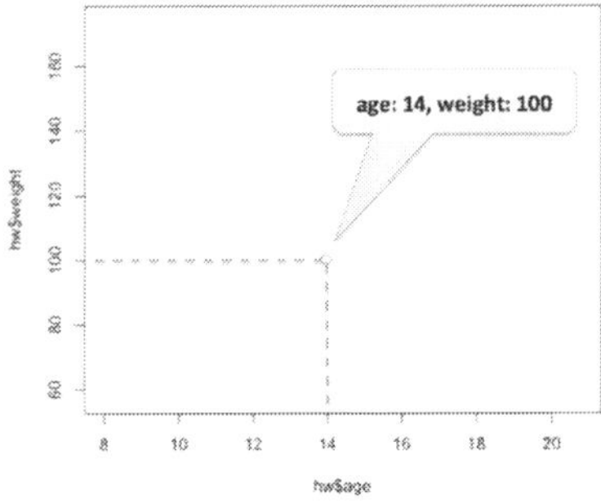

Figure 36: Each point on a scatterplot represents two attribute values of a single row of data.

We might also encounter scatterplots where higher values of one attribute tend to imply lower values for some other attribute. Can you imagine how the scatterplot for such a situation would look?

Figure 37 shows the case of a retail company that has sold the same product at various price levels in various stores at various points in time. The figure shows that points with higher prices tend to have lower sales quantities and vice versa. As before, we can only make a qualified statement because of the many obvious exceptions to that general trend.

Figure 37: Price vs. demand for a product.

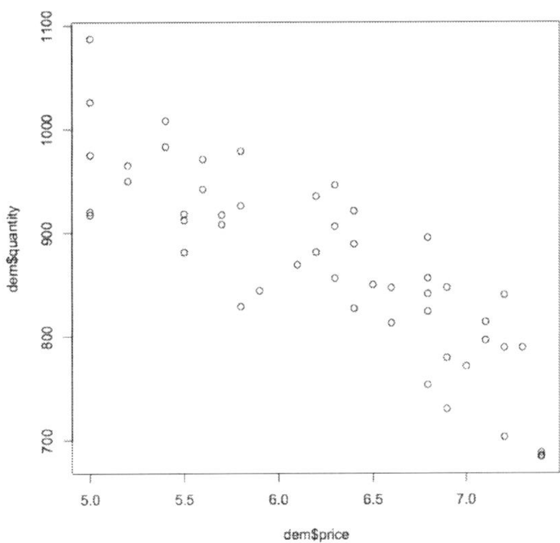

Consider the height-weight data gathered from a different set of people and available in file *height-weight-2.csv*. Figure 38 shows scatterplot of *age* and *weight*.

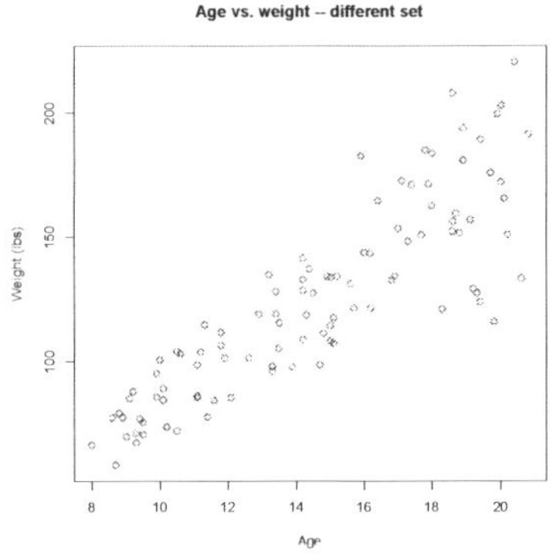

Figure 38: Age vs. weight for another group.

Figure 38 also exhibits the same general trend that points

with higher values for *age* also tend to have higher values for *weight*.

Compare the scatterplots of Figures 35 and 38. In which of these two does the relationship between *age* and *weight* seem "tighter" – in the sense that a higher *age* more closely associates with a higher *weight*?

We can answer the question by finding which of the two figures has fewer exceptions to the rule that a higher *age* means higher *weight*. Clearly Figure 38 harbors many more exceptions. You can see this especially clearly in the lower left portion of the figure when compared with the same region of Figure 35. We can see many points here for which we can find other points that have lower age, but a higher weight. We find far fewer such cases in Figure 35. Although you can more easily spot these cases on the lower left of the diagrams, you can actually see examples throughout the plot.

When the points in a scatterplot fall more closely along an imaginary straight line, they show a greater relationship than otherwise because we can then make statements like "a higher age implies a higher weight" with greater confidence. Analysts usually look for *linear relationships* between quantitative attributes – in which we want the points to cluster close to an imaginary *straight line* – because these are simpler to interpret and easier to model, and not because they reflect reality more closely.

We prefer *linear* relationships in which the points tend to fall close to an imaginary *straight line.*

You now see that scatterplots help us to visually see the strength of linear relationships between various numeric attributes. Usually we have data files with many numeric attributes. Generating scatterplots for various pairs of attributes can be very time consuming. Being able to generate a combined scatterplot – called a *scatterplot matrix* for several attributes at a time can be very convenient.

Try the following R command on the original height-weight data from "height-weight.csv":

```
> pairs(~age+height+weight, data = hw)
```

In the above command, we use the *pairs* function to generate the scatterplot. The expression ~ *age+height+weight* seems strange indeed. It specifies the attributes we want to include in the scatterplot. We indicate the attributes we want to include by starting the expression with a ~ and then specifying all the attributes as shown above, connected with plus signs. We will encounter such expressions later in the course and will explain them in more detail then. Did you get what Figure 39 shows?

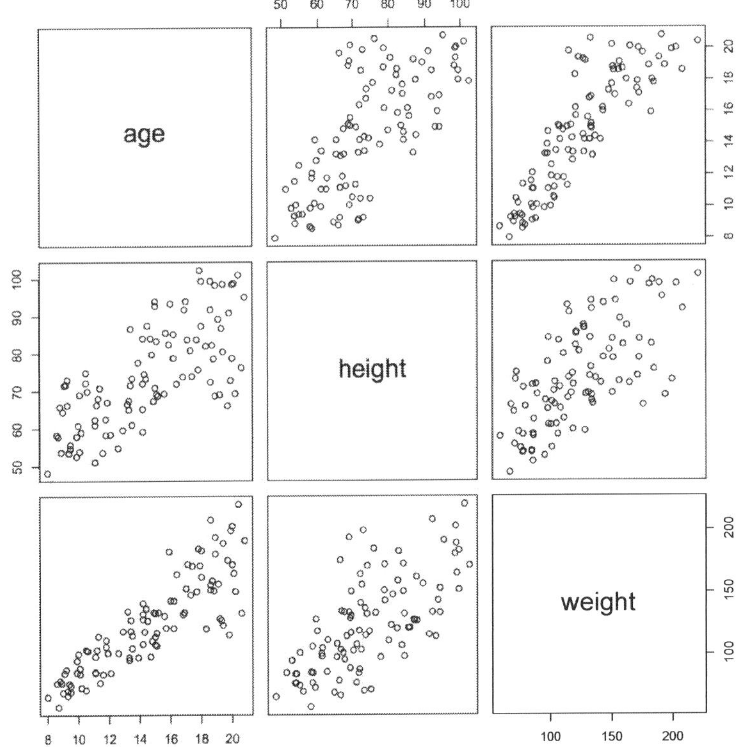

Figure 39: A scatterplot matrix showing scatterplot of three attributes simultaneously.

Scatterplot matrix

The scatterplot matrix shows a lot of relationship information in a compressed form and can prove extremely useful while exploring a data set before deciding upon what kinds of data analytics activities might be useful.

To understand the figure, note that the scatterplot matrix of Figure 39 has 9 rectangles, three per row in three rows. The main diagonal starting from the top left simply lists the attributes being plotted. Let us first look at the middle rectangle of the first row. Looking at the vertical axis of this chart, we see that it has *age* to its left. Looking at the horizontal axis, we see that it has *height* below. Therefore this sub-chart plots heights on the x axis and ages on the y axis. Conversely, first chart on the second row plots ages on the x axis (*age* appears along the horizontal axis) and heights on the y axis (*height* appears along the vertical axis).

- What does the first chart on the third row plot?
- How about the third chart on the second row?
- Which attribute seems more closely related to *age* – *height* or *weight*?

First chart on the third row: *age* on the *x* axis and *weight* on the *y* axis

Third chart on the second row: *weight* on the *x* axis and *height* on the *y* axis

The points in the plot of *age* and *weight* fall much more closely on an imaginary straight line than those of the plot of *age* and *height*. Thus *weight* more closely relates to *age* than does *height*.

Correlation

You now understand the role of scatterplots in visualizing relationships between attributes, However you might have found some of the language of the above discussion – for example: "points with higher age tend to have higher weight as well" and "the points in the second plot cluster together near an imaginary straight line more closely than those of the first plot" – somewhat vague and unsatisfying. Of course, statisticians have that covered too. They have numerical measures of relationship which make the above notions very concrete.

As we have already stated, we concern ourselves here with *linear relationships* only.

Measures of linear relationship:

- **Covariance:**
- **Correlation coefficient:**

We see that when two attributes have a close linear relationship, the scatterplot shows that their values cluster closely along an imaginary straight line. The closer they fall to the line, the stronger is the relationship.

Covariance

We will consider *covariance* as our first measure of linear relationship. Look at the term *covariance* – *co* means "together" and *variance* means "change." As its name indicates, *covariance* measures the extent to which two attributes "vary together" – that is, the extent to which a change in one attribute's value also reflects a somewhat predictable change in the value of the other attribute.

Applying the idea to our earlier age-height-weight example, we can see that older people weigh more. Thus if given two people in the age group of 7 to 21, one of whom is older than the other, we would also generally expect the older person to be heavier. So, age and height tend to change together or "co-vary."

Whereas the above example illustrated a situation where the two attributes changed in the same direction – when one increased, so did the other and when one decreased, so did the other – it could very well be the case that they change in opposite directions. In our price vs. units sold example (Figure 37), we saw that as price increased, the number of units sold tended to decrease and vice versa. When both attributes tend to change together in the same direction – increase together or decrease together they exhibit a positive relationship. When two attributes tend to change in opposite directions – when one increases the other tends to decrease and vice versa – then we have a negative relationship. Both positive and negative relationships can be strong or weak.

As we have already seen, in some cases, the relationships discussed above could occur with greater regularity and predictability than in others. When they are more regular and predictable, then we have a greater level of relationship – or a stronger relationship.

Let us think a little more deeply about what we mean by a strong positive relationship between two attributes in the context of our age and weight data. Let us say we are looking at many cases in our data set that fall close to the higher end of the age range – that is, close to 21. If the relationship between age and weight is strongly positive, where would we expect most of the weights for these cases to fall? Near the top of the weight range or somewhere else?

Clearly if age and weight are closely related positively, then we would expect that most of these people who fall in the higher end of the age range will also fall into the higher end of the weight range.

Similarly, given a set of cases with age near the average age, we would also expect that the weights for this set would generally be near the average weight.

Covariance exploits the above logic to attach a concrete number to the strength of relationship.

The following step-by-step description of covariance calculation might enable you to grasp the notion. We present the mathematical formula as well below.

- Calculate the average *age* and average *weight*. Let us call these *mean_a* and *mean_w*
- Take each case one by one. Let us call the age of the ith case as a_i and the weight of the ith case as w_i. Compute $(a_i - mean\_a)\,(w_i - mean\_w)$. Add up the values obtained for every case and divide by n, the number of cases. This is the covariance.

In general, we calculate the covariance of two attributes X and Y as:

$$cov(X,Y) = \frac{\sum_{i=1}^{n} (x_i - mean_X)(y_i - mean_Y)}{n}$$

In the above expression, we use lowercase letters when referring to individual attribute values and uppercase letters when referring to all values of an attribute. You can use the R function *cov* to compute the *covariance*:

```
> cov(hw$age, hw$weight)
```

The formula is all well and good, but how do we interpret the covariance? What do high positive values represent? What do high negative values mean?

How about low values in general whether they are positive or negative?

We can reason from the formula for covariance exactly under what conditions we might get high and low values.

Let us first consider the scenario shown in Figure 40

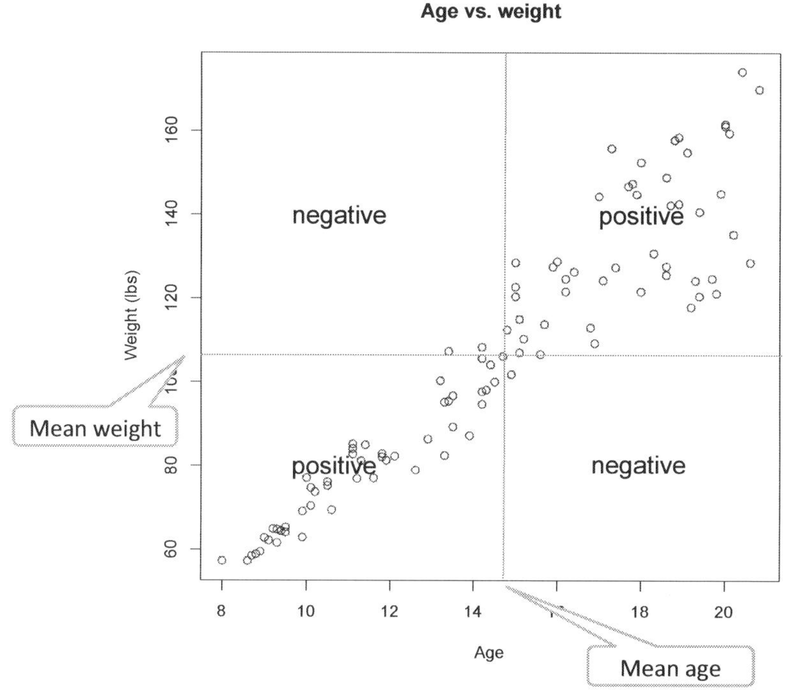

Figure 40: Magnitude of $(x_i - mean_x)\,(y_i - mean_y)$ in the four quadrants: high positive covariance case.

Let us look at Figure 40 closely. We have chosen to show the horizontal and vertical lines corresponding to the mean values of weight and age respectively. In the first quadrant (top right), both age and weight are above their respective averages and hence each of the two difference terms $(a_i - mean\_a)$ and $(w_i - mean\_w)$ is positive. Thus every point in this quadrant contributes a positive value to the covariance calculation. In the third quadrant (bottom left) age and weight are both below their respective averages and hence each difference term is negative, but their product is positive. Thus every point in this quadrant also contributes a positive value. In the other two quadrants, one attribute is above its mean and the other is below. So points falling in both of these contribute negative values. In the figure, since almost all values fall in the first and third quadrants, the overall covariance is highly positive showing a strong positive relationship.

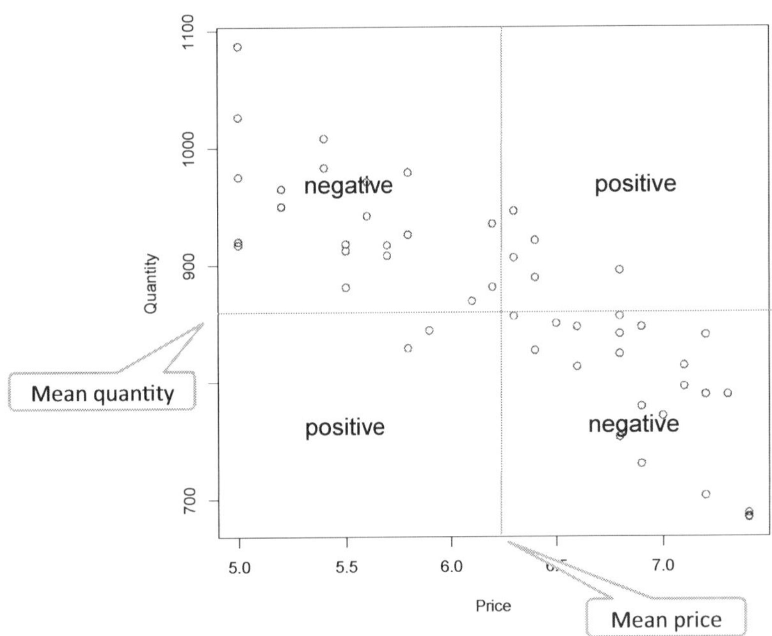

Figure 41: Magnitude of $(x_i - mean_x)(y_i - mean_y)$ in the four quadrants: high negative covariance case.

Let us look at Figure 41 and reason as above. Here, almost all the points fall in quadrants that contribute negative values and hence the overall covariance will be highly negative. Indicating a strong negative association.

Continuing the same process of reasoning, if a scatterplot has points scattered in all quadrants, the negative values from quadrants 2 and 4 will cancel out the positive values from quadrants 1 and 3, and we will end up with a value close to zero (could be either positive or negative depending on the actual cases). This reveals a weak relationship (or the absence of one if the covariance come our as exactly zero).

Summarizing, high positive covariance indicates strong positive relationship. High negative covariance indicates a strong negative relationship. Low covariance values, positive or negative, indicate a weak relationship.

Of course, strong relationships positive or negative indicate that one of the attributes can be very useful as a predictor for the other. Suppose we have a situation with a high positive covariance and we know the value of one of the attributes to be higher than its mean. The high positive covariance tells us that we can expect the other attribute to also have a value higher than its mean. With a weak relationship, one attribute does not serve us well as a predictor of the other.

So far so good. Analogous to our discussion with *variance*, we ask, what are the units of *covariance*?

Looking at the formula, we see that in our age-weight example, the units are "years-lbs" – pretty hard to wrap our brains around. That could be a problem. If we were looking at two sets of data, both of which have the same covariance units, then comparing the numbers could be meaningful. However, if we need to compare the strength of relationships between two very different pairs of attributes, then *covariance* will not help much. However, we discussed *covariance* only as a means to introduce something important: enter *Correlation coefficient*!

Correlation coefficient

Recognizing the weaknesses of *covariance* because of its weird units, statisticians have given us a good solution – the *correlation-coefficient*. Do you recall how we refined our measures of dispersion starting from *variance* till we reached the *coefficient of variation*?

There the standard deviation corrected the problem with the hard-to-interpret units for variance. However, because standard deviation had units, it was not useful for comparing sets of attribute values that had inherently different magnitudes or units. By dividing the standard deviation by the mean, we arrived at the unit-less *coefficient of variation* – a measure that we can use to successfully compare apples and oranges – yes, it is possible to do that if you are a statistician!

We can adopt the same approach to rectify the issues with

covariance. Just as dividing the *standard deviation* by the mean helped us to get rid of the units, here we can use the product of the *standard deviations* of the two attributes to achieve a similar effect.

Let us look at the formula for correlation coefficient first:

$cc\,(X,Y) = \frac{cov(X,Y)}{sd_X sd_Y}$

We divide the *covariance* by the product of the standard deviations of the two attributes. This makes the final result unit less and thus we can compare the strength of relationships between arbitrary pairs of attributes, no matter what units we measure them in.

We can look at the formula for *correlation coefficient* in a different way that makes intuitive sense as well. The formula below yields the same result as the earlier one. but can be more easily compared with the one for covariance.

$$cc(X,Y) = \frac{1}{n}\sum_{i=1}^{n} \frac{(x_i - mean_X)}{sd_X}\frac{(y_i - mean_Y)}{sd_Y}$$

For *covariance* we multiplied the absolute difference from the mean for the two attributes. We can view the formula for the *correlation coefficient* as nearly the same thing, except that we divide each of those differences from the mean by the standard deviation of the corresponding attribute. This way, for each attribute value, we simply find how many standard deviations away from the mean it is – a unitless value. Thus we normalize each term before we multiply it. This process makes the final result unitless and much more useful.

Another bonus is that the *correlation coefficient* always has a value between -1 and +1. A value of +1 indicates the strongest possible positive linear association and a value of -1 indicates the strongest possible negative linear association – both possess high predictive utility. A value of 0 indicates a complete lack of relationship, which means that looking at one of the attribute values tells us absolutely nothing about the possible value for the other attribute.

Figure 42 [16] shows several scatterplots and their corresponding correlation coefficients.

[16] Wikipedia. Pearson product-moment correlation coefficient, January 2014b. URL `http://en.wikipedia.org/wiki/Pearson_product-moment_correlation_coefficient`

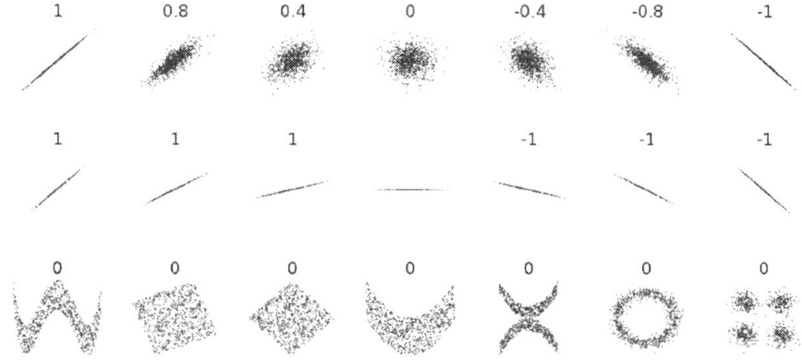

Figure 42: Various scatterplots and their corresponding correlation coefficients.

Lab 6: Dealing with missing data

Pre-requisite(s)

✓ You should have completed the Introduction to **R** lab on page 17.

Objective

After completing this lab, you will be able to:

✓ Correctly load files that contain missing data.

✓ Eliminate cases that have missing values for attributes to create clean data files for analysis.

Overview

Although we will provide "clean" data files for all labs and lab assignments in this book, real-life does not treat us quite so well. We will come across interesting data sets with missing attribute values for some of the cases; we will have to deal with these.

If we have a lot of data, we can afford the luxury of eliminating all cases that have any missing values, and still have enough data to work with. In this lab, we will assume that this is indeed the case and show you a way of eliminating cases that have missing attribute values.

What we show in this activity might not always be the best thing to do. For example, if a data set has 10 attributes and the value of one attribute is missing for a particular case, we will eliminate the case and thus lose useful information on 9 attributes. If 5 different cases are each missing one attribute value – but each one for a different attribute, then we will lose 5 cases and 45 useful attribute values.

Data analysts use certain techniques to fill in the missing attribute values with reasonable fillers so as to salvage the remaining data. We will not cover such techniques in this book.

Activity steps

1. **Read the first data file:** Read the data file *na-example-1.csv* into a data frame called *nax1*:

```
> nax1 <- read.csv("na-example-1.csv")

> # Display the values
> nax1
```

   We see that rows 6 and 13 have "NA" for the attribute *Income*. This indicates that the values are *Not-Available* – which is different from a zero value.

   If you look at the original file *na-example-1.csv*, you will see that these values were absent in the file. If you open the file in a spreadsheet program you will find these cells to be empty.

2. **Read the second data file:** Read the data file *na-example-2.csv* into a data frame called nax2:

```
> nax2 <- read.csv("na-example-2.csv")

> # Display the values
> nax2
```

   From the output you see that cases 6 and 13, are still missing *Income*. However, cases 9 and 20 have blank values for *Car_type*, but R does not show them as "NA". If we look at the file, we see that cases 9 and 20 also have blank values for *Car_type*. Why does R not show these as "NA"?

3. **Understand R's treatment of blanks in data files:** For attributes with numeric values, R treats blanks as "NA". However, for attributes with textual values, by default, R treats a blank as just another category value. This is

why the missing *Car_type* values did not show up as "NA".

4. **Read missing textual values correctly:** While using *read.csv* we can tell R to treat an empty cell as a missing value or as "NA" by doing the following:

```
> # In the following, na.strings = "" tells
> # R that a an empty value in a file signals NA
> nax2 <- read.csv("na-example-2.csv", na.strings = "")

> # Display the values
> nax2
```

When we now see the output, we see that **R** shows "<NA>" for *Car_type* in rows 9 and 20. It uses the angle brackets to help us to distinguish these values from real category names – after all, it is conceivable that "NA" might be the actual value of a categorical attribute. If the data file had a specific code for missing values like say "##", then we could indicate that too:

```
> # In the following, na.strings = "##" tells
> # R that "##" as an attribute value for an attribute signals NA
> nax3 <- read.csv("na-example-3.csv", na.strings = "##")

> # Display the values
> nax3
```

Even when we use the above approach, R will treat blank values for numeric attributes as "NA", but we also have the option of explicitly marking them with some special notation.

5. **Dealing with "NA":** As we have discussed, our approach will be to just eliminate the cases that have even a single missing attribute. As discussed in the overview, we assume that we will have lots of data and can afford to throw away some of it. In the following command, we will create a new data frame with just the *complete cases* – cases with no missing attributes. Using the data file *na-example-2.csv*, we should expect to retain only 20 of the original 24 cases because we are missing two attribute values for *Income* and two for *Car_type*.

```
> # first read the data
```

```
> nax4 <- read.csv("na-example-2.csv", na.strings = "")

> # Create a new data frame called naxnew
> # without the missing values
> naxnew <- nax4[complete.cases(nax4), ]

> # Get the number of cases in naxnew
> nrow(naxnew)
```

We can now see that *naxnew* has only the 20 clean cases – those that have no missing attribute values and are *complete*.

6. **Imputing missing values:** In this book, we take the approach of eliminating any row that has even a single missing value. This might be fine when we have lots of data.

   The main advantage of this approach is its obvious ease. However, its downside is that we might be throwing away useful information on the non-missing attributes.

   To avoid throwing away useful information, people sometimes *impute* missing values. For example, a missing value for a numeric attribute can be replaced with the average of that attribute. Alternately, we can randomly sample a value from the attribute. For categorical attributes, we can either replace the missing value with the most frequently occurring value or with a randomly drawn value. We do not resort to either approach in this book.

Classification

In this section we will introduce the *classification* problem through an example. This section does not cover any specific technique for *classification* – we will encounter three in subsequent sections.

Classification problems – a case study

Linda and Jason sat exhausted at the admissions office conference table at the Beecham Business School (BBS) of Biltmore University. The conference room afforded a great view of the manicured university lawns with its idyllic lake and snow-white swans gracefully gliding over the water. The view could have done much to soothe Linda and Jason. At the moment the room felt more like a cave in which they had found refuge from a hungry, growling, man-eating lion.

The twenty-year old Biltmore University had appointed Ludmilla Adams as its new Vice President of Admissions after seeing increasing numbers of students leaving the school during their freshman and sophomore years. Around 10% of such seats falling vacant because of drop-outs could be filled through incoming transfer students, but most remained vacant for the remaining period. Drop-outs certainly did not help the school in fulfilling its mission. Additionally the school lost a lot of potential revenue that it would have earned had these students stayed for four years.

Ludmilla's predecessor Byron Smith had been given the ultimatum a few years ago, but had not been able to reverse the trend. Axed. During the period Byron was trying to reverse the trend, he spent a lot of time talking to some of the students who were about to drop out and also to their professors to understand what could be done.

The admissions office at Biltmore understood that the problem had to be addressed at many different levels. They wondered if they could do something in the admissions decision to reduce the drop-out rate.

Linda Bright, the Director of Admissions, and Jason Rodriguez, the Admissions Manager, had made the final admissions decisions for the past three years. They examined each application and the comments on these from the admissions committee. They also took into account the SAT scores of the applicants before making their decision.

This time around, Ludmilla had explained the dire situation to them and asked Linda to first gather data and come to an *evidence-based* decision rather than base their actions on anecdotal evidence – which she accused Byron of. Although Ludmilla tried to remain calm, the higher-ups in the university were very concerned, and the tone of her voice and her sense of urgency conveyed tension. Privately, Linda and Jason now started to worry for the security of their jobs.

After some preliminary discussion and analysis, Linda and Jason found that poor-performers formed an overwhelming majority (97%) among students who left. Furthermore, they also found that around 50% of the poor-performers left after the first year. They knew that the problem could be addressed at many levels – quality of teaching, student advising, academic and other support systems for students and on and on.

However, given the very close connection between poor-performance and dropping out, as well as considering the information they could readily gather, they decided to see if they could somehow predict the first-year performance of students based on information available at the time of admission. Until now, they had relied mostly on SAT score cutoffs for admissions decisions, but wondered if they needed to rethink this. Were their current admissions criteria somehow allowing in too many under-performers and to some extent contributing to the high drop-out rate?

Linda used their computer-based admissions system to gather information on admitted students over the past years and how they had performed during their first year at Biltmore. Realizing that admissions not only had the job of avoiding under-performers, but also had the task of admitting as many high-performers as possible, she had classified student performance into three categories: *High*, *Medium* and *Low* based on their GPA at Biltmore.

At the end of the process, they had a large data file with

3,400 cases. Table 18 shows 10 cases from the file – just to show you the attributes. From the application information, Linda had gathered data on the number of academic-related projects that applicants had completed in high-school outside of any high-school course, as well as the number of hours of community service these applicants had done at the time they had applied.

SAT	GPA	Projects	Community	Gender	Performance
1300	3.41	4	10	M	High
1210	3.23	2	15	M	Medium
1250	3.45	2	5	M	Medium
1350	3.62	1	10	M	Medium
1320	3.39	2	5	F	Medium
1120	3.18	3	0	F	Medium
1480	3.63	4	5	F	High
1250	3.16	3	0	F	Medium
1340	3.3	3	0	F	Medium
1270	3.39	2	10	M	Medium
...	...	...	...	...	...

Table 18: Structure of Linda's data – college performance of admitted students, current and past.

How can data analytics help?

In the admissions context, we have to consider the error of admitting a wrong candidate – *Low* performer – in preference to one who would have performed better. We also have to consider the error of not admitting a candidate who will likely turn out to be a *High* performer and admitting a *Medium* or *Low* performer instead.

Since the data in Table 18 comes from admitted candidates, we do not have any information about people whom the school did not admit. We can therefore only try to analyze the first type of error – admitting a *Low* performer.

What can we do with the historical data?

We have data on students from the time they applied (*SAT*, *GPA*, *Projects*, *Community Service* and *Gender*) and also data on how these applicants subsequently performed. Can we use some data analytics technique to identify patterns that would tell us reliably who would perform at what level based only on information available at application time?

Colleges can make good use of such patterns or *models*. Let us say we have an applicant, for whom we have the values of all attributes, except of course, how they will actually perform in college. However, we can employ our *model* to determine their potential performance and make our decision based on it. If the model is good, we could reduce the chances of offering admission to potential poor-performers and hence reduce drop-outs.

We are presented here with a *classification* problem – given an applicant's *SAT*, *GPA*, *Projects*, *Community Service* and *Gender*, we have to *classify* the applicant as a *High*, *Medium* or *Low* performer.

Before looking at any classification technique, let us look at the kind of results we might get and how we might use the results.

Figure 43 shows a possible *error matrix* or *classification-confusion matrix* that we might obtain after we apply a classification technique on this data. For now, don't worry about how we arrived at the matrix. We will soon see methods to create these.

	Predicted (data analytics)		
Actual	High	Medium	Low
High	22	17	0
Medium	8	427	3
Low	0	8	25

Figure 43: Error matrix produced by data mining for college admission example.

The first row of data in the figure shows us that the technique classified 22 students who actually performed at a *High* level as *High* performers. It classified 17 actual *High* performers as *Medium* and did not classify any *High* performers as *Low*.

To get an idea of the usefulness of the model, we would want to compare the performance of the data analytics technique with that of the methods that the university had employed in the past – let us call this the *current* method. We therefore need the comparable error matrix for the *current* method.

Figure 44 shows us what this would look like.

	Predicted (current)	
Actual	High or medium	Low
High	39	0
Medi um	438	0
Low	33	0

Figure 44: Error matrix for the *current method.*

Since the data only represents people whom the university already admitted, clearly the *current* method did not consider any of the students to be *Low* performers – otherwise they would not have admitted them in the first place. Furthermore, at the time the university admitted these students, they did not formally distinguish between *High* and *Medium* performers or even if they did, we do not have that information. So we can assume that each admitted student was expected to perform at a *High* or *Medium* level.

What can we do with this?

We can see that the data analytics technique identified 25 *Low* performing students (5% of the applicants) as such. Given that the data comes from admitted students, the *current* screening method clearly did not identify these 25 students as potential under-performers.

If the school admits 600 students each year, this would mean that the data analytics technique will identify 5%, or 30 of these as *Low* performers – which the *current* method would not catch.

Assuming that the school will be able to replace these applicants with better performing students, data analytics can prevent the associated drop-outs. Let us now put a dollar figure on this benefit.

The school has observed that 50% of the *Low* performing students leave. Thus data analytics can enable us to prevent 15 such losses each year. Conservatively assuming that the tuition loss per drop-out per year is $15,000 and that we would lose two years worth of tuition for every student who leaves, each lost student costs the university $30,000. By saving 15 losses each year, data analytics can save the school 15*$30,000 or $450,000 per year. Not bad at all for a few hours of number crunching at a computer!

Data analytics can provide additional benefits if it helps us to not just identify *Low* performers, but to also spot characteristics of *High* performers, so that we can reduce the error of rejecting good students and thereby improve the overall quality of students.

We will talk more about this when we look at specific classification techniques.

For more examples of situations where classification techniques can be used consider the following:

- Suppose we have a dataset consisting of data about various people and would like to select those to whom we will mail promotional offers. Clearly we would like to mail the offers to people who are likely to respond by buying our product. We would therefore like to classify each person as a *potential buyer* or *potential non-buyer*. With a limited budget, we have to select the people with the highest likelihood of being buyers.

- Consider Gmail or a similar mail service. For each mail that reaches its server, it has to determine whether the mail is *genuine* or *spam* and use this determination to either put the mail into a user's inbox or spam folder. It thus has to classify incoming emails as *spam* or *non-spam*.

- A used car dealership might have data on a set of cars, some of which it wants to purchase. To determine the best among these to buy, it might want to classify each car's reliability as *high*, *medium* or *low*.

Each of the above exemplifies the task of *classification* where we need to categorize each case into one among a set of predetermined categories. We aim only to box the cases into categories and not arrive at a numerical prediction.

We will later see that in *regression* tasks, we would like to ascribe a specific number to a case – for example, Netflix might want to *predict* what someone's rating (a value between 1 and 5) for a movie might be. We will learn more about this in the chapter on *Regression* (page 231).

Some data analytics books use the term *prediction* to refer to what we have referred to as *regression*. They thus talk about *classification* and *prediction* and the two types of *predictive analytics*. We avoid this usage because of the scope for confusion.

What type of target attribute signals the use of a *classification* technique?

Clearly, since aim to assign each case to a category, the target attribute must be categorical. If a situation arises where the target attribute is numeric and we still want to use a classification method, then we first need to convert it to a categorical attribute before we can proceed; we will cover that too.

In this chapter, we will look at three useful classification techniques – *K-Nearest Neighbors*, *Classification Trees* and *Naive Bayes*. The first two can also be used for regression, but in this chapter we only consider their application to classification. The chapter on *Regression* covers their use for regression.

Review 7: Classification

You can find the answers to these questions on page 365

For each of the following tasks which the concerned entities will carry out based on historical data, indicate if the task involves *classification* or *regression*.

1. An on-line store wants to calculate the possible rating that a specific customer might assign to a product and decide whether or not to present the product to the customer.

2. A company wants to examine its list of customers and mark each customer as one who is likely to switch to a competing product or not, and base some promotions on this determination.

3. A credit card company looks at every card transaction and wants to label it as fraudulent or not.

4. A store wants to find out how many units of a specific product will sell during a certain time period.

5. A bank is planning to invite some of its existing clients for a dinner event to promote a new financial product. It therefore wants to look at each current client predict if they will adopt the product. They plan to invite customers who seem likely to adopt the product.

K-Nearest Neighbors (KNN) for classification

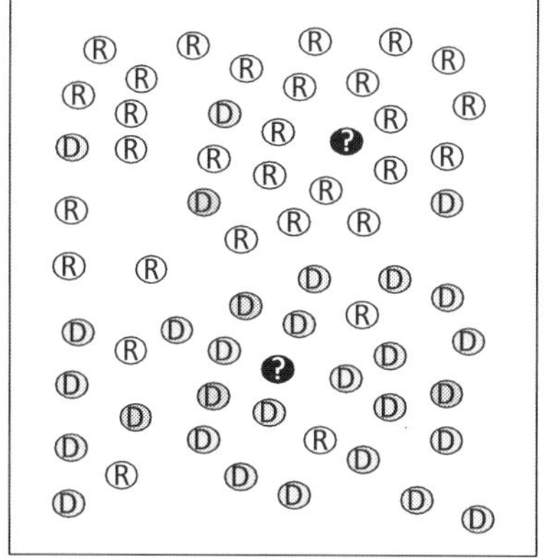

Figure 45: Voting preferences in a neighborhood.

Figure 45 shows the geographic location of homes in a fictitious neighborhood in a US city. Each circle represents a household with the voting preference of a household – R for Republican and D for Democratic. We have 30 households voting for each political party and two households for which we do not know the voting preference. We seek some way of classifying these two households as "D" or "R."

Like the country as a whole, this neighborhood also seems to be quite polarized; voters for each party cluster together pretty closely. It sure looks like the households are clustered geographically by voting preferences . Can we use this information and try to classify a household based on the voting preferences of its close neighbors?

Using KNN in the voting preference example

Specifically, for each household we could look at the *nearest* three *neighbors* and classify it based on the majority voting preference among these three neighbors. For example, suppose the household had two D neighbors and one R, then we would classify it as D. Suppose all its neighbors were R, then we would classify it as R, and so on.

There you have it – the essence of the K-Nearest Neighbors approach to classification – KNN for short.

We considered three neighbors above, that is, k=3. In general we could use any number for *k* and go with the majority category among of the *k* neighbors. In our example we have two *classes* "R" and "D". If we have two classes, choosing an even numbered value for *k* leaves open the possibility for ties to occur. To avoid ties, we can use odd values for *k*. If we have more than two classes, we cannot avoid ties just by choosing an odd value for *k*, but with more classes, the possibility of a tie also decreases.

In KNN, if ties do occur in classifying a case, then we select one of the tied classes randomly as the classification for the case in question.

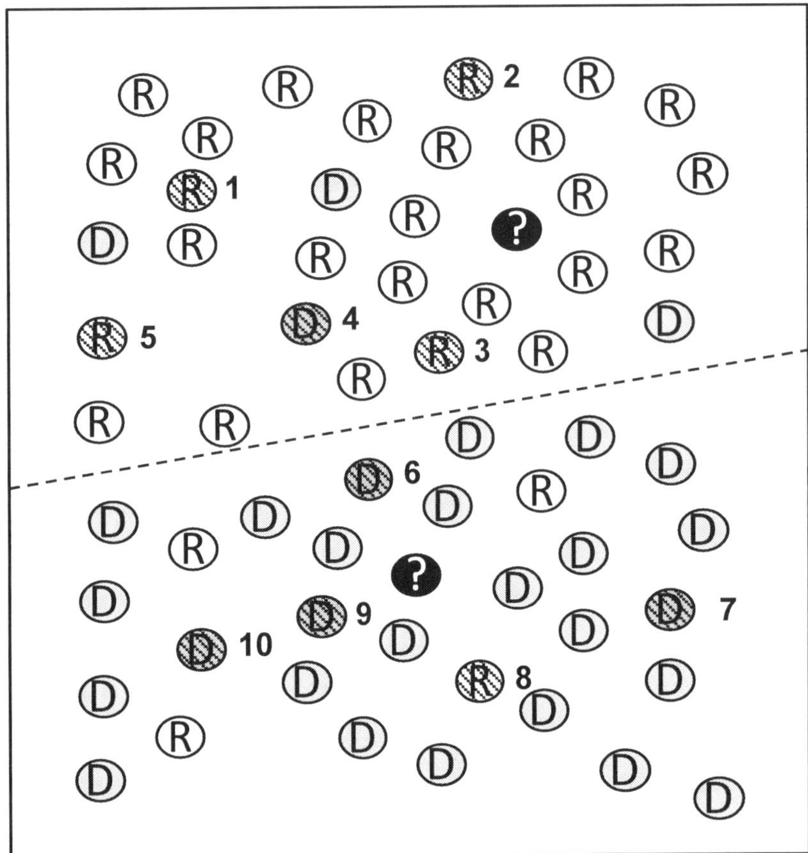

Figure 46: Testing the method by classifying some households for which we already know the classification.

If we applied this method to the two households marked with "?" we would classify the one in the top half as "R" and the other as "D" because of the majority class among three neighbors for each.

To evaluate the performance of this approach, let us pretend that we do not know the voting preference of some households for which we actually do know the preferences, and try to use this method to classify them. We can evaluate the quality of the method based on the number of errors we see.

We would like to use our approach to classify the cross-hatched households in Figure 46. For convenience, we have numbered each cross-hatched household. Table 19 shows the results for $k = 3$.

So KNN gets eight households out of 10 correct for a performance level of 80%. Do you feel that this performance is satisfactory?

Household no	Classification and explanation	Correct?
1	R. All of its neighbors are R	Yes
2	R. All of its neighbors are R	Yes
3	R. All of its neighbors are R	Yes
4	R. All of its neighbors are R	No
5	R. Two out of three neighbors are R	Yes
6	D. All of its neighbors are D	Yes
7	D. All of its neighbors are D	Yes
8	D. All of its neighbors are D	No
9	D. All of its neighbors are D	Yes
10	D. Two out of three neighbors are D	Yes

Table 19: Classifying based on the three nearest neighbors to each case – that is, KNN with $k = 3$.

Whether or not we consider this performance satisfactory would depend on how we plan to use the analysis and the costs of making mistakes. We do not have that information for our hypothetical situation and hence cannot make the determination.

However, we are always interested in how much improvement data analytics yields. How much does it improve over the baseline performance? How do we establish the baseline performance?

Leaving out the two households for which we do not know the classification as well as the cross-hatched ones for which we pretended not to know the classification, we have 50 households, equally divided between the two parties. If we were to classify a random household in this neighborhood without the benefit of location information and data analytics, the best we can do is to go with the overall numbers. Given the equal division, we would have to toss a coin to decide. That is, let us suppose that we are given a random household for which we do not know the voting preference and are asked to determine it knowing only that 50% of the households vote R and 50% vote D. All we can do is to make a random guess – perhaps flip a coin and give our decision. If we did that, we would be right about half of the time and have a success rate of 50%. Using KNN, we can achieve 80%. Thus KNN helps us to improve the classification performance from 50% to 80% for a *lift* of 1.6 – 80/50. Alternately we can see this as a 60% improvement over the baseline performance of 50%.

Having grasped the spirit of KNN for classification, let us look at a more complete example.

Boat purchase example for KNN

Jolly Boats Inc (JBI) wants to identify prospective buyers for its boats. It has promoted its boats to people in the past and has demographic information on the people as well as whether or not they purchased a boat. It wants to send out promotional brochures to many people in an area who do not already have boats, and has their demographic information. JBI only wants to send out brochures to those people its model identifies as prospective buyers.

Game on – we have a *classification* problem!

Table 20 shows the historical information that JBI has on past campaigns. It shows, for 24 people, their annual income, the number of cars they own and whether or not they purchased a boat in response to a prior campaign.

A few points before we forge ahead – our data set serves only to illustrate the process. For a real data analytics exercise we would need more rows as well as many more predictor attributes. We can hardly expect a model that uses just *income* and *number of cars* to provide good results. Therefore please treat this example as just an explanation of the process of using KNN for classification, and not as a realistic case study. However, don't let the simplicity of the example obscure the fact that it still accurately illustrates the very same principles that would apply in real-life situations. The ensuing lab and lab assignment are based on larger data sets.

Income ($)	Num cars	Outcome
144,000	3	Buyer
117,000	4	Buyer
154,000	2	Buyer
70,000	1	Non-buyer
124,000	3	Buyer
73,000	1	Non-buyer
62,000	1	Non-buyer
105,000	3	Buyer
74,000	1	Non-buyer
115,000	7	Buyer
106,000	2	Buyer
76,000	2	Non-buyer
109,000	2	Buyer
60,000	2	Non-buyer
98,000	2	Non-buyer
76,000	2	Non-buyer
58,000	1	Non-owner
104,000	3	Buyer
130,000	3	Buyer
161,000	2	Non-buyer
92,000	2	Non-buyer
105,000	2	Buyer
111,000	2	Buyer
56,000	2	Non-buyer

Table 20: Fictitious data on boat ownership for illustrating KNN classification.

Take a close look at the data. You might have spotted a major glitch already in applying the essence of our motivating discussion. The notion of neighbors does not seem to apply to this example. How do we calculate the *neighbors* of a given case? This data has nothing to do with spatial distances.

Look at the data carefully. Can you find some easy way of classifying the cases?

In the voting example, we used only the location information to classify a person as R or D. In other words, we used geographical location as a predictor attribute and exploited its relationship to the target attribute. We relied on the logic of "people with similar location coordinates have similar voting preferences" and in our example that was adequate.

While we used spatial distance as a pivotal concept in the voting example, we used it to identify the cases in the data set that were *similar* to a given case. In the current example, we have not one, but two attributes and therefore want to base our notion of *similarity* of cases on both attributes.

Clearly we cannot use the notion of spatial distance to find neighbors in this example.

For example, take the case on the first row, (144,000, 3) – we represent a case here as a set of two coordinates (income, no of cars). No other case matches this one exactly. But which of the other cases in the data set seems most similar to this one?

You will most likely agree that the case on row 19, (130,000, 3) seems to be the closest – it has the same number of cars and the income differs by only a little. So even though we cannot calculate spatial distances, we see the possibility of measuring the similarity between cases by how closely their attribute values match.

We can establish the degree of similarity between cases by looking at how closely their attribute values match

So suppose we have the above data set and we get a new case for which we do not know the classification. We can see which cases it is most similar to in terms of the two predictor attributes and arrive at a classification based on this.

Classifying a new case based on historical cases to which it is *similar*

In KNN, when we talk about *distance* we are really taking about a measure of *similarity*. Let us now turn our attention to quantifying the notion of *similarity*, based on the values of multiple attributes.

From your geometry classes, you might recall that we can calculate the *distance between any two points in space* by applying the Pythagorean Theorem (see figure 47).

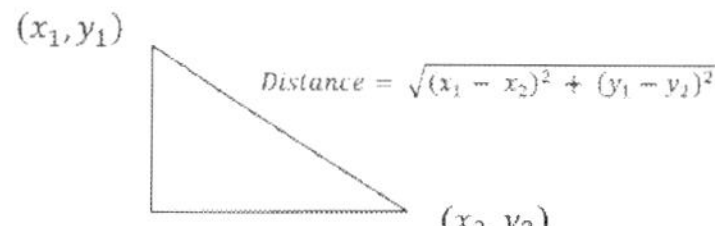

Figure 47: Calculating the distance between two points in two-dimensional space using the Pythagorean Theorem.

Can we borrow the same idea to calculate the distance between two cases in a data set? That is, can we find a way to mathematically determine the "neighbors" of a given case in such a way that cases that are very similar have short distances and dissimilar ones, long?

In fact we have already hinted at this by the way in which

we earlier represented each case by two numbers enclosed in parentheses.

Before going much further, we can already see that KNN absolutely depends on distance between cases calculated using the values of the predictor attributes of the cases. Therefore, *to use KNN, all predictor attributes must be numeric.*

KNN requires all predictor attributes to be numeric

Also, as noted earlier, to use any classification method, the target attribute (or dependent attribute) must be categorical. Let us calculate the "distance" between (144,000, 3) and (130,000, 3) by using the distance formula. We could calculate it as:

For any classification problem, the target attribute must be categorical

Distance computation

$$\sqrt{(144,000 - 130,000)^2 + (3-3)^2}$$

and arrive at 14,000 as the distance.

Consider the following two pairs of cases:

$(144,000,3)$ and $(130,000,3)$, and
$(144,000,3)$ and $(130,000,10)$

The cases in the second pair are much more different than the ones in the first pair. Why?

One case in the second pair has 7 more cars, but the incomes are identical to the cases in the first pair. We should expect the cases in the second pair two cases to be "further" away from each other than the cases in the first pair.

Incomes dominate the distance computations

Using the formula, we find the distance in the cases of the second pair to be 14,000.001756 – practically the same as the earlier case!

Now consider the pair:

$(144,000,3)$ and $(131,000,3)$,

Which we would consider to be very similar to each other and hence result in a small distance. In fact the distance between these two is 13,000, much less than the almost similar cases compared earlier.

What is going on?

To recap, we found that changing the number of cars from 3 to 10 had no impact on the distance, whereas changing the income from 130,000 to 131,000 had a huge impact. Put differently, a small percentage change in income has a much larger impact on the distance than even a huge percentage change in number of cars.

Clearly, the distance formula in its raw form does not work

for us. Can you identify the issue?

By now you might have found the reason – the raw income numbers are much larger and hence dominate the distance computations. Can we somehow bring both income and the number of cars to the same scale so that neither dominates? Of course people have figured out the solution and given us not one, but two options.

- **Adjust the range to (0,1):** The first approach adjusts the values such that the range becomes [0,1] – that is, the largest value becomes 1, the smallest, 0 and the rest fall proportionately in between. For example, consider the attribute values 50, 20, 70 and 60. The numbers fall in the range 20 to 70. In adjusting the range, we want to covert this range to be between 0 and 1, so that 20 becomes 0 and 70 becomes 1 and the remaining two values fall in between at levels proportionate to their magnitudes.

  Adjusting the range to [0,1]

  Consider 50. We have a range of 50 between the largest and smallest values – the difference between 70 and 20. Where does the original value of 50 fall on this range?

  50 is 30 above the minimum and hence is three-fifth of the way between the minimum and maximum. So its value will be three-fifth or 0.6.

  Similarly 60 is 40 above the minimum and falls four fifths of the way between 20 and 70. Thus it becomes 0.8.

  So the original values of 20, 50, 60 and 70 now have range-adjusted values of 0, 0.6, 0.8 and 1 respectively.

  More formally, if we use *min* and *max* to represent the smallest and largest values, then a value x would be adjusted as:

  $adjusted\_x = (x - min)/(max - min)$

- **Standardize:** The second *standardizes* the values. That is, it treats the average or mean as zero and every other value as the number of standard deviations away from the mean the value falls (values below the mean get standardized into negative values). For example, if we have the heights of many people with the mean height as 70 inches and the standard deviation as 5 inches. A 70 inch tall person is right at the mean and would standardize to 0. A 75 inch tall person falls one standard deviation (5 inches) above the mean and standardizes to 1. Someone who is 77.5 inches tall would standardize to 1.5 because 77.5 is 1.5 standard deviations away from the mean of 70. A person 65 inches tall would standardize to -1, because 65 is one standard deviation below the mean 70.

  Standardizing or normalizing attribute values

  More generally, if *mean* and *sd* stand for the mean and the standard deviation respectively, then the standardized value of x is:

  $standardized\_x = (x - mean)/sd$

When you need to use any method that relies on distance computations, you can use either of the above two approaches. Of course for a particular data set you should use the same approach for all the predictor attributes.

Continuing with the boat purchase example, Table 21 shows the range-adjusted values corresponding to the original boat ownership data in 20. For each attribute, we used the first approach; we set the largest value and the smallest value to 1 and 0 respectively. We used the following values for scaling – minimum income: 56,000, maximum income: 154,000, minimum cars: 1, maximum cars: 7. Incidentally, you will not have to perform any of these calculations by yourself – we will soon show you how to use **R** to do all this painlessly. We are showing every step here just to ensure that you understand the process.

Table 21: Boat ownership data with [0,1] range-adjusted income and number of cars (rounded to three decimal places).

Income ($)	Num cars	Range-adjusted income	Range-adjusted cars	Outcome
144,000	3	0.898	0.333	Buyer
117,000	4	0.622	0.500	Buyer
154,000	2	1.000	0.167	Buyer
70,000	1	0.143	0.000	Non-buyer
124,000	3	0.694	0.333	Buyer
73,000	1	0.173	0.000	Non-buyer
62,000	1	0.061	0.000	Non-buyer
105,000	3	0.500	0.333	Buyer
74,000	1	0.184	0.000	Non-buyer
115,000	7	0.602	1.000	Buyer
106,000	2	0.510	0.167	Buyer
76,000	2	0.204	0.167	Non-buyer
109,000	2	0.541	0.167	Buyer
60,000	2	0.041	0.167	Non-buyer
98,000	2	0.429	0.167	Non-buyer
76,000	2	0.204	0.167	Non-buyer
58,000	1	0.020	0.000	Non-buyer
104,000	3	0.490	0.333	Buyer
130,000	3	0.755	0.333	Buyer
61,000	2	0.051	0.167	Non-buyer
92,000	2	0.367	0.167	Non-buyer
105,000	2	0.500	0.167	Buyer
111,000	2	0.561	0.167	Buyer
56,000	2	0.000	0.167	Non-buyer

We had calculated the distances between (144,000, 3) and (130,000, 3) and (144,000, 3) and (130,000, 10) and found that the distances turned out to be very similar even though we would consider these two cases to be very dissimilar. Let us now repeat the calculations with range-adjusted values.

Looking at Table 21 we see that the adjusted value for an income of $144,000 is 0.898 and for $130,000 is 0.755, for 3 cars is 0.333 and for 7 cars is 1. Although we do not have a case with an income of $131,000, we use it in the illustration below. Its adjusted value would be 0.765.

Table 22 compares the distances calculated using the adjusted and unadjusted values. You will note that the distances computed using the adjusted values are much smaller in magnitude. The absolute magnitude does not mean anything; we are interested only in the relative magnitudes.

Look at rows 1 and 2. The unadjusted computation shows the same distance for both pairs (the minuscule difference has vanished in rounding), although the cases in the second row are far more different than those in the first. The distances based on the adjusted values show a lot of difference, with the second being more than four times the first.

Row 5 is very instructive too. Although the cases are very different, the unadjusted computation sees them as practically identical – the distance of 4 pales in comparison with the general magnitude of distances computed with the other unadjusted values. On the other hand, the a distance computation with adjusted values shows that these two cases are highly dissimilar.

We can see that under adjusted computations similar cases (rows 1, 3 and 4) have relatively small distances and dissimilar cases have large distances. Unadjusted calculations do not possess this important property because they allow attributes with generally high values to dominate and drown out significant differences in other smaller-valued attributes.

We could very well have done these computations using standardized values (the second approach described above) and would have obtained similar relative distances.

Row	Cases	Unadjusted distance	Adjusted distance
1	(144,000,3) and (130,000,3)	14,000	0.143
2	(144,000,3) and (130,000,7)	14,000	0.682
3	(144,000,3) and (131,000,3)	13,000	0.133
4	(130,000,3) and (131,000,3)	1,000	0.010
5	(130,000,3) and (130,000,7)	4	0.667

Table 22: Comparison of distances calculated with adjusted and unadjusted data.

Now that we have found a way of objectively establishing the extent of similarity between cases, we are ready to apply KNN. In what follows, we will use the adjusted distances for illustrating the steps of KNN for classification.

Recall that we aim to use this data set to build a model that we can later apply to classify as *Buyer* or *Non-buyer* people whose *income* and *number of cars* we know.

Not only do we want to build a model, but we also want to evaluate its performance before deploying it (using it for classifying future cases). Recall from the introduction that we use data partitioning to achieve this. For KNN, we use three partitions that we call – *Training.A*, *Training.B* and *Test*. We will partition the data set and then explain how the method works.

Tables 23, 24 and 25 show the three random partitions – note that we have added case numbers within each partition for facilitating discussion. Also note that we first range-adjusted the data before partitioning it. Scaling after partitioning would be incorrect.

Table 23: Training.A partition for boat purchase data.

Case no	Income ($)	Num cars	Adjusted income	Adjusted cars	Outcome
1	144,000	3	0.898	0.333	Buyer
2	154,000	2	1.000	0.167	Buyer
3	70,000	1	0.143	0.000	Non-buyer
4	124,000	3	0.694	0.333	Buyer
5	73,000	1	0.173	0.000	Non-buyer
6	62,000	1	0.061	0.000	Non-buyer
7	105,000	3	0.500	0.333	Buyer
8	74,000	1	0.184	0.000	Non-buyer
9	115,000	7	0.602	1.000	Buyer
10	106,000	2	0.510	0.167	Buyer
11	76,000	2	0.204	0.167	Non-buyer
12	60,000	2	0.041	0.167	Non-buyer

Table 24: Training.B partition for boat purchase data.

Case no	Income ($)	Num cars	Adjusted income	Adjusted cars	Outcome
1	109,000	2	0.541	0.167	Buyer
2	117000	4	0.622	0.500	Buyer
3	98,000	2	0.429	0.167	Non-buyer
4	76,000	2	0.204	0.167	Non-buyer
5	58,000	1	0.020	0.000	Non-buyer
6	104,000	3	0.490	0.333	Buyer

Table 25: Test partition for boat purchase data.

Case no	Income ($)	Num cars	Adjusted income	Adjusted cars	Outcome
1	130,000	3	0.755	0.333	Buyer
2	61,000	2	0.051	0.167	Non-buyer
3	92,000	2	0.367	0.167	Non-buyer
4	105,000	2	0.500	0.167	Buyer
5	111,000	2	0.561	0.167	Buyer
6	56,000	2	0.000	0.167	Non-buyer

We first pick a value for k – let us say $k = 1$. We then classify each case of the Training.B partition using the Training.A partition. We explain this process in detail below.

For each case of the Training.B partition, find the k nearest neighbors in the Training.A partition and classify the Training.B case as the majority class among the neighbors.

Let us take the first case of the *Training.B* partition. To classify this case, we compute its distance (using the adjusted values, of course) to each case of the Training.A partition.

For convenience, we have shown the distances for each of the cases in the Training.B partition to each of the cases in the

Training.A partition in Table 26. When you use **R** to apply this method, all of this will happen in the background and you will not have to mess with any of this.

Incidentally, although we have shown the distances in Table 26, in reality we can skip the step of computing the square root and just use the squared distances. After all, we are only interested in the closest neighbors; leaving out the square root step will not change the relative magnitudes of the numbers.

	Training.B partition case no					
Trg.A case no	1	2	3	4	5	6
1	0.394	0.322	0.498	0.714	0.939	0.408
2	0.459	0.504	0.571	0.796	0.994	0.537
3	0.431	0.693	0.331	0.178	0.122	0.481
4	0.226	0.181	0.313	0.517	0.751	0.204
5	0.403	0.672	0.305	0.169	0.153	0.460
6	0.508	0.752	0.403	0.220	0.041	0.543
7	0.172	0.207	0.181	0.340	0.584	0.010
8	0.394	0.665	0.296	0.168	0.163	0.453
9	0.836	0.500	0.851	0.923	1.157	0.676
10	0.031	0.352	0.082	0.306	0.517	0.168
11	0.337	0.535	0.224	0.000	0.248	0.331
12	0.500	0.670	0.388	0.163	0.168	0.479

Table 26: Distances from each case of the Training.A partition to each case of the Training.B partition.

Since we are working with k = 1, we need to look at just one nearest neighbor. We find from Table 26 that case 10 of the Training.A partition (income:106,000, cars:2, outcome: Buyer) is closest to the first case of the Training.B partition – distance 0.031. Because the nearest neighbor is a *Buyer*, we classify the first case of the Training.B partition as *Buyer* – and this turns out to be correct.

Figure 48 shows the nearest neighbor for the first three cases of the Training.B partition.

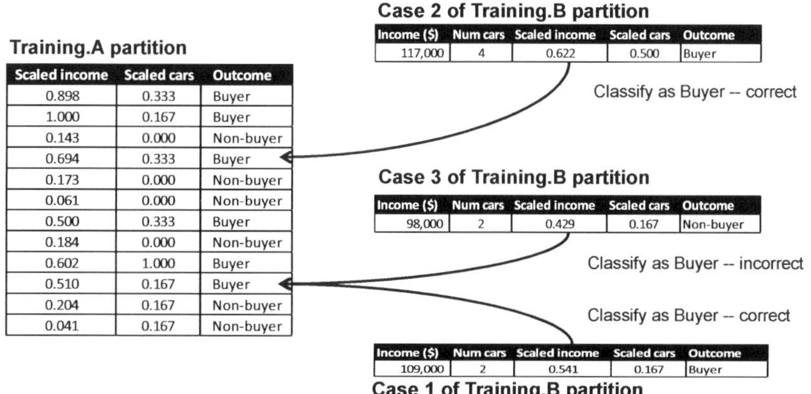

Training.A partition
Scaled income | Scaled cars | Outcome
0.898 | 0.333 | Buyer
1.000 | 0.167 | Buyer
0.143 | 0.000 | Non-buyer
0.694 | 0.333 | Buyer
0.173 | 0.000 | Non-buyer
0.061 | 0.000 | Non-buyer
0.500 | 0.333 | Buyer
0.184 | 0.000 | Non-buyer
0.602 | 1.000 | Buyer
0.510 | 0.167 | Buyer
0.204 | 0.167 | Non-buyer
0.041 | 0.167 | Non-buyer
Case 2 of Training.B partition
Income ($) | Num cars | Scaled income | Scaled cars | Outcome
117,000 | 4 | 0.622 | 0.500 | Buyer
Classify as Buyer -- correct
Case 3 of Training.B partition
Income ($) | Num cars | Scaled income | Scaled cars | Outcome
98,000 | 2 | 0.429 | 0.167 | Non-buyer
Classify as Buyer -- incorrect
Classify as Buyer -- correct
Income ($) | Num cars | Scaled income | Scaled cars | Outcome
109,000 | 2 | 0.541 | 0.167 | Buyer
Case 1 of Training.B partition

Figure 48: KNN with $k = 1$: Nearest neighbor (shown with arrows) for each of the first three cases of Training.B partition.

In similar vein, we find that the nearest neighbor to the second Training.B case happens to be case 4 of the training partition and we also correctly classify this as a *Buyer*.

We classify case 3 of the Training.B partition incorrectly as a *Buyer* because it falls closest to case 10 of the Training.A partition – a *Buyer*.

Continuing thus, we can classify all the Training.B cases. Table 27 shows the results. You should also verify these using the distances in Table 26.

Training.B case	Actual class	KNN classification
1	Buyer	Buyer
2	Buyer	Buyer
3	Non-buyer	Buyer
4	Non-buyer	Non-buyer
5	Non-buyer	Non-buyer
6	Buyer	Buyer

Table 27: KNN performance on Training.B cases with $k = 1$.

We see that of the six Training.B cases, KNN, with $k = 1$ classifies five correctly for a 83.33% performance or a 16.67% error rate.

The error rate of 16.67% has arisen from the misclassification of a single non-buyer as a buyer. With more cases in the Training.B partition, we might have had the other kind of error too – classifying buyers as non buyers, and we might want to know the break-up.

In *classification*, we usually create the *error matrix* or the *classification-confusion matrix*, which gives the break-up of errors.

Figure 49 shows the *error-matrix (classification-confusion matrix)* for our Training.B partition. Can you explain why the numbers in the matrix add up to 6?

We classified 6 cases in the Training.B partition.

The first row of data indicates that, of the actual buyers, KNN classified three out of three as buyers and none as non-buyers. The second row tells us that, of the three actual non-buyers (total of all the numbers on that row), KNN classified one, incorrectly, as a buyer and classified the remaining two correctly. The numbers on the diagonal from the top left to the bottom right tell us what KNN got correct. The numbers on the other diagonal tell us what KNN got wrong. The total of all the numbers, of course, tells us the total number of cases in the Training.B partition. We see that KNN got one case out of six wrong, for an overall error rate of 16.67%. However, it correctly classified all the buyers for a 0% error rate or 100% performance on these. It got one out of three non-buyers wrong for an error rate of 33.33% or a 66.67% correctness performance.

		KNN result	
		Buyer	Non-buyer
Actual class	Buyer	3	0
	Non-buyer	1	2

Figure 49: KNN Error matrix (or classification-confusion matrix) for Training.B partition of boat buying example with $k = 1$.

We can assess the performance of a classification technique like KNN based on its overall error rate. However, this might not always be appropriate. We have two types of errors – that of classifying a buyer as a non-buyer and vice versa. The overall error rate lumps the two types of errors together. This implicitly assumes that they are equally undesirable. In reality, one kind of error might be much more costly than the other.

For example, suppose we classify individuals among a group of people as buyers or non-buyers and then mail promotional brochures to the people we classify as buyers. Suppose it costs $10 to mail a brochure and that we stand to make a profit of $100 if we make a sale. Thus if someone buys the product as a result of the promotion we gain $100. In this scenario, classifying a non-buyer as a buyer costs us $10 because we wastefully mailed a brochure to them. Classifying a buyer as a non-buyer costs us $100 – because if we had mailed a brochure to them we would have made a sale. The latter error is thus ten times as costly!

asymmetric costs

Such situations reflect *asymmetric costs* – that is, the cost of the two types of errors are not equal. In these cases, we might not necessarily assess the performance of a classification method by overall error rate alone.

What would the baseline performance be? That is, how might we perform without the benefit of data analytics?

The original data set has equal numbers of buyers and non-buyers and without the benefit of data analytics, we would just have to guess, ending up being wrong about half the time. Our performance would be 50%. So, it looks like KNN with $k = 1$ seems to be performing well at a correctness rate of nearly 84%.

We are not done yet though. We still have to try out other values of k – we might find a value that yields even better results.

Another, even more important point, is that, to be more confident about the model's performance, we need to test it on data that we have not at all used in the model building process. This is why we created the third partition, *Test*. Once we have tried several values of k on the Training.B partition, we will choose the k-value that performs best. We will then see how that value of k performs on the *Test* partition. Only then can we get an unbiased estimate of our model.

Having tried $k = 1$, let us try $k = 3$. Why not $k = 2$?

Suppose we chose $k = 2$ and for a particular case we find one neighbor to be a buyer and another to be a non-buyer – a tie. We would have to pick a class randomly to resolve the tie. We therefore avoid even values for k when we have two values for the target attribute.

Figure 50 shows the three nearest neighbors of the first Training.B case. Since all of these represent buyers, we classify the case as a buyer – correctly as it happens.

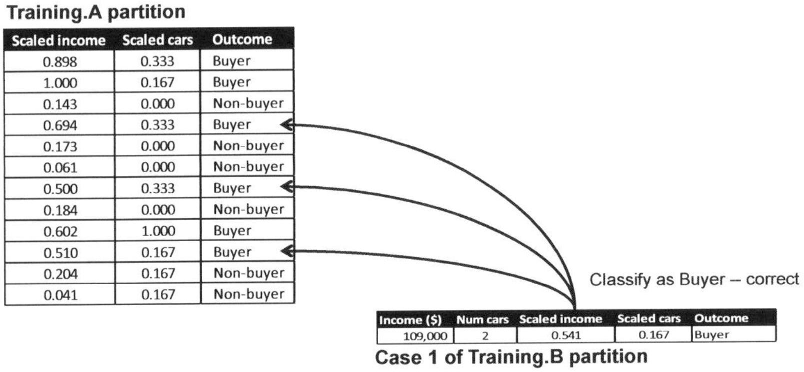

Training.A partition

Scaled income	Scaled cars	Outcome
0.898	0.333	Buyer
1.000	0.167	Buyer
0.143	0.000	Non-buyer
0.694	0.333	Buyer
0.173	0.000	Non-buyer
0.061	0.000	Non-buyer
0.500	0.333	Buyer
0.184	0.000	Non-buyer
0.602	1.000	Buyer
0.510	0.167	Buyer
0.204	0.167	Non-buyer
0.041	0.167	Non-buyer

Classify as Buyer – correct

Income ($)	Num cars	Scaled income	Scaled cars	Outcome
109,000	2	0.541	0.167	Buyer

Case 1 of Training.B partition

Figure 50: KNN with $k = 3$: Three nearest neighbors (shown with arrows) for the first case of the Training.B partition.

Again, using the distances in Table 26 we see that with $k = 3$, we get the same results as we got for $k = 1$, which we showed in Table 27 and thus get the error or classification-confusion matrix as before (see Figure 49).

With a larger data set, we might try bigger values for k. In general we do not use values for k beyond 9.

With $k = 1$ and $k = 3$ giving identical results, which of the two should we use as out "best" value?

We choose the lower value for k in such cases, because, computation-wise, using a higher value for k requires the computer to do more work. With large data sets, this could take up significant extra time – for no gain, because we will not be getting any better results.

Now that we have chosen our best k, let us see how KNN performs with this value on the six cases in the *Test* partition. That would be the real test as the data in this partition was not used in finding the best value for k. The test partition contains unbiased data.

For convenience, we once again show the distances from each of the cases in the Test partition to each of the cases in the

Training.A partition in Table 28. Using these distances, we can easily determine how KNN performs on each case in the test partition. Table 29 shows the results.

As before, we still have just one error in the six cases for the same overall error rate of 16.67%. Once again the error involves classifying a non-buyer as a buyer and thus the classification-confusion or error matrix is identical to what we saw earlier (see Figure 49).

Trg.A case no	1	2	3	4	5	6
1	0.143	0.863	0.556	0.431	0.376	0.913
2	0.296	0.949	0.633	0.500	0.439	1.000
3	0.697	0.190	0.280	0.394	0.450	0.220
4	0.061	0.664	0.367	0.256	0.213	0.714
5	0.670	0.207	0.256	0.367	0.422	0.241
6	0.770	0.167	0.349	0.469	0.527	0.178
7	0.255	0.479	0.213	0.167	0.178	0.527
8	0.662	0.213	0.248	0.358	0.413	0.248
9	0.684	0.999	0.866	0.840	0.834	1.028
10	0.296	0.459	0.143	0.010	0.051	0.510
11	0.576	0.153	0.163	0.296	0.357	0.204
12	0.733	0.010	0.327	0.459	0.520	0.041

Table 28: KNN for boat example: Distances from Training.A cases for each of the six Test partition cases.

Test case	Actual class	KNN classification
1	Buyer	Buyer
2	Non-buyer	Non-buyer
3	Non-buyer	Buyer
4	Buyer	Buyer
5	Buyer	Buyer
6	Non-buyer	Non-buyer

Table 29: KNN with $k = 1$: Performance on each of the Test partition cases.

We had earlier advised against using even numbered values for k. On occasions, we have to depart from this advise. While using classification techniques, we sometimes want the method to just give us the probability of a case belonging to a class rather than actually doing the classification for us. If we are using KNN for obtaining just the *raw probabilities*, then we can use even values. For example, suppose, we were working with $k = 3$ and for a particular case we find two of the three nearest neighbors to be buyers and one to be a non-buyer. In this case the raw probability of this case being a buyer is 2/3 or 66%. Suppose we use an even value for k and find a tie between buyer and non-buyer, then we can just report a raw probability of 50%.

Review 8: KNN for Classification

You can find the answers to these questions on page 366

Table 30 shows fictitious data on some people's age, family income and the type of smart phone they own.

Age	Family_income	Phone_type
14	50,000	iPhone
17	80,000	Android
23	70,000	Android
30	100,000	Android
40	120,000	iPhone
60	200,000	Other
16	40000	iPhone
13	48,000	iPhone
17	80,000	Android
22	71,000	Android
29	100000	Other
41	120000	iPhone
60	210000	Other
16	42000	iPhone

Table 30: Table for KNN review question.

Table 31 shows the original and standardized values of the 10 cases in the Training.A partition.

Age	Family_income	Phone_type	Age_z	Family_income_z
14	50000	iPhone	-0.895	-0.842
17	80000	Android	-0.709	-0.281
23	70000	Android	-0.337	-0.468
30	100000	Android	0.098	0.092
40	120000	iPhone	0.718	0.466
60	200000	Other	1.959	1.960
16	40000	iPhone	-0.771	-1.029
13	48000	iPhone	-0.957	-0.879
17	80000	Android	-0.709	-0.281
22	71000	Android	-0.399	-0.450

Table 31: Training.A partition for KNN review question

Table 32 shows the original and standardized values of 4 cases in the Training.B partition.

Age	Family_income	Phone_type	Age_z	Family_income_z
29	100000	Other	0.035	0.092
41	120000	iPhone	0.780	0.466
60	210000	Other	1.959	2.146
16	42000	iPhone	-0.771	-0.991

Table 32: Training.B partition for KNN review question

1. Use Excel (or anything else) to calculate the **three** nearest neighbors in the Training.A data for the second row of the Training.B data.

2. Based on the above calculations, how would you classify the item on the second row of the Training.B data? Don't confuse this with what the table already shows; your classification might be the same, or could be different.

Lab 7: Adjusting and standardizing attributes in **R**

Pre-requisite(s)

- ✓ You should have **R** installed on your computer.
- ✓ You should have downloaded and stored the data files for the book and pointed **R** to the location of your data files.
- ✓ You should have downloaded all the code files for this book and stored them in your **R** working directory.
- ✓ You should have read the section on *KNN for Classification* on page 117 and answered the associated review questions.

Objective

After completing this lab, you will be able to:

- ✓ Adjust or standardize attributes in preparation for data analytics methods that rely on distance computations

Overview

Many data analytics techniques rely on the notion of *similarity* between different cases in data sets. They use some measure of distance to assess similarity. When we have data sets with more than one attribute, the relative magnitudes of the attribute values might differ drastically. If so, attributes with relatively high values will dominate the distance calculations and render the other attributes ineffective as predictors. We combat this by either adjusting the range of all predictor attributes to [0, 1] or by standardizing all of them.

In our earlier example, we saw that the values of incomes are much higher than those of the number of cars that people own. In such cases, the attributes with higher numerical values dominate distance calculations and can hence drown out the effect of other attributes. To prevent this from happening, data analysts convert all attributes to a uniform scale – usually 0 to 1, or they standardize the values. Either approach works fine so long as you use the same approach for all the predictor attributes involved.

In this lab, we will learn how to use **R** for performing these conversions.

Activity steps

1. **Load the data file:** We will load the data in the file *knn-smart-ph.csv* and prepare its attributes for KNN analysis in the next lab. Load the file now into a variable called *sp*.

```
> sp <- read.csv("knn-smart-ph.csv")
```

2. **Look at the data:** Use the appropriate command to see the data in the variable *sp*. Note that the attribute names are: *Age*, *Family_income* and *Phone_type*.

Use the command *sp* to see the values in the data frame.

3. **See the smallest and largest values for each attribute:** You can use the *max* and *min* **R** functions to see the maximum and minimum values for an attribute in a data frame. Type the command *max(sp$Family_income)* to see the highest value for *Family_income*.

Recall that we can use the $ operator to get at a named attribute in a data frame.

use: *min(sp$Age)*, *max(sp$Age)*.

You can also use the column position notation as in *max(sp[,1])* to get the highest age

4. **Range-adjust the Age values:** We will first see how to adjust the values so that the minimum and maximum are 0 and 1 respectively. We assign all in-between values proportionate to where they fall in the range.

   Enter the following command to adjust the ages and store them in a new attribute in the data frame. We will explain the command shortly.

```
> sp$Age_s <- (sp$Age -  min(sp$Age))/
    (max(sp$Age) - min(sp$Age))
```

   In **R** when we want to perform the same operation on all rows of data, we do not need to process each row separately. The single command above processes all the rows of the data frame. You can see that we have used the *max* and *min* functions to calculate the highest and lowest age. We have then computed the adjusted value of age for every row and stored the results in a new attribute called *Age_s*. We could have called the new attribute anything at all, but *Age_s* seems reasonable. Look at the data in the variable *sp* to see the new attribute. Note how the highest age of 60 has been adjusted to 1 and the lowest one, 13, has been adjusted to 0.

5. **Adjust the Family_income values:** Based on the above, now enter the command to adjust the *Family_income* values. Again, examine the data frame to ensure that the highest and lowest values were properly adjusted.

sp$Family_income_s <- (sp$Family_income - min(sp$Family_income))/ (max(sp$Family_income) - min(sp$Family_income))

6. **A note:** We repeat that you can use either range-adjusting or standardizing to apply KNN and other distance-based data mining techniques. You do not have to do both. Nevertheless, we show you both techniques here.

7. **Standardize the income values:** As we have already seen, to standardize an attribute, for each value of the attribute we calculate the number of standard deviations away from the mean the value lies. **R** provides a prebuilt function – called *scale* – to achieve this. Type the command

```
> sp$Family_income_z <- scale(sp$Family_income)
```

The above command computes the standardized values of income and stores the results in a new attribute called *Family_income_z*. We attached a "z" at the end the attribute name because statisticians call these standardized values as Z values.

Based on the above, now type the command to calculate the standardized value of *Age* and store the result in an attribute called *Age_z*.

sp$Age_z <- scale(sp$Age)

8. **Standardizing several attributes together:** Quite often, we will need to standardize several attributes in a single data frame. Entering a separate command for each one can be tedious. The book's code has a convenience function to standardize several attributes in one command.

To ready the convenience function for use, perform the following steps:

a First read the file *dar2ed-scale-many.R* into **RStudio** by using the menu option *File/Open File*. The file should now be open in the top left pane. This code defines a convenience function called *dar2ed.scale.many*; we will not explain the code in this book.

b Make the function available in the **R** environment by clicking on the *Source* button in the top right of the pane with the code. This reads the function definition into **R**.

To standardize both *Age* and *Family_income* in one command, enter:

```
> # Load the data file afresh since we have already
> # standardized the attributes in
> # the earlier data frame
> sp <- read.csv("knn-smart-ph.csv")
> # Now standardize multiple attributes
> # Use the c function to specify the column numbers of
> # the attributes to standardize
> # You should load the code in the file
> # dar2ed-scale-many.R first
> sp <- dar2ed.scale.many(sp, c(1,2))

> # This creates new attributes with _z
> # appended to the old attributes names. Check it.
> sp
> # or use RStudio to display the data frame sp
```

You should now have two new attributes called *Age_z* and *Family_income_z*.

To use the function *dar2ed.scale.many*, be sure to do the following:

a Load the code for the function, as described earlier

b Pass, as the first argument, the data frame on which you are operating

c Pass the vector of column numbers as the second argument. As shown above, You can construct this vector using the *c* function.

d Assign the result to the data frame variable so that the data frame now has the standardized columns in addition to the original ones.

Lab 8: KNN for classification

Pre-requisite(s)

✓ You should have read the portions of the text dealing with classification in general (page 111) and with KNN in particular (page 117) and answered the associated review questions.

✓ You should have completed the prior labs on *Introduction to* **R***data frames* (page 17), **R** *packages* (page 55) and *Standardizing attributes* (page 133).

Objective

After completing this lab, you will be able to:

✓ Prepare data for classification using KNN.

✓ Run KNN for classification on a data set.

✓ Interpret the results of a KNN for classification run.

Overview

In this lab we will run the KNN classification algorithm in **R** for a small data set of 40 rows. We will build a model to classify cases as *Buyer* or *Non-buyer*. You can use the same steps for data sets of any size.

As discussed earlier, we will first standardize the data and create three partitions. We will then run KNN with various values of k and choose the one that gives the best results in terms of the classification-confusion matrix. We will finally see how the model performs on the test partition.

Activity steps

1. **Load the data:** Load the data from the file *vacation-trip-classification.csv* into a variable called *vac*.

   ```
   > vac <- read.csv("vacation-trip-classification.csv")
   ```

2. **Understand the data:** The file contains historical data from a fictitious tour operator. The tour operator operates special expensive adventure tours and is planning to invite a select group of people to a free promotional dinner event cum information session. If people accept the offer, the tour operator stands to make good money. Otherwise, the operator will lose around $50 per head for the free dinner and associated costs. The company wants to invite only those people who are likely to accept the offer. It wants to use the historical information to build a KNN model to classify people as buyers or non-buyers. In this activity, we will use *Income* and *Family_size* as predictor attributes and *Result* as the target attribute.

3. **Explore the data:** Before jumping into model building, we would typically explore the data.

   In this case, creating boxplots and histograms of the predictors will make sense:

```
> boxplot(vac$Income)
> hist(vac$Income)
> boxplot(vac$Family_size)
> hist(vac$Family_size)
```

The above plots give us an idea of how the individual attributes are distributed. There is nothing surprising here.

In analytics, we want to understand relationships – especially, how the target attribute *Result* relates to the predictors. For examples, how do the family incomes of buyers and non-buyers compare? Side-by-side boxplots are a good way to examine such things.

```
> boxplot(Income ~ Result, data = vac, ylab = "Income")
> boxplot(Family_size ~ Result, data = vac,
      ylab = "Family size")
```

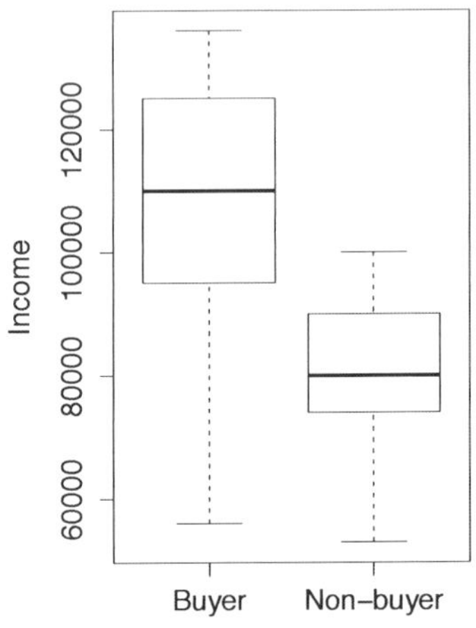

Figure 51: Side by side boxplots of Income by Result

Figures 51 and 51 show the results.

That was powerful! Let us understand the details.

Looking at the first line, the first argument to the *boxplot* function is *Income ~ Result*. This is an example of a *formula expression* that is used extensively in **R**. To understand how a formula expression works, consider that we are interested in seeing how the distribution of *Income* is affected by the level of the factor *Result*. To state it differently, we want to see whether or not the distribution of *Income depends* on *Result*.

That is, *Income* is like a *dependent attribute* and *Result* is like an *independent attribute*.

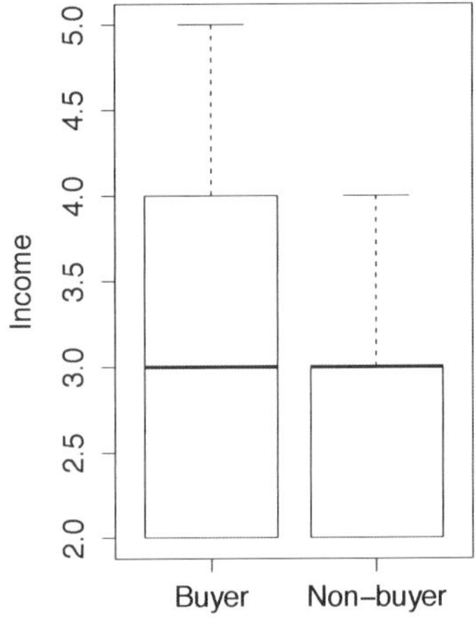

Figure 52: Side by side boxplots of Family_size by Result

In a formula expression, we place the dependent attribute on the left hand side of the tilde sign and the independent attribute(s) on the right. Since we are using just the attribute names, **R** will not be able to find these unless we indicate the data frame that contains them – hence the argument *data = vac*.

The above explorations tell us something that we might have expected all along – that people with higher incomes are much more likely to be buyers. As for family size, the picture does not seem very clear. We might have expected people with large families not to be buyers – because of the cost. However, while the median family size of both groups is about the same, many buyers seem to have relatively large families and very few non-buyers seem to have large families. Interesting!

4. **Standardize predictors:** KNN involves distance computations and so we need to standardize the attribute values for both *Income* and *Family_size*:

```
> # Standardize the attributes in the first two columns
> # we can do this one by one as below
> vac$Income_z <- scale(vac$Income)
> vac$Family_size_z <- scale(vac$Family_size)
> # Verify
> vac
```

   Instead of the above, we could have used the approach described in the lab on Standardizing attributes (page 133). How would you do that?

Hint:

- First load and execute the code for the function dar2ed.scale.many by loading the file first and then *sourcing* it in;
- Then execute the code vac <- dar2ed.scale.many(vac, c(1:2))

5. **Partition the data:** Our data set is too small for serious analysis. However, we will follow all the steps just for illustration. Recall that we need three partitions for running KNN. We use two partitions to build the model and the *test* partition to assess the quality of the model.

   The lab on *Data Partitioning* on page 60 showed you how to create two partitions. We did not include the steps to create three partitions because KNN is the only approach discussed in this book that requires three partitions.

   As already discussed, *Result* is our target attribute.

   We can easily modify the approach used there to create three partitions as shown below. We will do a 60-20-20 break-up.

```
> # Load the caret package
> library(caret)
> # Seed the random number generator
> set.seed(2015)
> samp <- createDataPartition(vac$Result,
      p = 0.6, list = FALSE)
> # Create the first training partition, train.a
> train.a <- vac[samp, ]
> # Store the rest of the data
> # in a new variable called rest
> rest <- vac[-samp, ]
> # We need to sample half of the rest into
> # the second training partition, train.b
> samp <- createDataPartition(rest$Result,
    p = 0.5, list = FALSE)
```

```
> train.b <- rest[samp, ]
> # Store the remaining rows in test
> test <- rest[-samp, ]
```

6. **Load the *class* package:** KNN analysis in **R** requires us to install and use the *class* package. In the lab on **R** packages (page 55), we already installed the *class* package (page 55). We can now load it by either checking *class* in the *Package* tab on the bottom right pane or by issuing the command:

   ```
   > library(class)
   ```

7. **Understand the partitioned data:** Before we jump into building the model, let us take a look at the data in relation our task. We aim to classify a person as a buyer or non-buyer of an adventure trip based on their income and family size. Instead of the raw values, we will be using the standardized values for these two predictor attributes. Our data partitions contain the original and the standardized values but we want to use only the standardized values in our analysis.

   Each of the partitions *Training.A*, *Training.B* and *Test* has five attributes: *Income*, *Family_size*, *Result*, *Income_z* and *Family_size_z*, with the last two representing standardized values. We will be classifying based only on the last two attributes; our target attribute *Result* is in the third column.

   Recall that in KNN, we classify the cases in the *Training.B* partition based on their proximity to cases in the *Training.A* partition. We will use only the standardized values.

   Thus the relevant data in *Train.A* is *train.a[,4:5]* – we will take all rows, but use only the fourth and fifth columns (standardized values of the predictor attributes) from each row. Our target attribute is *Train.A*[,3] because the third column contains the correct classification.

   Similarly, our *Train.B* data resides in *train.b[,4:5]*.

8. **Inputs to the knn function:** In using KNN we will invoke the *knn* function from the *class* package. The function requires the following inputs:

   a **Training.A data:** For us that will be *train.a[,4:5]*

b **Training.B data:** *train.b[,4:5]*

c **Correct classification in training data:** *train.a[,3]*

d **Value to use for k:** Whatever we choose. We could start with 1 and the try successive odd numbers.

9. **Recap of KNN mechanics:** KNN uses both the training partitions to build the model. It takes each row of the *train.b* partition and finds the k nearest neighbors to it in the *train.a* partition. It then classifies each *train.b* row based on whichever class forms a majority in the neighbors found (if k is even and there is a tie, then it breaks ties arbitrarily). For example, suppose it takes the first row of the *train.b* partition and finds its three nearest neighbors (if k = 3) in the *train.a* partition. If two or more of these three are *Buyer* then it will classify this case as *Buyer*.

10. **Building the model:** We are now ready to call the function that builds the model. Classifying Training.B cases for different values of k is the model building process. In fact, the final "model" is nothing but the best value of k, along with the *train.a* partition!

    As you will see in Figure 53, the *knn* function call returns the predicted values for each case of the *train.b* partition. We first ask you to enter the command and then explain the individual components of the command. Enter the command:

```
> train.b$pred.1 <- knn(train.a[,4:5],
      train.b[,4:5], train.a[ ,3], 1)
```

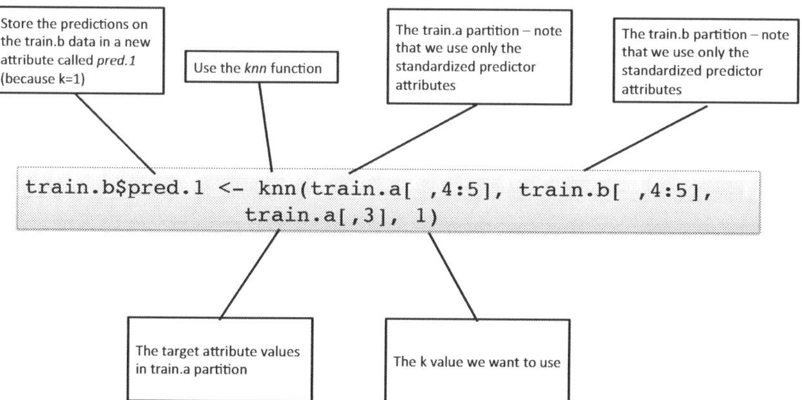

Figure 53: Details of the knn function call

Figure 53 explains the individual components of the *knn* function call.

11. **Examine and tabulate the results:** Now that we have completed running knn for k=1, let us see the results. We simply have to look at the *train.b* partition and compare the actual ownership status against what knn arrived at. Table 33 shows the results. We can see that it correctly classified all of the cases.

Income	Family_size	Result	Income_z	Family_size_z	pred.1
88000	4	Non-buyer	-0.3221423	1.2220288	Non-buyer
100000	3	Non-buyer	0.21606968	0.1110935	Non-buyer
120000	3	Buyer	1.1130896	0.1110935	Buyer
100000	4	Non-buyer	0.21606968	1.2220288	Non-buyer
100000	2	Buyer	0.21606968	-0.9998418	Buyer
90000	2	Non-buyer	-0.2324403	-0.9998418	Non-buyer
95000	4	Buyer	-0.0081853	1.2220288	Buyer
130000	5	Buyer	1.56159957	2.3329641	Buyer

Table 33: KNN predictions for the training.b partition with k=1.

We can guess what the error matrix or the classification confusion matrix will look like. However, let us see the commands to generate it.

```
> tab.1 <- table(train.b$Result, train.b$pred.1,
        dnn = c("Actual", "Predicted"))

> # Now print the table
> tab.1
```

The *table* function cross-tabulates the values of the two attributes. It computes the number of matches and mismatches of the values. This gives us the classification-confusion matrix.

Figure 54 explains the details and Figure 55 shows the result.

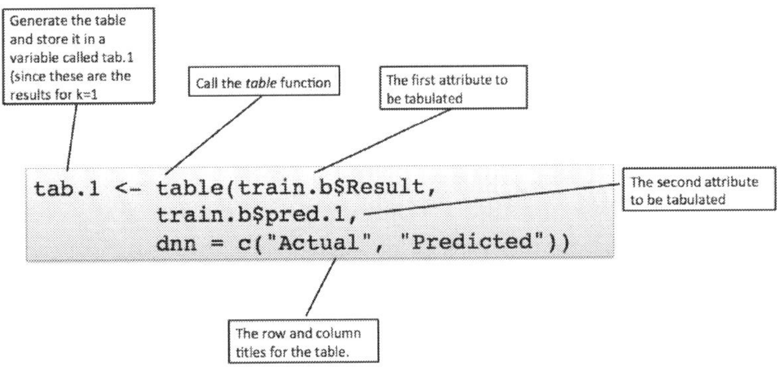

Figure 54: Details of the *table* function call

```
                Predicted
Actual          Buyer Non-buyer
  Buyer             4         0
  Non-buyer         0         4
```

Figure 55: Classification-confusion matrix for k=1

From the error matrix we can calculate the overall error rate. The total number of cases is the sum of all the numbers in the matrix. The number of cases that the model classified correctly is the sum of the numbers on the main diagonal – the one from the top left to the bottom right of the matrix.

In the present case, since the model got everything correct, we can directly say that the model performance is 100%.

In KNN, we try different values for k and see which one gives the best results. In our case, k=1 already gave us perfect results and we cannot better this.

Nevertheless, just for practice, let us repeat the process for k=3.

12. **Repeat for k=3:** We can repeat the above process for k=3 and generate the corresponding classification confusion matrix.

```
> train.b$pred.3 <- knn(train.a[,4:5],
      train.b[, 4:5], train.a[ ,3], 3)
> tab.3 <- table(train.b$Result,
      train.b$pred.3,
      dnn = c("Actual", "Predicted"))
> tab.3
```

Figure 56 shows the resulting error-matrix.

We find that this model is worse than the one for k=1. The model's correctness performance is 7/8 or 87.5%.

```
              Predicted
Actual        Buyer Non-buyer
  Buyer           3         1
  Non-buyer       0         4
```

Figure 56: Classification-confusion matrix for k=3

In general, you can expect to find that as we increase k from 1, the model's performance improves until some point and then starts deteriorating. We choose the value of k that provides the best performance. Sometimes the performance improves, then deteriorates and then improves again. In such cases, we have to use our judgment in selecting the best value of k.

13. **Evaluating model quality:** How good is the model? Our data set had 21 buyers and 19 non-buyers. So, 52.5% of the cases were buyers. Without the help of a model, we can do no better than relying on the *naïve* approach of classifying everyone as belonging to the majority class – as *buyer* in this case. This will give us a 52.5% performance rate. With the model (using the best

k), we get a performance of 100%.

The ratio of the performance with the model to that without the model is called *Lift*.

Our model therefore provides a *Lift* of 100/52.5 or 1.90.

Based on the definition of *Lift*, it is clear that we want values above 1. The higher the better.

We cannot evaluate a model based solely on its absolute performance or *Lift*. Only in context can we evaluate the model. In some situations, a 1% improvement might be a lot and in others, even a 50% improvement might not be adequate. If we are able to put a concrete monetary value on the improvement, then we will be in a good position to evaluate a model.

In the above, we have assumed that all errors are born equal. However, this might not be the case. The cost of classifying a buyer as a non-buyer might be much higher than the other way around. If we make this error we stand to lose the profits from a sale. If we classify a non-buyer as a buyer, then our cost might just be that of inviting someone who does not buy the product. If this were the case, we would have *asymmetric costs* and might tend to choose a value of k that has a higher overall error rate but does better on classifying buyers as buyers – at the expense of classifying more non-buyers also as buyers.

14. **Using the test partition to assess the model:** Having built a model and possibly found its performance to be adequate, we must now test it on independent data that we have not used to build the model. Remember, our performance evaluation of the model thus far has been on data that we used to build the model itself. Relying on the performance measure based on this would surely be biased. This is why we kept away some of the data in the form of the *test* partition. Our best value for k was 1. Let us see how our model with k=1 performs on the test data.

    Enter the command to run *knn*, but replace the references to the *train.b* partition with the *test* partition.

```
> test$pred.1 <- knn(train.a[,4:5],
        test[, 4:5], train.a[ ,3], 1)
> tab.test.1 <- table(test$Result, test$pred.1,
```

```
        dnn = c("Actual", "Predicted"))
> tab.test.1
```

Table 34 shows the *test* partition with the predictions appended.

Income	Family_size	Result	Income_z	Family_size_z	pred.1
78000	3	Non-buyer	-0.7706522	0.1110935	Buyer
95000	4	Buyer	-0.0081853	1.2220288	Buyer
94900	2	Buyer	-0.0126704	-0.9998418	Non-buyer
53000	3	Non-buyer	-1.8919272	0.1110935	Non-buyer
128000	2	Buyer	1.47189757	-0.9998418	Buyer
82000	3	Buyer	-0.5912483	0.1110935	Non-buyer
80000	3	Non-buyer	-0.6809503	0.1110935	Non-buyer

Table 34: KNN predictions for the test partition with k=1

Figure 57 shows the error matrix. This is very much worse than what we got on the training data. With large data sets we would not expect to see such a big difference between the performance on the training and test data. With the very small data set, this is not very surprising.

```
              Predicted
Actual        Buyer Non-buyer
  Buyer           2         2
  Non-buyer       1         2
```

Figure 57: Classification-confusion matrix for k=1 on the test partition

The correctness rate on the *test* partition is 4/7 or 57.1% – which still gives some *Lift*!

15. **More tabulating options:** We used the *table* function above to generate cross-tabulations containing raw numbers. Sometimes we might also want to see proportions in place of these numbers. In the present tables we have very small numbers and percentages really would not make much sense. However, let us go ahead and generate them anyway for practice.

Try the following. In this command, we use the previously generated table and get a new table showing the proportions that comprise each cell of the table. Compare the results with those from the previous table.

```
> prop.table(tab.test.1)
```

The *prop.table* function shows overall proportions. If we add all the numbers, we should get 1.00.

We might not want so many decimal places to be displayed. We can round off to a certain number of digits by using the *round* function. Below, we round the results to two decimal places:

```
> round(prop.table(tab.test.1), 2)
```

We do not have to use the *prop* function only on tables that we have previously generated and stored. Instead, we can apply it on the fly as well, as the code below shows.

```
> prop.table(table(test$Result, test$pred.1,
        dnn = c("Actual", "Predicted")))
```

Of course you can multiply the results from the above commands by 100 to display percentages.

```
> round(prop.table(tab.test.1)*100, 2)
```

All of the above tables show overall proportions or percentages. Sometimes we might want row-wise or column-wise proportions. For example, suppose we want to look at what proportion of actual buyers the method classifies as buyers and the proportion of actual non-buyers the model classifies as buyers. This would require us to find row-wise percentages. We can get those easily as well. For row-wise proportions supply the second argument as 1 to the *prop.table* function call.

```
> prop.table(tab.test.1, 1)
```

For column-wise proportions supply the second argument as 2 to the *prop.table* function call.

```
> prop.table(tab.test.1, 2)
```

16. **Summary:** Table 35 summarizes the steps.

Lab assignment 4: KNN For Classification

You can find the answers to this assignment on page 368. The

file "academic.csv" contains historical data that a professor maintained about her students. The file contains the score that students obtained on the first test of one of her courses and the student's attendance record till the first test. The file also

Table 35: Summary of steps for *KNN for classification.*

Step no	Description	R command	Remarks
1	Read the data into a frame called vac	`vac <- read.csv( "vacation-trip-classification.csv")`	
2	Understand and explore the data		Look at the data; generate scatterplots, scatterplot matrices, boxplots, histograms, density plots, etc.
3	Standardize the predictors	`vac$Income_z <- scale(vac$Income)` `vac$Family_size_z <- scale(vac$Family_size)`	We can do this one by one, or use the convenience function *dar2ed.scale.many*

4	Create three partitions	`library(caret)`
		`set.seed(2015)`
		`samp <- createDataPartition(vac$Result, p = 0.6, list = FALSE)`
		`train.a <- vac[samp, ]`
		`rest <- vac[-samp, ]`
		`samp <- createDataPartition(rest$Result, p = 0.5, list = FALSE)`
		`train.b <- rest[samp, ]`
		`test <- rest[-samp, ]`	

5	Be clear about model elements		Note down the columns in the train.a and train.b partitions that contain the predictors and the target.
6	Load the "class" package	`library(class)`	
7	Build model for k=1	`train.b$pred.1 <- knn(train.a[,4:5], train.b[, 4:5], train.a[ ,3], 1)`	Be clear about what goes where in this command.
8	Compute and display error matrix for k=1	`tab.1 <- table(train.b$Result, train.b$pred.1, dnn = c("Actual", "Predicted"))` `tab.1`	Tabulate and print the actual and predicted values
9	Repeat above steps for several values of k and select one with acceptable error	Change the above command suitably for other k values	We found k=1 to be the best for this data. Use the appropriate k value for the next step based on your context.
10	Generate predicted values on test partition with chosen k	`test$pred.1 <- knn(train.a[,4:5], test[, 4:5], train.a[ ,3], 1)`	
11	Generate error matrix for test partition	`tab.test.1 <- table(test$Result, test$pred.1, dnn = c("Actual", "Predicted"))` `tab.test.1`	Compare this with the error matrix on the train.b partition

has information on the overall performance of each student classified as *Acceptable* or *Not-acceptable*.

The professor wants to see if she can build a model to predict how students will perform based on the score in the first test and their attendance record. She wants to use this information to spot potential poor performers and counsel then in advance to enhance their chances of success.

1. Load the data now into a data frame called *students*.
2. List the data in the **R** data frame *students* that you created in the previous step.
3. What is the target attribute?
4. What are the predictor attributes?
5. Take a look at the data. What are the maximum and minimum values of the two predictor attributes?
6. What additional processing do you need to do to the data so that you can use KNN?
7. Store the standardized values of the two predictor attributes in two new attributes in the same data frame.
8. What do you need to do next to set up for KNN analysis?
9. Create three partitions with a 70-15-15 breakup (remember to set the seed to 2015 if you want to match your answers to those given in the book).
10. Run KNN for k=1, 3 and 5. For each one, generate the classification-confusion matrix.
11. Based on the classification-confusion matrices you obtained, select a value for k to use.
12. Use the chosen value of k and generate the classification-confusion matrix for the test partition. Did it turn out to be better or worse than the performance on the training data?
13. Without the use of data analytics, what would have been your error rate? Does the KNN approach provide any lift? If so, how much?

Attribute Conversion

We have seen that the KNN technique for classification can only be applied when the data set has numeric predictor attributes and a categorical target attribute. As we proceed to look at other techniques, we will find that each one imposes specific restrictions. What if our data does not have the characteristics that a method demands, but the method otherwise seems very applicable in principle? Are we doomed?

Fortunately mathematicians have devised ways to convert attribute values from one type into another as needed. In some cases we lose some information in the conversion process, but the process still frequently proves useful.

Categorical to numeric

Look at the data in Table 36, specifically at the categorical data in the attribute *State*. Suppose we have chosen a technique requiring this to be numeric. What do we do?

Age	State	Height	Income
23	New Jersey	61	5000
13	New York	55	1000
36	New Jersey	66	3000
31	Virginia	64	4000
58	New York	70	30000
29	Texas	63	10000
39	New Jersey	67	50000
50	Virginia	70	55000
23	Texas	61	2000
36	Virginia	66	20000

Table 36: Sample data to illustrate dummy attributes or variables

Of all things, *dummy* attributes (also called *dummy* variables) can get us off the hook. Table 37 shows the solution. Take a close look at the values for the attributes *State* and the new attributes *New Jersey*, *Virginia* and *Texas* before reading on.

Age	State	New Jersey	Virginia	Texas	Height	Income
23	New Jersey	1	0	0	61	5,000
13	New York	0	0	0	55	1,000
36	New Jersey	1	0	0	66	3,000
31	Virginia	0	1	0	64	4,000
58	New York	0	0	0	70	30,000
29	Texas	0	0	1	63	10,000
39	New Jersey	1	0	0	67	50,000
50	Virginia	0	1	0	70	55,000
23	Texas	0	0	1	61	2000
36	Virginia	0	1	0	66	20,000

Table 37: The three columns following *State* demonstrate how to convert it to numeric through three *dummy* attributes. Note that for any row, at most one of these three attributes has a value of 1.

Note that the attribute *State* has four different values (New Jersey, New York, Virginia and Texas). To make it numeric, Table 37 has added three new attributes – called *dummy* attributes – with each one being the name of a possible value of *State*. The first row with *State* "New Jersey" has the corresponding *dummy* attribute set to 1 and the rest set to 0. More generally, for a given value of *State*, the attribute corresponding to its name has a value of 1 and the others have a value of 0. Look at the table and verify each case for correctness.

Wait a minute ... New York has no corresponding *dummy* attribute. Although *State* has four different values in the table, we have chosen to keep only three *dummy* attributes. Why?

Note that rows with "New York" as their *State*, have 0 for the values for all the three *dummy* attributes. Thus, while looking at the converted data, we can already figure out which rows have "New York" as the *State*; adding an extra column would be redundant. When data sets have redundant columns, some of the data analytics methods fail to work properly if we include the redundant attributes.

As a rule, when converting categorical attributes with n distinct values to numeric, we need to add only $n - 1$ *dummy* attributes. The upcoming lab shows you how to create dummy attributes in **R**. You will see that methods that we will discuss for creating dummy attributes create new attributes corresponding to *all* values of the categorical attribute. However, when we use the data for modeling, we have to take care to exclude one of the dummy attributes corresponding to each categorical attribute.

Numeric to Categorical

Look at Table 36 again. If we are using a data analytics method that requires *Income* to be categorical, we would need to convert it appropriately. Looking at the data, we see some very low incomes ($10,000) and below. We might categorize these as "Low" and categorize the values between $10,000 and $31,000 as "Medium" and the rest as "High" – as the *Income Category* attribute of Table 38 shows.

With a very large data set, we might find incomes spread quite evenly unlike in our table. In such cases, we run into some problems. Using the approach adopted in Table 36, we would consider an income of $9,999 to be *Low* and $10,000 as *Medium* and this could seem very arbitrary. In such cases, we

Age	State	Height	Income	Income Category
23	New Jersey	61	5,000	Low
13	New York	55	1,000	Low
36	New Jersey	66	3,000	Low
31	Virginia	64	4,000	Low
58	New York	70	30,000	Medium
29	Texas	63	10,000	Low
39	New Jersey	67	50,000	High
50	Virginia	70	55,000	High
23	Texas	61	2,000	Low
36	Virginia	66	20,000	Medium

Table 38: Attribute *Income category* shows the converted categorical values of *Income*.

can consider dividing numerical attributes into two categories, say *High* and *Low*. To achieve this, we can first decide on three categories like we did in Table 36 and then leave out the middle category – cases classified as *Medium*. That way we would have a robust division between cases classified as *High* and those classified as *Low*. Of course we would need to have enough data that allows us the luxury of discarding some of our data.

Review 9: Attribute conversion

You can find the answers to these questions on page 371

1. **Categorical to numeric:** Let us suppose that a data file has 5 attributes with two of these being categorical. One of the categorical attributes has three possible values and the other has four. If someone adds just the correct number of dummy attributes to the data file while retaining the original attributes as well, how many attributes will the data have overall after the addition of dummies?

2. **Numeric to categorical:** Suppose a data file has information on many stores of a grocery chain. The file contains a numeric attribute *return_on_investment*. A data miner wants to apply a classification technique to this file to be able to classify stores as *High_ROI* or *Low_ROI* and wants to convert this numerical attribute to categorical. Assuming that the data file has many rows of data, how might the data miner proceed?

Lab 9: Converting data

Pre-requisite(s)

- ✓ You should have completed the lab on *Introduction to* **R** *data frames* on page 17.
- ✓ You should have completed the lab on **R** packages on page 55.
- ✓ You should have downloaded and stored the data files for the book and pointed **R**'s working directory to the location of your data files.
- ✓ You should have read the section on attribute conversion (page 149) and answered the associated review questions.

Objective

After completing this lab, you will be able to:

- ✓ Convert categorical attributes to numeric when needed.
- ✓ Convert numeric attributes to categorical when needed.

Overview

Every data analytics technique requires its attributes to be of specific types. We have just seen that KNN for classification requires numeric predictor attributes and a categorical target attribute. We will see later that linear regression requires all attributes to be numeric. We might therefore need to convert attributes from one type to another before using an analytical technique. In this lab we will learn how to convert from categorical to numeric and vice versa.

Activity steps

1. **Read the file:** Read in the file *conversion.csv* into a data frame called *students*.

   ```
   > students <- read.csv("conversion.csv")
   ```

   Take a look at the data. You see the data in Table 36 from before.

2. **Load the *dummies* package:** In the lab on **R** packages on page 55 you should have installed the *dummies* package. Now load it by checking its name in the *Packages* tab of the bottom right pane.
   Alternately you can use:

```
> library(dummies)
```

3. **Create dummy attributes for *State*:** We now want to create dummy attributes for *State*. We will show you the command first and then explain what it does. Enter the command:

```
> students <- cbind(students, dummy(students$State, sep="_" ))
> # See the attribute names now
> names(students)
```

Figure 58 explains the components of the above command.

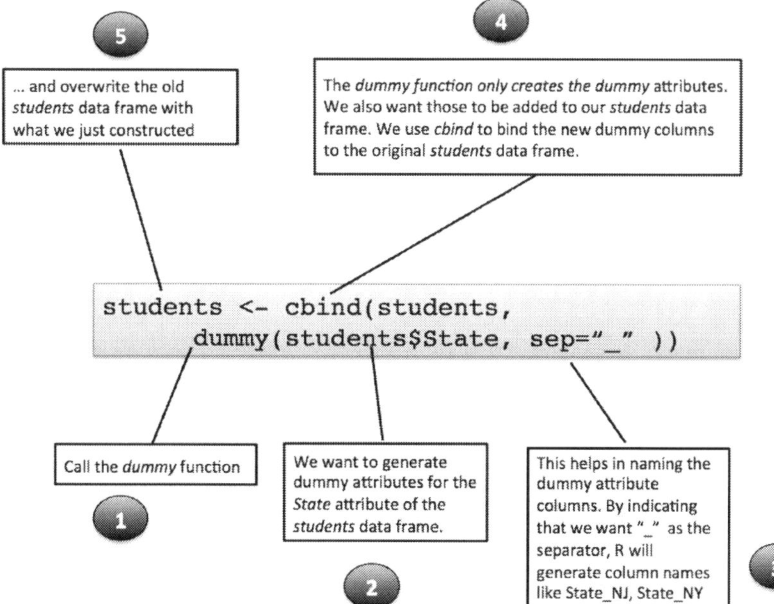

Figure 58: Explanation of the *dummy* function

4. **Converting many categorical attributes:** When we need to convert just a single attribute, the above approach works fine. However, we often have to convert many – sometimes more than 10; the process could then be unnecessarily repetitive. We offer a convenience function for this as well.

   Load the file *dar2ed-dummy.R* into **RStudio** and *source* it in by clicking on the *Source* button on the pane where the code is displayed. Then execute:

```
> mags <- read.csv( "dummy-example-2.csv")
> mags
```

Note that this file has two categorical attributes: *Origin* and *Gender; name* is not really categorical. We could create dummies for each one separately. Or we can use the function *dar2ed.dummy* and convert both in one shot. These attributes are in columns 3 and 4.

```
> mags <- dar2ed.dummy(mags, c(3,4))
> names(mags)
```

5. **Create categorical attribute for *Income:*** We do not have any set rules for how to convert numerical attributes to categorical. For the present, let us assume that we want to categorize rows with income less than or equal to $10,000 as "Low", those above $10,000 but $31,000 or below as "Medium" and the rest as "High". **R** provides a *cut* function to do this easily. We will show the code and explain:

```
> # First create a vector of the breakpoints
> # Inf stands for Infinity
> breaks = c(-Inf, 10000, 31000, Inf)

> # Then create the names we want to call the groups
> names = c("Low", "Medium", "High")

> # Note that names has one less element than the breaks
> # The 4 items in breaks define three intervals
> # (-Infinity to 10000], (10000 to 31000] and (31000 to +Infinity]
> # The left parenthesis in each group shows that
> # the number on the left is not part of its group
> # The square right brackets show that the second
> # number of each interval is included in its group

> # Now assign each income to its category using
> # the cut function
> students$Income_cat = cut(students$Income, breaks, names)

> # Verify
> students
```

Be sure to understand *breaks* and *names* and their relationship

. You can now check the data to see that the conversions were correct.

Classification Trees

Look at the data in Table 39 and see if you can see any underlying patterns. For example, what seem to be the attributes common to people who own *Luxury* cars? How about *Economy*?

Of course we have simplified the data for our discussion. In reality we would hardly be convinced that income and family size alone would play a big role in someone's car choice, but try nevertheless.

Income	Family size	Type of car
200,000	4	Luxury
30,000	4	Compact
75,000	3	Economy
90,000	6	Economy
30,000	2	Compact
125,000	2	Luxury
130,000	6	Economy
300,000	2	Luxury
250,000	3	Luxury
128,000	5	Economy
35,000	1	Compact
...	...	...

Table 39: Hypothetical data on car ownership.

With the available data, you might have noticed that all cases earning $\$200,000$ or more own *Luxury* cars. Those earning $\$35,000$ or below own *Compact* cars and those with incomes between $\$100,000$ and $\$200,000$ own *Luxury* cars if their family size is less than 3 and own *Economy* cars if their family size is 5 or greater.

In the above, we found some *rules* underlying the data. To make the *rules* very clear, we can express some of them more formally as shown below:

IF $Income \geq 200,000$ THEN Luxury
IF $Income \leq 30,000$ THEN Compact
IF $(100,000 \leq Income < 200,000)$ *and* $(Family\_size < 3)$ THEN Luxury

We can represent the complete set of rules as a *tree* as Figure 59 shows. (Although it hardly looks like a tree, we can see some resemblance if we turn it upside down.)

Each rounded rectangle represents a *node* of the tree. We call the node at the top the *root* node and those at the very bottom (sharp cornered rectangles) as *leaf* nodes; the rest are *interior* nodes.

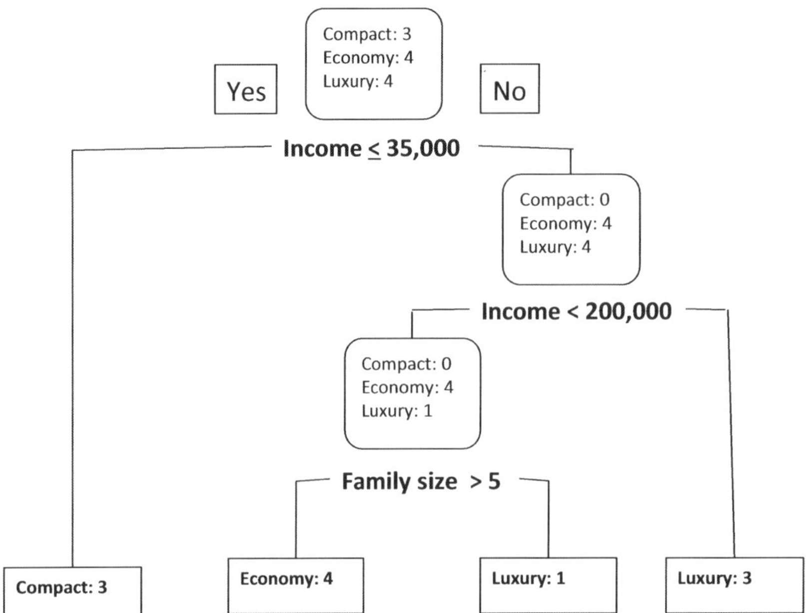

Figure 59: Complete classification tree for first luxury car example

In the *classification tree* approach, we first look at historical data and *build* the tree. We can then use the tree to classify new cases.

Let us first understand the information that the tree provides.

Inside each node we see the number of cases from our data that satisfy the conditions for reaching that node. We have 11 cases overall with 4 *Economy* and *Luxury* cars and 3 *Compact* cars in our data set and we see this information in the root node. Of these 11 cases, 3 have income below $35,000 and all of them are *Compact* cars. The leftmost *Leaf* node shows this.

Note that each leaf node has cases of only one type; we have shaded them for clarity.

Using the tree to classify a case

Given a new case, let us see how we can classify it using the tree. Consider a case with income $180,000 and family size of 6. We start at the root node. The condition below the node says "Income <= 35,000" and our case does not satisfy the condition. Next to the root node we see a legend that indicates "No" to the right and "Yes" to the left. Since our case does not satisfy the condition, we branch to the right child node. The condition under this node says "Income < 200,000" and our case satisfies that condition and so we branch to the left child node. Now we encounter the condition "Family size >= 5" and our node meets that condition too. So we branch again to the left child and reach a leaf node which is of class *Economy*. The tree thus classifies the case as *Economy*.

At the bottom of every non-leaf node we see the condition on which the node branches. We take a case from our data and apply the condition under the root node. If the condition holds, we examine the child node to the left; otherwise we go right. We keep doing this till we reach a leaf node and cannot branch any further. We classify the case as the class corresponding to the leaf node we reached.

Take a few cases from the data set and work through the tree. Verify that the tree classifies them correctly.

So we see the possibility of unearthing hidden rules in large volumes of data. How can we use the above idea in a data analytics context?

If we are a luxury car dealership and would like to solicit future customers based on their likelihood of being interested in a luxury car, then we might be able to use such rules to identify good candidates. We might do this by looking for rules hidden in past data about people's demographic information and whether or not they purchased luxury cars. We can then apply the rules to data about people who do not currently own a luxury car and then solicit those that our rules classify as *Luxury*.

Real-life applications of classification trees

Considering another example from before, an email provider might want to identify rules based on some of the characteristics of an incoming email to enable it to classify the email as spam or normal.

The university admissions officers from our earlier example could look for rules that might enable them to classify prospective students as high, medium or low performers based on information available at admissions time.

When faced with very large data sets, we cannot hope to manually find the rules as we were able to do in the toy example above. The task becomes more and more complex as the number of attributes increases. There could be complex rules involving several attributes that we might not be able to ferret out by just eye-balling the data.

Cannot manually find classification trees for very large data sets

In the *Classification Tree* approach to data mining, we present the computer with a large data set and it automatically *learns* the inherent rules.

In our synthetic example, we obtained perfect rules – that is, the tree classified every case in our data set correctly. That

We do not expect to finding perfect trees on real-life data

would be too much to ask for in the real world. For example, we could have two families with identical income and family size and yet own different type of cars. This happens because we are not considering every factor that could affect car ownership. We also have to remember that the real world does not necessarily operate around rules – these rules merely represent our efforts to inject some order into a complex real-world situation.

As with our discussion of *KNN for classification*, *Classification Trees* also require us to partition the data so as to be able to test the quality of the model on an independent *holdout* data set. We will get into those details shortly.

We do not expect to obtain classification trees that provide perfect answers, even on the training partition, let alone the *holdout* data that we reserve for unbiased testing of the model. Instead we seek rules that have an *acceptable* level of error. What do we mean by *acceptable* level of error? 1%? 5%? 10%? 40%?

You might be quite surprised to see that even error-rates that seem pretty high might not be as bad as they seem, and conversely, error rates that seem very low might not be as good as they seem.

Suppose that we have a large set of people whose car-ownership we would like to classify. Let us also assume that the data in Table 39 quite accurately represents the larger set of car buyers and that we can use the classification tree from Figure 59. Let us suppose that using the classification tree gives us a 60% performance – or a 40% error rate. At first sight this looks terrible – if we classify 100 cases, we are going to get 40 of them wrong!

Despite first appearances, we should not let the absolute numbers fool us. We can only evaluate the performance of a data mining method by comparing it to the results we would have achieved without the benefit of its results.

We should evaluate an analytics method by comparing its performance with what we might have done in its absence

In the absence of any data analytics support, let us suppose that we are able to classify 40% of the cases correctly – that is, we have an error-rate of 60%. Viewed against this, the classification tree's 60% correct performance represents a 50% improvement over what we were able to achieve without it! Nowhere near perfect, but a good boost nevertheless. If, as a result of using data mining a car dealership is able to identify 5 more *Luxury* car buyers each month and stands to gain $5,000 from each, then data analytics can yield $300,000 per year.

Remember, we do not expect perfection with data analytics approaches. We only look at how much better we can do with it than without. Often even small improvements can be very useful.

Seemingly poor performance can be useful . . .

Conversely, seemingly excellent performances might not be as good as they appear in some situations. Suppose there is a fatal disease that affects one in 1000 babies. Furthermore, suppose that, if identified early, this condition can be treated with a very expensive medical procedure that should only be applied to babies with this condition.

. . . and seemingly stellar performance can also be useless!

So when a baby is born, doctors might want to determine if the baby is likely to be a candidate for the medical procedure. A particular doctor is able to provide a correct diagnosis in 99.9% of the cases. Impressive, right?

Suppose we found out that the above doctor simply classified every single baby as not having the condition. He would be incorrect in only 1 out of 1000 cases, because the condition is rare and affects only 1 out of 1000 babies! That error translates into a 99.9% correct performance overall! However, that doctor would be 100% wrong on cases where the babies have the condition – abysmal performance indeed!

After the next section which gives you a chance to review the concepts, we will learn how to use **R** to generate classification trees.

Review 10: Classification Trees-1

You can find answers to these questions on page 372

Look at the classification tree in figure 60. The tree is based on historical data about some students' performance in the first test of a course, their attendance record until the first test and their overall performance at the end of the course as *Acceptable* or *Not-acceptable* – these have been shortened in the tree diagram.

The tree in Figure 60 looks slightly different from the one we saw in Figure 59. Each interior node of the tree in Figure 59 showed the count of cases of each class satisfying the condition for the node. The tree in Figure 60 shows the proportion of cases of each class in the node, labels each node based on the majority class and also shows (at the bottom of the node) the overall percentage of cases satisfying the conditions for the

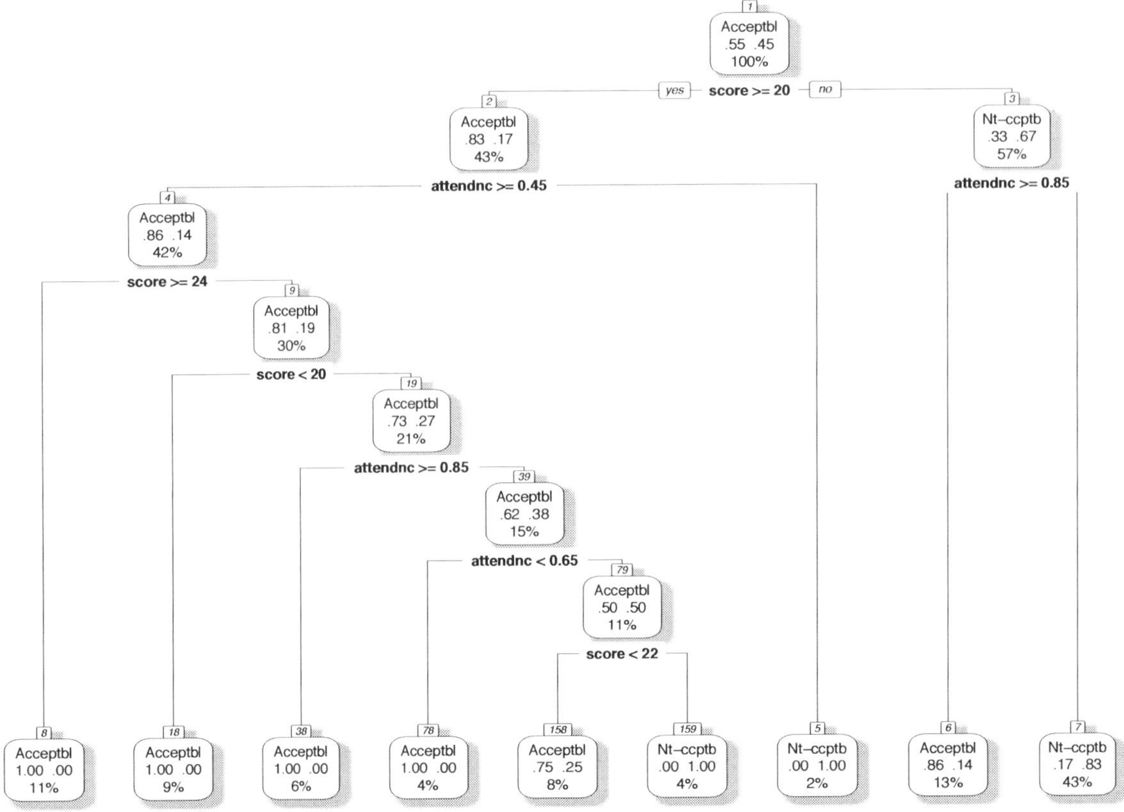

Figure 60: Classification tree for review questions

node. Each node also has a node number and we refer to those numbers in the questions below. Despite these differences, the two figures contain the same kind of information. Use the tree in Figure 60 to answer the following questions:

1. How many leaf nodes does the tree have?
2. Look at the node numbered 2. What conditions do the cases in that node satisfy?
3. What proportion of the overall cases satisfy the condition for node 2?
4. What proportion of the cases satisfying the condition for node 2 had *not-acceptable* performance?
5. Using this tree for classification, how would you classify someone who had a score of 18 and an attendance of 0.95? Which leaf node did you end up at?

6. Using this tree for classification, how would you classify someone with a score of 21 and attendance of 0.43? Which leaf node did you end up at?

7. Did this tree classify every case correctly? How did you find out?

8. Under what conditions would it be impossible to find a perfect tree – that is, a tree which can classify every case correctly?

Lab 10: Classification Trees 1

Pre-requisite(s)

- ✓ You should have installed **R** on your computer.
- ✓ You should also have downloaded and stored the data files for the book, and pointed **R** to the location of your data files. **R**
- ✓ You should have read the section on *Classification trees* on page 155 and answered the associated review questions.

Objective

After completing this lab, you will be able to:

- ✓ Use **R** to generate the complete classification trees for small data sets.
- ✓ Interpret the textual and tree outputs from the model.

Overview

In this introductory lab on classification trees, you will learn to build the complete tree for a small data set, and to interpret the tree output and the detailed textual output from the process.

This lab covers some preliminaries of using **R** for classification trees and therefore we will not partition the data or evaluate the model on hold-out or test data. We start by doing some exploratory data analysis. We then build the complete tree and interpret the results. We will see the full-blown process with partitioning in the next lab.

In the following section you will see that the complete classification trees for real-life applications tend to be very large and impractical to use. They also tend to *overfit* – a concept that we also discuss later. We will therefore look at ways to control the size of the generated tree. After these additional inputs on controlling tree-size, the next lab will enable you to apply the technique on a large data set.

Activity steps

1. **Load the data:** Load the data from the file *luxury-car-ownership.csv* into a data frame called *lc*.

```
> lc <- read.csv("luxury-car-ownership.csv")
```

2. **No partitioning:** In this activity, we only aim to learn how to build the complete classification tree and to interpret the output. We will therefore not partition the data and instead use all the 24 rows to build the tree. In a later lab we will go through the whole process including partitioning.

3. **Look at the data:** Issue the **R** command to see the data in the data frame *lc*. Alternately, click on *lc* on the *Environment* tab in the top left pane.

   You see that the data frame has three attributes *Income*, *Family_size* and *Car_type*. We used this very data set in our discussion of the details of classification trees (on page 155)

   From that you probably recall that our target attribute is *Car_type* and the remaining two are predictors.

```
    Income           Family_size        Car_type
 Min.   : 13800   Min.   :1.000   Luxury    :12
 1st Qu.: 46725   1st Qu.:3.000   Non-Luxury:12
 Median : 59450   Median :3.000
 Mean   : 63642   Mean   :3.125
 3rd Qu.: 79400   3rd Qu.:4.000
 Max.   :145100   Max.   :6.000
```

Figure 61: Summary for the car ownership data.

4. **Exploratory analysis:** Exploratory data analysis often gives us some key insights and we should resort to it before jumping into predictive analytics. In real-life, we will need to do some exploratory analysis to even figure out what method to use. Although we have already decided to use classification trees, let us still do a little bit of analysis to get a feel for our data.

   a **Summary:** Almost always, the very first step would be to look at an overall summary. Issue the **R** command to do this. Figure 61 shows the summary statistics that **R** generates. We can see immediately that it has treated the two predictor attributes as numerical and the target attribute *Car_type* as categorical – note that in the latter case it has just given us the counts of the cases belonging to the two classes *Luxury* and *Non-luxury*, which happen to be equal – 12 each.

summary(lc)

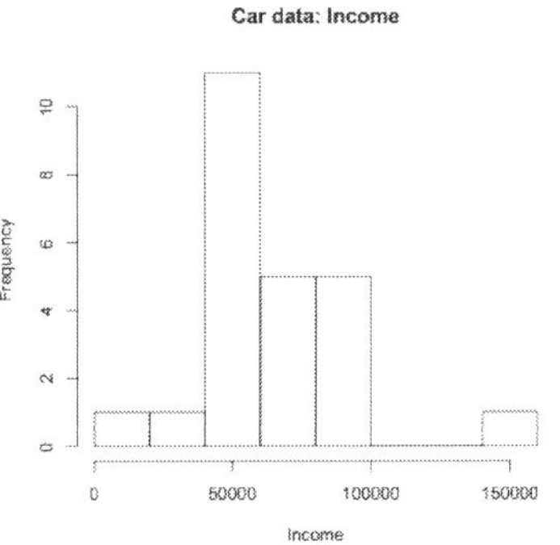

Figure 62: Car data: Income histogram.

We can also see that for both of the predictor attributes, the mean and median are very close, indicating the absence of significant skew. However, it might be a good idea for us to see how the values for these two are distributed.

b **Histograms:** Issue the commands to generate the histograms for the two predictor attributes.

```
> hist(lc$Income)        # or
> hist(lc$Income,main="Car data: Income", xlab="Income")
# and
> hist(lc$Family_size) # or
> hist(lc$Family_size, main="Car data: Family size",
    xlab="Family size")
```

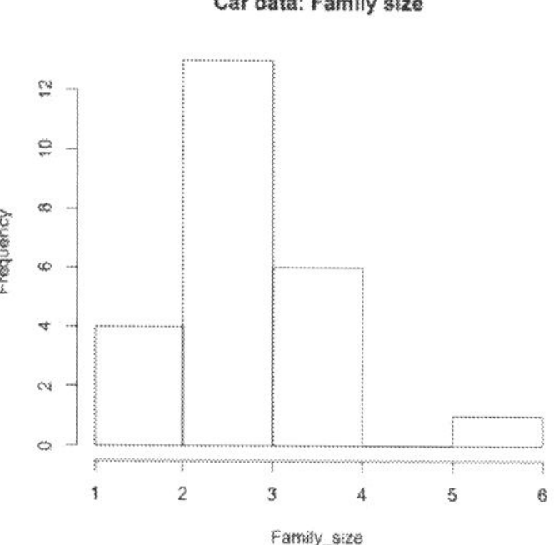

Figure 63: Car data: Family size histogram.

Figures 62 and 63 show the two resulting histograms.

The two histograms reveal nothing unexpected – both of these attributes have almost balanced shape with the bulk of the values in the middle – which is what we expect since the mean and median for each attribute were close. However, if we look closely at the histogram for family size, we do see that a majority of the values are between 2 and 3. In fact if we go back to the main data, we see that only two of these have a value of 2. Of course, based on our understanding of family sizes these days, this might not be completely unexpected either. Nevertheless, we have learned something about the data. With a small data set like this, the insight might not be great, but when dealing with large data sets, the overall grasp that we gain by this kind of exploratory analysis can be very helpful and protect us from being overwhelmed by the mountain of data.

c **Boxplots:** Just to round off matters let us also do the boxplots for these two attributes. Figure 64 shows the boxplots.

```
> boxplot(lc$Income, main="Car data: Income",
    xlab="Income")

> boxplot(lc$Family_size, main="Car data: Family size",
    xlab="Family size")
```

The two boxplots reveal some surprises in the form of outliers – 2 for family size and one for income. Because we now know that we have outliers, we might consider dropping them later if our data mining methods do not give suitable results.

d **Scatterplot:** We have two numerical attributes. Let us see if we can spot any correlation between them. That is, do people with high incomes have larger families or smaller families or is there no correlation? Let us generate a scatterplot as shown in Figure 65.

```
> plot(lc$Income, lc$Family_size,
```

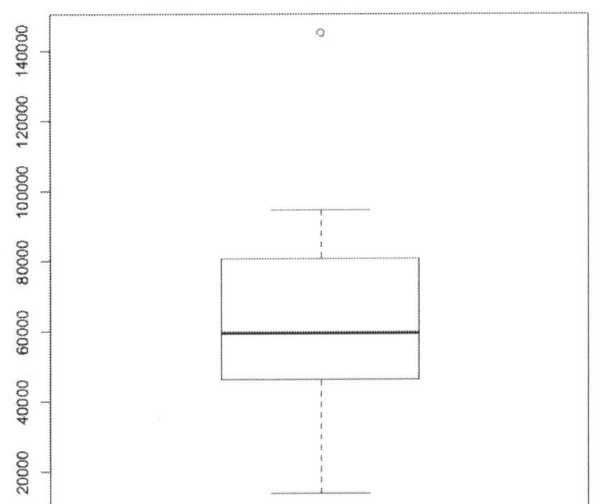

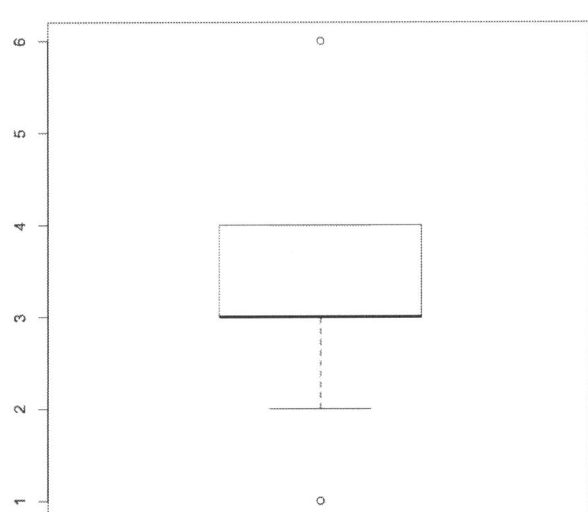

Figure 64: Car data: boxplots

```
main="Car data: Income vs. family size",
xlab="Income", ylab="Family_size")
```

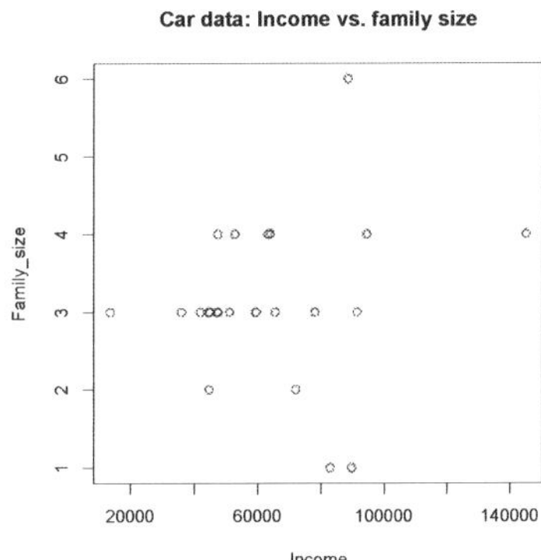

Figure 65: Car data: Income vs. family size.

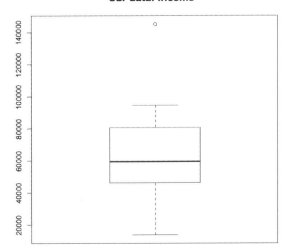

From the figure, we cannot quite make out if there is a very faint hint of a linear relationship. Let us calculate the correlation coefficient just to check. Recall that the correlation coefficient measures linear relationships between attributes and is always between -1 and 1 with the values at the extremes indicating a strong relationship.

```
> cor(lc$Income, lc$Family_size)
```

We get a value of 0.1266, indicating no linear relationship.

We now know that the two predictor attributes are not correlated with each other – which is always a good thing and we will broach this topic later in the book. However, what about the relationship of the target attribute with each of the predictor attributes? In other words, how do the incomes and family sizes of luxury car owners relate to those of non-owners? Off-hand we might expect that luxury car owners generally have higher incomes. We can check out the data to see if it harbors any surprises for us.

e **More advanced boxplots:** You will recall that data analytics often relies on exploiting relationships between attributes. With a quantitative target attribute, we could look at its correlation with the predictor attributes through scatterplots and correlation coefficients to spot relationships. With a categorical one, as we now have, we cannot calculate a correlation coefficient. However, we can still utilize boxplots to study relationships.

For instance we can compare the boxplots of income and family size for luxury car owners with the corresponding boxplots for non-luxury car owners. Let us first generate the boxplots of income separately for luxury car owners and non-owners. Use the following two commands. First see the result of the first command before issuing the second command.

```
> # The command has two equals signs
> # Don't type just one -- you will
> # get weird results
> boxplot(lc$Income[lc$Car_type=="Luxury"],
      main="Incomes of luxury car
       owners")

> boxplot(lc$Income[lc$Car_type=="Non-Luxury"],
      main="Incomes of non-luxury
      car owners")
```

In the first command above, we are passing only the incomes corresponding to luxury car owners (by stating the condition within square brackets – note the "==" used for checking for equality). The details are a little intricate and we will not go into them here.

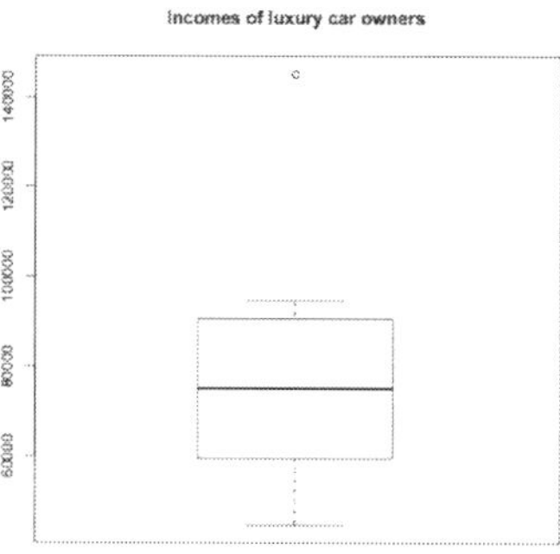

Figure 66: Incomes of luxury car owners

This produces the two boxplots in Figures 66 and 67.

At first sight it looks as if the incomes of non-luxury car owners are generally higher. However, on closer inspection – given that the two plots have different scales – we see, as we would expect, that luxury car owners tend to have higher incomes. However, comparing the two was cumbersome to say the least.

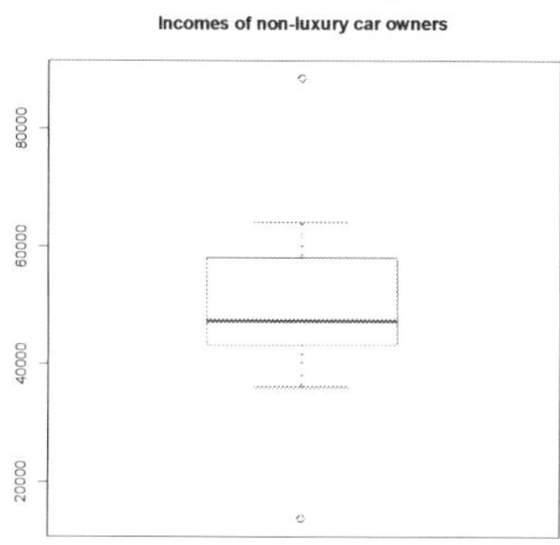

Figure 67: Incomes of non-luxury car owners

Wouldn't it be nice if we could have the two side-by side?

Recall from page 138 in the lab on KNN that we were able to use side-by-side boxplots to show the relationship between a categorical attribute and a numeric one. Here we can try and see how *Income* and *Family_size* relate individually to *Car_type*.

```
> boxplot(Income ~ Car_type,
      data = lc, ylab = "Income")
> boxplot(Family_size ~ Car_type,
      data = lc, ylab = "Family size")
```

Figures 68 and 69 show the results.

That reveals quite a surprise! The family sizes of non-luxury car owners are consistently higher. In fact no luxury car owner has a bigger family size than *any* non-luxury car owner. Even in such a small data set, that would have been very difficult to catch without side-by-side boxplots. Pretty powerful indeed! Since it does seem as if the two

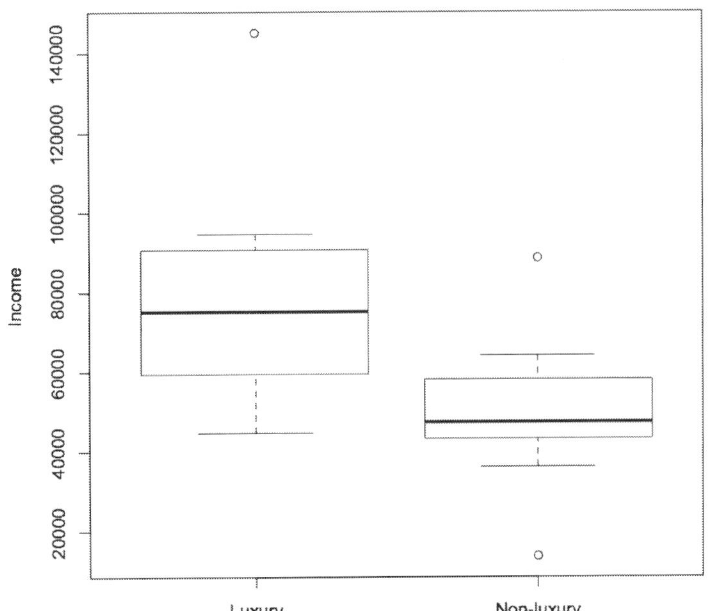

Figure 68: Side-by-side boxplots of incomes of luxury car owners and non-owners.

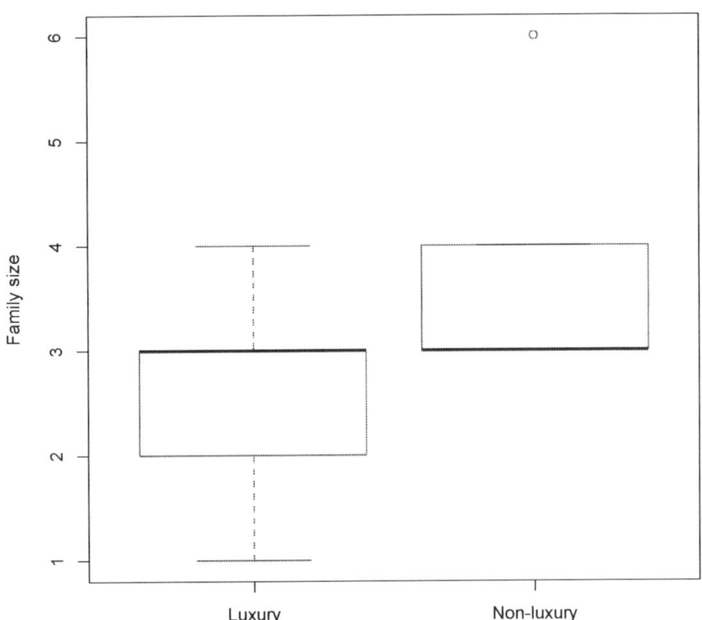

Figure 69: Side-by-side boxplots of family sizes of luxury car owners and non-owners.

predictors are not mutually correlated and yet have an influence on the target attribute, classification trees can be expected to work well. Let us proceed.

5. **Load the necessary packages:** In the lab on **R** packages (page 55), we had already installed the two packages needed to build and plot classification trees. Let us now load these:

```
> library(rpart)
> library(rpart.plot)
> # alternately, you can just check
> # the boxes for these two in the packages tab
```

6. **Build the tree:** We have a small data set and aim only to build the tree. The following command builds the *complete tree* model and stores the result in an **R** variable called *car.tree*:

```
> car.tree <- rpart(
       Car_type ~ Income + Family_size,
       data = lc, control = rpart.control(minsplit = 2, cp = 0))
```

Figure 70 explains.

We will *never* build the *complete* tree on real-life data sets – the trees would be huge. We are doing it here just for illustration.

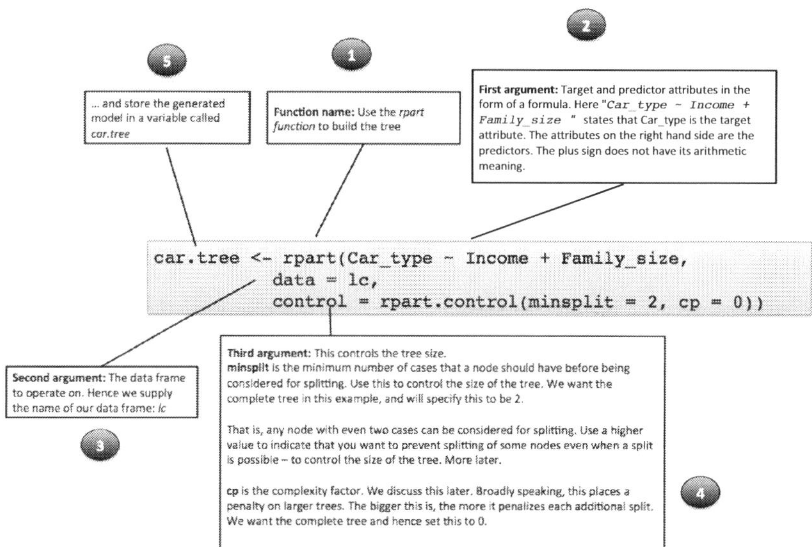

Figure 70: Using the rpart function for building the complete classification tree.

That's it – the tree is available in the variable *car.tree* and we can start looking at it.

7. **Look at the tree:** Having generated a tree, we might want to first take a look at it. The *prp* function from the *rpart.plot* package to print a tree has numerous optional parameters that we can use to customize the look. The command below shows one set of options that I particularly like. You can use it almost as is, except to substitute the name of the tree model based on context. Enter the command:

```
> prp(car.tree, type = 2, extra = 104,
        nn = TRUE, fallen.leaves = TRUE,
        faclen = 4, varlen = 8,
        shadow.col = "gray")
```

Figure 71 shows the full tree.

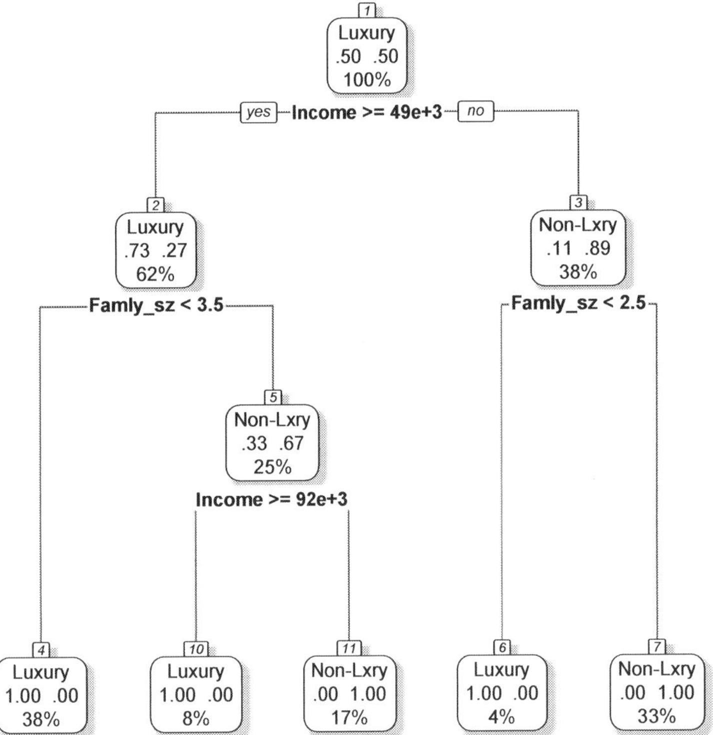

Figure 71: The complete classification tree.

You will notice from the figure that the class name *Non-luxury* has been shortened as has the attribute name *Family_size*. When trees get big, spelling these out in full can clutter the figures and so we used an option to cut their display sizes.

8. **Try to understand the information the tree provides:** Is this picture indeed worth the clichéd thousand words? Let us see what information it packs. Here are some questions for you to consider before reading on:
   - How good is the tree? How many cases of our data does it classify correctly?
   - How many rules did it generate?
   - Do the rules make sense?
   - How many cases from our data satisfied the condition for each rule?

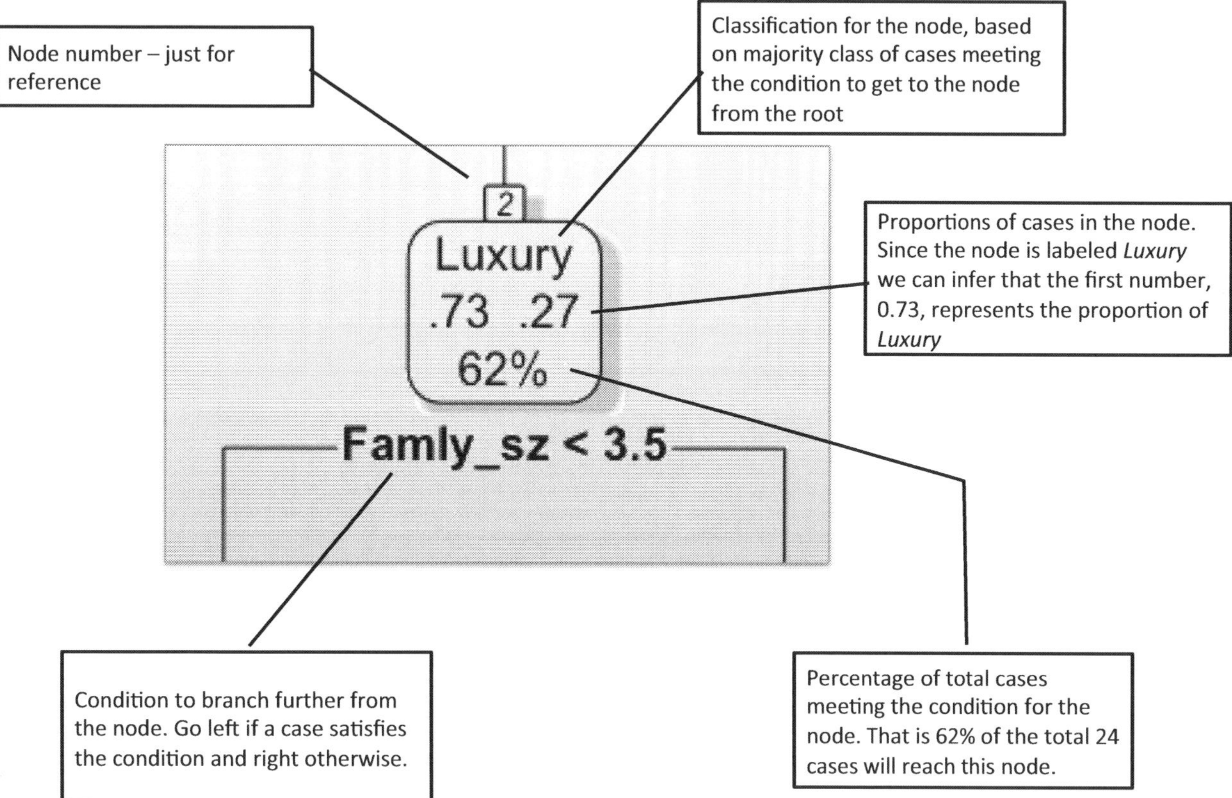

Figure 72: Information in a classification tree node

9. **What the tree says:** In your efforts to make sense of the tree, you might have unearthed some or all of the following points. Figure 72 explains the information associated with each node. The following points amplify that information.
   a. **Node number:** At the very top of each node is a small rectangle with a number. For example, the root node has the number 1. This number is just an identifier assigned to a node and is useful for cross-referencing the tree figure

with the textual output that we will later discuss. For now, just note that each node has a unique number. Also note that the child nodes of a node numbered n are always numbered $2n$ and $2n + 1$. Verify this – node 1 has children 2 and 3. Node 3 has children 6 and 7 and so on. This convention eases navigation of the text representation.

b **Branching condition:** Right below each node is the branching condition to go further from the node. For example, right under the root node we see *Income >= 49e+3* (49e+3 is scientific notation for 49,000; it represents $49 * 10^3$. Actually we will see in the text output that this is 49,350 and has been simplified for display.). All cases that meet the condition proceed to the left child of the root (namely, node 2) and those that don't, go to the right child – node 3.

c **Classification rules:** Most critically, the tree tells us the classification rules that the classification tree method found. Let us look at that first. Note that under each non-leaf node we have a condition. Note also that the legends on the lines going from the root node say *Yes* on the left branch and *No* on the right branch. Thus if a case meets the conditions, then we go to the left child node. Otherwise we go to the right child node.
Look at the tree and see if you can figure out how it would classify a person whose income is $80,000 and family size is 1. What did you get? I am sure that you got *Luxury*. This is because the income is greater than or equal to 49,000 and therefore the case satisfies the condition. So we take the left branch, to node 2. Since this is not a leaf node, we continue. The condition under node 2 says *Family_size <* 3.5 and our case meets this condition too. So we go left again, to node 4, which happens to be a leaf node labeled as *Luxury*, and hence the tree classifies our case as *Luxury*.
Look at the tree and come up with a case that the tree will classify as *Non-luxury*.
You can easily do this by tracing the path from the root to any leaf node labeled as *Non-luxury* and creating a suitable case. For example, let us trace the path from the root to node 7. The associated conditions are *Income < 49,000* and *Family_size >= 2.5*. Therefore a case with income $48,000 and family size 3 will reach this node and be classified as *Non-luxury*.

d **Leaf nodes:** All the leaf nodes are at the very bottom of the figure. We chose a plotting option that does this for ease of reading.

e **Node composition:** Inside each node, we see two numbers in the middle row. These state the proportions of cases that satisfy the condition for the node and belong to each class of the target attribute. In the root node we see 0.5 and 0.5 to indicate that in our data set we have equal numbers of *Luxury* and *Non-luxury* car owners. In node 2 we see 0.73 and 0.27 and so we know that of all cases that satisfy the condition for node 2 (*Income* $\geq$ 49000), 73% belong to one class and 27% to the other. But which is which? Read on.

f **Node classification:** Although we expect to see a classification only for the leaf nodes (those that have no nodes below them), we see that the every node of the tree shows a classification. For example, the node numbered 2 is classified as *Luxury*. In this representation, each node is classified as the dominant class among the cases that satisfy its condition. In node 2, because it is labeled as *Luxury* we know that the dominant class is *Luxury*. Therefore 0.73 must represent the proportion of *Luxury* car owners among those that satisfy the condition for node 2. Thus we can infer that the first number in the middle row of each node represents the proportion of *Luxury* and the second one the proportion of *Non-luxury*.

g **Examining some node classifications:** What should the root node be classified as? Given that we have equal proportions of the two classes, the algorithm has chosen to classify the root node – randomly – as *Luxury*. In the case of a tie this is what happens. Can you explain why nodes 5 and 7 are classifies as *Non-luxury*? Why is node 10 classified as *Luxury*? Does the tree tell us how many cases met the conditions for each node? Sure. Read on.

- Node 5: Non-luxury, because 67% of its cases are Non-luxury
- Node 7: Non-luxury, because 100% of its cases are Non-luxury
- Node 10: Luxury, because 100% of its cases are Luxury

h **Number of cases in each node:** The last row in each node tells us the percentage of the overall cases that met the conditions for each node. No wonder the root node has 100%. Of course every case satisfies the condition for the root node – namely no condition – because we have not yet started branching! The numbers in nodes 2 and 3 clearly tell us that 62% of the overall cases meet the condition for node 2 and 38% of the cases meet the condition for mode 3. Since we had 24 cases in all to start with, we can then say that 62%, or 15 of these fell into node 2 and 9 into node 3. Incidentally, note that the percentages in the nodes have been rounded for convenience. Thus the 62% in node 2 is actually 62.5% rounded down and the 38% in node 3 is actually 37.5% rounded up. With bigger numbers, these approximations will not matter – all we want is a good idea of the magnitudes. Do you see any connection between the percentages in the very last row (leaf nodes) and the proportions in the middle row of the root node?

The root node says that 0.5 or half of the initial cases are *Luxury* and half are *Non-luxury*. Adding up the percentages on the leaf nodes we see that 50% of the cases are *Luxury* and 50% are *Non-luxury*. They do match, as they must.

i **Leaf node classifications:** You might have noted that in the leaf nodes, the proportions are (0, 1) or (1, 0). This means that every leaf node is pure and that the method was able to find a perfect tree. This happened only because of our toy example. With real-life data we should be very suspicious if this happens – if things were that cut and dried, we would have known the result all along and not needed data analytics to figure it out!

10. **Understand the textual output:** To see a basic textual

output of the model, type the command (basically the name of the model alone):

```
> car.tree
```

This produces the output shown in Figure 73. Let us examine this line by line:

```
node), split, n, loss, yval, (yprob)
      * denotes terminal node

 1) root 24 12 Luxury (0.5000000 0.5000000)
   2) Income>=49350 15  4 Luxury (0.7333333 0.2666667)
     4) Family_size< 3.5 9  0 Luxury (1.0000000 0.0000000) *
     5) Family_size>=3.5 6  2 Non-Luxury (0.3333333 0.6666667)
      10) Income>=91600 2  0 Luxury (1.0000000 0.0000000) *
      11) Income< 91600 4  0 Non-Luxury (0.0000000 1.0000000) *
   3) Income< 49350 9  1 Non-Luxury (0.1111111 0.8888889)
     6) Family_size< 2.5 1  0 Luxury (1.0000000 0.0000000) *
     7) Family_size>=2.5 8  0 Non-Luxury (0.0000000 1.0000000) *
```

Figure 73: Basic text output from *rpart* for classification for car ownership example.

In essence, this listing contains the same information as the tree figure, but in a different form. Since it lists raw numbers, you can more readily get some information from this than from the tree display.

Figure 74 points out some of the details in the textual output.

The node numbers correspond to those in the tree and thus you can cross-reference between the two. For example, looking at node 2 in the tree diagram, we cannot immediately know (but can infer) how many actual cases met the conditions for the node or how many actual cases were *Luxury*. However, if we turn to the text representation, we can immediately see that 15 cases meet the condition for node 2, of which 4 do not belong to the majority class. We also see more accurate numbers for the proportions. So using both together can be useful.

On the textual output, leaf nodes are marked with an asterisk at the end.

11. **Using the model to classify cases:** Now that we have the model (that is, a classification tree) we can use it to classify cases. Since we did not partition the data, we have no hold-out data in a *test* partition to evaluate the

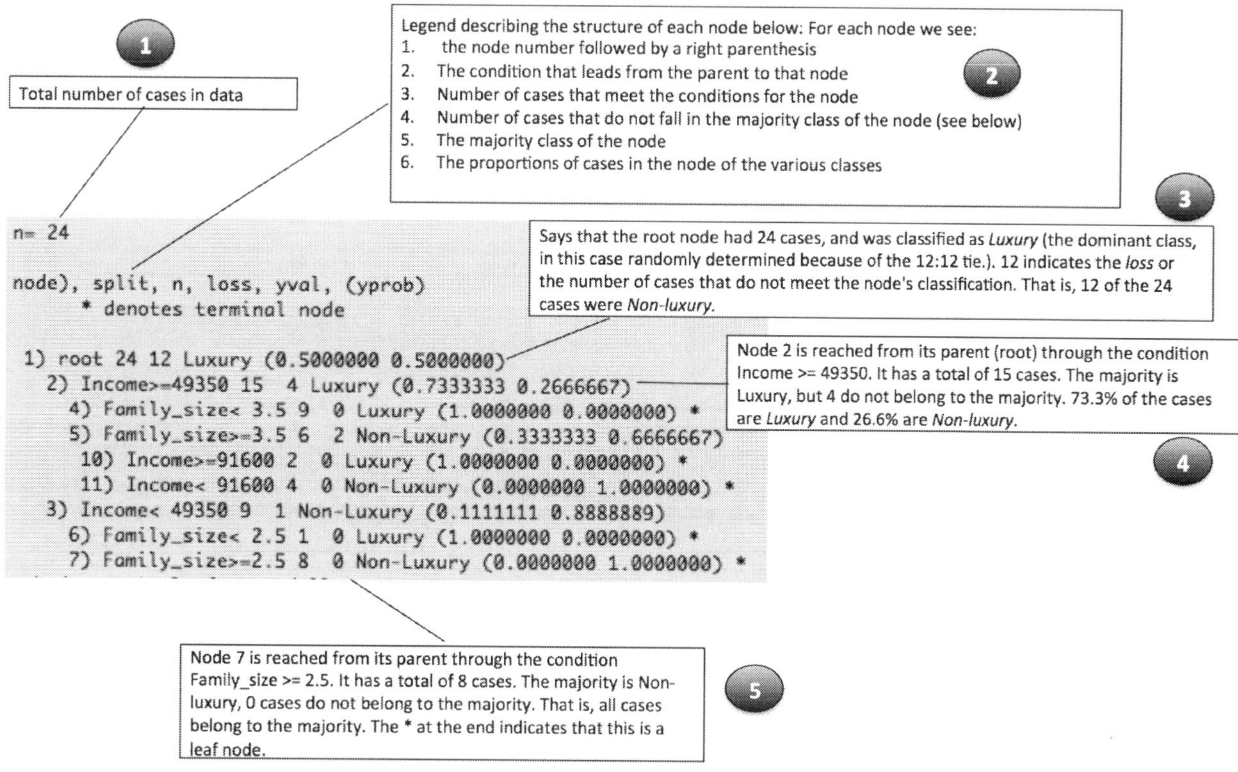

Figure 74: Details of the basic text output from rpart classification tree.

model on. We already know that the complete tree is perfect and correctly classifies every case in the training partition.

Just to foreshadow what is to come when we work with a large data set where we will partition, let us learn how to use the model to classify cases. Enter the command (Figure 75 explains):

```
> # Generate the model classification for each case of the
> # training partition and store it in a
> # new variable pred.lc. Note that
> # pred.lc is not in the data frame lc
> pred.lc <- predict(car.tree, lc, type = "class")
> # print out original values and
> # predictions
> data.frame(lc, pred.lc)
```

Table 40 shows the original values in the data frame *lc* along with the predictions. We see for each case, the actual class and the model's classification – of course we knew that all of them would be correct!

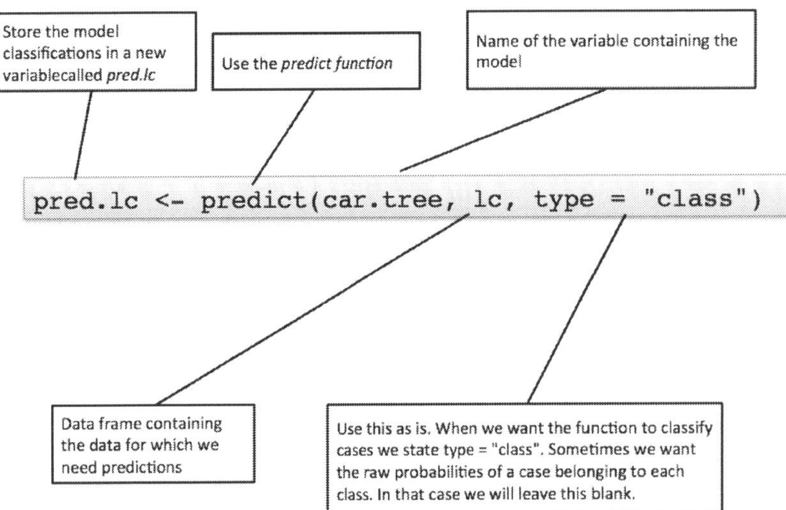
Store the model classifications in a new variablecalled pred.lc
Use the predict function
Name of the variable containing the model
pred.lc <- predict(car.tree, lc, type = "class")
Data frame containing the data for which we need predictions
Use this as is. When we want the function to classify cases we state type = "class". Sometimes we want the raw probabilities of a case belonging to each class. In that case we will leave this blank.

Figure 75: Using the classification tree model to classify cases

You can now generate the classification-confusion matrix as before, by using the command:

```
> table(lc$Car_type, pred.lc,
      dnn = c("Actual", "Predicted"))
```

```
              Predicted
Actual          Luxury Non-Luxury
  Luxury            12          0
  Non-Luxury         0         12
```

Figure 76: Error matrix on training partition

This produces the predicted results as Figure 76 shows.

12. **Review questions :** You can find the answers to these questions on page 374
Answer the following general questions on classification trees:

    a In some tree diagram for a classification problem, you see a node numbered 10 with two child nodes. What numbers will its two child nodes have?

    b If a tree has 25 splits, how many leaf nodes will it have? Draw a few small trees and you will see a pattern – you just have to draw trees in which you have one root node and each node can have zero or two child nodes. Your trees do not need to have any other details like branching conditions to answer this question.

    c If a tree has 30 leaf nodes, how many splits were made? The logic of the previous answer should help you to answer this.

    d Assuming that in a particular situation, we have two classes for the target attribute (like *Luxury/ Non-luxury* or *Buyer/Non-buyer*), and we are able to obtain a *perfect* tree. In this case, what would you expect the proportions of the two classes to be in the leaf nodes?

    e Same as above, but we have three classes. What would be the proportions of the three classes in the leaf node?

Table 40: Results of tree model classification

Income	Family_size	Car_type	pred.lc
89800	1	Luxury	Luxury
47500	4	Non-Luxury	Non-Luxury
45000	3	Non-Luxury	Non-Luxury
44700	2	Luxury	Luxury
59500	3	Luxury	Luxury
36100	3	Non-Luxury	Non-Luxury
63300	4	Non-Luxury	Non-Luxury
52900	4	Non-Luxury	Non-Luxury
78200	3	Luxury	Luxury
145100	4	Luxury	Luxury
88600	6	Non-Luxury	Non-Luxury
65600	3	Luxury	Luxury
44500	3	Non-Luxury	Non-Luxury
94600	4	Luxury	Luxury
59400	3	Luxury	Luxury
47300	3	Non-Luxury	Non-Luxury
72100	2	Luxury	Luxury
83000	1	Luxury	Luxury
64100	4	Non-Luxury	Non-Luxury
42100	3	Non-Luxury	Non-Luxury
91500	3	Luxury	Luxury
51200	3	Luxury	Luxury
13800	3	Non-Luxury	Non-Luxury
47500	3	Non-Luxury	Non-Luxury

f In the problem that we took for this lab we were able to get a perfect classification tree – every leaf node had only cases of one class. Can you change any one of the data rows (cases) in such a way that it would be impossible to get a perfect tree?

13. **Review questions – Luxury car problem :** Use the information in the tree diagram (Figure 71) and the textual output (Figure 73) to answer the following questions:

    You can find the answers on page 374

    a How would this tree classify a case with income 70,000 and family size 1? Which leaf node with the case end up at?

    b Why is node 3 is marked as *Non-Luxury*?

    c What conditions does a case have to satisfy to reach node 5?

    d Of the 24 cases in total, how many meet the conditions for node 5?

    e What conditions does a case have to satisfy to reach node 11? State it as simply as you can.

    f Use the text output to find how many cases do not belong to the majority case in nodes 2 and 5.

14. **Summary:** Table 41 shows the steps we employed.

Table 41: Summary of steps for *Classification tree.*

Step no	Description	R command	Remarks
1	Load the required packages	`library(rpart)` `library(rpart.plot)`	
2	Read the data	`lc <- read.csv(` `     "luxury-car-ownership.csv")`	

3	Explore	`summary(lc)`
		`hist(lc$Income)`
		`hist(lc$Family_size)`
		`plot(lc$Income, lc$Family_size)`
		`boxplot(Income ~ Car_type,`
		`    data = lc, ylab = "Income")`
		`boxplot(Family_size ~ Car_type,`
		`    data = lc, ylab = "Family size")`
			Look at the data; generate histograms, boxplots, scatterplots, etc.

4	No partitions		Given our small data frame, we did not partition. In a real life application, you should use partitioning.

5	Build the tree	`car.tree <- rpart(`
		`    Car_type ~ Income + Family_size,`
		`    data = lc,`
		`    control = rpart.control(`
		`       minsplit = 2, cp = 0))`	

6	Print the tree	`prp(car.tree, type = 2, extra = 104,`
		`       nn = TRUE, fallen.leaves = TRUE,`
		`       faclen = 4, varlen = 8,`
		`       shadow.col = "gray")`
			Use the *prp* function for a pretty picture

7	Look at the text output	`car.tree`	
8	Generate model predictions on the data used to build the tree	`pred.lc <- predict(car.tree,` `    lc, type = "class")`	Since we did not partition, we do not have a test partition. From the tree we already know that the model is perfect.
9	Generate the error matrix	`table(lc$Car_type, pred.lc,` `   dnn = c("Actual", "Predicted"))`	

Classification Trees: Under the Hood

We have seen how *Classification trees* can learn rules inherent in large data sets and then help us to classify future cases. How does the computer accomplish this?

In this section, we get under the hood to see the internal workings.

We take a slightly bigger data set now, but extend the same car-ownership example. Consider the data in Table 42.

If we run the *Classification Tree* data mining method on this data (without partitioning), we might get the tree shown in Figure 77.

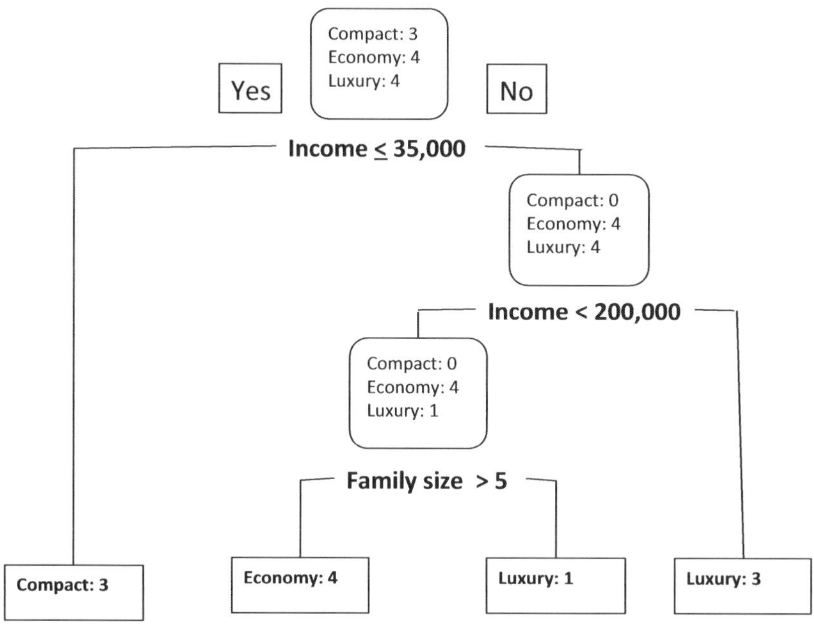

Figure 77: Classification tree for data in Table 42

We will now describe how the computer constructed the *Classification tree*. Of course, you will never have to manually carry out these operations. Nevertheless, looking at the process in detail can give you a deeper insight into the method and could add some nuance to how you interpret the results. We have to admit though that you will be able to use the technique even if you skip these under-the-hood details.

We will explain the process largely visually by using a scatterplot of the two attributes *Income* and *Family Size* (see Figure 78). For data sets with more predictor attributes, such a visualization would not be possible, although the underlying ideas

Income	Family_size	Car_type
89,800	1	Luxury
47,500	4	Non-Luxury
45,000	3	Non-Luxury
44,700	2	Luxury
59,500	3	Luxury
36,100	3	Non-Luxury
63,300	4	Non-Luxury
52,900	4	Non-Luxury
78,200	3	Luxury
145,100	4	Luxury
88,600	6	Non-Luxury
65,600	3	Luxury
44,500	3	Non-Luxury
94,600	4	Luxury
59,400	3	Luxury
47,300	3	Non-Luxury
72,100	2	Luxury
83,000	1	Luxury
64,100	4	Non-Luxury
42,100	3	Non-Luxury
91,500	3	Luxury
51,200	3	Luxury
13,800	3	Non-Luxury
47,500	3	Non-Luxury

Table 42: Data for classification tree discussion.

are exactly the same.

Before we jump into the problem at hand, let us consider what a classification tree does to the cases in the data set. Look back at the classification tree of Figure 77. If we take any specific case and run it through the tree, we will end up at one of its leaf nodes. If we combine all the cases that end up at the leaf nodes, we will get back the original data set. If we visualize the tree as a complex sieve into which we *pour* all the cases, we can think of the sieve as depositing each case into one of the leaf nodes. In this sense, the classification tree partitions the original data set into as many subsets as the number of rules in it. Each path from the root node to a leaf node represents one complete rule.

If the tree is perfect (as is the case in Figures 59 and 77), then the subset corresponding to each leaf node will contain only nodes of a single class – or be *pure*.

We cannot expect to get perfect trees all the time. In fact, on real-life data, we should be very suspicious if that ever happens. Even if the tree is imperfect, we would still expect cases belonging to one class to predominate within each leaf node. Only then will classifying any case that satisfies the associated rule as belonging to the majority class in the set make sense.

We want the majority case in every leaf node to predominate among the cases in that node

This means that we would like a set of rules such that for

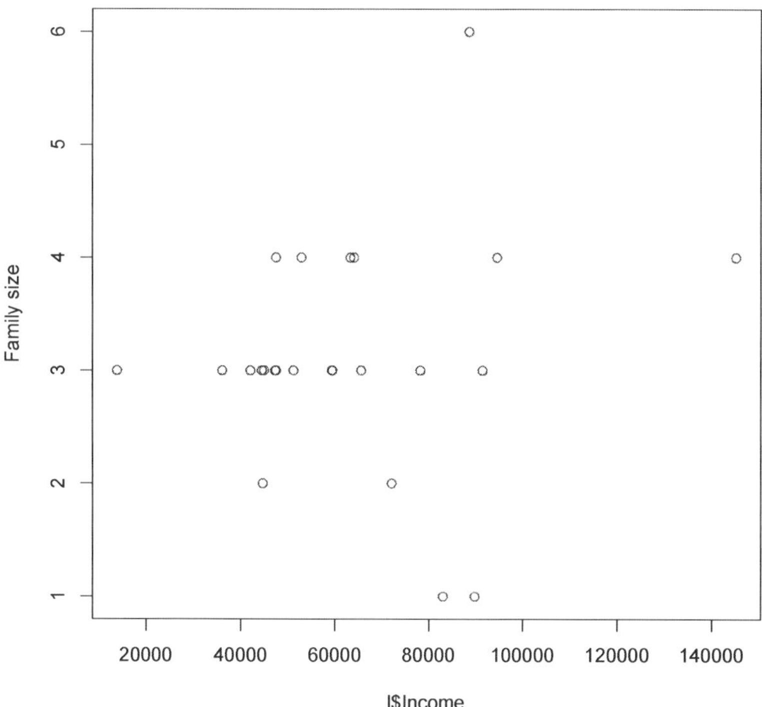

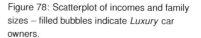

Figure 78: Scatterplot of incomes and family sizes – filled bubbles indicate *Luxury* car owners.

each rule, the set of cases that satisfy the rule are as pure or as homogeneous as possible. That is, as far as possible, they belong to the same class.

Consider the scatterplot shown in Figure 78. We have shown the cases corresponding to *Luxury* cars with filled bubbles and the rest with open bubbles.

Note how the condition under the root node (income $\geq$ 65e+3, using scientific notation for 65,000) divides the whole region into two parts. Figure 79 makes this clear by placing a vertical line at $Income = \$65,000$. The points to the left of the line represent all the cases for which the income is less than $\$65,000$ and those to the right show the remaining cases.

Now comes the important point – why did the computer choose to split the root node as $income = 65e + 3$? Why not some other value? Why not split on *Family size* instead?

Look back at the classification tree in Figure 59. Each leaf node contains only one class of cases (*Compact*, *Economy* or *Luxury*) – a perfect classification tree. Ideally, our classification

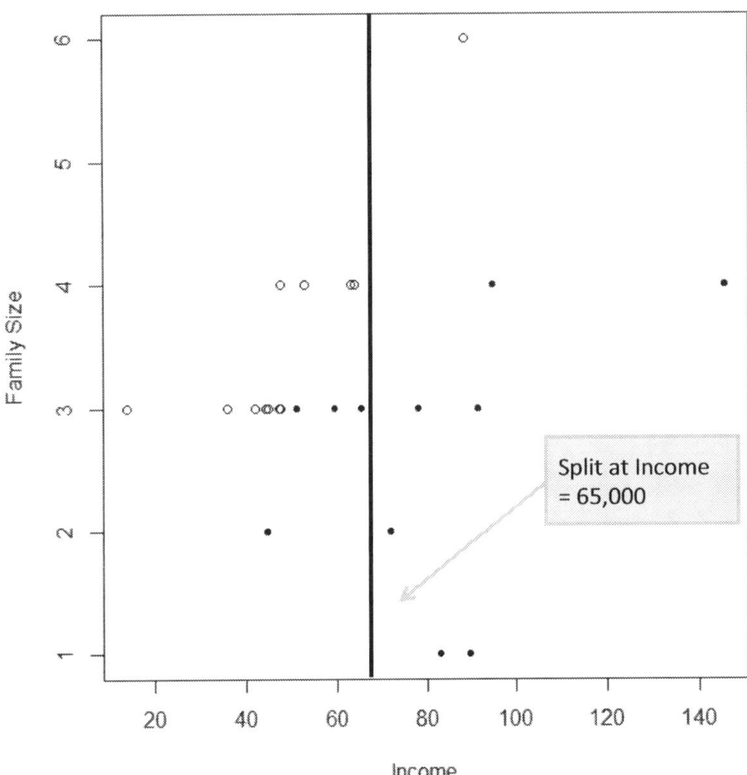

Figure 79: Scatterplot of incomes and family sizes – effect of first split at $income = 65,000$.

tree should end up with such *pure* leaf nodes, or at least come close. We therefore want each new split to create areas that take us closer and closer to the ideal.

At the root node we have a perfectly heterogeneous mixture – 12 cases each of *Luxury* and *Non-luxury* – the root node is as *impure* as it can possibly be. After the first split at the root node, the right child node (represented by the left region in Figure 79) has the 15 cases out of the original 24 with $Income < 65,000$ and the left child node (represented by the right region in Figure 79) has the 9 cases where $income \geq 65,000$. Of the 15 cases on the left region, 11 are *Non-luxury* and of the 9 cases on the right region, 8 are *Luxury* (although only 7 are discernible because two points overlap). Clearly, from our original situation where we had equal numbers of the two classes in the root, the first split created two *purer* nodes than the root.

Figure 80 shows this pictorially. Figure 81 shows that the right child node corresponds to the region on the left of Figure 79 and the left child node corresponds to the region on the right.

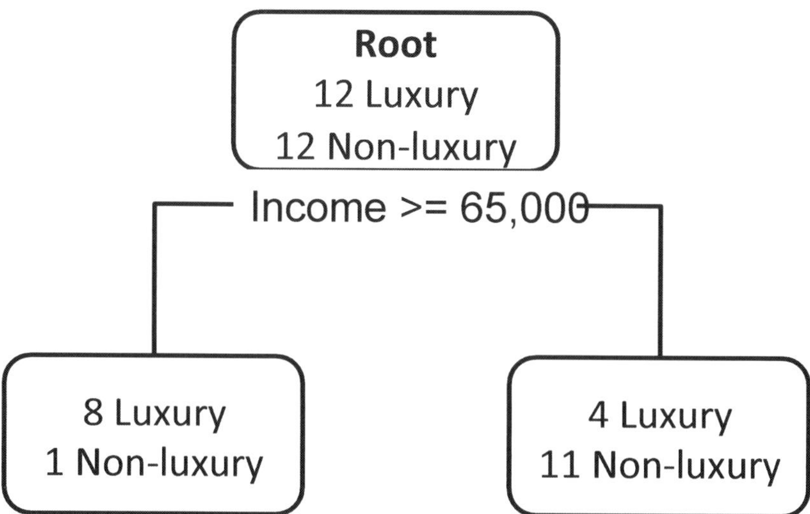

Figure 80: Impact of the first split – two vastly more homogeneous nodes than the root.

Returning to the original question of why the computer chose to split at $income \geq 65,000$, you might have guessed that this was perhaps the *best* option. That is, among all possible splits at the root node, this split produced the *greatest level of homogeneity or purity* in the resulting regions. We can see in an intuitive way that the overall purity has increased, but unless we have an objective measure, we cannot claim that the first split maximized purity or homogeneity. How might we measure homogeneity or purity?

The first split created two child nodes, each much purer than the root.

Given a set of people, we can identify the tallest among them because we have an objective measure of height. Similarly, we need an objective measure of purity to see which split maximizes it.

We need an objective measure of the purity of a node.

Before looking at the actual measure of purity that *Classification trees* use, let us discuss a simpler intuitive measure that helps to grasp the concept. Be warned though that the measure that we are about to describe is not what classification trees actually use and for good reason. However, we describe this first because it is much easier to understand. Having grasped it, you will be in a position to understand the actual measure that classification trees use.

Using a simplified measure of purity – for illustration only this is not what classification trees actually use

Suppose a node has 100 cases and all of them are *Luxury*. We might say that the *purity* of the node is 1 – since it represents complete purity. A node in which the predominant class comprises 80% of the cases could then be 0.8 pure. We therefore choose to represent the purity of a set of cases in a node as the proportion of the majority class at that node.

So we now have a possible measure of purity of a node.

When we have only two classes, as in our current scenario – *Luxury* and *Non-luxury* – the smallest possible value for *purity* is 0.5 (when we have equal numbers of both classes), and the largest value is 1, when all cases are of the same class.

For brevity, let us represent the *purity* of a node n as $u(n)$.

For simplicity, we first consider the purity of a node as just the proportion of the majority class at that node. We will change this shortly.

Using this approach for our problem, $u(root) = 0.5$ because we have equal numbers of the two classes to start with. When we have just the root node, its purity measure alone suffices to represent the purity measure of the whole tree. However, after one or more splits, we have multiple nodes and we need to look at the purity measure of the classification tree as it stands. Let us represent the purity of a classification tree after m splits by $U(m)$. We use the uppercase for the purity measure of the tree and lowercase for the purity measure of a node.

Thus $U(0) = 0.5$ because, before any splits, all we have is the root node whose purity is 0.5.

Figure 80 represents the tree after a single split at income=$65,000. What is $U(1)$, the purity measure after the first split?

To calculate this, we first find the u value of each of the two leaf nodes and combine these into a single U value for the whole tree at that point.

If we call the left child of Figure 80 as L and the right child as R, then we can calculate the following:

$u(L) = \frac{8}{9} = 0.89$

$u(R) = \frac{11}{15} = 0.73$

Each of these independently improves upon the root node, but we are interested in the measure of homogeneity of the whole tree at this point, rather than just one node or other. How can we combine $u(L)$ and $u(R)$ into a single meaningful value?

Can we just add up the values for each node?

No – because adding up the scores of many impure nodes can yield a high purity value, even greater than 1, which would not make sense. Furthermore if we have two nodes each of which has a purity value of 0.5, we will see that simple addition yields an overall purity of 1 – clearly incorrect. Instead of adding, we could just take the average. That would be an improvement, but considering that **R** has more cases than L we should allow **R** to have a greater influence on the overall value. A weighted average, with the number of cases in a node as the

How to combine the purity measures of leaf nodes into a purity measure for the whole tree?

Using the weighted average of the purity measures of the leaf nodes as the purity measure of the whole tree.

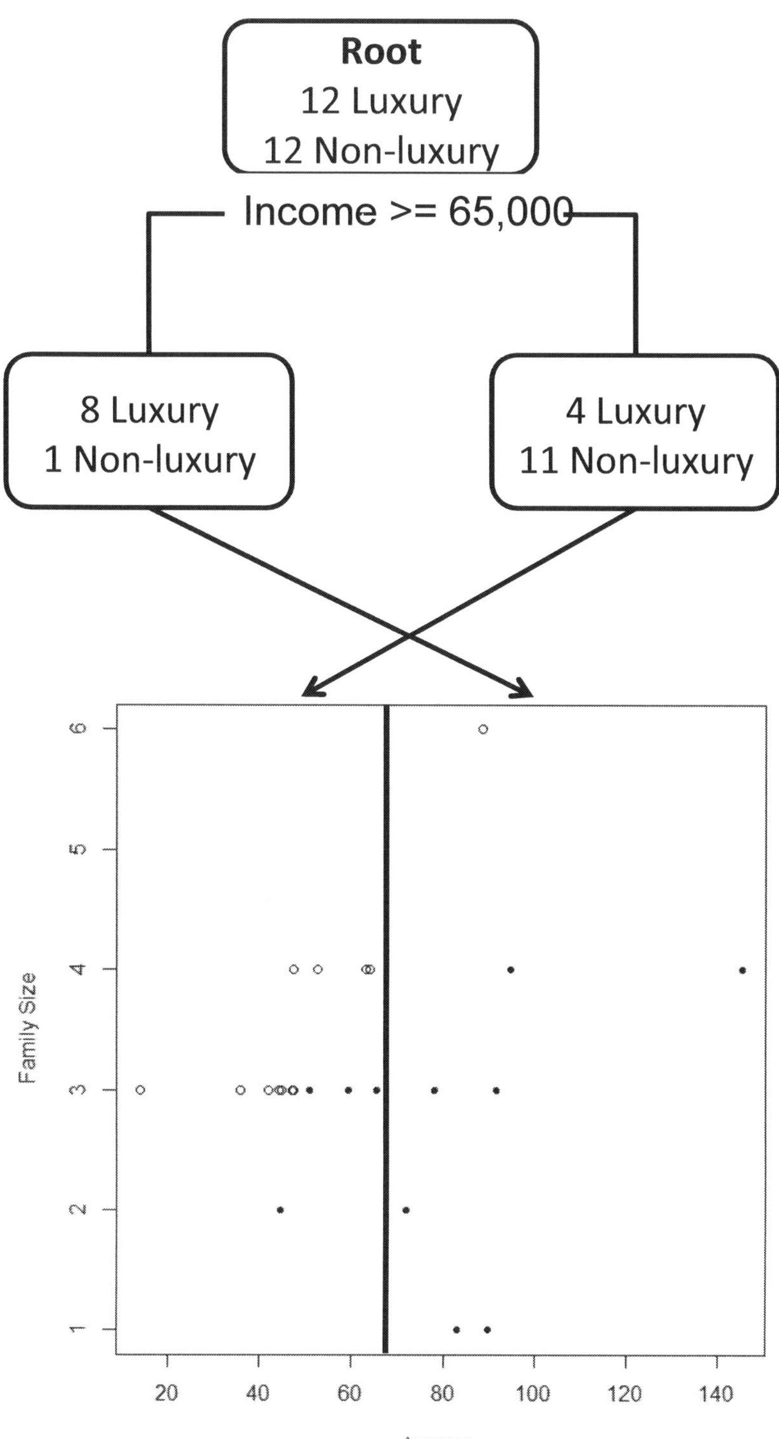

Figure 81: Mapping the nodes from the first split to the corresponding regions on the scatterplot.

weight would be much better. We can thus calculate $U(1)$ the overall purity after a single split as:

$$U(1) = \frac{9*0.89 \quad + \quad 15*0.73}{9+15} = 0.79$$

So the first split has improved the homogeneity from 0.5 to 0.79 – using our approximate method.

We can now return to our original question of why the computer chose that specific split at the root node. The *Classification Tree* method considered *every possible* split at the root node, and chose the one that provided the greatest improvement in purity.

Do we not have an infinite number of possible splits at the root node? After all, we can split on any value between the maximum and minimum income or family size. For example, we can split on $Income = 13,800.01$, $Income = 13,800.02$ and so on. We can immediately see that both of these splits divide the cases into the same two subsets and hence they are essentially the same. We need not waste time by considering both. We only need to consider splits that divide the cases differently.

Therefore, what splits are possible at the root node?

Determining all possible splits at the root node

The root node consists of all the cases in the data file. The set of possible *Income* values from smallest to largest is:

{13800, 36100, 42100, 44500, 44700, 45000, 47300, 47500, 47500,51200 , 52900, 59400, 59500, 63300, 64100, 65600, 72100, 78200, 83000, 88600, 89800, 91500, 94600, 145100}

We can split these values by placing dividers half-way between any two consecutive values. Thus the first possible split could be anywhere between 13,800 and 36,100 – say mid-way at 24,950. The next could likewise be mid-way between 36,100 and 42,100 – at 39,100. You can verify that the next possible split could be at 43,300. In all we have 23 possible income splits.

In similar vein, we see that the possible *Family size* values are { 1, 2, 3, 4 } and hence the possible splits could be at 1.5, 2.5 and 3.5. We thus have 23+3=26 possible splits at the root.

The system has considered each of the above 26 splits and calculated the purity values that the tree from each split yielded. It then chose the split that gave the highest overall purity value.

We had earlier indicated that the measure we have used thus far is not the real thing. Why not? It seems to make perfect sense.

What if we have three classes? In this case, our earlier ap-

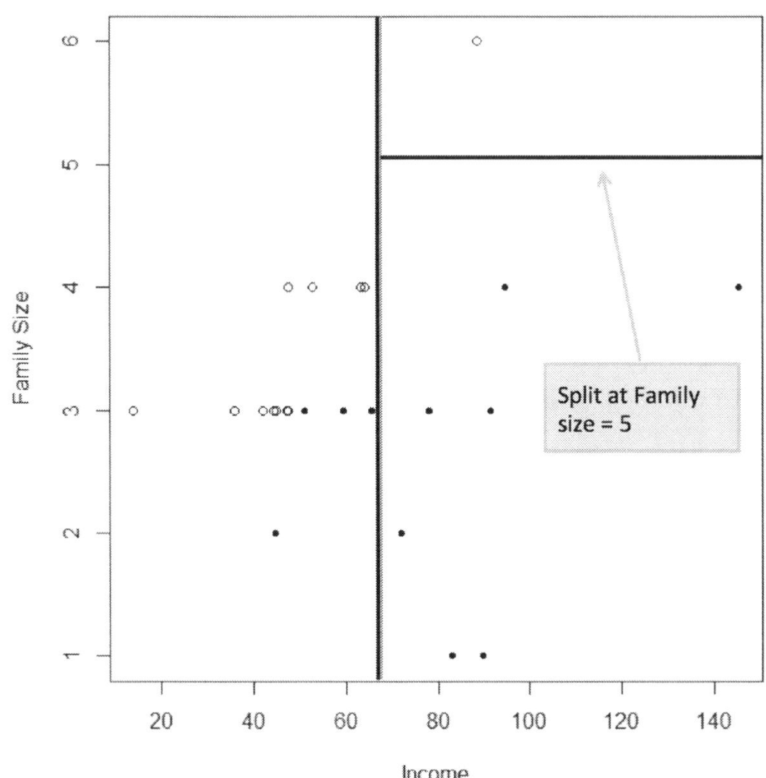

Figure 82: Luxury car example. Second split – at Family size = 5

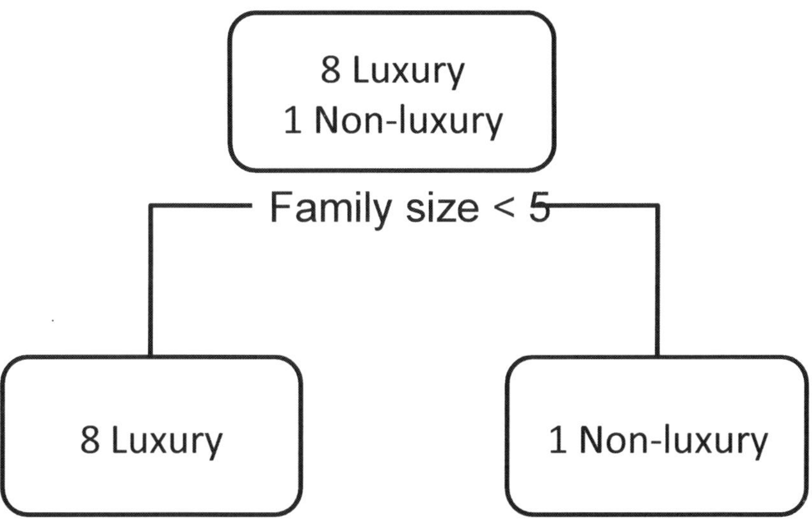

Figure 83: Impact of the second split – at Family size = 5

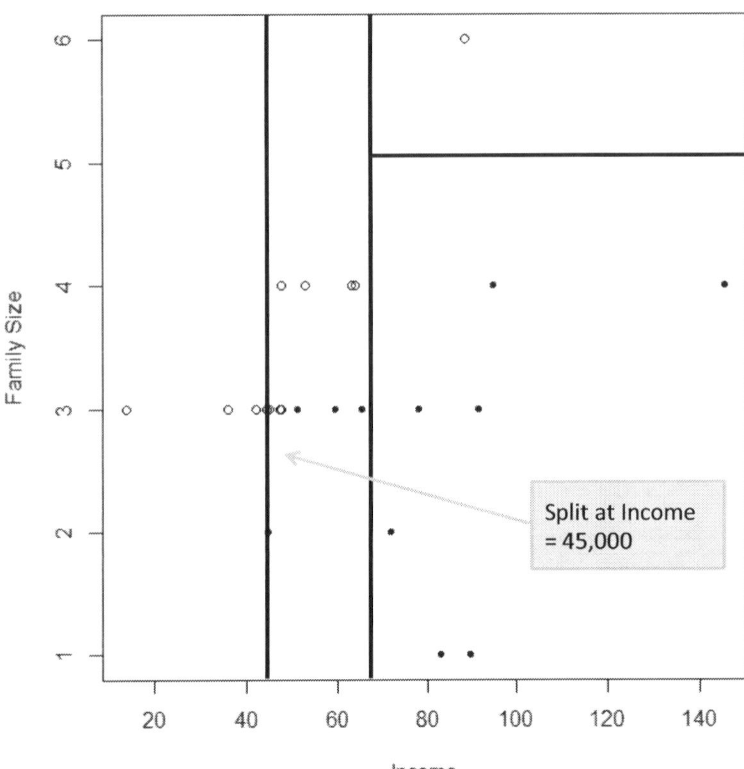

Figure 84: Luxury car example. Third split – at Income = 45,000

proach of using the proportion of the dominant class as the purity measure of a node will not work. For example, if we have three cases *Luxury*, *Mid-size* and *Compact* and we have one node with proportions (0.5, 0.25, 0.25) and another with proportions (0.5, 0.3, 0.2). Based only on the predominant class, our method would give the same purity measure to both, whereas they are different. Clearly, we need a method that is able to consider all the proportions.

Classification Trees use one of two measures of *impurity* – *Gini* index and *Entropy* – that work well even if we have more than two classes. While running these methods on a computer, we will have the option of specifying the measure to use.

Let us suppose that we have 3 classes and that at some point we have a node x with proportions (0.5, 0.25, 0.25) of the three classes. Then

$$Gini(x) = 1 - (0.5^2 + 0.25^2 + 0.25^2)$$

More generally, if we have k classes and have a proportion of r_i of the ith class then:

$Gini\,(x) = 1 - \sum_{i=1}^{k} r_i^2$

To calculate the entropy, we can use:

$Entropy\,(x) = \quad -(0.5 * \log_2 0.5 + 0.25 * \log_2 0.25 + 0.25 * \log_2 0.25)$

More generally:

$Entropy\,(x) = -\sum_{i=1}^{k} r_i \log_2 r_i$

Using any one of the above measures of impurity, the method first computes the impurity of each leaf node at any point in time. Later, as we did, it computes the overall impurity as the weighted average. Among all possible splits at a given stage, it chooses the split that yields the lowest overall impurity – which is the same as looking for the highest purity, if we define purity as $(1 - impurity)$.

Figure 83 shows how the second split breaks up the cases. From these two figures we can see that the second split produces two pure leaf nodes.

Let us walk through the process using *Gini*. The process if we use *Entropy* would be very similar.

For our situation: $Gini\,(root) = 1 - (0.5^2 + 0.5^2) = 1 - 0.5 = 0.5$

Using the first split at $Income = 65,000$, we obtain the situation shown earlier in Figure 80. As before, if we name the left and right nodes as L and R respectively, we get:

$Gini\,(L) = 1 - \left(\frac{8}{9}\right)^2 - \left(\frac{1}{9}\right)^2 = 0.1975$

$Gini\,(R) = 1 - \left(\frac{11}{15}\right)^2 - \left(\frac{4}{15}\right)^2 = 0.3911$

So the overall Gini after the first split is: $GiniOverall\,(1) = \frac{0.1975*9+0.3911*15}{24} = 0.3185$

We see a reduction in impurity from 0.5 to 0.3185 after one split at $Income = 65,000$.

From Figure 77 we see that the second split occurs at $Familysize = 5$. This split affects only those cases for which $Income \geq 65,000$ – the cases in the right half of the scatterplot of Figure 79.

Figure 82 shows this on the scatterplot and Figure 83 elaborates.

In similar vein, Figures 84 and 85 show the impacts of the third and fourth splits.

Figure 86 shows the progressive reduction of the overall Gini

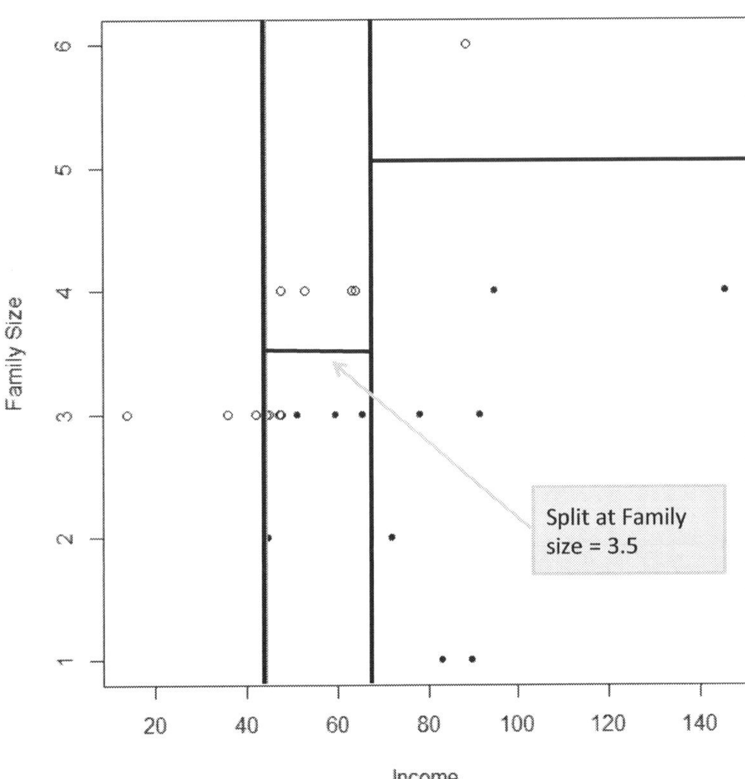

Figure 85: Luxury car example. Fourth split – at Family size = 3.5

at every stage.

On large data sets from the real-world, carrying on the above process till no more splits are possible will yield gigantic trees. Using such a tree would be impractical.

We need to trade-off accuracy for tree-size. *classification tree* methods therefore use *pruning* techniques to keep the tree down to a manageable size. We will discuss these issues in a later section.

Review 11: Classification Trees-2

There is no single correct answer for this question and so no answer is provided.

Assume that the table below shows the high school GPA, SAT score and the first semester performance in college for a set of students. Just by examining the data (that is, without using **R** or any other tool), build a decision tree that is perfect – meaning that it correctly classifies every single case – any tree

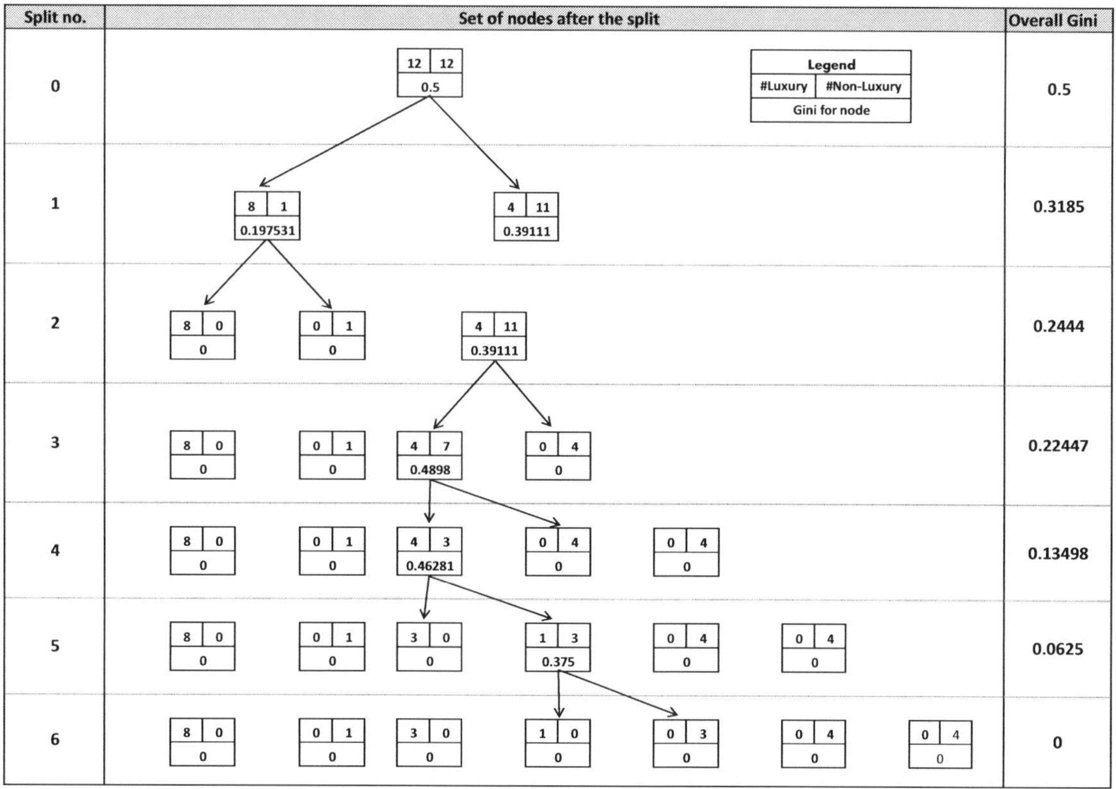

Figure 86: Set of nodes after each split. Each node shows the number of cases of each class and the Gini score for the node. The right-most number of each row shows the overall Gini score at that stage. Note how the Gini score has reduced from the maximum possible value of 0.5 (for the two-class case) to 0.

will do; it does not have to be good in any sense..

GPA	SAT	Performance
3.5	1200	Medium
3.9	1400	High
2.5	1420	High
2.8	1100	Low
2.7	1080	Low
3.4	1190	Medium
3.6	1230	Medium
3.9	1200	High

Answer the following questions based on the tree you arrived at:

1. How many splits does your tree have?
2. What is the Gini index for the root node – that is, before any splits?

3. What is the Gini index after the first split?
4. What is the Gini index after all splits?
5. Draw the error matrix for your tree.

Over-fitting

We had earlier ruled out the possibility of generating and using complete trees for practical data, because the trees would be huge and impractical.

We want to use this opportunity to explain an important data mining concept lurking here – *over-fitting*.

Let us start with an analogy – what, according to you, makes clothes to be *well-fitting*?

Especially when looking at suits, but even generally, we do not want clothes to be too baggy or too tight – we want them to be *just right*. If they match the contours of our body too well then we will be uncomfortable even if we had a nice meal!

For another example, consider the situation of someone training for an examination with a set of questions and their answers. For some reason, let us suppose that some of the answers provided are incorrect because of typos or other issues. Instead of learning the general principles and concepts, the student somehow rationalized those incorrect answers and learned some incorrect *principles* from them.

Clearly, if the student then applied the incorrect principles on the real test, they would perhaps perform very poorly, although they learned *everything* correctly from the training questions.

Both of these situations are analogous to *over-fitting* in data analytics.

When we build data analytics models, we do not want the models to slavishly follow the training data and get perfect results. Why not? Why would we not want a model that performs as well as possible on the training data?

Let us assume for a moment that our training data were *perfectly* representative of data that the model will encounter in actual use. That is, there is not even a single case that is anomalous. In this case we should build as good a model as we possibly can with the training data.

However, real life data contains anomalies.

Suppose for example, our luxury car data had one case of

a person with an income of $8,000 who owned a luxury car – a freak case, perhaps representing someone who inherited the car, but is otherwise in dire straits. Given that no other income is that low, a model that made no mistakes at all would create a rule that says, in effect, "if income <=8,000 then classify the case as a luxury car owner." In doing this, it would be taking a freak case, unrepresentative of reality, and basing a rule on it. So we might get a model that performs superbly on the training data. However, our test data (as well as the data on which the model would later be applied) will contain genuine cases of people with low incomes owning non-luxury cars; our over-fitted, *perfect* model could perform very poorly on the test cases. It would be a disaster to use that model in practice.

With large data sets, we should expect our training data to have many such freak cases. Building a perfect model on the training data that somehow accounts for these freak cases will result in *over-fitting*. *Over-fitting* helps to improve the performance on the training partition. However, when we apply the model to our test data, some rules that helped to correctly classify freak cases in the training data will contribute to poor performance.

If we have a sufficiently large amount of training data, we can expect it to be broadly representative of reality. However, not every single case in the training data and not every single nuance holds useful information. If we tried to capture everything in our model then the model will be too closely fitted for that specific training data – *over-fitted* – and have lots of misleading detail when applied to general data. *Over-fitting*, despite helping to improve performance on the training partition, depresses performance on the test data.

Recall that test data are data that we do not use at all in the process of developing a model

In general, when the performance on the training data is too good, we have to watch for *over-fitting*. In data analytics, you will observe a general "U" shaped relationship between model refinement and performance on the hold-out data, as Figure 87 shows. In that figure, we use the phrase *degree of refinement of model* to stand for how elaborate the model is. For example, a classification tree with more nodes would be more refined or elaborate than one with fewer nodes. A model using more predictor attributes would also be more refined.

The figure shows that as the model gets more and more refined (for example, as we consider more and more splits on a classification tree), its performance on the training data keeps on improving, perhaps up to some possible minimum value.

As we make our models more and more complex, we might improve the performance on the training partition. Beyond a certain point we will overfit and the performance on the holdout partition will begin to suffer.

The performance on the hold-out data on the other hand shows improvement up to a point, but then starts deteriorating. Why does this happen? Because at some point the model becomes too refined and starts over-fitting the training data and latching on to features peculiar to some cases in the training data. It is therefore no more representative of real data and hence starts failing on more and more hold-out cases.

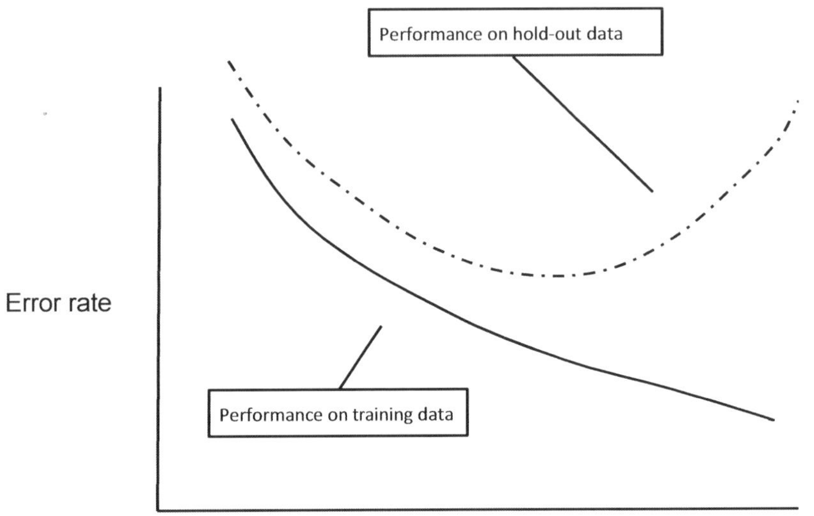

Figure 87: As we refine the model more and more, we usually get better and better performance on the training data, but after a point, the performance on the hold-out data starts deteriorating and the model starts to *over-fit*.

The ideal level of refinement therefore is where the performance on the test data is best. Figure 88 shows this.

Classification trees for real-life data – pruning

Having seen how the best tree that we can find on the training data will generally be huge and additionally run the risk of *over-fitting*, let us consider what we can do to control the size of the tree and attack both of these problems – size and over-fitting

This section discusses some fairly involved concepts and you can skip it if you choose to. However, our steps for building classification trees in **R** incorporate these ideas. Therefore, even if you skip this section, be sure to do the lab that follows so that you will learn how to properly use **R** to build classification trees on large data.

We have already seen that as a classification tree becomes larger (by having more and more splits) its performance on the

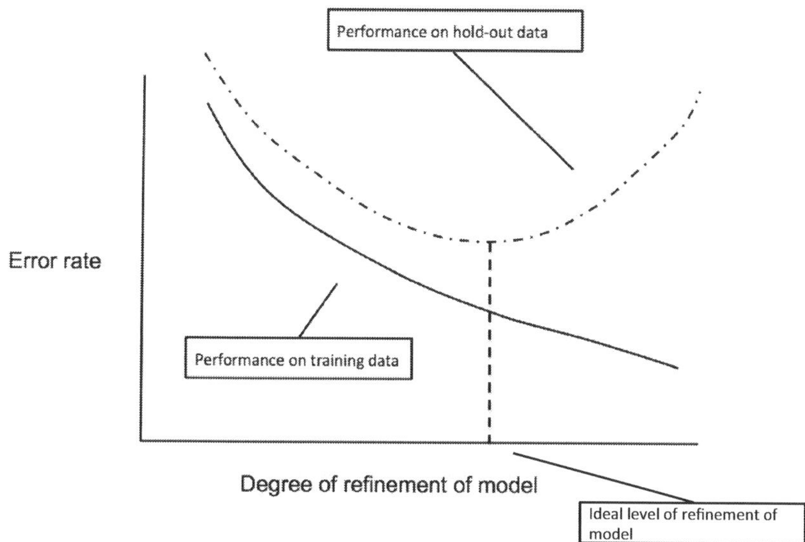

Figure 88: Ideally we should choose the level of refinement leading to the best performance on the hold-out data.

training data improves. However, we also know that the tree becomes bigger and more complex and runs the risk of over-fitting as well. We face the challenge of finding the *ideal* tree.

Before going further, let us see how we might make a tree smaller. Of course that would mean eliminating some nodes. Compare the two trees shown in Figure 89.

What difference do you see? In the original tree, node 3 was split, but in the new tree it has become a leaf node, even though it is not *pure*. It has 1 luxury and 8 non-luxury cases and is therefore classified as *Non-Luxury*.

The tree on the left classifies all 24 cases correctly, but the one on the right gets one case incorrect - it classifies a luxury car owner as a non-luxury car owner. We got a smaller tree, but it has more errors.

Now consider the tree in Figure 90. It shows the same situation, but with just one split.

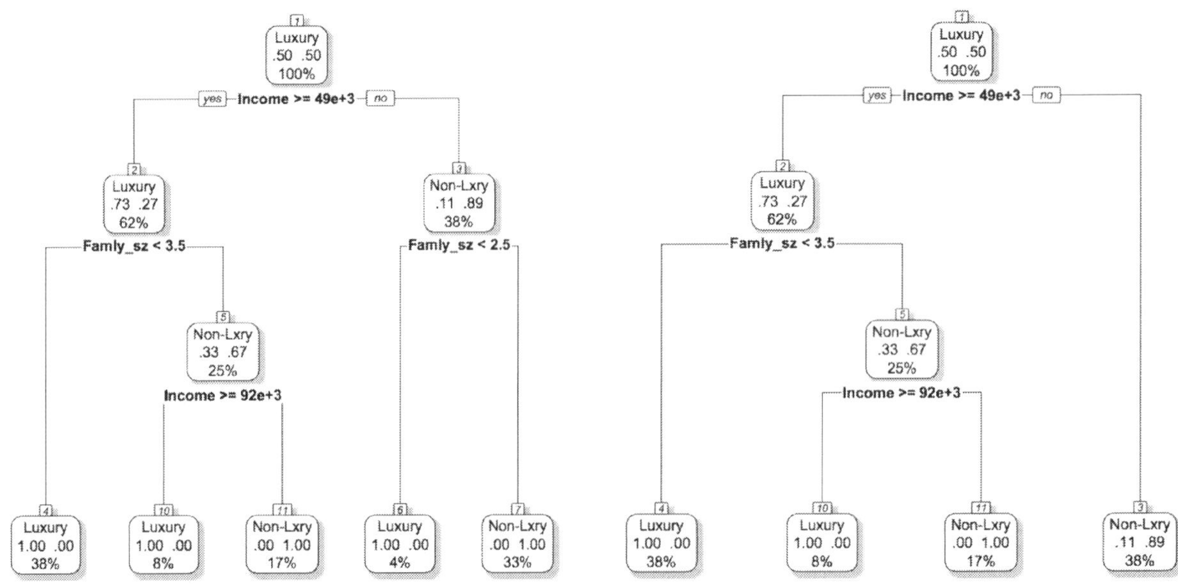

Figure 89: Original tree and tree with one less split

This tree has two leaf nodes, with both impure. The left leaf mis-classifies 4 cases and the right one 1, for a total error of 5 cases out of 24. This tree is even smaller, but the error is higher.

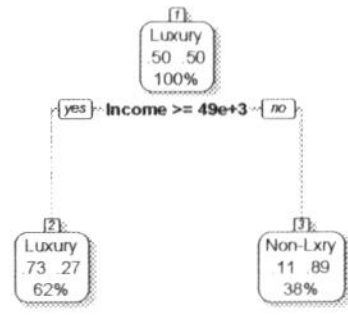

Figure 90: Even smaller tree

If we consider the simplest tree possible in this case – just the root node alone, then we see that it will classify every case as *Luxury* and make 12 errors.

The above process, where we took the whole tree and collapsed it to a tree with just the root node is called *pruning* and it involves a few more concepts that we will discuss now.

From this example, we can see that as we grow the tree, we improve its performance on the training data. In this case, as we increase the tree size from just the root node to the complete tree we decrease the total number of errors from 12 to 0.

Look at the tree shown in Figure 91.

Figure 91 shows one huge tree indeed. In case you missed it, note that it shows two rows of leaf nodes at the bottom. On real-life data, the complete tree will almost always be huge. Sure, it will probably have a low error rate – but it will be very cumbersome to use. Furthermore, it will likely over-fit the data.

Classification tree methods obtain a tree of moderate size by

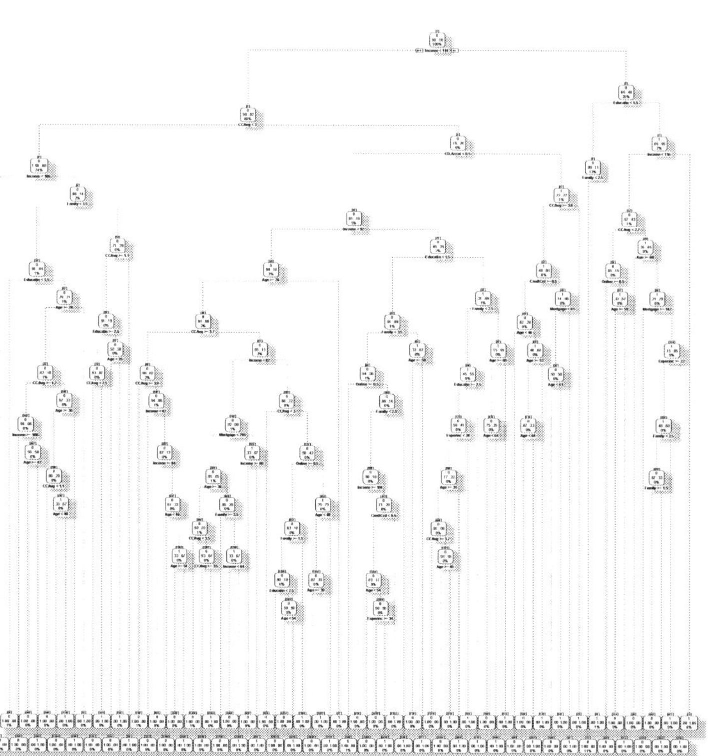

Figure 91: Complete classification tree from a real life data set – too big to be useful.

trading off size for performance on training data. They do this by imposing a cost on each additional node generated.

Suppose each error costs 0.05 and the cost of each additional node (called the complexity factor) is 0.02, then if a tree makes 100 errors and has 50 nodes, then the overall cost of that tree is 100*0.05 + 49*0.02. As we increase the number of nodes, the error goes down and the first term decreases. However, as the tree grows, the second term increases. Initially the total cost will decrease as the tree grows, but at some point, the cost will start to rise. We want the tree that has the lowest cost.

If the complexity factor is 0, then additional nodes cost nothing and the best tree will be the full tree – because that tree has the lowest error.

On the other hand, if the complexity factor is very high, then even a single split will increase the cost a lot and so the best tree will be just the root node alone – classify every case as simply the class of the majority case in the training data – using what we earlier called the *Naïve rule*.

Classification tree methods can build the whole tree and help us to prune it to the optimal level. The *rpart* package that you installed earlier has the features to generate the tree and to prune it down to the best size based on the complexity factor as we just discussed. In the process it performs some additional calculations that we will not go into in this book.

Lab 11: Classification Trees 2

Pre-requisite(s)

✓ You should have completed the prior classification tree lab starting on page 161.

Objective

After completing this lab, you will be able to:

✓ Use **R** to generate *pruned* classification trees for large real-life data sets.

✓ Interpret the textual and graphical results of the process.

✓ Evaluate the model's performance on test data.

Overview

Having already seen the basics of building classification tree models and interpreting the results on a toy example, we now apply it to a large data set. We will partition the data and evaluate its quality on the holdout data.

We will revisit the Boston Housing data[17,18]. You might recall that it had an attribute *MEDV* reflecting the median value of the homes in a neighborhood. To make it suitable for a classification problem, we have included another attribute called *MEDV_CAT* in which we have categorized *MEDV* into *High* and *Low*.

Table 43 provides a brief description of each attribute in the file.

We will build a classification tree for this modified data set.

In the previous lab you generated the complete tree for a small data set.

[17] D. Harrison and D.L. Rubinfeld. Hedonic prices and the demand for clean air. *J. Environ. Economics & Management*, pages 81–102, 1978

[18] K. Bache and M. Lichman. UCI machine learning repository, 2013. URL `http://archive.ics.uci.edu/ml`

Attribute	Description
CRIM	per capita crime rate by town
ZN	proportion of residential land zoned for lots over 25,000 sq.ft.
INDUS	proportion of non-retail business acres per town.
CHAS	Bounds Charles River or not (1 if tract bounds river; 0 otherwise)
NOX	nitric oxides concentration (parts per 10 million)
RM	average number of rooms per dwelling
AGE	proportion of owner-occupied units built prior to 1940
DIS	weighted distances to five Boston employment centres
RAD	index of accessibility to radial highways
TAX	full-value property-tax rate per $10,000
PTRATIO	pupil-teacher ratio by town
B	$1000(Bk - 0.63)^2$ where Bk is the proportion of blacks by town
LSTAT	% lower status of the population
MEDV_CAT	Median value of owner-occupied homes categorized into *High* or *Low*

Table 43: Boston Housing attribute descriptions.

We already know that the complete tree for a large data set would be huge. This time, we will take steps to generate a pruned tree as we discussed in the section on page 192.

We will then evaluate the performance of the pruned tree model on the holdout data in the test partition.

Activity steps

1. **Load the data:** Load the data from the file *boston-housing-classification.csv* into a data frame called *bh*.

   ```
   > bh <- read.csv("boston-housing-classification.csv")
   ```

   Table 43 provides the column descriptions.

2. **Explore the data:** How many rows of data do we have?

   nrow(bh)

   How many attributes? What are their names?

   names(bh)

   Look at the first 10 rows of data.

   bh[1:10,] or head(bh, 10)

   You can also use head(bh) to see the first six rows and tail(bh) to see the last 6 rows

   Since *MEDV_CAT* is categorical, we can apply Classification Trees to this data. For classification trees we need a categorical target attribute and numeric, categorical or ordinal predictor attributes. Our data file is thus ready for processing.

3. **Compute the a-priori probabilities in the original data:** We find the total number of cases in our data to be 363. We can find the number of cases in each class using one of two ways:

   nrow(bh)

```
> summary(bh$MEDV_CAT)
> table(bh$MEDV_CAT)
```

From the above we can see that 52.34% of the cases have *High MEDV* and the rest have *Low MEDV*. Therefore, if we randomly picked a case from the original data set, we have a 0.5234 probability of getting a *High* case and a 0.4766 probability of getting a *Low* case. If we had no model to predict the class of a case and were given a case at random and asked to predict its *MEDV_CAT*, what should we do? A little reflection tells us that the best we can do is to predict every case as belonging to the majority class, *High*. Another example might clarify this. if we are given a group of people and told that 80% are women. If we are told that someone has picked a person at random from this group and without giving any further information, asks us to predict the gender of the person, we would obviously be better off predicting the gender as female – the majority class. We call this the *naïve* rule.

A-priori probabilities

In analytics we refer to the proportions of the different classes of the target attribute in the original data as the *a-priori* probabilities. If we follow the *naïve* rule then we can expect to be correct 52.34% of the time. That represents our base performance – or performance without the help of a model. We will build a model and see how much better it can do.

4. **Partition the data:** Classification trees only require two partitions. We want to build a model to classify the median home values in a neighborhood as *High* or *Low*. Therefore *MEDV_CAT* will be our target attribute. Recalling what we did in the lab on creating partitions, we can use the following code for creating the training and test partitions with 70% and 30% of the cases respectively:

```
> library(caret)
> set.seed(2015)
> sam <- createDataPartition(bh$MEDV_CAT,
       p = 0.7, list = FALSE)
> train <- bh[sam, ]
> test <- bh[-sam, ]
```

Now *train* has the training partition and *test* has the test partition.

5. **Build the tree model:** For now, let us use all attributes other than the target as predictors. With Classification Trees, we do not need to worry too much about eliminating predictor attributes. The way the methods works automatically ignores attributes that have low predictive power.

   Unlike in the previous lab on classification trees, we will not attempt to build the complete tree. Since the classification at the leaf nodes is based on proportions, they will make sense only if the total number of cases in each leaf node is reasonably large, say at least 10. For this lab, we will initially set a value of 10 for *minbucket* to ensure this. We will leave *cp* at zero. You might recall that in the earlier lab, we had specified *minsplit* – the minimum number of cases in a node before it is considered for splitting. Here we have specified *minbucket*. We can specify one or the other of these two. Instead of specifying *minbucket* as 10, we could have specified *minsplit* as 30.

   The *rpart* package provides many more controls, but we will not go into them. You can do a lot with just what we have covered.

   Enter the command (see Figure 92 for details):

```
> library(rpart)
> bh.tree <- rpart(MEDV_CAT ~ .,
      data = train, control = rpart.control(minbucket = 10, cp = 0))
```

   The tree model is now in the variable *bh.tree*.

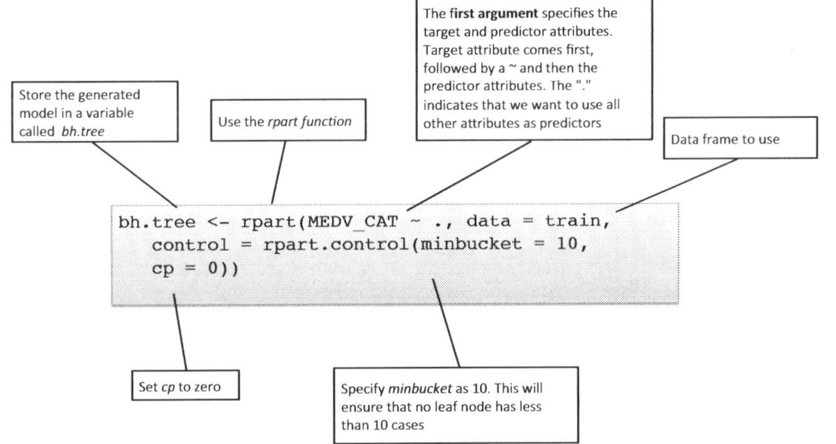

Figure 92: Using the *rpart* function to build the classification tree.

In the above command, we have specified the model formula with the target attribute first, and then, following the tilde sign "~", the predictor attributes – by using "." here we have asked **R** to use all attributes *other than the target* as predictors. Following that, we have indicated the training data as *train*.

6. **Print the tree:** As before, we can print the tree with the command:

```
> library(rpart.plot)
> prp(bh.tree, type = 2, extra = 104,
       nn = TRUE, fallen.leaves = TRUE,
       faclen = 4, varlen = 8,
       shadow.col = "gray")
```

Figure 93 shows the resulting tree.

Figure 93: Tree for the Boston Housing data with *minbucket=10*

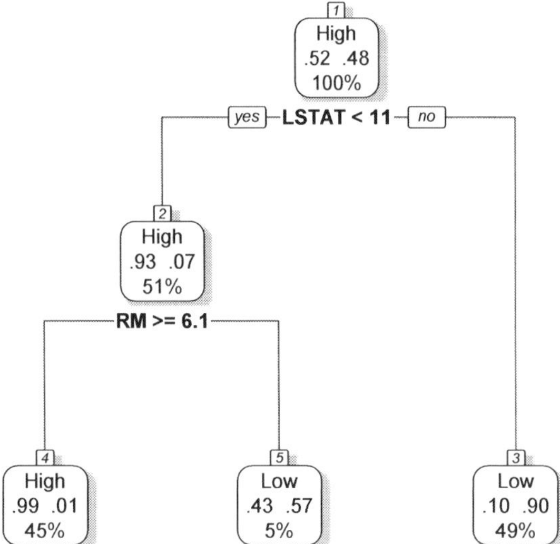

This tree is quite small as it is and hence we will not try to prune it any further. We will illustrate pruning in a later step after deliberately generating a large tree.

Let us also generate the text output.

```
> bh.tree
```

Figure 94 shows the result.

For each node, the text output shows the following:

- the node number
- the condition that resulted in that node (just *root* for the root node)
- total number of cases in the node
- the number of cases that belong to the non-majority class(es)
- the classification of the node
- and the relative proportions of the various classes.

For the root node, we see that it has:

- node number as 1
- condition – just *root*
- 255 cases in all (the size of the training partition)
- 122 of these belong to the minority class
- this node is classified as *High*
- proportions of *High* and *Low* as (0.521568627 0.478431373)

```
n= 255

node), split, n, loss, yval, (yprob)
      * denotes terminal node

1) root 255 122 High (0.521568627 0.478431373)
  2) LSTAT< 11.375 129   9 High (0.930232558 0.069767442)
    4) RM>=6.0985 115   1 High (0.991304348 0.008695652) *
    5) RM< 6.0985 14   6 Low (0.428571429 0.571428571) *
  3) LSTAT>=11.375 126  13 Low (0.103174603 0.896825397) *
```

Figure 94: Textual output of tree for Boston Housing with *minbucket=10*

7. **Preliminary evaluation:** We see that **R** was able to create a very simple classification tree. Just by splitting on a two attributes it got what looks like a *good* tree.

   How can we say that? If you look at the leaf nodes, we see that the proportions for the nodes numbered 4 and 3 which make up 94% of the overall cases are (0.99, 0.01) and (0.10, 0.90). These nodes are quote close to being pure. Node 5 is not very pure, but accounts for only 5% of the cases.

   We can also see from the textual output that, of the 255 cases, the leaf nodes mis-classify only 20 cases (node 3 mis-classifies 13, node 4 just 1 and node 5 mis-classifies 6). So the overall performance is 235/255 or 92.2%.

We know the a-priori performance to be 52.34%. The lift therefore is 92.2/52.34 or 1.76 or a 76% improvement over the base performance.

We can generate the error matrix on the training partition by:

```
> pred.train <- predict(bh.tree, train, type="class")
> table(train$MEDV_CAT, pred.train,
      dnn = c("Actual", "Predicted"))
```

```
        Predicted
Actual High Low
  High  114  19
  Low     1 121
```

Figure 95: Classification confusion matrix for Boston Housing – training data

Figure 95 shows the result.

Even though things seem to look pretty rosy, we still have to see how it does on the test data. Without this step we will not know if the model is good.

8. **Evaluation using holdout data in the test partition:** To evaluate the model's performance on the test partition, we need to first use the model on that partition to see how the model classifies those cases. We can then compare the actual value against the model results to see if the model is useful.

   Enter the command (similar to what we did in the first classification tree lab):

```
> pred.test <- predict(bh.tree, test, type="class")
```

   The variable *pred.test* contains the predictions. Note that it is not a part of the data frame *test*.

   Now generate the classification-confusion matrix:

```
> table(test$MEDV_CAT, pred.test,
      dnn = c("Actual", "Predicted"))
```

```
        Predicted
Actual High Low
  High   49   8
  Low     2  49
```

Figure 96: Classification confusion matrix for Boston Housing – test data

   Figure 96 shows the resulting matrix.

   What error rate does the model generate on the test partition? It made a total of 10 errors on 108 cases – 9.25% – compared to 7.84% on the training partition. Decent.

   The correctness rate on the test data is 98/108 or 91%. The lift on the test data is 91/52 = 1.75, or a 75% improvement over the base performance.

   To summarize, we were able to identify simple, but

very effective, decision rules from a large data set, quickly.

9. **Pruning:** Our tree turned out to be very simple, but effective. However this did not allow us to illustrate pruning at all. So in this step, we will deliberately generate a larger tree by setting *minsplit=10* and then prune it.

```
> bh.tree <- rpart(MEDV_CAT ~ ., data = train,
      control = rpart.control(minsplit = 10, cp = 0))
> prp(bh.tree, type = 2, extra = 104, nn = TRUE,
      fallen.leaves = TRUE, faclen = 4, varlen = 8,
      shadow.col = "gray")
```

Figure 97 shows the resulting tree.

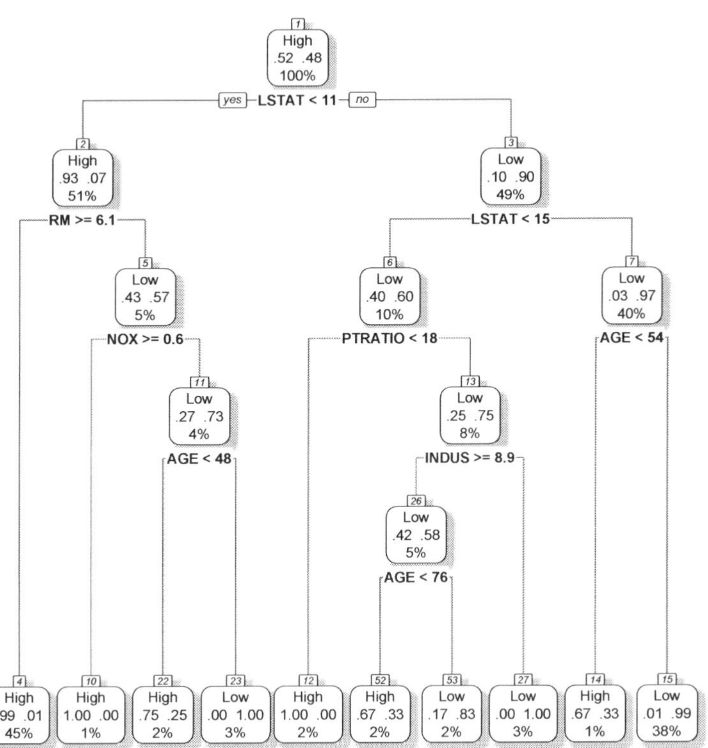

Figure 97: A bigger tree for the Boston Housing data

Looking at the leaf node proportions in Figure 97 quickly tells us that the tree is pretty good. However, we might not want a tree that is quite so large. This calls for *pruning*.

Recall that we generated the tree with *minsplit=10*. This means that any node with even 10 cases would be considered for splitting.

Consider leaf node 10. It has 1% of the cases – which means it has 1% of the 255 cases or 3 cases. That is hardly sufficient to base a rule on. In fact, other than leaf nodes 4 and 15, all the rest have too few cases. This clearly calls for *pruning*.

Note: Don't panic if you do not understand the following paragraph. You do not need to know these details to properly use classification trees.

When *rpart* runs, other than generating the tree, it goes through an additional process called *cross-validation* that we will not go into. In that process, it generates trees of various sizes (number of leaf nodes) and computes the average and standard deviation of the error for trees of each size. In addition it also computes the complexity factor that leads to trees of various sizes.

We can use this information to *prune* the tree. We will only describe the steps here without going into the underlying mathematics.

We first generate a plot of *cp* and tree size versus the error rate. Actually since the error rates will vary vastly from situation to situation, we will plot the *relative error rate*. This is just a scaled version of the actual error rate with the highest error rate (for a tree with just one node) being converted to 1 and all other error rates proportionately scaled.

```
> plotcp(bh.tree)
```

Figure 98 shows the result – **your chart can differ because of random factors**.

Note that the minimum size of tree is 1 node (root node only, no splits) and the maximum size is 10 – which is the number of leaf nodes in the tree that Figure 97 shows.

We would like to select the tree with the lowest error rate. In practice we allow for some random variation and select the tree that corresponds to the leftmost point on or below the dashed line. This will correspond to a tree of smaller size whose error is within one standard deviation of the error of the smallest tree. In this situ-

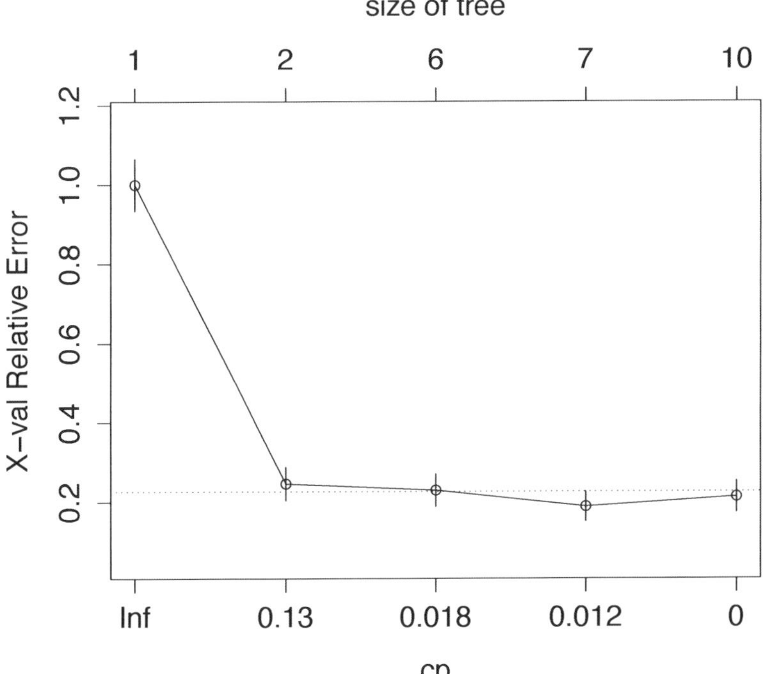

Figure 98: Output of *plotcp*

ation, we would therefore choose the tree with size 6, corresponding to the complexity factor of 0.018 – your plot could be different and you should go with the *cp* as per your plot. Look at your plot and determine the *cp* factor for the leftmost point below the line. If, for some reason, that value is not shown on the axis, resize the plot area till the value shows up.

To generate and plot the pruned tree:

```
> # Change the second argument as per
> # your cp value
> bh.pruned <- prune(bh.tree, 0.018)
> prp(bh.pruned, type = 2, extra = 104, nn = TRUE,
    fallen.leaves = TRUE, faclen = 4, varlen = 8,
    shadow.col = "gray")
```

Figure 99 shows the smaller, pruned, tree.

10. **Evaluating the pruned tree on the test data:** Run the following code:

```
> pred.test <- predict(bh.pruned, test,
       type = "class")
> table(test$MEDV_CAT, pred.test,
```

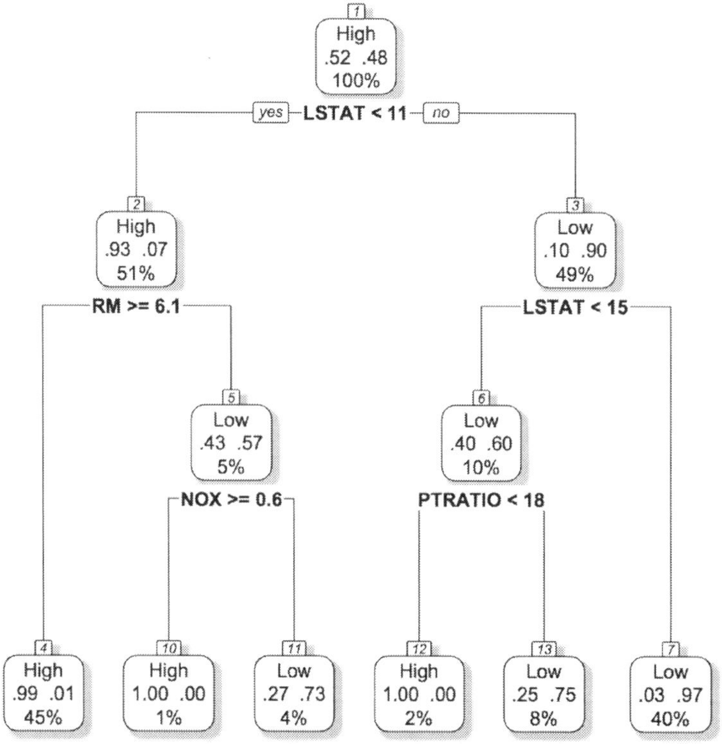

Figure 99: Pruned tree

```
      dnn = c("Actual", "Predicted"))
```

Figure 100 shows the resulting error matrix – yours might differ based on your *cp* value.

The correctness rate is 89.8%; lower than the much smaller tree that we initially generated. Being a bigger tree, this might be over fitting a little.

```
         Predicted
Actual  High  Low
  High    52    5
  Low      6   45
```

Figure 100: Error matrix on test partition for the pruned tree

Naïve Bayes

ChipsR'us Inc makes semi-conductor chips. and has a 0.1% defect rate. This means that, on the average, we can expect 1 out of every 1,000 chips the company produces to be defective.

Someone shows you a chip made at that facility. With no additional information, the person then asks you to guess whether the chip is defective or not. How would you answer? Of course, with no further help, you can only guess, and neither of the two possible answers guarantees success. But what

Table 44: Summary of steps for *Classification tree*.

Step no	Description	R command	Remarks
1	Read the data	`bh <- read.csv("boston-housing-classification.csv")`	

2	Create partitions	`library(caret)`
		`set.seed(2015)`
		`sam <- createDataPartition(bh$MEDV_CAT, p = 0.7, list = FALSE)`
		`train <- bh[sam, ]`
		`test <- bh[-sam, ]`
			We need two partitions for Classification tree analysis

3	Build the tree	`library(rpart)`
		`bh.tree <- rpart(MEDV_CAT ~ .,`
		`data = train,`
		`control = rpart.control(minbucket = 10, cp = 0))`
			Using minbucket = 10. This means that no leaf node will have less than 10 cases.

4	Print the tree	`prp(bh.tree, type = 2,`
		`extra = 104, nn = TRUE, fallen.leaves = TRUE,`
		`faclen = 4, varlen = 8, shadow.col = "gray")`	

5	Look at the text output	`bh.tree`	
6	Generate model predictions on the training data	`pred.train <- predict(bh.tree, train, type="class")`	
7	Generate the error matrix on the training data	`table(train$MEDV_CAT, pred.train, dnn = c("Actual", "Predicted"))`	
8	Generate the predictions and the error matrix on the test data	`pred.test <- predict(bh.tree, test, type="class")` `table(test$MEDV_CAT, pred.test, dnn = c("Actual", "Predicted"))`	

9	Build (and print) a bigger tree just to illustrate pruning	`bh.tree <- rpart(MEDV_CAT ~ .,`
		`data = train,`
		`control = rpart.control(`
		`minsplit = 10, cp = 0))`
		`prp(bh.tree, type = 2, extra = 104, nn = TRUE, fallen.leaves = TRUE,`
		`faclen = 4, varlen = 8, shadow.col = "gray")`
			Using minsplit = 10; a node must have at least 10 cases to be considered for splitting/ – bigger tree than before

10	Plot the *cp* table	`plotcp(bh.tree)`	Select *cp* factor as leftmost one below line

11	Prune and print new tree	`bh.pruned <- prune(bh.tree, 0.018)`
		`prp(bh.pruned, type = 2,`
		`extra = 104, nn = TRUE,`
		`fallen.leaves = TRUE, faclen = 4, varlen = 8, shadow.col = "gray")`
			Replace 0.018 with your *cp* factor

12	Generate error matrix on pruned tree	`pred.test <- predict(bh.pruned, test, type = "class")` `table(test$MEDV_CAT, pred.test, dnn = c("Actual", "Predicted"))`	

guess will give you the highest chance of being correct?

Given that the company produces 99.9% non-defectives, we would be prudent to label that specific chip as non-defective. Why? Because a non-defective chip is almost 1,000 times more likely than a defective one. Of course we could still be wrong – that specific piece could be defective. However, the odds favor the chip being non-defective.

If we were given 10,000 chips and asked to classify them as defective or not, how many can we expect to get wrong if we classify every piece as non-defective?

Given the 0.1% rate of defectives, the 10,000 pieces would contain roughly 10 defectives. We would get these wrong because we classified every piece as non-defective. We would have an error rate of only 0.1% by following this strategy. Certainly does not look like a bad error-rate!

Naïve Approach: Classify every case as belonging to the majority class

In the above, we used a strategy of classifying all items as belonging to the majority class – the *naïve* approach.

To take another example of the use of the *naïve* approach, let us suppose that a particular company's stock had a price of $50 or more on 300 days of the past year. Someone picks a random day from the past year and asks us to guess, without providing any additional information, whether the price of the stock was $50 or more on the chosen day. Given that the price was $50 or more on 300 of the 365 days of the prior year, the *naïve* approach would guide us to say that the price was $50 or more because that is the majority class (with a probability of 300/365 or 0.822).

Going beyond the Naïve approach ...

In the semi-conductor chip example above, the *naïve* approach helped us to achieve a correct prediction rate of 99.9% – however, do you think that it is useful? It predicts every non-defective correctly, but completely fails to identify even a single defective – because we predict every chip to be non-defective. So the seemingly good overall performance can mislead us.

Let us ease into another example to see how we might be able to get over our naïvete. We will use this example to describe a technique called *Exact Bayes*. Do not let the name make you expect that we are going to look at something fancy – you should find this technique very easy to grasp.

Gizmos Inc, a company that makes innovative new consumer electronics devices is about to introduce a revolutionary new product and expects that only 1% of the people will even be ready to try it out initially. Gizmos Inc feels that once these early adopters have tried their product, word of its usefulness will spread and product sales will pick up. The company now needs to find this minuscule subset and promote the product to the group. Gizmos had already done a pilot with 30,000 people and identified 300 adopters. As a result of this pilot, the company now has demographic information as well as information on whether they adopted the product or not, for the 30,000 who participated in the pilot. For each person who participated, the company has information on attributes like education level, ownership of certain other products, gender, whether self-employed or salaried, and so on, as well as whether or not they adopted the product. Table 45 shows the kind of data that Gizmos Inc has at this point.

Exact Bayes

Case	Educ	Gen	Smt ph?	Tablet?	Self-empl?	Hyb car?	Adopter?
1	UG	F	Y	Y	Y	Y	N
2	UG	F	N	Y	N	N	N
3	PG	M	N	N	N	N	N
4	HS	M	N	Y	N	Y	Y
5	UG	F	Y	N	Y	N	N
6	HS	M	Y	Y	N	N	N
...	...	...	...	...	...	...	...

Table 45: Kind of data Gizmos Inc had after its pilot. The full table would have 30,000 rows.

Before we go too far, What kinds of attributes does our Gizmos example have? All *categorical*. The target attribute as well as all predictors are categorical.

Exact Bayes and Naïve Bayes, the two main techniques that we discuss in this chapter require all attributes to be categorical. If we have any numerical attributes, we will first need to convert them before we can use them in these techniques.

Returning to Gizmos Inc, the company now wants to expand the market for the new product and plans to do a nation-wide product promotion to 100,000 people who are most likely to adopt the new product. It has purchased a mailing list with demographic information (like what it gathered in its pilot) on 3 million people who have not yet been exposed to the new product.

How can the company go about selecting the *best* 100,000 from the 3 million?

What would the company do if it used the *naïve* approach?

Using the *naïve* approach, the company would classify all 3 million cases as non-adopters – the overwhelming majority class – and hence will not approach anyone at all – the *naïve* approach leads to inaction! Even though the decision would be correct for 99% of the cases, it would still be perfectly useless.

What exactly might the phrase "*best* 100,000 from the 3 million" mean? Remember, no matter how we choose the 100,000 from the 3 million, we can never be sure that they will all be adopters. If, based on the patterns from our pilot data, we can somehow identify the 100,000 people who have the highest likelihood or *probability* of being adopters, then we should promote the product to these people.

To make it easy for us to see the whole picture, let us suppose that we have 10 people instead of 3 million and we have to select *best* 2 from the 10. Without worrying about "How?" let us say that we are somehow able to generate the data shown in Table 46 for the 10 people.

If we need to select only two persons from the 10, who should they be?

Person no.	Probability of adoption
1	0.55
2	0.02
3	0.98
4	0.75
5	0.33
6	0.89
7	0.65
8	0.39
9	0.44
10	0.87

Table 46: Probability of adoption for a set of 10 people. We will soon see how we can use Exact Bayes to calculate such probabilities.

Person 3 with a probability of 0.98 of being an adopter is the best, and person 6 with a probability of 0.89 is the next best and we should select these two. If we had to select 3, then we can add on person 10.

Let us now see how we can generate such probabilities.

Returning to Gizmos Inc, what would we need so as to be able to find the best 100,000 from 3 million? Applying what we saw from the simple example of Table 46, if we can somehow compute the probability of adoption for each of the 3 million in the mailing list, we can easily select the 100,000 with the highest probabilities.

We now discuss how the data in Table 45 from the pilot study can potentially help us to calculate such probabilities.

Suppose we examine the data from the pilot and find that there were 40 female self-employed people with a post-graduate degree who own a hybrid car. Of these let us suppose that we find 32 (or 80%) adopted the product.

In statistics, 40 would usually be considered as a sufficiently large number of cases to base important conclusions on – even 30 would generally suffice. Therefore, based on these 40 cases, we can expect that roughly 80 % of the people with a similar profile (female, self-employed, post-graduate degree, hybrid car owner) will be adopters.

We can express the same thing differently: a person with the above profile (female, self-employed, post-graduate degree, hybrid car owner) would have an 80% probability of being an adopter.

Similarly, if we find that the pilot data had 30 salaried males with a post-graduate degree who did not have a hybrid car. Of these, suppose 3 were adopters. Again, given that we have sufficient number of cases for reasonable generalization, this tells us that people matching this profile (male, salaried, post-graduate degree, no hybrid car) have a 10% probability of being adopters.

Voilà. We can use the pilot data from Table 45 to find all possible combinations of attribute values, and for each one, find the probability of adoption.

With 3 possible values for Educ (UG, PG and HS), and two each (Y and N) for the five other predictor attributes, we have a total of 3*2*2*2*2*2 or 96 distinct combinations of predictor attributes. In other words, we could construct something like Table 47 – the table only illustrates a few of the rows, with made up data. The complete table would have 96 rows and we will need all the data from the pilot to computer the actual numbers.

In Table 47 we have arrived at the values in the column *Probability* by dividing the number of adopters by the no of cases.

Combination	Educ	Gen	Smt ph?	Tablet?	Self-empl?	Hyb car?	No. cases	No. adopt	Probability
1	UG	F	Y	Y	Y	Y	100	2	0.02
2	UG	F	Y	Y	Y	N	400	45	0.11
3	UG	F	Y	Y	N	Y	300	1	0.00
4	UG	F	Y	Y	N	N	350	3	0.02
5	UG	F	Y	N	Y	Y	200	1	0.00
6	UG	F	Y	N	Y	N	90	1	0.01
7	UG	F	Y	N	N	Y	450	0	0.00
8	UG	F	Y	N	N	N	387	10	0.03
...	...	...	...	...	...		...	...	...
...	...	...	...	...	...		...	...	...
96	HS	M	N	N	N	N	296	5	0.02

Table 47: Calculating the probabilities for all 96 possible combinations of attribute values based on Gizmos Inc Pilot data.

Armed with this table we can ascribe a probability of adoption for each of the 3 million persons based on the person's profile, and then select the 100,00 people with the highest probabilities.

You have just learned the *Exact Bayes* method.

Why the word *Bayes* in the name? The technique is based on *conditional probabilities* (which we will see shortly), which in turn is the subject of the hugely important *Bayes' Theorem*[19] or *Bayes' Law* in the field of statistics.

Bayes' Theorem is named for its inventor Thomas Bayes

[19] Wikipedia. Bayes' theorem, February 2014a. URL http://en.wikipedia.org/wiki/Bayes'_theorem

Victory at last! We have just used *Exact Bayes* to fully solve Gizmos Inc's problem.

Exact Bayes cannot usually be applied to real life problems.

Not so fast! Although *Exact Bayes* looks like a slam-dunk for such situations, we will encounter a major pitfall if we try to apply *Exact Bayes* to most real life situations. A variation on *Exact Bayes*, called *Naïve Bayes* helps to overcome the pitfall. We will soon discuss *Naïve Bayes*, but only after covering *conditional probabilities* (and in the process also clearly seeing the pitfall in applying *Exact Bayes* to most real-life problems).

Naïve Bayes adapts Exact Bayes for use in real-life problems.

Note for people with rusty mathematical skills: At this point, some of us might be excused for thinking "Probability is bad enough and now the author wants to torture me with *conditional* probability? I've had it." Actually we all– yes you too – routinely use conditional probabilities in our daily lives without even a second thought. So I bet that you will quite easily understand the discussion below. Also, in order to succinctly discuss conditional probabilities, we will need to use some mathematical notation – possibly daunting initially, but quite simple if you do not let the apparent complexity get to you.

Let us first understand the concept of conditional probability.

Suppose a company has data about a set of people who have been exposed to its product. Some among these purchased the product and the others did not. We have data on 36 persons and Table 48 shows a part of our data. As always, we start out with a simple example for ease of understanding.

Figure 101 pictorially depicts a part of the information. The filled circles represent buyers and the others non-buyers. Such pictures make it much easier to visualize and discuss conditional probabilities.

From Figure 101, we can see that 12 of the 36 people are buyers. So we can say that a randomly chosen person will have a *probability* of 12/36 or 0.33 of being a buyer.

Computing probabilities as relative frequencies

Some might find this last statement confusing. After all, a person is either a buyer or not. Where is this 0.33 coming from?

Case	Country	Status
1	Canada	Non-buyer
2	Canada	Non-buyer
3	US	Buyer
4	US	Non-buyer
5	Mexico	Non-buyer
6	US	Buyer
7	Mexico	Buyer
8	Canada	Buyer
9	US	Non-buyer
10	Mexico	Non-buyer
11	US	Non-buyer
12	Canada	Buyer
13	Mexico	Buyer
14	US	Buyer
..	...	...
..	...	...

Table 48: Cases showing people exposed to a company's product.

Actually this is not very different from saying that the probability of getting a head (or tail) in a toss of a fair coin is 0.5.

Another way to look at it is to consider that we repeat, a large number of times, the process of randomly choosing a person and checking whether or not he is a buyer (and putting this person back into the pile). Roughly a third of the time we can expect to choose a buyer.

So a probability of an event is the relative frequency with which the event occurs.

We can express probabilities more formally in mathematical notation:

$$P\left(Status = Buyer\right) = \frac{12}{36} = 0.33$$

$$P\left(Status = Non\text{-}buyer\right) = \frac{24}{36} = 0.67$$

These two probabilities represent the *a-priori* (sometimes just called *prior*) probabilities of *buyer* and *non-buyer*. They represent the probabilities of someone being a buyer or not *in the absence of any other information* – like the country to which a person belongs.

Figure 102 shows the country for each person as well. For convenience, we have chosen to draw an oval surrounding all the buyers. From this we can calculate some more probabilities. For example we can now see that 10 of the 36 are Canadian, and so on. Therefore:

$$P\left(Country = Canada\right) = \frac{10}{36} = 0.28$$

$P\left(Country = US\right) = \frac{17}{36} = 0.47$

$P\left(Country = Mexico\right) = \frac{9}{36} = 0.25$

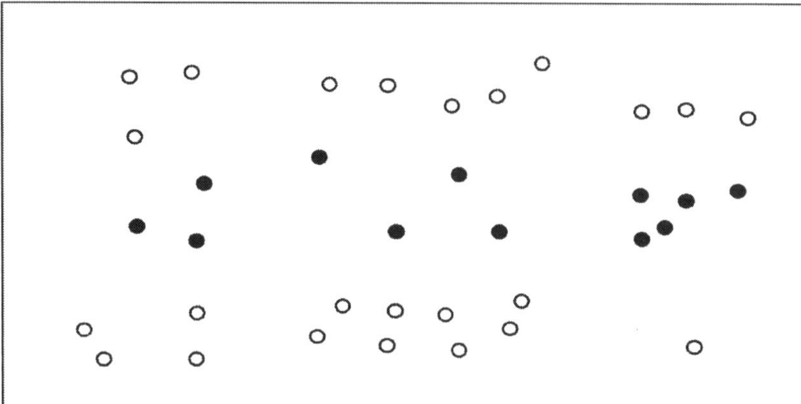

Figure 101: All customers: Filled circles represent buyers.

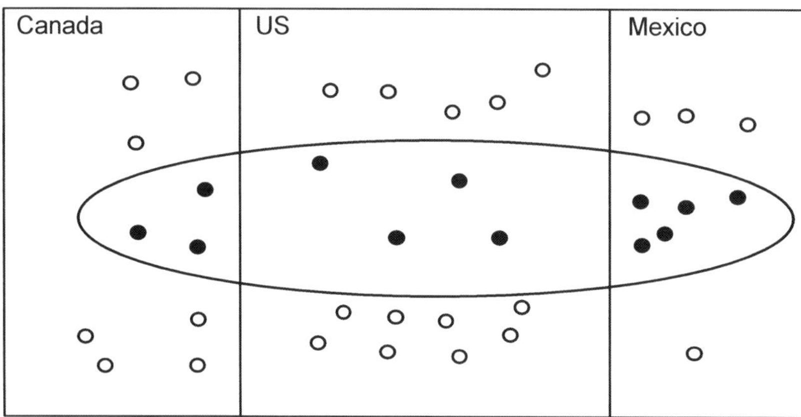

Figure 102: Customers by country: Filled circles represent buyers.

All of the above represent *unconditional* probabilities because we are not placing any restrictions on the denominator – we consider all persons.

Conditional probabilities

Let us now turn our attention to *conditional* probabilities.

Suppose we randomly choose a person from among the set of Canadians in Figure 102. What is the probability that this person is a buyer?

Clearly this refers to a very different thing than the *a-priori* probability that a person chosen at random (without regard to country) is a *buyer*.

Statisticians state this probability as: Given the condition that the person is a Canadian, what is the probability of the person being a buyer? We denote it mathematically as

$P\left(Status = Buyer|Country = Canada\right)$

In the mathematical notation, we place the condition(s) after the vertical bar. We read the vertical bar as "given".

We read $P\left(Status = Buyer|Country = Canada\right)$ as "Probability of a person being a *Buyer* **given** that the person is from *Canada*."

Why do we call this a *conditional* probability?

Obviously because we have now placed an additional condition – that the person is from Canada.

Since we have been told that the person is Canadian, we have to confine our attention to just that part of the figure. Of the 10 Canadians, 3 are buyers and hence

$P\left(Status = Buyer|Country = Canada\right) = 0.3$

The probability is 0.3, which differs from the *a-priori* probability of 0.33 for *buyer* without the added condition that the person is Canadian.

Can the conditional and the unconditional or a-priori probabilities have the same value?

Of course that is possible if the numbers lined up that way. We will see an example later.

In similar vein, we can compute the following *conditional* probabilities:

$$P\left(Status = Non\text{-}buyer|Country = Canada\right) = \frac{7}{10}$$

$$P\left(Status = Buyer|Country = US\right) = \frac{4}{17}$$

$$P\left(Status = Buyer|Country = Mexico\right) = \frac{5}{9}$$

Figure 103 shows the same data in the form of a table, which makes it easier to calculate various conditional probabilities. Depending on the condition, we can use the appropriate row or column total as the denominator.

	Buyer	Non-buyer	
Canada	3	7	10
US	4	13	17
Mexico	5	4	9
	12	24	

Figure 103: Customer-country data in table form.

	Buyer	Non-buyer	
Canada	330	1000	1330
US	300	858	1158
Mexico	700	610	1310
	1330	2468	

Figure 104: Customer-country data in table form – larger numbers.

What was the point of all this? Let us suppose we have a much larger, and therefore more representative, data set about persons and countries with information about whether each person is a buyer or not. Then we can construct something like

Figure 104.

From Figure 104 we can compute the conditional probabilities of someone being a *buyer* as $P(buyer|Canada) = \frac{330}{1330}$, $P(buyer|US) = \frac{300}{1158}$ and $P(buyer|Mexico) = \frac{700}{1310}$. Similarly, we can also compute the conditional probabilities of someone being a *non-buyer*.

Now, given a new person and their nationality, we can use the above conditional probabilities to classify them as *buyer* or *non-buyer* based on which conditional probability is higher.

We could have done exactly the same with the data in Figure 103, but the numbers in that table are too small and hence we cannot reasonably generalize from those numbers to probabilities. For example, Figure 103 shows 5 of 9 Mexicans to be buyers. However it is possible that the 9 people we picked randomly were not representative of reality and that in reality, a significantly smaller or larger proportion of them are buyers. With large numbers though we greatly reduce the likelihood of getting results that are not representative of reality. Of course there is still a chance that it can happen, but it is small enough that we can often ignore the risk of being wrong.

(As with our discussion in earlier classification techniques, when we have asymmetric costs, we might not always go with the higher probability – more on this later.)

We will now return to our original data. Let us add one more predictor attribute to our data as shown in Figure 105. In our earlier table Canada had 3 buyers and 7 non-buyers. We now see the gender-wise break-up of these buyers and non-buyers. The figure shows the break-up for the other two countries as well.

We can now calculate various, more complex, conditional probabilities. Given a US female, we can calculate the probability of this person being a buyer as 1/7 and that of being a non-buyer as 6/7, because we have one buyer among the 7 US females in our data.

The mathematical notation will differ slightly now; we now have two conditions – the person is from the *US* and is *Female*. When this happens we place all the conditions after the vertical bar and separate the conditions with commas. In mathematical notation:

$$P(Status = Buyer|Country = US, Gender = Female) = \frac{1}{7}$$

		Buyer	Non-buyer	
Canada	Male	1	5	6
	Female	2	2	4
US	Male	3	7	10
	Female	1	6	7
Mexico	Male	4	1	5
	Female	1	3	4
		12	24	

Figure 105: Adding gender as a predictor attribute.

$$P\left(Status = \textit{Non-buyer} | Country = US, Gender = Female\right) = \frac{6}{7}$$

Going by our earlier logic, we would classify this person as a non-buyer because of the higher probability of that class.

How would we classify a Mexican male?

Buyer, of course, because our data shows 4 of the 5 Mexican males as buyers for a probability of 4/5 of being a buyer.

To recap our discussion thus far, we had data with categorical predictor attributes (*country* and *gender*), and a categorical target attribute (*buyer* or *non-buyer*). We then constructed a table showing, for each possible combination of the values of the predictor attributes, the number of buyers and non-buyers. Given a person and their *country* and *gender*, this table enabled us to classify the person based on their conditional probabilities of being a buyer or non-buyer. That is, we can compute the following for all values of *country* and *gender* that appear in our data set:

$$P\left(Status = Buyer | Country = \ldots, Gender = \ldots\right)$$

$$P\left(Status = \textit{Non-buyer} | Country = \ldots, Gender = \ldots\right)$$

The above procedure illustrates the *Exact Bayes* approach to classification. Easy enough! Why do we need to look beyond this at all to *Naïve Bayes*?

Thus far, we have worked with a toy example to illustrate the concepts. We have three possible values for *country* and two for *gender* for a total of six possible combinations of the predictor attributes. In real-life examples, we should expect many more predictor attributes. To make matters concrete, let us add two more predictor attributes *Employment_status* and *Education*.

Figure 106 shows the scenario without actual numbers. With three possible values for *country*, two for *gender*, three for *employment-status* and three for *education*, we have 54 possible combinations. Even if we had 1,000 rows of data, that would mean an average of less than 20 cases per combination to be split across buyers and non-buyers – not a lot to base our probability computations on. Real-life data sets generally have even more predictors and the number of possible combinations explodes. Even with seemingly large amounts of data, we might not have enough cases for each combination of predictors. Even worse, we might have no data for many of the possible combinations and hence be unable to classify such cases.

Curse of dimensionality

Suppose for example, we had 8 predictors with an average of 3 distinct values for each. This would yield 3^8, or 6,561 possible distinct combinations. In such a case, even a data file with 30,000 rows would be too small. With so many possible distinct combinations, often we will find no cases or very few cases for many of the possible combinations and hence be unable to classify those cases reliably, or even at all. Statisticians often refer to this situation as the *curse of dimensionality*. This is why *Exact Bayes* is generally inapplicable on real-life data sets.

The real reason why Exact Bayes cannot be applied to most real-life data sets

So when we have lots of data for every possible combination of predictor attributes *Exact Bayes* works. When not, it just fails, without making use of the partial information available in the data.

Naïve Bayes can be used when the curse of dimsionality prevents us from using Exact Bayes

To address this key issue, researchers have created a method called *Naïve Bayes* to help us calculate a good approximation for the conditional probability, even when we do not have as much data as we might like.

To get a concrete idea of what the approximation does, let us suppose that we have data with the structure that Figure 106 shows. We have already seen that the figure represents 54 different combinations of values of the predictor attributes *Country*, *Gender*, *Employment_Status* and *Education*. From the data in the figure, we can calculate the conditional probabilities for all possible combinations of values of the predictor attributes:

				Buyer	Non-buyer
Canada	Male	Self-empoloyed	High school		
			Undergrad degree		
			Graduate degree		
		Salaried	High school		
			Undergrad degree		
			Graduate degree		
		Unemployed	High school		
			Undergrad degree		
			Graduate degree		
	Female	Self-empoloyed	High school		
			Undergrad degree		
			Graduate degree		
		Salaried	High school		
			Undergrad degree		
			Graduate degree		
		Unemployed	High school		
			Undergrad degree		
			Graduate degree		
US	Male	Self-empoloyed	High school		
			Undergrad degree		
			Graduate degree		
		Salaried	High school		
			Undergrad degree		
			Graduate degree		
		Unemployed	High school		
			Undergrad degree		
			Graduate degree		
	Female	Self-empoloyed	High school		
			Undergrad degree		
			Graduate degree		
		Salaried	High school		
			Undergrad degree		
			Graduate degree		
		Unemployed	High school		
			Undergrad degree		
			Graduate degree		
Mexico	Male	Self-empoloyed	High school		
			Undergrad degree		
			Graduate degree		
		Salaried	High school		
			Undergrad degree		
			Graduate degree		
		Unemployed	High school		
			Undergrad degree		
			Graduate degree		
	Female	Self-empoloyed	High school		
			Undergrad degree		
			Graduate degree		
		Salaried	High school		
			Undergrad degree		
			Graduate degree		
		Unemployed	High school		
			Undergrad degree		
			Graduate degree		

Figure 106: Curse of dimensionality.

$$P(Status = Buyer|Country = \ldots, Gender = \ldots, Employment\_status = \ldots, Education = \ldots)$$

and

$$P(Status = Non\text{-}buyer|Country = \ldots, Gender = \ldots, Employment\_status = \ldots, Education = \ldots)$$

With enough data for each combination, we can apply *Exact Bayes* and use the conditional probabilities to classify any new case based on its predictor attribute values.

Without sufficient data for each possible combination of predictor attributes, we will be unable to compute the above conditional probabilities and hence be unable to use *Exact Bayes*. However, it is very likely that we will have enough data to compute the following simpler conditional probabilities for all possible predictor attribute values:

$P(Country = \ldots|Status = Buyer)$
$P(Gender = \ldots|Status = Buyer)$
$P(Employment\_status = \ldots|Status = Buyer)$
$P(Education = \ldots|Status = Buyer)$

$P(Country = \ldots|Status\text{=}Non\text{-}buyer)$
$P(Gender = \ldots|Status\text{=}Non\text{-}buyer)$
$P(Employment\_status = \ldots|Status\text{=}Non\text{-}buyer)$
$P(Education = \ldots|Status\text{=}Non\text{-}buyer)$

The *Naïve Bayes* technique uses the above conditional probabilities to compute a good approximation (based on Bayes' Theorem) to the more complex conditional probabilities discussed above.

Let us review what we have learned so far and then use **R** to perform *Naïve Bayes* analysis.

Review 12: Naive Bayes

You can find the answers to these on page 377

Assume that the table below shows the high school GPA, SAT score and the first semester performance in college for a set of students. All data are categorical.

Calculate the following:

GPA	SAT	Performance
High	Medium	Medium
High	Medium	High
Low	High	High
Low	Medium	Low
Low	Low	Low
Medium	Medium	Medium
High	Medium	Medium
High	Medium	High

1. $P(Performance = High)$
2. $P(GPA = Low)$
3. $P(SAT = Medium)$
4. $P(GPA = High|Performance = High)$
5. $P(SAT = Low|Performance = Low)$

Lab 12: Naïve Bayes Classification using **R**

Pre-requisite(s)

✓ You should have set up **R**, downloaded the practice data files and pointed **R** to the location of the files.

✓ You should have read the section on Naïve Bayes on page 206 and answered the associated review questions.

Objective

After completing this lab, you will be able to:

✓ Use **R** to perform a Naïve Bayes analysis.

✓ Interpret the results

✓ Use the resulting model to classify new cases

Overview

In this lab you will learn how to use **R** to perform a Naïve Bayes analysis. We will work with a small data set so that you can grasp all the details.

However, because the data set is small, we will not get a model with great predictive power. The lab assignment allows you to practice with a larger data set.

We will build a model to predict whether someone will buy a product based on some demographic and other attributes.

Activity steps

1. **Read the data file:** Read the data from the file *nb-example.csv* into a data frame called *nb*.

```
> cust <- read.csv("nb-example.csv")
```

   Note how small the data set is – just 16 cases. We chose this deliberately so that you can check some of the model calculations.

2. **Look at the data:** The data set has some information on a small set of people: education, gender, whether they have a smart phone, whether they have a tablet and whether or not they purchased a certain product. We will build a Naïve Bayes model to predict whether or not future cases for whom we know the demographic details will be purchasers. Note that the data frame has only categorical attributes. Naïve Bayes only works under this condition. Table 49 shows the data.

Education	Gender	Smart_ph	Tablet	Purchase
C	M	N	N	No
B	F	Y	Y	Yes
A	M	N	Y	No
C	M	Y	Y	Yes
C	M	Y	N	No
C	M	Y	N	No
A	F	Y	N	No
B	M	Y	Y	No
A	F	Y	Y	Yes
B	F	Y	Y	Yes
B	F	N	N	No
B	M	N	Y	Yes
C	F	N	N	Yes
A	M	N	Y	Yes
A	F	N	N	No
C	M	Y	Y	Yes

Table 49: Electronics purchase data.

3. **Partition the data:** Even though we have only a very small data set, we will still partition the data to see the whole process. Naïve Bayes requires two partitions. Using *Purchase* as the target we can do:

```
> library(caret)
> set.seed(2015)
> sam <- createDataPartition(cust$Purchase,
       p = 0.7, list = FALSE)
> train <- cust[sam, ]
> test <- cust[-sam, ]
```

4. **Build the model:** You can build the model by invoking the **R** function *naiveBayes* from the *e1071* package. We first load this package – either by the *library(e1071)* command or by checking the package name in the *Packages* tab.

   Since we are interested in whether or not someone will make a purchase, our target should be *Purchase*. As usual, we explain the function call later. Enter the commands:

   ```
   > library(e1071)
   > cust.nb <- naiveBayes(Purchase ~ . ,
               data = train)
   ```

   That is all there is to it! The **R** variable called *cust.nb* now has the model and we can use it to classify new cases.

   Before jumping ahead, let us dissect the above command a bit. Figure 107 explains.

   The period following the tilde is extremely important! If we want to predict the target attribute based on *all other attributes in the data frame*, then we do not have to spell them out individually and can just use the period after the tilde.

   Of course if we do not want to use all attributes in the data frame other than the target, then we are out of luck as far as using this shortcut is concerned. We will then have to spell out every predictor attribute as Figure 107 explains.

5. **See the model:** We can certainly go ahead and mechanically use the commands to put the model to use for classifying new cases. But it might be worthwhile to understand what *cust.nb* really contains. Type the command *cust.nb* all by itself. You get the output shown in Figure 108. Let us look at it piece by piece.

6. **Explore the model:** You will now learn to read and interpret the output of the model.

   a **First three lines:** The first three lines of the output give general information about the function call.

   b **A-priori probabilities:** The segment starting with *A-priori probabilities* contains useful information. It tells us that half of the cases in the training partition had a value of *No* for the target attribute and half had *Yes*.

summary(train$Purchase)

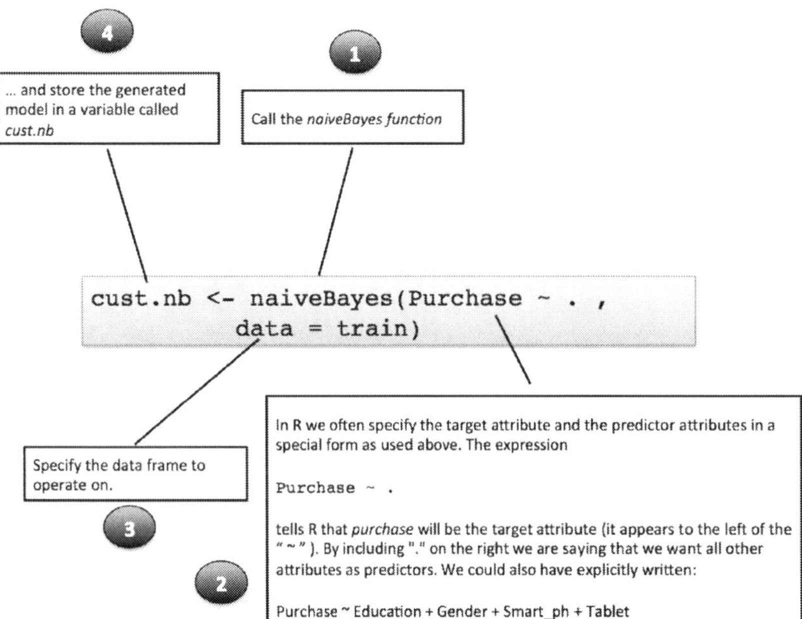

Figure 107: Details of the *naiveBayes* function call.

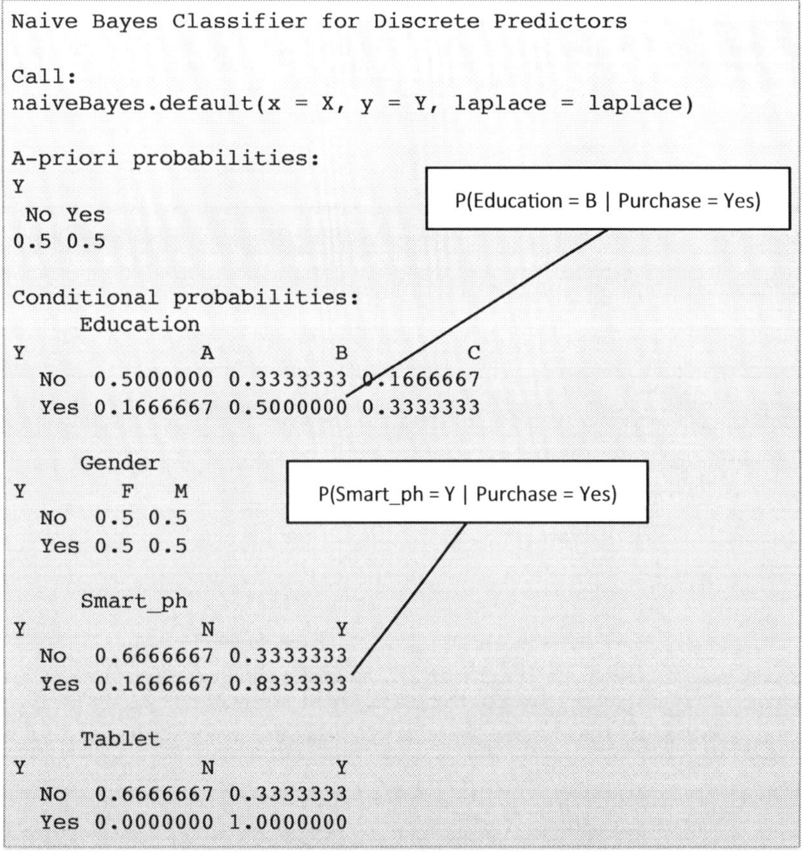

```
Naive Bayes Classifier for Discrete Predictors

Call:
naiveBayes.default(x = X, y = Y, laplace = laplace)

A-priori probabilities:
Y
 No Yes
0.5 0.5

Conditional probabilities:
     Education
Y             A         B         C
  No  0.5000000 0.3333333 0.1666667
  Yes 0.1666667 0.5000000 0.3333333

     Gender
Y       F   M
  No  0.5 0.5
  Yes 0.5 0.5

     Smart_ph
Y             N         Y
  No  0.6666667 0.3333333
  Yes 0.1666667 0.8333333

     Tablet
Y             N         Y
  No  0.6666667 0.3333333
  Yes 0.0000000 1.0000000
```


Figure 108: Naïve Bayes output (with two conditional probabilities indicated).

We can check the training partition and see that 6 of the 12 cases were *No* and the rest were *Yes*.

A-priori probabilities represent the baseline performance for evaluating classification methods

In classification problems, *a-priori* probabilities tell us the proportions of the occurrences of the various values of the target attribute in the data set analyzed. If we had partitioned the data and run some analysis on the training partition alone, then the *a-priori* probability figures pertain to the training partition alone.

We are generally more interested in the *a-priori* probabilities on the overall data. How might we use them?

On the overall data, we have a 50-50 split between *Purchase=Yes* and *Purchase=No*.

In data analytics, it makes little sense to look at the performance of various methods in absolute terms. The value of a method has to be evaluated in comparison to the baseline. For classification problems, *a-priori* probabilities represent that baseline. To see why, suppose we were given the above data and then given a random case to classify as *Yes* (buyer) or *No* (non-buyer) without any additional information about the person. In this situation, since we have equal numbers of buyers and non-buyers, without analytics we can only guess randomly for a 50% performance. We can evaluate the performance of analytics based on how much it improves over this baseline.

We can calculate lift by dividing the correctness percentage of a classification method by the majority *a-priori* probabilities on the whole data

If data analytics can help us to be right 70% of the time, then that would represent a lift of 70/50 or 1.4; a 40% improvement.

c **Conditional probabilities:** The segment starting with *Conditional probabilities* shows the various conditional probabilities that Naïve Bayes will use in calculating the appropriate probability of a specific case falling in a particular class. At this point we will do well to recap our goal. With reference to the specific task on hand, given a new case with specific values for the predictor attributes *Education*, *Gender*, *Smart_ph* and *Tablet*, we would like to classify the case as *Yes*, meaning buyer, or *No*, meaning non-buyer. For example, given a case with *Education* = *B*, *Gender* = *M*,

Smart_ph = *Y* and *Tablet* = *N*, how should we classify it? To do this, we need to calculate the following:

$$P\left(Purchase{=}Yes|Education{=}B, Gender{=}M, Smart\_ph{=}Y, Tablet{=}N\right)$$

We have already seen that because of the curse of dimensionality, we might not have sufficient data to calculate the above probability and that *Naïve Bayes* uses the following individual conditional probabilities to calculate a good approximation for the above expression:

$$P\left(Education = B|Purchase = Yes\right)$$
$$P\left(Gender = M|Purchase = Yes\right)$$
$$P\left(Smart\_ph = Y|Purchase = Yes\right)$$
$$P\left(Tablet = N|purchase = Yes\right)$$

Figure 108 shows us that the Naïve Bayes method has calculated precisely these kinds of conditional probabilities.

d **Verify a few calculations:** What value has Naive Bayes calculated for

$P\left(Education = B|Purchase = Yes\right)$?

Under the conditional probabilities, in the *Education* section, we see 0.5 in the row for *Yes* and the column for *B*. How did it arrive at that number?

Looking at the data in the training partition, we can see that we have 6 cases with *Purchase* = *Yes*. Of these three have *Education* = *B*. Therefore the conditional probability evaluates to 3/6, or 0.5.

In similar vein, can you find the probability in the output and explain how the system arrived at the number for

$P\left(Smart\_ph = Y|Purchase = Yes\right)$?

Did you get 5/6 or 0.833333? We find this number in the *Smart_ph* section of the conditional probabilities in the row for *Yes* and the column for *Smart_ph* = *Y*. Going back to the data, we see 6 cases with *Purchase=Yes*, of which 5 have *Smart_ph* = *Y*. The conditional probability therefore is 5/6 or 0.8333333.

7. **Generate the error matrix on training data:** We first check the quality of the model on the training data:

```
> pred.train <- predict(cust.nb, train)
> table(train$Purchase, pred.train,
      dnn = c("Actual", "Predicted"))
```

Figure 109 shows the error matrix on the training partition.

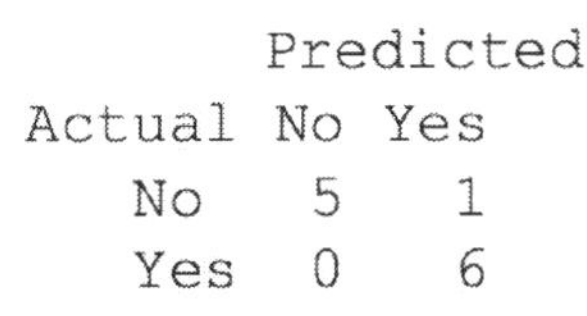

```
         Predicted
Actual No Yes
   No   5   1
   Yes  0   6
```

Figure 109: Error matrix on the training partition

8. **Use the model for classification:** Now that the model contains all the conditional probabilities, we can use it to classify new cases.
   We can use the *predict* function to classify the cases in the test partition and create an error matrix:

```
> pred.test <- predict(cust.nb, test)
> table(test$Purchase, pred.test,
      dnn = c("Actual", "Predicted"))
```

   Figure 110 explains the command's components. Figure 111 shows the resulting error matrix.
   Given the extremely limited data we used, we cannot really hope for a good model and the performance on the test partition shows that. With a 50% performance it provides no lift.

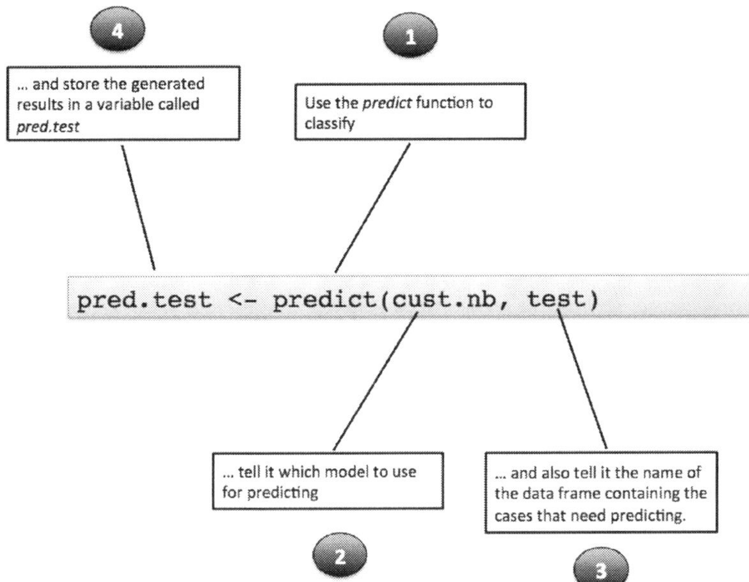

Figure 110: Making predictions with a Naïve Bayes model.

9. **Summary:** We have now seen all the steps involved in running Naïve Bayes on a small data set. You can use exactly the same steps on a large data set as well. Table 50 briefly recaps all the steps.

```
         Predicted
Actual No Yes
   No   2   0
   Yes  2   0
```

Figure 111: Error matrix on the test partition

Table 50: Summary of steps for *Naive Bayes Analysis*.

Step no	Description	R command	Remarks
1	Read the data	`cust = read.csv("nb-example.csv")`	

2	Partition	`library(caret)`
		`set.seed(2015)`
		`sam <- createDataPartition(cust$Purchase,`
		`p = 0.7, list = FALSE)`
		`train <- cust[sam, ]`
		`test <- cust[-sam, ]`	

3	Build the model	`library(e1071)`
		`cust.nb <- naiveBayes(Purchase ~ . ,`
		`data = train)`	

4	Look at the output	`cust.nb`	Explore the conditional probabilities and the a-priori probabilities

5	Check the model's performance on the training partition	`pred.train <- predict(cust.nb, train)`
		`table(train$Purchase, pred.train,`
		`dnn = c("Actual", "Predicted"))`
			First generate the predictions and then generate the error matrix

6	Check the model's performance on the test partition	`pred.test <- predict(cust.nb, test)`
		`table(test$Purchase, pred.test,`
		`dnn = c("Actual", "Predicted"))`
			Compare performance on training with that on test

Lab assignment 5: Naïve Bayes

You can find the answers starting from page 378

Load the file *car-classification.csv*[20] into **R**. Take a look at the data. It has input information about *price, maint, doors, persons, boot* and *safety*. The variable *acceptability* gives the level of acceptability of a car with specific values for these input attributes. We would like to build a classification model to classify new cases for their acceptability. All attributes, even though shown as numbers are actually categorical. Before starting your work, convert all attributes to categorical (factors).

[20] M Bohanec and V Rajkovic. Expert system shell for decision making. *Sistemica*, pages 145–147, 1990

1. What is the target attribute?
2. How many rows does your data frame have?
3. All attributes other than *acceptability* have numeric values and **R** will treat them as such by default. Recall that *Naïve Bayes* requires all of the attributes to be categorical. Convert all attributes other than *acceptability* to factors.
4. Partition the data into two partitions (70-30) as needed for Naïve

Bayes.

5. Build a Naive Bayes model based on the data in the training partition.
6. From the model created – what is the a-priori probability of *acc*?
7. Which value of *acceptability* has the highest a-priori probability ?
8. Look at the conditional probabilities for *safety*. Explain what the three elements on the first row mean. What conditional probabilities do they represent?
9. What do you see that is common to every single row of every conditional probability matrix generated by the model? Why is this so?
10. What is the name of the **R** function you use to classify new cases?
11. Use the model to classify the cases in the training and test partitions and store the results in a new variable. Generate the error matrix for each partition.
12. Based on the error matrix of the training partition, what proportion of acceptable cars (*acc*) were classified as acceptable (*acc*)?
13. Based on the error matrix of the test partition, what proportion of acceptable cars (*acc*) were classified as acceptable (*acc*)?
14. What was the overall percentage of errors on the training partition?
15. What was the overall percentage of errors on the test partition?
16. What lift does data mining provide in this case based on overall error rate?

Regression

In the chapter on *Classification*, we studied techniques that assigned cases to categories like *Buyer* and *Non-Buyer* or *Normal mail* and *Spam mail*. Sometimes though, just assigning a case to a category does not suffice and we need to predict a precise number.

We have already encountered an example of this in our early discussion of the Netflix competition (on page 5). Netflix wanted a method to predict the ratings (a number between 1 and 5) that its customers would assign to movies that they have not yet seen.

People might want a numerical prediction in the following situations as well:

- A company wants to predict the number of people who will visit its kiosks at an industry expo so as to plan out the number of kiosks to make available.
- A stock broker wants to predict the price of a specific stock.
- A cruise operator, in the process of designing a new cruise route, wants to predict the average number of customers per voyage during a specific period.
- From outside the world of business, weather forecasters routinely need to determine the high and low temperatures for future time periods.

In this chapter we cover techniques for making specific numerical predictions.

Quality of a Regression Model

Before looking at specific regression models, let us look at how we will evaluate the quality of a regression model.

Recall that we used the *classification-confusion matrix* or the *error matrix* to evaluate the performance of classification models. How about regression models? Clearly the closeness of the predicted values to the actual values of the target attribute will play a big role in the process. But what exactly? Let us consider an example.

Suppose a resort has built a model to predict the amount of money that each family that has a future reservation will spend at the resort. For the present discussion, we will not need to talk about the predictor attributes used in the model. We concern ourselves with just the actual and predicted value of the target attribute, *Spending*

As with classification models, we first evaluate the model's quality on the data using which it was built – the *training* partition. If this meets our expectations, we then evaluate the model's performance on independent hold-out data – the *test* partition – to check if the performance obtained still holds up.

Accordingly, we first compare the model predictions against the actual values. Table 51 shows some hypothetical data on model predictions and actual values.

Case	Spending-$	Prediction-$
1	500	550
2	1,000	900
3	800	1,000
4	300	500
5	950	930
6	450	550
7	670	550
8	300	400
9	700	700
10	780	700

Table 51: Hypothetical actual and predicted values.

From the data in Table 51, we can calculate the error and the squared error for each case as shown in Table 52. The table also shows the mean (average) of the squared errors and also the square root of this, the *Root Mean Square* or *RMSE*.

The mean of the squared errors tells us the squared error that the model produced per case, and square root of this gives us the *Root Mean Square Error* or *RMSE*.

If we let (as is conventional) $\hat{y}$ stand for the model prediction, and y_i stand for the value of the target attribute for the ith case, then we can calculate the total sum of squared errors *SSE* as:

$$SSE = \sum_{i=1}^{n} (\hat{y} - y_i)^2$$

and, assuming n cases, we can calculate $RMSE$ as:

$$RMSE = \sqrt{\frac{SSE}{n}}$$

Case	Spending-\$	Prediction-\$	Error	Sqr err
1	500	550	50	2500
2	1000	900	-100	10000
3	800	1000	200	40000
4	300	500	200	40000
5	950	930	-20	400
6	450	550	100	10000
7	670	550	-120	14400
8	300	400	100	10000
9	700	700	0	0
10	780	700	-80	6400
			Mean squared error	13,370
			Root Mean Squared Error or RMSE	115.6

Table 52: Errors, squared errors and RMS error.

The error in each row of Table 52 has units of \$, and the squared errors and the mean squared error have units of \$^{2} – not particularly meaningful. However, once we take the square root of the mean squared error, we return to having \$ as the unit.

The $RMSE$ tells us that, on the average, we can expect the model prediction to be off by \$ $\pm$ 115.6 on the average. If this seems acceptable, then we can use the model. Data analysts do not use any hard and fast rule to determine the acceptable values of $RMSE$. The context alone can guide us on this.

Simple Linear Regression

For regression tasks, we want to use data analytics to find a way of computing the values of the target or dependent attribute based on the independent or predictor attributes. Specifically we had said that we seek a function f:

$$target\ attribute = f\left(predictor_1,\quad predictor_2,\quad predictor_3 ...\right)$$

Take a look at the following two equations:

$$y = 32 + 5x$$

$$spending = 254 + 1.37 * family\_size + 0.08 * income + 70 * days$$

The above examples represent *linear* equations. Note from the above that the variables on the right hand side of each of the above equations (x in the first example and $family\_size$, $income$ and $days$ in the second) appear at the first power – they are not squared or cubed and so on.

In *Simple Linear Regression*, we seek to find a linear function of just a single predictor attribute to calculate the value of the target attribute. This might not seem like a realistic task. Getting good predictions on real-life data would require us to use many more predictors. However, we will use this discussion of *Simple Linear Regression* as a way to ease into *Multiple Linear Regression* where we can have many predictor attributes. We explain the important concepts through *Simple Linear Regression*.

In *Simple Linear Regression*, we seek a linear function f:

$$predicted\_target = f\,(predictor)$$

We named the left hand size as *predicted_target* to distinguish it from the actual value of the target attribute. Recall that during the model development phase in data mining we do have the actual value of the target attribute available to us. The above equation only helps us to calculate a predicted value for it so that we can compare it with the actual value to see how well the model performs.

Let us make things more concrete.

Suppose in some situation, we are trying to predict the level of spending during a business trip, based on the number of days of travel. We have lots of historical information for the number of days and the corresponding spending. Let us suppose we have used *linear regression* and obtained the following equation which does a good job on the available data:

$$predicted\_spending = 50 + 74.5 * days$$

For future cases, given only the value of *days*, we can use the above equation to predict *spending*. For each future case that we consider, the value of *days* could be different. In that sense *days* is a *variable*. However, the 50 and 74.5 remain fixed no matter what the new case is. In this sense they are *constant*.

More generally, *Simple Linear Regression* seeks an equation of the form:

$$predicted\_target = \beta_0 + \beta_1\ predictor$$

In a general case, we would not know the values of the constants and have hence used β_0 and β_1 to represent the constants. People commonly use Greek letters (often with numeric subscripts, as above) to represent *constant values* – don't let these scare you.

Why do we seek a *linear* function? Why not something more complex? Do real-life phenomena tend to exhibit linear behavior?

In statistics, linear regression has a long legacy. This, despite the fact that real-life phenomena seldom exhibit linear behavior. For example, if it takes one towel an hour to dry under the sun, how long does it take ten towels to dry? Would you consider that linear?

Despite a very complex, non-linear real world, linear regression has arguably been the most widely used data analysis technique mainly because of its relative simplicity and its ability to provide reasonably good results when used "properly." We will discuss later what we mean by "proper" use. In fact *Linear Regression* has become so widely used, especially in the social sciences and business that some scholars seem to have forgotten that we use it only for convenience and that it is usually not synonymous with *truth*.

We should use *linear regression* only when we suspect that there is at least an approximately linear relationship between the predictor and target attributes. To check this, we can eyeball the relationship through a scatterplot. For an illustration, let us revisit the Boston housing data[21] [22] which shows data on several Boston neighborhoods. Although the data set has 14 attributes, we will look at only two of them *RM*, which shows the average number of rooms in homes in a neighborhood, and *MEDV*, which shows the median value of home prices in a neighborhood.

[21] D. Harrison and D.L. Rubinfeld. Hedonic prices and the demand for clean air. *J. Environ. Economics & Management*, pages 81–102, 1978

[22] K. Bache and M. Lichman. UCI machine learning repository, 2013. URL `http://archive.ics.uci.edu/ml`

Figure 112 shows the scatterplot. From it we can see an approximate linear relationship. If the relationship were perfectly linear, then all the points would have been on a straight single line. As the average number of rooms increases, so does the median value of homes. However, we can find many exceptions too.

Several neighborhoods with higher average number of rooms than some others have lower median values. Can you spot any?

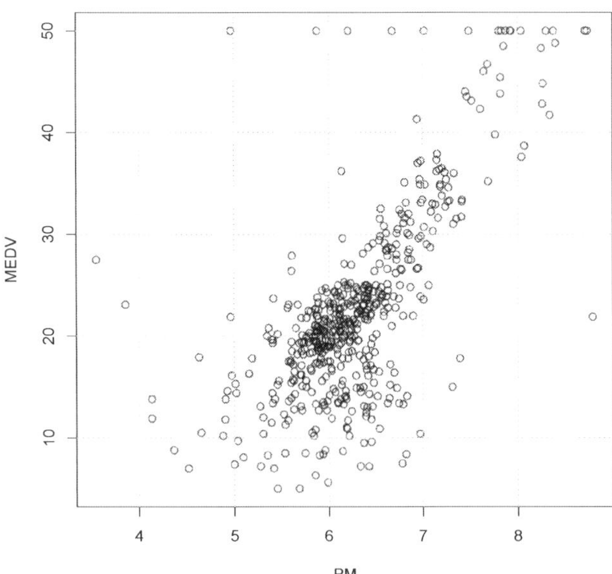

Figure 112: Scatterplot of average number of rooms and median home values of Boston neighborhoods from the Boston Housing data set

Figure 113 shows one example. Why do such anomalies exist?

Number of rooms alone does not determine a home's value. We would need to look at various other factors. For example, homes in upscale areas of downtown Boston might have fewer rooms than those in many suburbs, but would likely be priced much higher. In this example, we are looking at just one predictor and should not be surprised that it does not completely account for the price.

Recall from our discussion on page 44 that we cannot realistically seek perfect answers from data analytics and that doing even marginally better as a result of the process can be very beneficial.

Now let us understand how exactly *Simple Linear Regression* finds the linear function described earlier. We will skip the mathematical details – let **R** deal with those – and just convey the underlying intuition.

Consider the simplified hypothetical scatterplot (Figure 114) of heights and weights of schoolgirls in a certain age group in a particular school. The scatterplot also shows a line that seems to capture the essence of this approximately linear relationship. We would like to see if we can use this line as the linear function that we are looking for – our linear model.

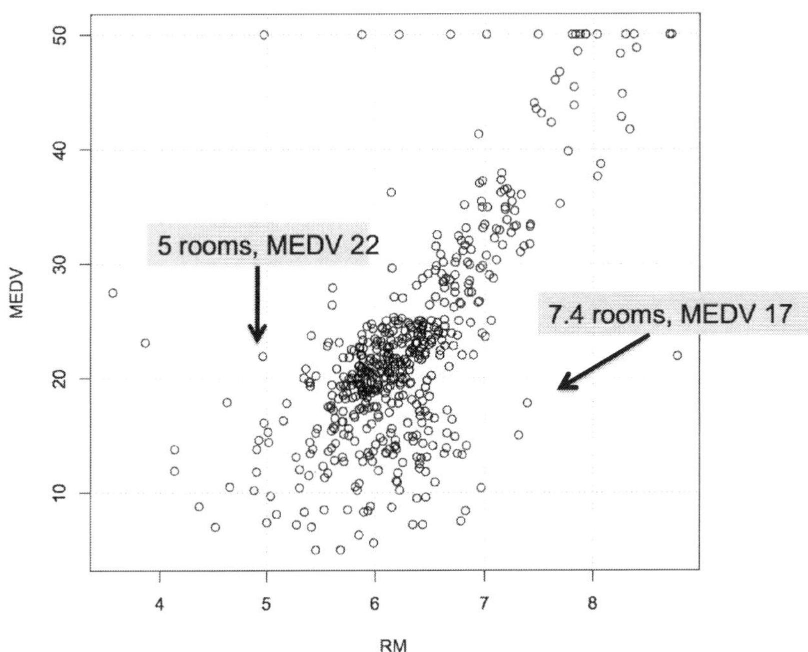

Figure 113: One example of a neighborhood having lower average number of rooms and higher MEDV

As expected, we see only an approximate linear relationship, with the points scattered close to the line.

If we use this line as our linear model, then we would use the line to predict the weight of a student whose height is given to us.

Figure 115 shows the same scatterplot with the line, and a specific case labeled as A. Case A does not fall on the line. If we used this line as our linear model, then we would have some error for this point – six kgs, to be precise. For a height of 165 cms, our model would predict a weight of 70 kgs. The actual *weight* is 64 kgs. The difference represents the error that the model would make for this case.

Continuing in the same vein, Figure 116 shows the error for three cases. Clearly, we can calculate the error for all the cases and add up all the errors to get an idea of how good a line we have got. If the line were perfect, then it would run through all the points and the total error would be zero. On the other hand, if the line were far away from many points then the total error would be high. Thus the lower the error, the closer the line is to many points.

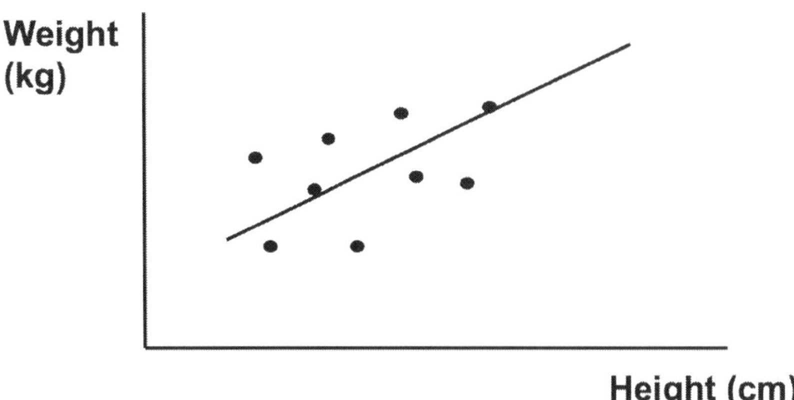

Figure 114: Hypothetical scatterplot of heights and weights of schoolgirls.

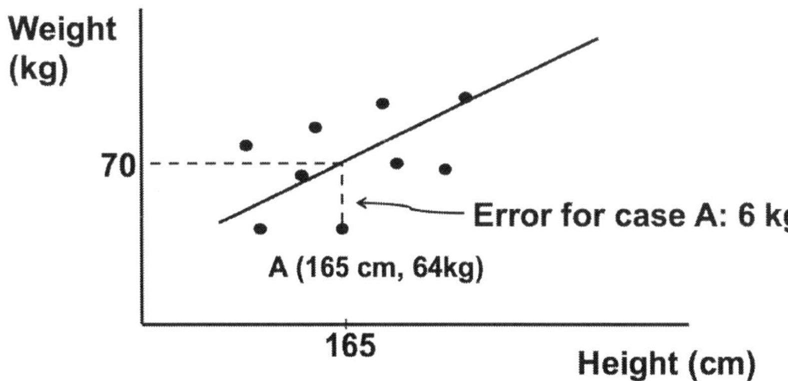

Figure 115: Scatterplot showing the error – length of the dashed line – for case A.

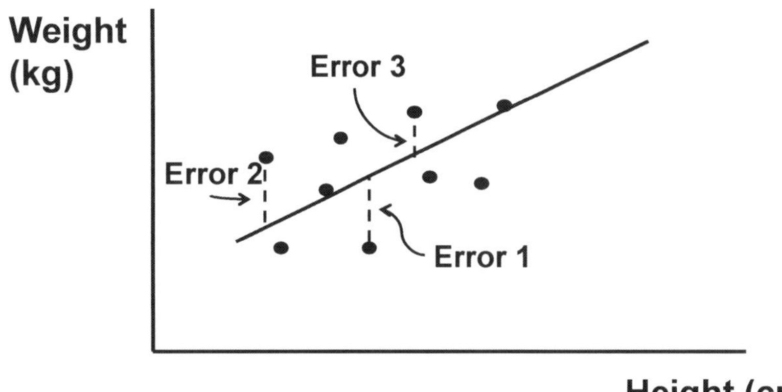

Figure 116: Scatterplot showing the error for three cases.

Table 53 shows some hypothetical cases and the errors for each.

Case	Height (cms)	Actual weight (kgs)	Predicted weight (kgs)	Error
1	158	64	61	-3
2	162	68	64	-4
3	159	59	62	3
4	165	68	65	-3
5	175	68	72	4
6	170	62	69	7
7	166	69	66	-3
8	177	73	73	0
9	185	82	78	-4
10	177	75	73	-2

Table 53: Computing the error for each case.

If we calculate the error for a case as (*predicted value* − *actual value*) then the error would be positive for cases below the line (*predicted value* > *actual value*); negative for cases above the line (*predicted value* < *actual value*) and zero for points on the line. If we simply add up the errors for each point then the positives and negatives will cancel out and we might get a small total error even though many points did not fall on the line. To avoid this problem, statisticians get rid of the negative sign by squaring each error to get the *squared error*. They then add up the *squared errors* to get the *total squared error*.

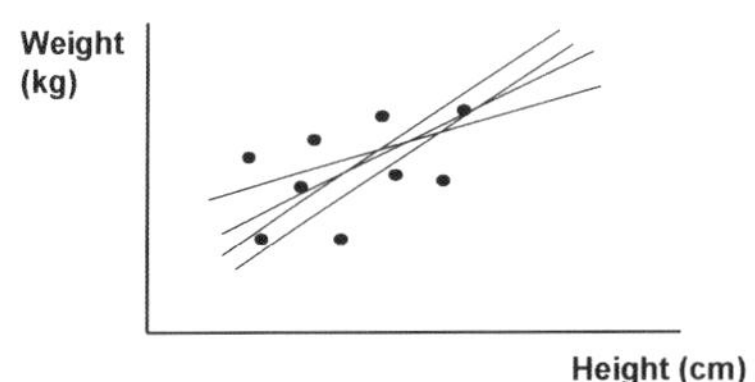

Figure 117: We can draw an infinite number of lines through a set of points on a scatterplot ....

Figure 117 shows that we can draw any number of lines through the scatterplot. Which one does *Simple Linear Regression* choose?

We have already seen how to compute the *total squared error* for a line. So it would be possible to calculate the *total squared error* for each possible line and choose the one that has the lowest *total squared error*. This would be the line that stays closest to as many points as possible. Statisticians call this the *Least Squares Line*.

We face a small glitch however. How do we find this *Least Squares Line*? Can we try each possible line and calculate the error for it? Given that we have infinitely many possible lines, we would never finish this process!

Fortunately for us, Sir Isaac Newton invented Calculus to solve just such thorny problems. We will not go into the details here, but the good news is that we can find the best line without trying infinite lines by applying a fairly simple formula. **R** will perform the computation when we use it for *Simple Linear Regression* and *Multiple Linear Regression* later.

To summarize, *Simple Linear Regression* finds the *Least Squares*

Line, the line that runs as close as possible (in the least squares sense) to the points on the scatterplot.

Let us now see the connection between the line and the equations that we saw earlier. In *Simple Linear regression* we seek to find an equation of the form:

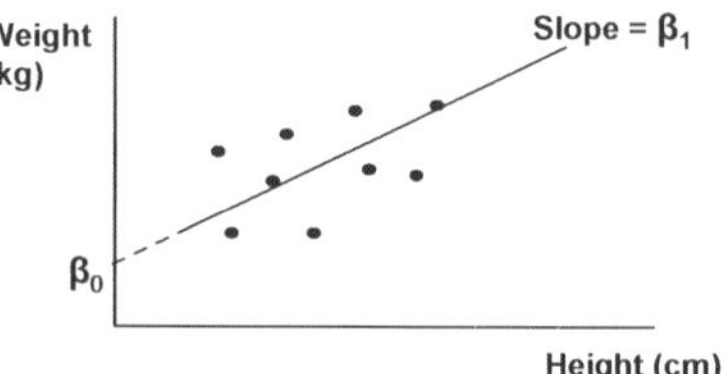

Figure 118: Intercept and slope of the least squares line.

$$predicted\_weight = \beta_0 + \beta_1 height$$

Figure 118 shows the least squares line for our scatterplot and extends the line to intersect with the x axis – which it meets at β_0.

β_1 represents the slope of the line – the change in predicted weight for a unit change in height.

Figure 118 brings us to an important point about the proper use of the regression results. We computed (or asked **R** or some other tool to compute) the regression equation for us so that we could use it to compute the weights of future cases for whom we knew the heights.

Let us suppose that we find that the following regression equation works well for our data.

$$predicted\_weight = 45.35 + +0.095 * height$$

The equation says that the weight of someone with a height of zero would be 45.35 kg – absurd; and that someone who is 190 cm tall would weigh around 64 kgs – quite unlikely for a healthy person over six feet tall. Despite these absurdities, the regression equation might still be very good *for the range of data on which it was developed*. Suppose we had developed the model on data on a large number of eighth grade girls in the US, the regression model might be very valid when used in that specific group, but we should be wary of using it on third graders or even to eighth grade girls from Kenya.

Use regression results only for data in the range used to develop the model

Quality of a Linear Regression Model

Given a set of cases, **R** or any number of other tools can always find a regression equation for us. Before using the model, we need to determine the quality of the model.

As we discussed earlier on page 231, we can use the *Root Mean Square Error* or *RMSE* as a measure of the performance of the regression model. However, with linear regression, we have other measures as well, which we describe below.

After running a regression, we get a lot of output information beyond just the regression equation. The tools give us much of this additional information to help us decide if the model is good enough for our needs. We will now see some important concepts that will help us interpret the output properly.

As before, we need a baseline to measure the regression against. That is, we need to look at what we might have done without any predictive model.

Once again, let us say that we have data on the heights and weights of various students and have built a regression model to predict the weight given the height. If we are given a new person and not told their height, what would be our best prediction for the weight?

In the absence of any predictor information – information about the height – our best approach would be to predict the weight of the person to be the average weight across all the cases. That approach does not guarantee a very good prediction, but over many attempts, this will give us the best chance of minimizing the average error.

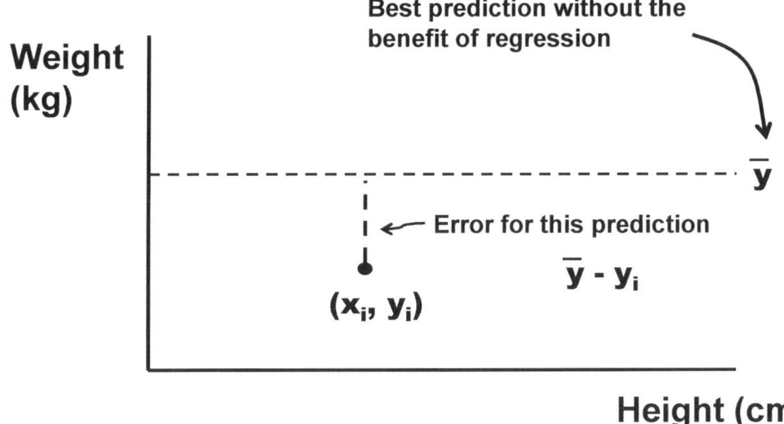

Figure 119: Baseline: In the absence of a regression model and the value of the predictor attribute *height*, our best strategy would be to predict the weight of any person to be the average weight across the data set.

Figure 119 shows this scenario. In the figure, we have labeled the case as (x_i, y_i) considering this to be the ith case. Here x stands for the *height* and y for the *weight* and the subscript indicate the case number within the data set.

For the ith case, in the absence of any predictor information, we will predict the weight as the average $\bar{y}$. and therefore the error would be $(\bar{y} - y_i)$.

Before the regression model and without knowing the value of the predictor attribute *height*, we might have wondered why the weight for this case is below average. Once we are given the value of *height*, we might say "Aha, this person is quite short. No wonder they are below average in weight." Of course we can only make this statement because we believe that height and weight are related – as confirmed by the regression.

Without the benefit of the regression, we can see the variation in the students' weights, but we do not know the reason. Once we run the regression and see the results, we see that height and weight are related and therefore say that the regression *explains* the variation in weights.

Does our regression explain *all* of the variation in weight?

If that was true, then all of the points would have been exactly *on* the regression line. Since that fortuitous event has not occurred, we know that our regression does not *explain* all of the variation. The proportion of variation that the regression line explains determines its quality. That is, the more of the variation the regression explains, the better the model is. Let us see how we can calculate this proportion.

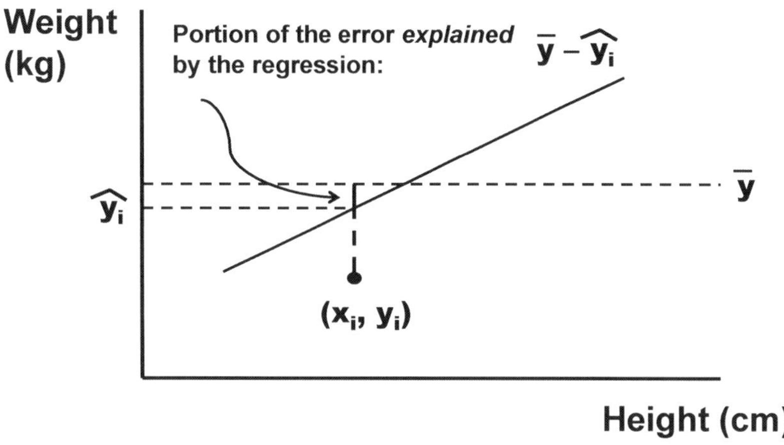

Figure 120: Armed with the regression, our prediction is now on the regression line and better than before.

Figure 120 shows that with the regression line available, our prediction is a little closer to the actual value. We use the "hat" sign to denote model predictions and hence have used $\hat{y}$ in the figure to represent the regression prediction. The distance between the mean $\bar{y}$ and $\hat{y}$ represents the amount of variation for this case which the regression *explains*.

As shown in Figure 121, the regression line does not *explain* the rest of the error $\hat{y} - y_i$. We now have a basis to calculate

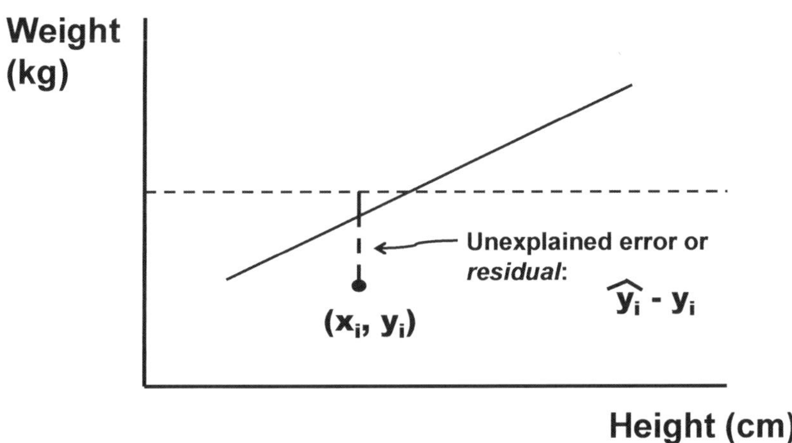

Figure 121: The part of the total error that the regression cannot *explain*.

the quality of the regression – consider the proportion of the error that the regression *explains*. To explain the concept of the proportion of error that a regression model explains, we have based our foregoing discussion on just one case. However, we cannot base our evaluation of the regression on one case alone. We must consider all the cases in the data set. We describe below how we can extend the above discussion from one case to the overall data set.

Recall from our discussion of data partitioning on page 49 that we evaluate the quality of a model using data that we never used in building the model. Before doing this, we first see how the model performs on the data that we used to build the model. If the model does poorly even on this, then we need not even bother trying to use new data on it and can discard it right away. In the following discussion, when we refer to data set, we mean the training partition.

Let us look first at the baseline. In the absence of the regression model we would have predicted the mean as the value of the target attribute for each case. The error for case i would then be $\bar{y} - y_i$. We have already seen that statisticians use squared errors instead of raw errors to get rid of negative signs. Therefore, assuming that we have n cases, we can calculate the total squared error across all cases, the *Total Sum of Squares* or *TSS* as:

$$TSS = \sum_{i=1}^{n} (\bar{y} - y_i)^2$$

TSS represents the baseline amount of squared error that

we can expect in the absence of the regression model. Once we have the regression model, we know that for case i the regression *explains the* difference between the regression's prediction and the mean or $\hat{y} - \bar{y}$. Again aggregating this across all cases, we get the *Sum of Squares Regression* or *SSR* as:

$$SSR = \sum_{i=1}^{n} (\hat{y}_i - \bar{y})^2$$

We had calculated the unaccounted error for a single case to be $\hat{y} - y_i$. Aggregating across all cases as above yields the *Sum of Squared Errors* or *SSE* as:

$$SSE = \sum_{i=1}^{n} (\hat{y}_i - y_i)^2$$

Figure 122 summarizes these variability measures.

Therefore the proportion of the total error that the regression explains – the *Coefficient of Determination*, usually referred to as R^2 can be calculated as:

$$R^2 = \frac{SSR}{TSS}$$

For simple linear regression R^2 and the *correlation coefficient* are equal.

$$TSS = \sum (y - \bar{y})^2$$

Measure of total variability in the dependent variable

$$SSR = \sum (\hat{y} - \bar{y})^2$$

Variability accounted for by the regression

$$SSE = \sum (y - \hat{y})^2$$

Unaccounted variability

Figure 122: Variability measures in linear regression

Review 13: Simple Linear Regression

You can find the answers to these questions on page 381

Table 54 shows a portion of a large data set that contains the annual restaurant expenses of families and their annual income per member (annual income divided by number of family members). We would like to build a simple linear regression model to predict the annual restaurant expense for future cases knowing only the annual income per member for a family.

rest_exp	income_pm
500	20000
600	30000
510	15000
520	25000
650	35000
...	...

Table 54: Per member family income and family annual restaurant expenses.

Answer the following questions based on Table 54.

1. Using the column headings as attribute names, what is the target attribute?
2. What is the predictor attribute?
3. Which of the following represent correct forms of simple linear regression models for the problem (with the Greek letters representing the regression coefficients or constants). Select **all** applicable options. As is conventional, we have used the "hat" notation to indicate the predicted value for an attribute.
   a. $\widehat{income\_pm} = \beta_0 + \beta_1\, rest\_exp$
   b. $\widehat{rest\_exp} = \beta_0 + \beta_1\, income\_pm$
   c. $\widehat{rest\_exp} = \beta_0 + \beta_1\, income\_pm + \epsilon$
   d. $\widehat{rest\_exp} = \beta_0 + \beta_1\, income\_pm^2$
   e. $income\_pm = \alpha_0 + \alpha_1\, rest\_exp + \epsilon$
   f. $\widehat{rest\_exp} = \delta_0 + \delta_1\, income\_pm$
   g. $rest\_exp = \beta_0 + \beta_1\, income\_pm$
4. Let us assume that we have built a simple linear regression model for the above situation and find the intercept to be 366 and the regression coefficient for the predictor attribute to be 0.0076.
   a. What would the predicted annual restaurant expense be for a family with zero annual income per member?

b. If the annual income per member increases, would the predicted annual restaurant expense increase or decrease?
c. If the annual income per member increases by $10,000, by how much would the predicted annual restaurant expense change?
d. Given a family with an annual per-member income of $200,000, what would the family's predicted annual restaurant expense be?
e. Let us suppose that a family has an annual per-member income of $12,000 and an annual restaurant expense of $850. What is the error (or, more correctly, *residual*) for this case based on our regression model?

5. The regression coefficients mentioned in Question 4 were actually arrived at using only the first six rows of Table 104 Answer the following based on the data in Table 104 and the slope and intercept mentioned in Question 4.

   a. Compute TSS (total sum of squares), SSE (sum of squared errors) and SSR (sum of squares regression)?
   b. Do the numbers add up?
   c. How much of the variation in the target attribute does the regression explain?

Lab 13: Simple Linear Regression using **R**

Pre-requisite(s)

✓ You should have read the portions of the book dealing with regression (page 231), quality of a regression model (page 231) and simple linear regression (page 233) and answered the associated review questions.

✓ You should have set up **R**, downloaded the practice data files and pointed **R** to the location of the files.

Objective

After completing this lab, you will be able to:

✓ Use **R** to perform a *Simple Linear Regression* analysis.

✓ Interpret the results and construct the regression equation.

✓ Use the model to classify new cases.

Overview

In this lab, we will learn how to apply simple linear regression in **R**.

In data analytics, we will seldom have just a single predictor attribute. We however, use *SImple Linear Regression* as a way to ease our way into multiple-linear regression.

The base **R** installation includes linear regression analysis and hence we will not need to load any specialized package for this.

We will take data on some attributes of various automobiles and build a simple linear regression model to predict *mpg* using *horsepower*. That is, *mpg* will be our target attribute and *horsepower* will be the predictor attribute.

So we are trying to build the following linear model:

$$\hat{mpg} = \beta_0 + \beta_1\, horsepower$$

Note the "hat" on top of *mpg*. Recall that it refers to the value that the model computes – as opposed to the real *mpg*.

Activity steps

1. **Read the data file:** Read the data from the file *auto-mpg.csv* into a data frame called *auto*.

```
> auto <- read.csv("auto-mpg.csv")
```

2. **Look at the data:** The data frame has information about 398 automobiles[23]. Table 55 shows an extract of the data. The attributes should be self-explanatory.

[23] J Ross Quinlan. Combining instance-based and model-based learning. In *ICML*, page 236, 1993

No	mpg	cylinders	displacement	horsepower	weight	acceleration	model_year	car_name
1	28	4	140	90	2264	15.5	71	chevrolet vega
2	19	3	70	97	2330	13.5	72	mazda rx2 coupe
3	36	4	107	75	2205	14.5	82	honda accord
4	28	4	97	92	2288	17	72	datsun 510 (sw)
5	21	6	199	90	2648	15	70	amc gremlin
6	23	4	115	95	2694	15	75	audi 100ls
7	15.5	8	304	120	3962	13.9	76	amc matador
8	32.9	4	119	100	2615	14.8	81	datsun 200sx
9	16	6	250	105	3897	18.5	75	chevroelt chevelle
10	13	8	318	150	3755	14	76	dodge d100
...	...	...	...	...	...	...	...	...

Table 55: Extract of automobile data.

   We will build a regression model to predict *mpg* based on *horsepower* alone. We will not use any of the other available attributes as predictors now.

3. **Look at the relationship:** We can examine the strength of the linear relationship between the target and predictor attributes.

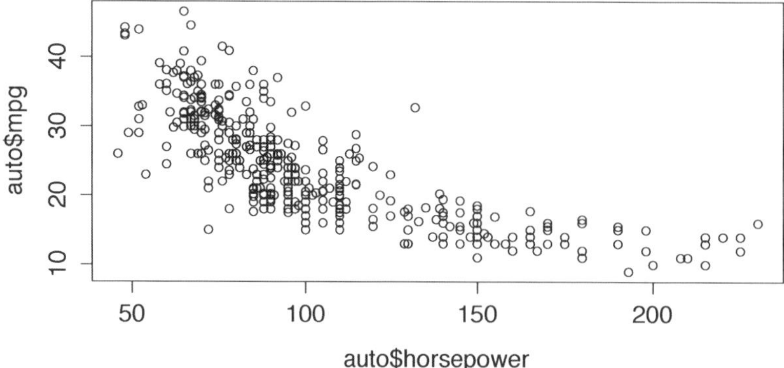

Figure 123: Scatterplot of *horsepower* vs. *mpg*.

From Figure 123 we see the expected negative relationship. The relationship seems non-linear in the sense that we would expect that a smooth curved line will fit the data better. Nevertheless, we will go ahead and build a linear model. (With such an obvious non-linear relationship, we would ordinarily not build a linear model directly. We could either build a non-linear model (perhaps one with a quadratic term), or build a linear model to predict *log(mpg)* based on *horsepower*. We will not look at those options here.)

4. **Partition the data:** Linear regression requires two partitions. Create them now:

```
> library(caret)
> set.seed(2015)
> sam <- createDataPartition(auto$mpg,
      p=0.7, list = FALSE)
> train <- auto[sam, ]
> test <- auto[-sam, ]
```

5. **Build the model:** You can build the model on the training partition by invoking the **R** function *lm* as shown below. As usual, we will explain the function call shortly.

```
> auto.lm <- lm(mpg ~ horsepower, data = train)
```

That is all there is to it! The **R** variable *auto.lm* now has the model and we can use it to find the regression equation, evaluate its performance and to classify new cases

Before jumping ahead, let us dissect the above command a bit. Figure 124 explains.

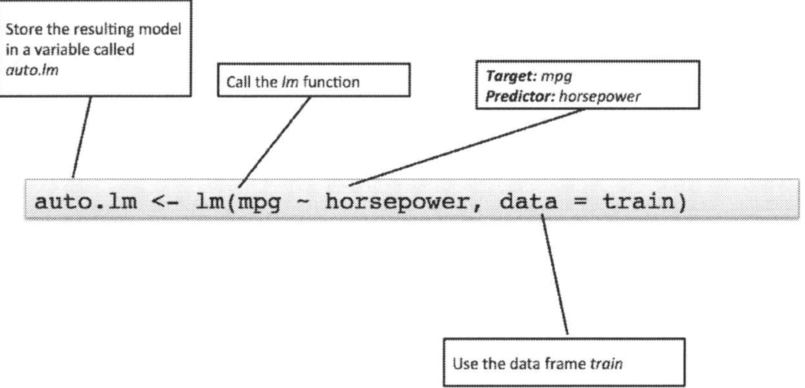

Figure 124: Details of the *lm* function call for linear regression.

6. **View the regression coefficients:** Let us first look at the basic elements of the model:

```
> auto.lm
```

Figure 125 shows the basic output you get by just typing the model name. This shows the regression coefficients β_0 – Intercept, and β_1 – coefficient of *horsepower*. Based on this output, the regression equation is:

$$\hat{mpg} = 39.5769 - 0.1543\, horsepower$$

```
Call:
lm(formula = mpg ~ horsepower, data = train)

Coefficients:
(Intercept)   horsepower
    39.5769      -0.1543
```

Figure 125: Regression coefficients output by *lm*.

7. **Explore the results in greater detail:**

To see more detailed model output, use the *summary* function with the name of the model as its argument:

```
> summary(auto.lm)
```

Figure 126 shows the more detailed output from the above call and Figure 127 highlights the following important points in the linear regression output:

- **Regression coefficients:** The coefficients shown in the previous output are also shown here. Sometimes you might see the coefficients in scientific notation. For example, consider a coefficient displayed as 1.5e3 (not on the figure). This stands for 1.5 multiplied by 10 raised to the third power, or 1.5 * 1000 or 1500.
- **Significance:** Given any data, linear regression can always calculate a regression equation. Before using a regression model though, we need to assess its quality. When working with relatively small samples from large data sets, we need to be careful to ensure that we do not infer a relationship (coefficient) when in the population there is none.

```
Call:
lm(formula = mpg ~ horsepower, data = train)

Residuals:
    Min      1Q  Median      3Q     Max
-9.5376 -3.1979 -0.4549  2.8608 13.6537

Coefficients:
             Estimate Std. Error t value Pr(>|t|)
(Intercept) 39.576877   0.813420   48.66   <2e-16 ***
horsepower  -0.154350   0.007292  -21.17   <2e-16 ***
---
Signif. codes:  0 '***' 0.001 '**' 0.01 '*' 0.05 '.' 0.1 ' ' 1

Residual standard error: 4.692 on 278 degrees of freedom
Multiple R-squared:  0.6171,	Adjusted R-squared:  0.6157
F-statistic:   448 on 1 and 278 DF,  p-value: < 2.2e-16
```

Figure 126: Simple linear regression output by *lm*.

The significance number for each coefficient tells us the probability that the coefficient is actually zero and that we are observing a different number just because of the quirks of the sample. The closer this coefficient is to zero, the better. The figure of "< -2e-16" tells us that the probability is less than $2 * 10^{-16}$ or extremely small. So we can say that the intercept and the coefficient are significant. The annotations to the right of the significance values can help us to quickly find the level of significance. "***" indicates an extremely high significance (or a probability of almost 0); "**" tells us that the probability is less than or equal to 0.01; "*" implies that it is between 0.01 and 0.05; "." implies that it is between 0.05 and 0.1 and the absence of an annotation tells us that the probability is greater than 0.1 – the coefficient is not significant.

- **RMS Error:** As discussed earlier on page 231 we can use the RMS error or RMSE as a measure of a regression model's quality. In fact when we have large numbers of rows, we do not need to bother about the significance of the regression coefficients (for linear regression). The RMS error of 4.692 tells us that the model's predictions

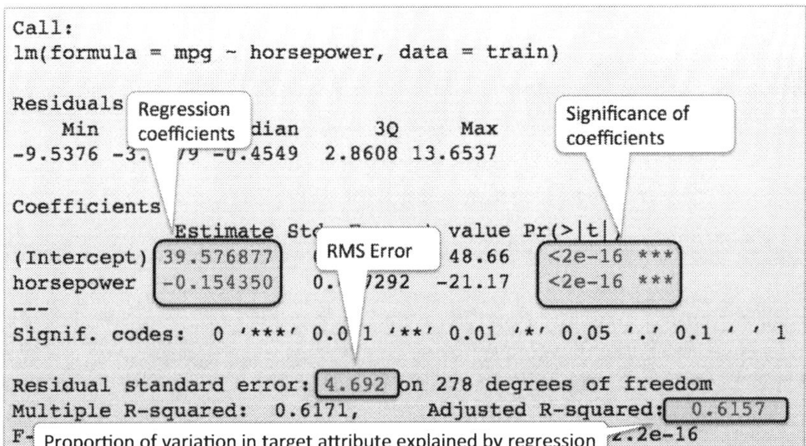

Figure 127: Simple linear regression output by *lm* – various components annotated.

deviate, on the average, by 4.692 from the actual values. We have to determine whether or not this represents a satisfactory value in our context. Is predicting the *mpg* of an automobile to within 4.692 miles per gallon good enough? Well that depends on what we will use the result for. Only the context can tell us if that level of performance is acceptable.

- **Adjusted R-squared:** This figure tells us the extent to which the regression *explains* the variation in the target attribute – as page 244 explained. We have an adjusted R-squared value of 0.6157. Our regression is able to explain 62% of the variation in *mpg*. In other words, 62% of the variation in the target attribute is because of the variations in the predictor attributes. As regressions go, this is a pretty good result. A value close to 1.0 would be extraordinary. This also means that 38% of the variation remains unexplained. Based on the scatterplot, we already know that we can never get a perfect model that explains all of the variation. That can heppen only if all the points lie on a straight line.
  With just a single predictor attribute, we generally cannot expect to get great results. By adding more attributes, we might be able to improve upon this through *Multiple Linear Regression*.

8. **Plot the result:** Let us plot the regression model on top of a scatterplot of the data. This will give us a visual feel for how well the line fits our data. First generate the scatterplot on the training partition:

```
> # In the following command, we first specify the
> # x axis and then the y axis
> # The xlab and ylab arguments below are optional
```

```
> plot(train$horsepower, train$mpg,
      xlab="Horsepower", ylab="mpg")

> # Alternately we could specify what to plot
> # through the familiar formula expression where we
> # specify mpg as the target and cause it to
> # appear on the y axis.
>
> # or we can avoid typing train$ many times and do
> plot(mpg ~ horsepower, data = train)

> # Having used one of the above  approaches to
> # get a scatterplot, now draw the regression line
> # by using the abline function on the already
> # created regression model auto.lm

> abline(auto.lm)
```

After those commands, we get the chart shown in Figure 128. Note that although we have a nice downward-sloping line, we see that the points are not located very close to the line. We have many points pretty far away from the line. This alerts us to the fact that this regression model is not extraordinarily accurate. We should hardly be surprised though – we have used just a single predictor to predict values for a phenomenon that we expect to be influenced by many attributes.

9. **A few caveats:** Sometimes, when using computers to crunch a lot of data, we tend to blindly accept the results without *interpretation*. What is the above regression equation actually telling us?

    - **Make causal inference with caution:** Let us assume that we use linear regression and get a good model based on a lot of data. In analytics, if we have chosen the predictors carefully, we can often use the model for predictions on future cases. However, we cannot implicitly assume that the predictor attributes are *causing* the target attribute to behave as it does. We are only seeing *correlation* and cannot be sure of *causation* and should not make such claims unless we manage to establish that by other means – which we do not cover in this book.
    - **Beware of range of applicability:** The regression equation is telling is that as *horsepower* goes up, *mpg* goes down. This is quite reasonable. It also tells us that at some high level of horsepower, mpg will become zero. We might

Figure 128: Scatterplot and regression line for *mpg* vs. *horsepower* on training partition.

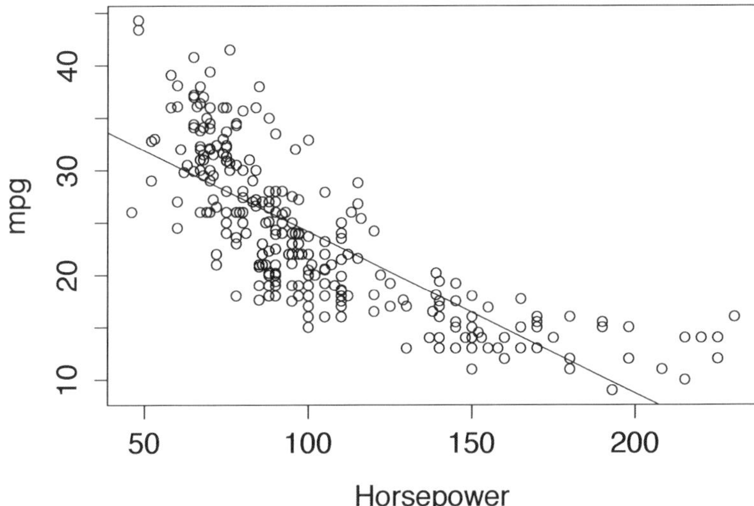

accept that. However, it tells us that for even higher values of horsepower, mpg will become negative – absurd. On the other side, it tells us that if horsepower is zero, then mpg will be 39.58 – also absurd. We should be very wary of using a regression model to infer things outside of its range.

10. **Looking at model predictions and RMSE:** We have some hold-out data in the test partition. We compare the model's predictions against the actual values to measure the model's quality. We can use the following command to calculate and store the predicted *mpg* values for each of our cases in a new variable called *pred.test* (we could have called this new variable anything). We use the *predict* function:

```
> pred.test <- predict(auto.lm, test)
```

Figure 129 explains the *predict* function call. Going beyond just linear regression, we use the *predict* function to predict values based on many types of models. Generally we have to pass the name of the variable containing the model as the first argument and the data on which we want to make predictions as the second argument,

Now, we can compare the actual *mpg* values in the

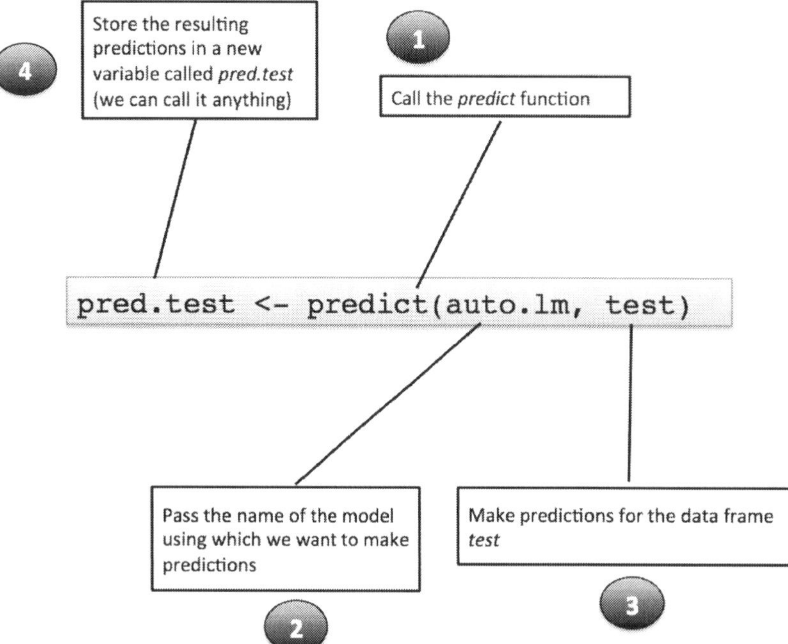

Figure 129: Using the *predict* function.

attribute *mpg* with the predicted or fitted ones in our new variable *pred.test* by entering the command:

```
> data.frame(test$mpg, pred.test)
```

As can be expected, the fitted (or predicted) values differ from the actual values by a little in some cases and by a lot in others.

When we explored the detailed output of the regression model, we saw that the RMSE was 4.692 (Figure 127). How does the model perform on the test partition? With the actual and fitted values available, we can compute the RMSE as follows:

```
> rmse <- sqrt(mean((test$mpg-pred.test)^2))
> rmse
```

We find the RMSE to be 5.486 – comparable to what we got with the training partition. Thus, if it is OK for our predictions to deviate from the actual values by about 5 miles per gallon, we can use this model. As discussed earlier, only the context can tell us whether this is acceptable.

Before using the model, we have to be careful about the earlier warning about using the model only within the range of the data used to build it. Additionally, we also have to be aware of the applicability of the historical data to future cases. In the present case, our data is actually from the 1980's. Given the technological changes that have occurred, this model cannot be used for making predictions about today's cars. However, we can replicate these steps with more recent data and get a model that we could possibly use now.

11. **Summary:** Table 56 summarizes the steps we used for simple linear regression. To use this table as a quick reference, substitute data frame and attributes names according to your usage context.

Table 56: Summary of steps for simple linear regression.

Step no	Description	R command	Remarks
1	Read the data	`auto <- read.csv("auto-mpg.csv")`	Ensure that file is in working directory.
2	Determine target and predictor		*mpg* and *horsepower*.

3	Partition the data	`library(caret)`
		`set.seed(2015)`
		`sam <- createDataPartition(`
		`    auto$mpg, p=0.7, list = FALSE)`
		`train <- auto[sam, ]`
		`test <- auto[-sam, ]`
			Linear regression requires two partitions

4	Build model on training partition	`auto.lm <- lm(mpg ~ horsepower,` `    data = train)`	
5	Draw a scatterplot	`plot(mpg ~ horsepower, data = train,` `   xlab = "horsepower", ylab = "mpg")`	
6	Add in the regression line	`abline(auto.lm)`	
7	Explore the model	`summary(auto.lm)`	Look at the coefficients, RMSE and adjusted r-squared.
8	Generate predictions on test	`pred.test <- predict(auto.lm, test)`	Look at the coefficients, RMSE and adjusted r-squared.

9	Compute RMSE on test	`rmse <- sqrt(mean(`
		`    (test$mpg-pred.test)^2))`
		`rmse`
			See if RMSE on training and test differ too much.

Lab assignment 6: Simple Linear Regression

You can find the answers to this assignment starting from page 384.

Load the data from the file *auto-mpg.csv* into an **R** variable called *auto*. The file contains information about various cars made between 1970 and 1982. The file contains 398 rows of data. Table 57 shows an extract of the first 10 rows to give you an idea of the data.

No	mpg	cylinders	displacement	horsepower	weight	acceleration	model_year	car_name
1	28	4	140	90	2264	15.5	71	chevrolet vega
2	19	3	70	97	2330	13.5	72	mazda rx2 coupe
3	36	4	107	75	2205	14.5	82	honda accord
4	28	4	97	92	2288	17	72	datsun 510 (sw)
5	21	6	199	90	2648	15	70	amc gremlin
6	23	4	115	95	2694	15	75	audi 100ls
7	15.5	8	304	120	3962	13.9	76	amc matador
8	32.9	4	119	100	2615	14.8	81	datsun 200sx
9	16	6	250	105	3897	18.5	75	chevroelt chevelle
10	13	8	318	150	3755	14	76	dodge d100
...	...	...	...	...	...	...	...	...

Table 57: Data for lab assignment

1. Summarize the data set. What is the mean of mpg?
2. What is the median value of mpg?
3. Which value is higher – mean or median? What does this indicate in terms of the skewness of the attribute values? What plots could you use to verify your answer?
4. Draw a histogram of mpg.
5. Draw a density plot of mpg.
6. Looking at the histogram and at the mean and median of mpg, can you explain the relative magnitudes of the mean and the median – that is, what about the histogram would lead us to believe that one would be higher than the other?
7. Draw a scatterplot matrix of all the relevant numeric attributes.
8. Based on the scatterplot matrix, which two attributes seem to be most strongly linearly correlated?
9. Based on the scatterplot matrix, which two attributes seem to be most weakly correlated (don't consider *No*)?
10. Produce a scatterplot of the two attributes *mpg* and *displacement* with *displacement* on the x axis and *mpg* on the y axis.
11. Partition the data and store the result in a variable called *adat*.
12. Build a linear regression model on the training partition with *mpg* as the target and *displacement* as the predictor. Answer the following questions based on the regression model.

a For your model, what is the value of the intercept β_0 ?
b For your model, what is the value of the coefficient β_1 of the attribute *displacement*?
c For your model, what is the value of the slope?
d What is the regression equation as per the model?
e For your model, does the predicted value for *mpg* increase or decrease as the *displacement* increases?
f By how much does the predicted *mpg* change for every unit change in *displacement*?
g Given a car with a *displacement* value of 220, what would your model predict its *mpg* to be?
h What is the RMSE on the training partition?
i What does this mean in terms of the data and the model?
j What proportion of the variability in *mpg* does the model explain?
k Are the intercept and the slope statistically significant?
l Compute and store the model predictions on the test partition in an attribute called *fitted*.
m What is the mpg of the car on the tenth test row? What is the model's prediction for this car?
n What is the RMSE on the test partition?

Multiple Linear Regression

Recall from our earlier discussion that simple linear regression predicts a value for the target attribute by finding a formula like the following hypothetical formula to predict a home's price based on its number of rooms.

$$predicted\_home\_price = 140000 + 30000\, rooms$$

More generally, given some data on the price of a number of homes and the number of rooms in each, we might seek to find values of β_0 and β_1 which yield *good* predictions.

$$predicted\_home\_price = \beta_0 + \beta_1\, rooms$$

We also know from prior discussions that by "*good* values for β_0 and β_1", we mean those values that yield the lowest sum of the squared differences between the predicted and actual values of the home prices – the *least squares* criterion.

Figure 130 recaps the situation.

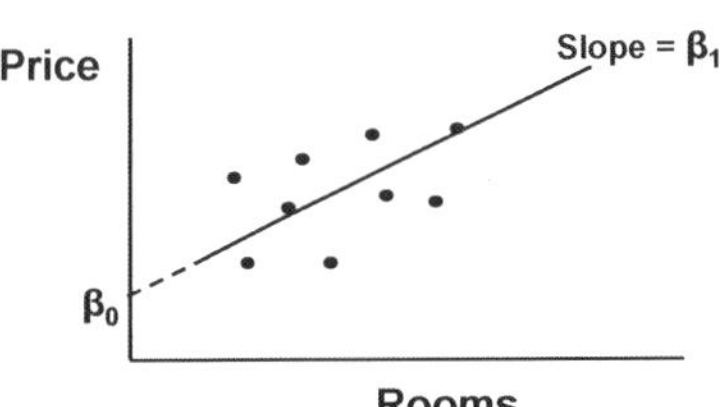

Figure 130: Regression line for Simple Linear Regression.

More generally, simple linear regression predicts the value of the target attribute based on the value of a single predictor attribute as the expression below shows:

$$predicted\_target = \beta_0 + \beta_1\, predictor$$

Multiple Linear Regression uses multiple predictor attributes instead of a single one – that's it.

Extending our home price example from above, we might build a model to predict a home's price based on the number of rooms, the total area and the age of the home (number of years). In this case the regression model will look like this:

$$predicted\_home\_price = \beta_0 + \beta_1\, rooms + \beta_2\, area + \beta_3\, age$$

Like *Simple Linear Regression*, *Multiple Linear Regression* seeks the values of β_0, β_1, β_2, ... based on the least squares criterion.

More generally, *Multiple Linear Regression* predicts the value of the target attribute based on the value of several predictor attributes, as the expression below shows:

$$predicted\_target = \beta_0 + \beta_1\, predictor_1 + \beta_2\, predictor_2 + ... + \beta_n\, predictor_n$$

Discussing *Simple Linear Regression* first helped us to see the underlying concepts. In reality we will rarely be able to use just a single predictor and hence will seldom be able to apply *Simple Linear Regression*. *Multiple Linear Regression* is perhaps the most widely used predictive technique and provides good results in many situations.

Studying *Simple Linear Regression* first also enabled us to illustrate many of the underlying concepts with two-dimensional figures. With two predictor attributes, we can still visualize the regression expression through a perspective drawing in three dimensions on a two-dimensional surface. In this case, the regression equation represents a plane in a three dimensional space as Figure 131 shows.

With three or more predictor attributes, we cannot pictorially represent the points or the regression hyperplane. Nevertheless, all the concepts that we had discussed for *Simple Linear Regression* apply unchanged.

This means that we can interpret the regression output in exactly the same way, and use the *RMS Error* as a measure of the quality of the model.

We now turn to a subtle distinction between the traditional use of linear regression as opposed to its use in a data-analytics context.

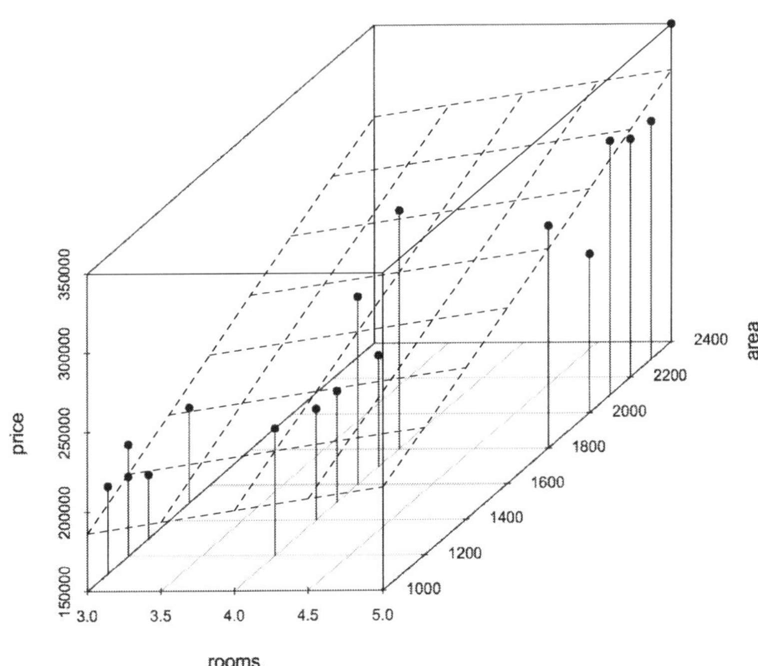

Figure 131: Visualizing the regression plane when we have two predictors.

Social science researchers often use linear regression in its traditional incarnation when they try to experimentally confirm theories about the influence of some attributes on others – that is, to make causal inferences. Most often these research studies operate on relatively small samples of data drawn from large populations and aim to make inferences about the populations based on the results of their analyses of the samples. That is, they aim to generalize their findings on the sample to the population and run the risk of generalizing without a strong basis. To reduce this risk, researchers in statistics have identified several conditions that the data must satisfy.

In a data analytics context, we usually work with huge amounts of data and face only a negligible risk of unwarranted generalization. So long as we obtain an acceptable *RMSE* on the data used to build the model (training partition) and a comparable *RMSE* on the hold out data in the test partition as well, we do not need to really bother much about whether the conditions for generalization really hold. We will therefore not get into discussing the more mathematical aspects of the conditions that must hold for the regression results to be generalizable.

Additionally, data analytics mostly focuses on prediction and hence does not need to worry about rigorously establishing causality. Hence predictive performance trumps most other considerations.

In large data sets, we often find numerous predictor attributes, not all of which have useful predictive power. Using attributes with questionable predictive power in a regression equation can hamper the results, as can using attributes which have only an indirect effect on the target attribute.

Statisticians use several techniques when faced with many predictor attributes.

- **Within linear regression**, people sometimes employ a (controversial) technique called *stepwise regression*, which comes in the following flavors:
  - **Forward selection:** This method starts with no predictor attributes and adds predictors one at a time based on their incremental explanatory power. This way the method aims to find the point at which the additional gain in predictive power from adding a new predictor starts to taper off. The researcher uses the predictive attributes in the model at that point. This method has drawbacks that we will not discuss – most scholars recommend that we should avoid this approach.
  - **Backward elimination:** This method starts with the complete model – including all predictor attributes – and starts removing predictors one by one based on their statistical significance until the leveling off point is reached as above. This approach also applies rules mechanically and runs the risk that we forget the underlying logic altogether. However, in a data analytics context, where we mainly seek predictive power, this approach makes sense.
  - **Bidirectional:** A combination of the above two approaches.
- In a more general context, when faced with a large number of predictor attributes people sometimes employ *Dimension Reduction* techniques to see if a model based on fewer attributes can explain the variability in the target attribute. They use techniques like *Principal Components Analysis* and *Factor Analysis*, which we address briefly later in the book.

Consider once again the example *Multiple Linear Regression* equation we had set up earlier:

$$predicted\_home\_price = \beta_0 + \beta_1\, rooms + \beta_2\, area + \beta_3\, age$$

Multiple Linear Regression can also handle so called *interaction effects*. In addition to just a linear expression on the individual predictor attributes as above, interaction effects consider the impact of attributes on the coefficients of other attributes. For example, we might want to add to our regression model the interaction of two attributes at a time. That is, we might want an equation of the form:

$$predicted\_home\_price = \beta_0 + \beta_1\, rooms + \beta_2\, area + \beta_3\, age$$
$$+\beta_{12}\, rooms * area + \beta_{23}\, area * age + \beta_{13}\, rooms * age$$

Likewise, we can also consider the impacts of three-attribute interactions and so on. We do not discuss interaction effects in this book.

We now have enough background to start learning how to use **R** for performing multiple linear regression analysis.

Review 14: Multiple Linear Regression

You can find the answers to these questions on page 390

Table 58. shows a portion of a large data set that contains information about many homes. For each home you can see number of rooms, the floor area, the age of the home in months and the price.

We would like to build a multiple linear regression model to predict the price for future cases when given only the number of rooms, the floor area and the age of the home in months.

Answer the following questions based on Table 58.

1. Using the column headings as attribute names, what is the target attribute?
2. What attributes should serve as predictors?
3. Which of the following represent correct forms of multiple linear regression models for the problem? Following convention, the Greek letters represent the regression coefficients or constants and the "hat" notation denotes the predicted value for an attribute . Select **all** applicable options.

   a. $\hat{price} = \beta_0 + \beta_1\, rooms + \beta_2\, area + \beta_3\, age$

   b. $\hat{rooms} = \beta_0 + \beta_1\, price + \beta_2\, area + \beta_3\, age$

rooms	area	age	price
3	1200	50	200000
4	1400	60	220000
3	1100	60	205000
4	1500	60	220000
4	1800	50	300000
4	1600	70	268000
3	1500	70	210000
4	1200	70	230000
5	2000	60	250000
5	1800	50	290000
5	2100	65	310000
5	2200	75	300000
4	1700	80	220000
3	1300	70	190000
3	1200	20	220000
5	2400	20	350000
5	2300	40	300000

Table 58: Extract from data about attributes of several homes.

c. $\hat{price} = \beta_0 + \beta_1\, rooms + \beta_2\, area + \beta_3\, age + \epsilon$
d. $\hat{price} = \beta_0 + \beta_1\, rooms + \beta_2\, area^2 + \beta_3\, age$
e. $\hat{price} = \alpha_0 + \alpha_1\, rooms + \alpha_2\, area + \alpha_3\, age$
f. $price = \beta_0 + \beta_1\, rooms + \beta_2\, area + \beta_3\, age$

4. Let us assume that we have built a multiple linear regression model for the above situation and obtained the following results: $\beta_0 = 105756.6$, $\beta_1 = 19054.8$,, $\beta_2 = 62.85$ and $\beta_3 = -627.01$ (the beta values correspond to the left to right order in which the attributes are listed in Table 58)

   a. What would the predicted annual price be for a 45 month old home having 3 rooms, measuring 1350 sq. ft?
   b. What could be a logical explanation for the signs of β_1, β_2 and β_3?
   c. Based on the regression coefficients mentioned above, what is the error (or, more correctly, *residual*) for the house on the first row?

5. The regression coefficients mentioned in Question 4 were actually arrived at using only the data in Table 58 Answer the following based on the data in Table 58 and the regression coefficients mentioned in Question 4.

   a. Compute TSS (total sum of squares), SSE (sum of squared errors) and SSR (sum of squares regression).
   b. Do the numbers add up?
   c. How much of the variation in the target attribute does the regression explain?
   d. What is the RMSE in this example and what does it say about the predictions that this model makes? If the average home price is \$250,000, what is the average percentage error that we can expect on the model's predictions?

Lab 14: Multiple Linear Regression

Pre-requisite(s)

✓ You should have read the general introduction to regression models (page 231), quality of regression models (page 231), simple linear regression (page 233) and multiple linear regression (page 257) and answered the associated review questions.

✓ You should have completed the lab on simple linear regression (page 246).

Objective

After completing this lab, you will be able to:

✓ Create appropriate partitions for linear regression.

✓ Provide correct inputs to the lm function call for performing linear regression.

✓ Interpret the results.

✓ Compute RMS error on the training and test partitions and determine whether the model is useful.

Overview

We will first use a fairly small data set that illustrates many important points, but does not result in a very good model. We then look at a data set where we get what would generally be considered as a good model.

In the first dataset we have some categorical attributes. The dataset also illustrates how to identify and eliminate outliers.

The second dataset is bigger, but has all numeric attributes and hence poses no special challenges.

Activity steps

1. **Read the first data set:** The file *education.csv*[24] contains data on the education expenses in several states along with some other attributes. Read it into an **R** data frame called *ed* now.

```
> ed <- read.csv("education.csv")
```

[24] P. J. Rouseeuw and A. M. Leroy. *Robust regression and outlier detection.* Wiley, 1987

2. **Look at the attributes:**

   Table 59 shows the attribute descriptions. We aim to build a multiple linear regression model to predict *expense* based on the region and the three numeric attributes. We will not use *state*.

Attribute	Description
state	US state code
region	Region (1=Northeastern, 2=North central, 3=Southern, 4=Western)
urban	Number of residents per thousand residing in urban areas in 1970
income	Per capita personal income in 1973
under18	Number of residents per thousand under 18 years of age in 1974
expense	Per capita expenditure on public education in a state, projected for 1975

Table 59: Education expense in various states.

3. **Explore:** Let us explore the ranges of the numeric attributes by creating boxplots. In the following code, we introduce a feature of **R** whereby we can directly type the attribute name without the containing data frame name – that is instead of typing *ed$urban* we can just type *urban*.

```
> # use attach to add a variable to the namespace
> attach(ed)
> # After attaching, You can then just use the
> # attribute name
> boxplot(urban)
> boxplot(income)
> boxplot(under18)
```

   In the boxplot of *under18* we see two outliers. The other two boxplots do not have any outliers. Generally outliers tend to disrupt linear regression models and we might do well to eliminate them before further processing.

4. **Eliminating outliers:** We will first find the outlier values and then eliminate them. To create a list of the outlier values enter:

```
> # Create a list of outlier values and
> # store the list in an R variable "outliers"
> # since we have already attached ed
> # we can avoid ed$ to refer to its attributes
> outliers <- boxplot(under18, plot=F)$out
```

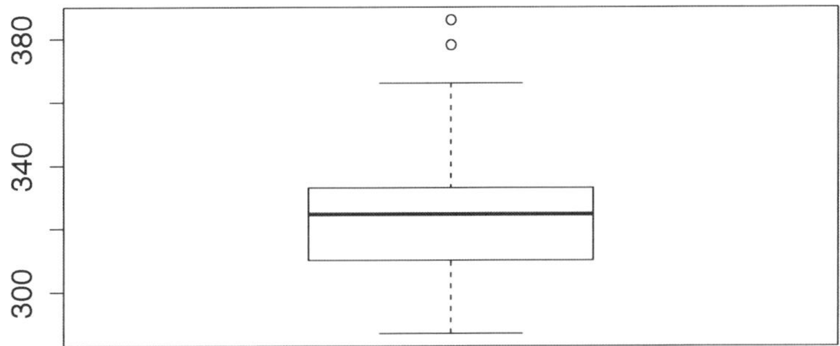

Figure 132: Boxplot of *under18*.

```
> # print the outlier values
> outliers
```

In the above command, we called the *boxplot* function, but asked it not to actually plot. However, whether or not we ask it to plot, the function returns a value which has, among other things, a list of outliers, in an attribute called *out*. We stored that in the variable *outliers*. We see that the cases 378 and 386 are the outliers. We want to remove the rows that contain these values.

```
> ednew <- ed[!(ed$under18 %in% outliers),]
```

In the above command the "!" represents the *not* operator or logical negation. The expression *ed$under18 %in% outliers* matches all the *under18* values that appear among the outliers. Negating it finds the values that do not appear in the list of outliers. We are thus finding the rows of *ed* whose values for the attribute *under18* do not belong to the collection of outliers, and copying these to *ednew*. We will now work with *ednew* which has 48 cases after removing the outliers.

5. **Create factors for categorical attributes:** In our data set, the attribute *region* has numeric values. However, we can clearly see that these values do not have any numeric significance. Unless we convert these to factors, **R** will treat these as numbers and give us misleading

results. Let us handle this:

```
> ednew$region <- factor(ednew$region)
```

6. **Dummy or not?:** From the earlier text, we can see that linear regression requires all attributes to be numeric. We have a categorical attribute *region*. In some of the earlier activities (for example in KNN), where we needed all predictor attributes to be numeric, we created dummies for categorical attributes. Does this mean that we need to create dummies for *region*?

   We do. But, conveniently for us, the **R** function for linear regression can automatically create dummies for all attributes marked as *factors* – as *region* is in our current data. We therefore need to do nothing special for this.

   We can now partition the data and proceed further.

7. **Create partitions:** Linear regression requires two partitions. Generate the partitions now:

```
> library(caret)
> set.seed(2015)
> sam <- createDataPartition(ednew$expense,
      p = 0.7, list = FALSE)
> train <- ednew[sam, ]
> test <- ednew[-sam, ]
```

8. **Build the regression model:** With the data properly treated and the partitions ready, we can build the regression model now. We should know our target and predictor attributes. We have already determined the target attribute to be *expense*. We will use all the other attributes other than *state* as predictors:

```
> ed.lm <- lm(expense ~ ., data = train[, -1])

> # We have stored the resulting model
> # in the variable ed.lm for future use.
```

   In the code above, we use a small trick to avoid typing out a long formula expression – we specified *data = train[,-1]*. In the resulting data frame – without the attribute *state* – we can use all the attributes other than *expense* as predictors and hence use the formula expression *expense* ~ . .

Once you have the model, you can see the details by using the command:

```
> summary(ed.lm)
```

Figure 133 shows the output.

```
Call:
lm(formula = expense ~ ., data = train[, -1])

Residuals:
    Min      1Q  Median      3Q     Max 
-65.762 -17.714  -1.467  17.335  67.428 

Coefficients:
              Estimate Std. Error t value Pr(>|t|)   
(Intercept) -130.02750  160.81803  -0.809   0.4254   
region2      -12.18171   20.81608  -0.585   0.5629   
region3       -5.57296   18.03390  -0.309   0.7595   
region4       22.83198   19.31246   1.182   0.2467   
urban          0.06266    0.06111   1.025   0.3137   
income         0.04618    0.01499   3.080   0.0045 **
under18        0.46407    0.41266   1.125   0.2700   
---
Signif. codes:  0 '***' 0.001 '**' 0.01 '*' 0.05 '.' 0.1 ' ' 1

Residual standard error: 33.94 on 29 degrees of freedom
Multiple R-squared:  0.6067,	Adjusted R-squared:  0.5254 
F-statistic: 7.457 on 6 and 29 DF,  p-value: 6.791e-05
```

Figure 133: Multiple linear regression output for school expense data.

9. **Examine the results:** First off, note that we have four predictors – *region*, *urban*, *income* and *under18* and would expect to see an intercept term and four regression coefficients. However, the output shows an intercept and *six* regression coefficients. What is going on?

   Well, since *region* is a factor or categorical attribute, the *lm* function automatically created dummies for it. In the original data set, *region* takes on values of 1, 2, 3 or 4. Thus **R** created four dummies for it and used just three of them – it left out the dummy corresponding to the *region* value of 1 and kept *region2*, *region3* and *region4*. You will see something like this whenever you apply *lm* on a data set with *factors*.

   From the output we see that the regression explains 52% of the variability in *expense* and hence seems like a poor model.

   The RMSE is 33.94 – we see this from the item *Residual standard error* in the regression output.

We also see that only the coefficient for *income* is significant. In such cases we should consider rebuilding the model with the significant attributes alone. Usually when we do this, the performance – in terms of Multiple R-squared – will deteriorate slightly, but we will end up with a simpler model with almost the same performance.

10. **Rebuild the model with the significant attributes:**

```
> ed.lm.1 <- lm(expense ~ income, data = train[, -1])
> summary(ed.lm.1)
```

As expected, we have a model with almost identical performance as before, but with just a single predictor.

11. **Examine performance on the holdout data:** We can now compute the RMSE on the holdout data in the test partition:

```
> pred.test <- predict(ed.lm.1, test[ ,-1])
> rmse <-  sqrt(mean((test$expense-pred.test)^2))
> rmse
```

We get 41.21. The mean of *expense* (on *ednew*) is about 278 and thus the prediction will be off on the average by 41.21/278 or about 14.8%.

Even though the model seems to explain only 45% of the variation in *expense*, if this RMSE helps us to make better decisions than what we could without the model, the model might still have some use.

12. **Summary:** Table 60 summarizes the steps we used for multiple linear regression on the education data. To use this table as a quick reference, substitute the data frame and attributes names according to your usage context.

We will now look at the process on a bigger data set, but with only numeric attributes and requiring no dummy attributes.

13. **Read the data:** We will be using the *Boston Housing* data set from before[25,26]. Read the data from the file *BostonHousing.csv* into a data frame called *bh*:

```
> bh <- read.csv("BostonHousing.csv")
```

[25] D. Harrison and D.L. Rubinfeld. Hedonic prices and the demand for clean air. *J. Environ. Economics & Management*, pages 81–102, 1978

[26] P. J. Rouseeuw and A. M. Leroy. *Robust regression and outlier detection.* Wiley, 1987

Table 60: Summary of steps for multiple linear regression with outlier elimination and model retrying with significant attributes.

Step no	Description	R command	Remarks
1	Read the data	`ed <- read.csv("education.csv")`	

2	Explored the data to find outliers	`boxplot(ed$urban)`
		`boxplot(ed$under18)`
		`boxplot(ed$income)`
			under18 has two outliers

3	Created a new data frame without the rows containing the outliers	`outliers <- boxplot(ed$under18,`
		`plot=F)$out`
		`ednew = ed[!ed$under18 %in% outliers), ]`
			Stored the outlier values in variable outliers Create new data frame without outlier rows.

4	Created factor for the categorical attribute region	`ednew$region <- factor(ednew$region)`	

5	Partitioned the data	`library(caret)`
		`set.seed(2015)`
		`sam <- createDataPartition(`
		`ednew$expense, p = 0.7,`
		`list = FALSE)`
		`train <- ednew[sam, ]`
		`test <- ednew[-sam, ]`	

6	Built the regression model and examined the results	`ed.lm <- lm(expense ~ .,`
		`data = train[, -1])`
		`summary(ed.lm)`
			Used lm function. Looked at RMSE, significance of coefficients and adjusted r-squared in model results.

7	Re-built the regression model with just the significant attribute(s)	`ed.lm.1 <- lm(expense ~ income,`
		`data = train[, -1])`
		`summary(ed.lm.1)`
			Used only significant attributes from earlier model. Looked at RMSE, significance of coefficients and adjusted r-squared in model results.

8	Computed the RMSE on the test partition	`pred.test <- predict(ed.lm.1, test[ ,-1])`
		`rmse <- sqrt(`
		`mean((test$expense-pred.test)^2))`
		`rmse`
			Compared this RMSE with RMSE on training partition.

Table 61 shows the attributes in the data set.

14. **Partition the data:** Create two partitions with a 70-30 split. Recall that the target attribute is *MEDV*.

```
> library(caret)
> set.seed(2015)
> sam <- createDataPartition(bh$MEDV,
       p=0.7, list = FALSE)
> train <- bh[sam, ]
> test <- bh[-sam, ]
```

Attribute	Description
CRIM	per capita crime rate by town
ZN	proportion of residential land zoned for lots over 25,000 sq.ft.
INDUS	proportion of non-retail business acres per town.
CHAS	Bounds Charles River or not (1 if tract bounds river; 0 otherwise)
NOX	nitric oxides concentration (parts per 10 million)
RM	average number of rooms per dwelling
AGE	proportion of owner-occupied units built prior to 1940
DIS	weighted distances to five Boston employment centres
RAD	index of accessibility to radial highways
TAX	full-value property-tax rate per $10,000
PTRATIO	pupil-teacher ratio by town
B	$1000(Bk - 0.63)^2$ where Bk is the proportion of blacks by town
LSTAT	% lower status of the population
MEDV	Median value of owner-occupied homes in $1000

Table 61: Boston Housing attribute descriptions

15. **Build and view the model:** We will build a model with *MEDV* as the target and all other attributes as predictors.

```
> bh.lm <- lm(MEDV ~ . , data = train)
> summary(bh.lm)
```

From the summary we see that the model has an RMSE of 4.76 and can explain about 73% of the variation in *MEDV*. Two of the coefficients are not significant – *INDUS* and *AGE*. We could rebuild the model without these, but we do not show those steps here. You can gain some practice by trying it out.

16. **Compute RMSE on test partition:**

```
> pred.test <- predict(bh.lm, test)
> rmse <- sqrt(
   mean((test$MEDV-pred.test)^2))
> rmse
```

We get an RMSE of 4.79 – very close to what we got on the training partition.

17. **Summary:** Table 62 summarizes the steps we used for multiple linear regression on the Boston Housing data. To use this table as a quick reference, substitute data frame and attributes names according to your usage context.

Table 62: Summary of steps for multiple linear regression on Boston Housing data.

Step no	Description	R command	Remarks
1	Read the data	`bh <- read.csv("BostonHousing.csv")`	

2	Partitioned the data	`library(caret)`
		`set.seed(2015)`
		`sam <- createDataPartition(bh$MEDV,`
		`p=0.7, list = FALSE)`
		`train <- bh[sam, ]`
		`test <- bh[-sam, ]`	

3	Built the regression model and examined the results	`bh.lm <- lm(MEDV ~ . , data = train)` `summary(bh.lm)`	Used MEDV as target and all the rest as predictors. Checked the model results – RMSE, coefficient significance and adjusted r-squared.

4	Computed the RMSE on the test partition	`pred.test <- predict(bh.lm, test)`
		`rmse <- sqrt(`
		`mean((test$MEDV-pred.test)^2))`
		`rmse`
			Compare this RMSE with RMSE on training partition.

Lab assignment 7: Multiple Linear Regression

You can find the answers starting from page 393

Load the data from the file *auto-mpg.csv* into **R**. The file contains information about various cars made between 1970 and 1982. Although the data are old, we can easily comprehend it, and provides good practice. The file contains 398 rows of data. Table 63 shows the first 10 rows to give you an idea of the data. We want to build a model to predict the fuel efficiency as measured by the *mpg*.

Table 63: Sample of *auto-mpg* data.

No	mpg	cylinders	displacement	horsepower	weight	acceleration	model_year	car_name
1	28	4	140	90	2264	15.5	71	chevrolet vega
2	19	3	70	97	2330	13.5	72	mazda rx2 coupe
3	36	4	107	75	2205	14.5	82	honda accord
4	28	4	97	92	2288	17	72	datsun 510 (sw)
5	21	6	199	90	2648	15	70	amc gremlin
6	23	4	115	95	2694	15	75	audi 100ls
7	15.5	8	304	120	3962	13.9	76	amc matador
8	32.9	4	119	100	2615	14.8	81	datsun 200sx
9	16	6	250	105	3897	18.5	75	chevroelt chevelle
10	13	8	318	150	3755	14	76	dodge d100
...	...	...	...	...	...	...	...	...

a We want to use all attributes other than *No*, and *car_name* as predictors. Which attributes can be used as is and which ones would need dummies? Do what is needed for these.

b Create a new data frame with just the target and the predictors we will use.

c Partition the data and run a linear regression to predict *mpg* in terms of the remaining attributes. Based on the output, what is the approximate RMSE? What does this mean in terms of the model's predictions on the average for the training partition?

d What percentage of the variation in the target attribute does the regression explain (use the adjusted R-squared value)?

e Which coefficients are significant at the 95% level?

f Build a linear regression model with only the statistically significant (at the 95% level) attributes from the previous model. This will involve typing out the predictor attributes explicitly. What percentage of the variation in the target attribute does the new model explain (use the adjusted R-squared value)? What is the RMS Error on the training partition?

g What is the RMS Error of the new model on the test partition? How does it compare with the RMS Error on the training partition?

K-Nearest Neighbors for Regression

KNN also works for regression!

The *K-Nearest Neighbors technique* that we had used for classification (page 117), also works for regression. If you have not already looked at that section, you should do so now because this section assumes that you understand the use of KNN for classification and only outlines the basic ideas.

Recap of KNN for classification

Let us recap the steps we used in KNN for classification:

1. **Check for the correct attribute types:** Verify that the data file contains only numeric predictor attributes and a categorical target attribute. If you have non-numeric predictor attributes or a numeric target attribute, then use the techniques described in the section on *Attribute Conversion* on page 149 to convert them.

KNN for classification requires numerical predictors and a categorical target.

2. **Standardize:** KNN relies on distance calculations and therefore we need to be careful not to let attributes with relatively high values dominate. So we should standardize the predictor attributes (see page 123).

3. **Partition the data:** Create the partitions Training.A, Training.B and Test, with approximately 70%, 15% and 15% of the rows respectively. We use the two training partitions for building the model and the test partition as the hold-out data to evaluate the model.

4. **Classify test cases:** For each value of k starting from 1 up to a reasonable number less than 10, do the following: For each case in Training.B, find the k nearest neighbors in Training.A. Classify

the Training.B case as belonging to the majority class among its k Training.A neighbors. Build the error matrix for k across all cases in the Training.B partition. (If the situation involves classifying into one of two cases, avoid even values of k because that could lead to ties and arbitrary tie resolutions.)

5. **Find the best value for k:** Compare the error matrices or classification confusion matrices for the various values of k and choose the value of k that performs best. In choosing the best value for k, we might not always go by the overall error rate if the costs of different types of errors are not the same – a situation of *asymmetric costs*. In such situations, we might be interested in getting a better performance on some of the classes for which an error is more costly, at the cost of slightly worse performance on others.
6. **Assess the chosen k on the test partition:** Use the chosen value of k to classify each case of the test partition. We do this just like we did for the cases in the Training.B partition, by checking the k nearest neighbors in the Training.A partition. Then see if the model performs acceptably. If so, deploy the model for classifying future cases. If the model turns out to be inadequate, go back and see if dropping a few predictor attributes or adding more helps. If those things still don't work, then perhaps KNN does not suit this situation; try a different classification technique.

KNN for regression relies on the same intuition – get the value for the target attribute of a case based on a set of *similar* cases in the training partition – as before, we will use distance as the measure of similarity and will thus need to standardize the values of the predictor attributes.

KNN for regression requires all attributes to be numeric – predictors and target.

However, since we now need a numerical prediction, the target attribute must also be numeric.

Unlike with KNN for classification, in KNN for regression, we cannot just go with the majority vote among the *k* nearest neighbors – because each neighbor does not belong to a class as was the case earlier. Instead, the target attribute of each of the neighbors has a numeric value, and KNN averages these to calculate the predicted value. A fully-explained example follows.

That's it! Given a case for which we need to compute the predicted value for the target attribute, KNN for regression finds k neighbors just like KNN for classification did. Having found the neighbors, it averages the value of the target attribute of the k neighbors to compute the predicted value for the target attribute. So the complete process for KNN for regression is:

Steps in KNN for regression.

1. **Ensure the correct attribute types:** Verify that the data file contains only numeric predictor attributes and a numeric target attribute.

Use the techniques described earlier in the section on *Attribute Conversion* page 149 to convert any non-numeric attributes to dummies.

KNN for regression predicts a value for the target attribute as the average of the values of the target attribute from the k nearest neighbors.

2. **Standardize:** KNN relies on distance calculations and therefore we need to be careful not to let attributes with relatively high values dominate. So we should standardize the predictor attributes. (See page 123). We should not standardize the target attribute.
3. **Partition the data:** KNN requires three partitions. Create the partitions Training.A, Training.B and Test, with approximately 70%, 15% and 15% of the rows respectively.
4. **Make predictions for the training.B cases:** For each value of k starting from 1 up to a reasonable number near 10, do the following: For each Training.B case, find the k nearest neighbors in Training.A partition. Compute the predicted value for the target attribute of the Training.B case as the average of the target attribute of the k Training.A neighbors. Then compute the RMSE (Root Mean Squared Error) for each value of k as discussed earlier. Since KNN for regression computes the average of the target attribute values from the k nearest neighbors, we can use even and odd values of k. Recall that with KNN for classification, we avoided using even numbers for k when we had two classes because of the scope for ties. The issue of tie resolution does not arise when we use KNN for regression.
5. **Find the best value for k:** Find the value of k that yields the lowest RMSE. If this value of RMSE seems acceptable then proceed further. Otherwise, you have to assess whether to use a different prediction method or add or drop predictor attributes and try again.
6. **Assess the chosen k on the Test partition:** Use the chosen value of k to make predictions for each case of the Test partition and compute the RMSE. If the RMSE is acceptable, deploy the model for predicting future cases. If the model turns out to be inadequate, go back and see if dropping a few predictor attributes or adding more helps. If those things still don't work, then perhaps KNN does not really suit this situation; try a different regression technique.

Income	Family_size	Expenditure
136000	3	765
78100	4	600
56100	2	350
75000	2	420
135000	2	740
102000	2	610
78500	3	525
67500	3	525
78000	2	420
78000	3	525
65000	3	525
125000	4	840
95000	4	700
67000	4	600
56000	2	350
136500	2	740
136000	3	765
136000	5	875
94900	2	510
50000	3	450

Table 64: Family vacation expenses.

Let us consider an example. Table 64 shows the fictitious historical vacation expenses at a resort for families that visited a resort. For cash flow planning, the resort manager wants to use data like this (with many more attributes) to predict the amount of money that families with reservations over next few months will spend. In what follows, we will only use the attributes from Table 64

We know that KNN requires us to standardize or scale the data and Table 65 shows both the original and the standardized values (*Income_z* and *Family_size_z*) for the predictor attributes (although the two tables have the same data, the tables differ in row ordering).

KNN requires us to create partitions. Although we will need many more rows of data to perform a true KNN analysis, we

Income	Family_size	Income_z	Family_size_z	Expenditure
102000.0	2	0.314	-0.987	610
125000.0	4	1.057	1.206	840
136000.0	5	1.413	2.303	875
50000.0	3	-1.366	0.110	450
78000.0	3	-0.461	0.110	525
94900.0	2	0.085	-0.987	510
67000.0	4	-0.817	1.206	600
95000.0	4	0.088	1.206	700
56100.0	2	-1.169	-0.987	350
136000.0	3	1.413	0.110	765
78500.0	3	-0.445	0.110	525
78100.0	4	-0.458	1.206	600
75000.0	2	-0.558	-0.987	420
65000.0	3	-0.881	0.110	525
135000.0	2	1.380	-0.987	740
136500.0	2	1.429	-0.987	740
67500.0	3	-0.801	0.110	525
78000.0	2	-0.461	-0.987	420
136000.0	3	1.413	0.110	765
56000.0	2	-1.172	-0.987	350

Table 65: Vacation expense data with standardized predictor values.

illustrate the process with just the 20 rows shown above. Tables 66, 67 and 68 show three random partitions of the data – we chose to keep 10 rows in the training partition and 5 each in the other two.

We now discuss the computations needed to perform KNN for this example. Remember however that when we perform KNN on real data sets, we will be using **R** to perform all these computations. This discussion only explains what **R** does – you will not have to ever do all this manually. Nevertheless, I urge you to verify at least some of the computations to help you understand what is going on.

As discussed under KNN for classification, we can find the neighbors of a case by using the Euclidean distance formula. For example, to compute the distance between the first Training.B case and the first Training.A case using the standardized values, we can evaluate the expression:

$$\sqrt{(-0.445 - 0.314)^2 + (0.110 + 0.987)^2}$$

This yields 1.334 as the distance between the first Training.B case and the first training case.

In a similar vein, we can compute the distances from every Training.A case to every Training.B case. Table 69 shows the results. For the column corresponding to each Training.B case, the highlighted cells show the distances of the three nearest

Trg row	Inc_z	Fam_sz_z	Exp
1	0.314	-0.987	610
2	1.057	1.206	840
3	1.413	2.303	875
4	-1.366	0.110	450
5	-0.461	0.110	525
6	0.085	-0.987	510
7	-0.817	1.206	600
8	0.088	1.206	700
9	-1.169	-0.987	350
10	1.413	0.110	765

Table 66: Training.A partition: Vacation expense data (attribute names have been truncated).

Val row	Inc_z	Fam_sz_z	Exp
1	-0.445	0.110	525
2	-0.458	1.206	600
3	-0.558	-0.987	420
4	-0.881	0.110	525
5	1.380	-0.987	740

Table 67: Training.B partition: Vacation expense data (attribute names have been truncated).

Test row	Inc_z	Fam_sz_z	Exp
1	1.429	-0.987	740
2	-0.801	0.110	525
3	-0.461	-0.987	420
4	1.413	0.110	765
5	-1.172	-0.987	350

Table 68: Test partition: Vacation expense data (attribute names have been truncated).

neighbors in the Training.A partition.

With this information, we can compute the knn predictions for the Training.B cases for k=1, 2 and 3. For example, using k=1, the closest neighbor for the first Training.B case is training case 5 with a distance of 0.016 (see the column named *case 1*). Thus, for the first Training.B case, KNN will predict the target attribute to be the value for the target attribute the fifth case of Training.A – which we can see from Table 66 is 525. Why did we not average anything? Because k=1, we have just one neighbor's value to consider and hence the average is the value itself.

	Distances to Training.B cases				
Trg.A row	case 1	case 2	case 3	case 4	case 5
1	1.334	2.325	0.872	1.622	1.066
2	1.860	1.515	2.724	2.227	2.217
3	2.874	2.168	3.835	3.174	3.290
4	0.921	1.424	1.362	0.485	2.957
5	0.016	1.097	1.101	0.420	2.143
6	1.218	2.259	0.643	1.461	1.296
7	1.158	0.359	2.208	1.099	3.104
8	1.219	0.546	2.286	1.464	2.546
9	1.314	2.306	0.611	1.134	2.549
10	1.858	2.168	2.255	2.294	1.097

Table 69: Distances from each Training.A case to each Training.B case – the three nearest neighbors for each Training.B case are highlighted.

What would KNN predict for the first Training.B case, with k=2?

We will now need to consider the two closest training neighbors.

From Table 69 we see these to be training rows 4 and 5. Thus the prediction is the average of the expenses for those training cases. looking again at Table 66, we see the actual expenses for cases 4 and 5 to be 450 and 525 respectively. The prediction is then the average of these two, or 487.5. We can use the same approach and compute the predictions for k=1, 2 and 3 for each of the Training.B cases. Table 70 shows the results.

k=1	k=2	k=3
525.0	487.5	525.0
600.0	650.0	608.3
350.0	430.0	490.0
525.0	487.5	525.0
610.0	687.5	628.3

Table 70: Vacation expenses: prediction for the Training.B cases: k=1, 2 and 3.

Table 71 shows the squared deviations of the KNN predictions for the Training.B cases for k=1, 2 and 3. It also shows the Root Mean Squared Error (RMSE) which is the square root of the sum of the average of the squared deviations, as discussed earlier in the section on *Quality of Regression Model* on page 231.

From Table 71, we can see that k=2 provides the lowest RMSE. The resort manager might consider an average error of $40 per family as pretty good and might want to use the model for future predictions. Of course, before deploying the

Training.B partition			KNN: predicted expenditure			Squared errors		
Income_z	Family_size_z	Expenditure	k=1	k=2	k=3	k=1	k=2	k=3
-0.445	0.110	525	525.0	487.5	525.0	0.00	1406.25	0.00
-0.458	1.206	600	600.0	650.0	608.3	0.00	2500.00	69.39
-0.558	-0.987	420	350.0	430.0	490.0	4900.00	100.00	4900.00
-0.881	0.110	525	525.0	487.5	525.0	0.00	1406.25	0.00
1.380	-0.987	740	610.0	687.5	628.3	16900.00	2756.25	12470.19
					RMSE	66.00	40.40	59.10

Table 71: Vacation expense data: RMS Error for k=1, 2 and 3 on the Training.B partition.

model she needs to first evaluate the model's performance on independent data – the hold-out data in the Test partition – on the chosen value of k=2.

Using exactly the same approach we used for computing the predicted expenses for the Training.B partition, we can compute the predicted expenditures for the Test partition and then see if we get an acceptable RMSE on that as well. Table 72 shows the results.

Use the numbers in Table 73 – which shows the distances from the test partition cases to the training partition cases, with the closest two neighbors highlighted – to verify the predicted expense computations.

Income_z	Family_size_z	Expenditure	Pred exp: k=2	Sqr err
1.429	-0.987	740	687.50	2756.25
-0.801	0.110	525	487.50	1406.25
-0.461	-0.987	420	480.00	3600.00
1.413	0.110	765	802.50	1406.25
-1.172	-0.987	350	400.00	2500.00
			RMSE	48.31

Table 72: Vacation data: RMSE computation for the Test partition.

	Distances to Test cases				
Trg.A row	case 1	case 2	case 3	case 4	case 5
1	1.115	1.564	0.775	1.552	1.486
2	2.224	2.157	2.668	1.153	3.127
3	3.290	3.116	3.786	2.193	4.184
4	3.002	0.565	1.422	2.779	1.114
5	2.185	0.339	1.097	1.874	1.307
6	1.344	1.409	0.546	1.722	1.257
7	3.139	1.097	2.222	2.484	2.222
8	2.571	1.411	2.261	1.720	2.529
9	2.598	1.157	0.708	2.805	0.003
10	1.097	2.213	2.171	0.000	2.808

Table 73: Vacation expenses: Distances to Test partition cases with the chosen value of k=2.

Review 15: KNN for regression

You can find the answers to these questions on page 396

A person collected data on many high school students. The data included *height*, *weight* and the *distance* that each student was able to throw a baseball. Using this data, the researcher is in the process of building a model to predict the distance that a high school student can throw a baseball, knowing only the student's height and weight. Table 74 shows the Training.A partition. For this assignment, we need only the target attribute *distance* and therefore we do not show the values of the other attributes in the table.

Training.A partition			
Case no	height	weight	distance
1	...	...	100
2	...	...	150
3	...	...	175
4	...	...	130
5	...	...	180
6	...	...	108
7	...	...	140
8	...	...	130
9	...	...	170
10	...	...	160

Table 74: Training.A partition: Distance some students threw a baseball.

Table 75 shows the Training.B partition and the three nearest neighbors (with the first being the nearest) in the Training.A partition to each case of the Training.B partition. You can assume that we also have a Test partition that we have not shown here.

Training.B partition				Neighbors in Trg.A		
Case no	height	weight	distance	1st	2nd	3rd
1	...	...	130	1	3	5
2	...	...	170	9	5	3
3	...	...	130	8	4	2
4	...	...	165	10	5	9
5	...	...	140	4	2	8

Table 75: Training.B partition and three nearest neighbors: Distance some students threw a baseball.

Answer the following questions based on the information in Tables 74 and 75.

a For k values of 1, 2 and 3 calculate the predicted distance thrown for the five cases of the Training.B partition and compute the RMSE for each k value.

b Assuming that you planned to consider only these k values, which one would you prefer? Why?

c Having chosen your preferred k as above, what would you need to do to check whether the model is ready for use in predicting for new cases?

Lab 15: KNN for regression

Pre-requisite(s)

✓ You should have read the text's general introduction to regression models (page 231), quality of regression models (page 231) and the discussion of KNN for regression (page 272) and answered the associated review questions.

✓ You should have completed the lab dealing with using KNN for classification (page 136).

Objective

After completing this lab, you will be able to:

✓ Provide correct inputs to the *knn.reg* function from the *FNN* package.

✓ Interpret and use the resulting model correctly.

✓ Compute RMS errors for various values of k.

✓ Select the best value of k.

✓ Test the model's performance on the hold-out data.

Overview

In this lab, we will work with a data set that deals with energy efficiency in buildings. We will build a KNN model to predict the energy efficiency of a building, based on several other attributes[27].

[27] Athanasios Tsanas and Angeliki Xifara. Accurate quantitative estimation of energy performance of residential buildings using statistical machine learning tools. *Energy and Buildings*, pages 560–567, 2012

Activity steps

1. **Read the data:** Read the data from the file *energy-efficiency.csv* into **R**.

```
> ee <- read.csv("energy-efficiency.csv")
```

The resulting data frame has 768 cases. Type the **R** command to list the complete data frame. Use the appropriate **R** functions to see the names of the attributes.

ee

names(ee)

2. **Understand the attributes:** Table 76 describes the attributes. We will build a KNN model with the first eight attributes as predictors to predict *Y1*, the *Heating load* of a building.

Attribute name	Description
X1	Relative compactness
X2	Surface area
X3	Wall area
X4	Roof area
X5	Overall height
X6	Orientation
X7	Glazing area
X8	Glazing area distribution
Y1	Heating load
Y2	Cooling load

Table 76: Attributes in the Energy Efficiency data set

3. **Prepare the data:** Attributes *X6* and *X8* are categorical, although they have numerical values. We need dummies for these. We will use the function *dar2ed.dummy* in the file *dar2ed-dummy.R*. Load that file in **RStudio** and *source* it in by clicking on the *Source* button on the top right of the pane that displays the file.

```
> ee <- dar2ed.dummy(ee, c(6,8))
> names(ee)
> # We see 20 attributes including the
> # dummies we just created above
```

We added ten dummy attributes corresponding to the four values of *X6 (Orientation)* and the six different values of *X8 (Glazing area distribution)*.

4. **Standardize:** We already know that KNN relies on distance computations and hence will need to standardize the predictor attributes. From the listing of attribute names above, you can see that our predictor attributes occupy positions 1 through 5, 7, 11 to 13 and 15 through 19. We leave out one dummy attribute from each set of dummy attributes. Since dummy attributes only have values 0 or 1, we need not standardize these. We will standardize the other predictor attributes.

   We had earlier seen the use of the *scale* function to standardize the predictors.

   When we have many attributes to scale, standardizing each attribute separately can be tedious. We have therefore created a convenience function called *dar2ed.scale.many* in the file *dar2ed-scale-many.R* to standardize several attributes with a single command. *Source* it in as explained earlier.

Then enter the following command:

```
> # Predictor attributes in columns 1 to 5, and 7
> ee <- dar2ed.scale.many(ee, c(1:5, 7))

> # Verify that the standardized attributes are there
> names(ee)
```

The function, through the message "Scaled 6 attribute(s)" informs you that all went well. The command to check the attributes in the data frame now shows us that the convenience function has added, for each predictor attribute we had indicated, a new attribute with '_z" suffixed to the attribute's name.

names(ee)

Figure 134 explains the *dar2ed.scale.many* function call. Note how we used *c(1:5, 7)* to indicate the specific columns we wanted to standardize from the data frame supplied as argument.

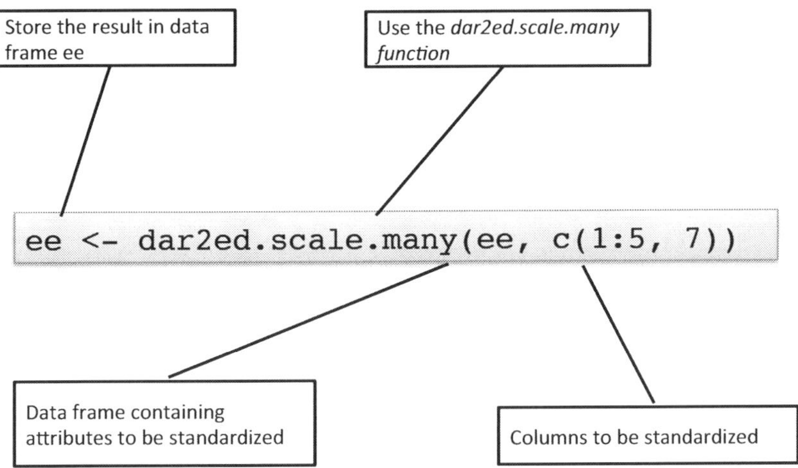

Figure 134: Convenience function for scaling many attributes with a single call

5. **Create a data frame with only the needed columns:** Sometimes when a data frame with dummy attributes and standardized attributes ends up with too many attributes, things can get confusing. We could remove some of the clutter by creating a new clean data frame with only what we need. In the code below, we retain

the standardized values of attributes $X1$ through $X5$ and $X7$. From each set of dummies, we leave one out.

```
> names(ee)
> ee.new <- ee[, c(9, 11:13, 15:19, 21:26)]
> names(ee.new)
 [1] "Y1"      "ee_X6_2" "ee_X6_3" "ee_X6_4"
 [5] "ee_X8_0" "ee_X8_1" "ee_X8_2" "ee_X8_3"
 [9] "ee_X8_4" "X1_z"    "X2_z"    "X3_z"
[13] "X4_z"    "X5_z"    "X7_z"
```

Going forward, we will use *ee.new*.

6. **Create partitions:** We know that KNN requires three partitions. Our data frame has 768 rows. We will use the default 70-15-15 split.

```
> library(caret)
> set.seed(2015)
> samp <- createDataPartition(ee$Y1,
       p = 0.7, list = FALSE)
> # Create the training partition
> train.a <- ee.new[samp, ]
> # Store the rest of the data in a new
> # variable called rest
> rest <- ee.new[-samp, ]
> # We need to sample half of the rest
> # into the second partition train.b
> samp <- createDataPartition(rest$Y1,
       p = 0.5, list = FALSE)
> train.b <- rest[samp, ]
> test <- rest[-samp, ]
```

You can now issue the appropriate commands to verify the sizes of these partitions.

```
nrow(train.a)
nrow(train.b)
nrow(test)
```

7. **Build the model:** Having standardized the predictors and partitioned the data, we are almost ready to build the model – *almost* because the function to run KNN for regression is in an **R** package called *FNN*. We already installed this in the lab on **R** packages (page 55). Load the package with the command:

```
> library(FNN)
```

Before you run the commands to build the model, you have to think through the data. We need to know the

Training.A predictor attribute values, Training.B predictor attribute values, the Training.A target attribute values and the Training.B target attribute values. From the detailed example in the text, you know that **R** will need all of these to be able to build the Training.B predictions and to compute the RMSE for each value of k. Table 77 shows the elements.

Table 77: Various elements to be clear about before building a KNN model.

Item	Value in our context
Training.A predictor attribute values	train.a[,2:15] – we need all rows of the standardized predictors
Training.B predictor attribute values	train.b[,2:15] – as above
Training.A target attribute values	train.a[, 1] – *Y1* is the target attribute and is in the first column
Training.B target attribute values	train.b[, 1] – as above

You know that with KNN we try out several values of k and then choose the one that gives the lowest RMS Error.

Execute the following commands to run KNN for k=1 and to compute the RMS error:

```
> library(FNN)
> # Try k = 1
> res <- knn.reg(train.a[ ,2:15],
      train.b[ ,2:15], train.a[ ,1], 1, algorithm="brute")
> rmse <- sqrt(mean(
      (train.b$Y1-res$pred)^2))
> cat("RMSE on training data for k=1: ", rmse)
```

Figure 135 explains the *knn.reg* function call.

We see that the RMSE is 4.72.

You can repeat the above process for k=2 through 5 – remember to replace the value for k in the call to *knn.reg*. Also change the value for k in the *cat* function call that prints the result. You will find the RMSE to be 2.771, 2.023, 2.079 and 2.222 respectively for k=2 through k=5.

However, to avoid the chore of repeating the same set of commands, we have provided two convenience functions that will do everything. Load the file *dar2ed-knn-reg-functions.R*. It has two functions. Then source in

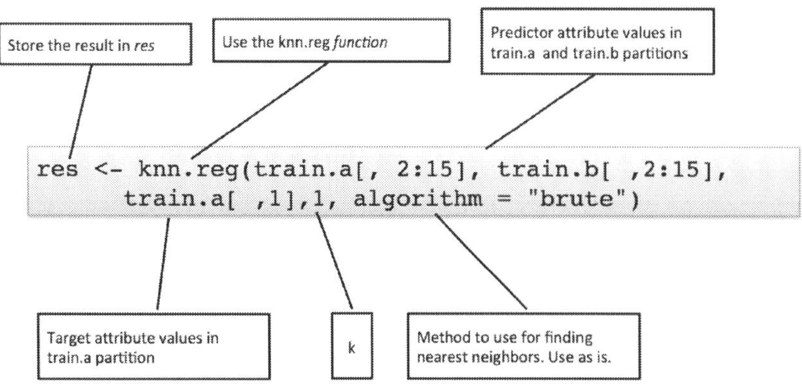

Figure 135: Convenience function to run KNN for regression and to compute RMSE.

the file to load the two functions. Then:

```
> # Source in the code in file
> # dar2ed-knn-reg-functions.R and then:
> dar2ed.knn.reg.multi(train.a[ ,2:15],
      train.b[ ,2:15], train.a[ ,1],
      train.b[ ,1],1,10)
```

Figure 136 explains.

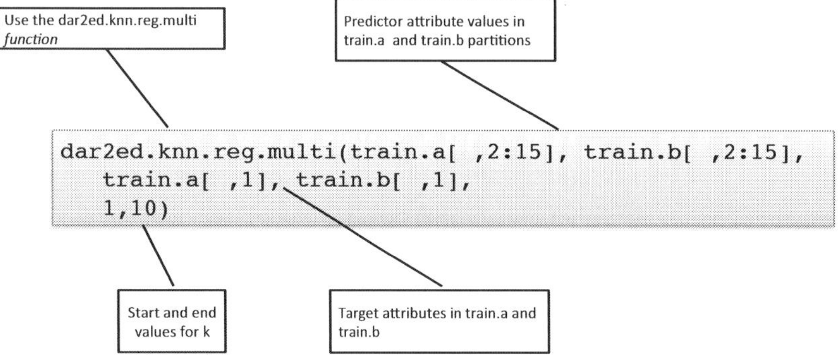

Figure 136: Convenience function to run KNN for regression and plot RMSE for multiple k values

If you use the above command, then you do not have to run the command separately for each value of k on the *train.b* partition. This single command will enable you to generate the RMSE for every value of k from a range. As a bonus it also plots the RMSE values so that you can pick the best k quickly. Figure 137 shows the plot. Clearly k=3 produces the lowest RMSE of 2.032.

The mean for *Y1* is 22.3. Assuming that predicting the *Heating load* to within about 2 points or 10% of the real value on the average is acceptable, we now need to

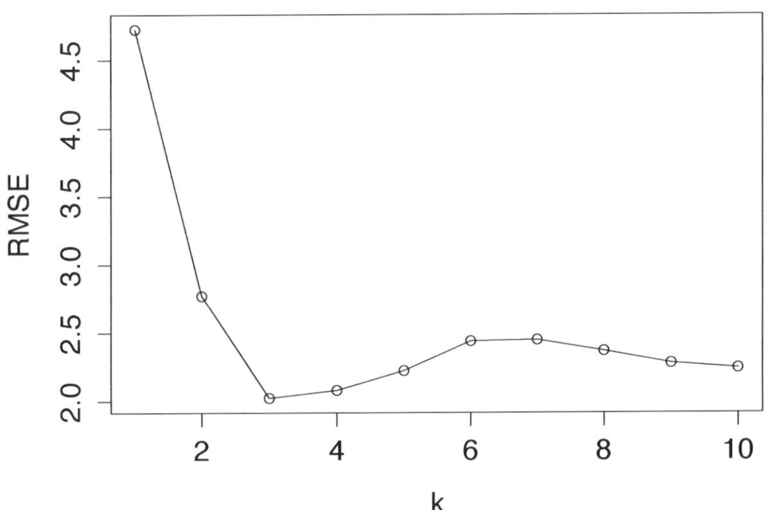

Figure 137: Graph produced by *dar2ed.knn.reg.multi*

see if we get similar results on the test partition.

8. **Verify on hold-out data in the test partition:** Since we will now run for just a single value of k, we can revert to using *knn.reg* as before and replace references to *train.b* with *test*. Enter the following command:

```
> res <- knn.reg(train.a[ ,2:15],
         test[ ,2:15], train.a[ ,1],
         3, algorithm="brute")
> rmse <- sqrt(mean((test$Y1-res$pred)^2))
> cat("RMSE  on test data for k=3: ", rmse)
```

   We now get an RMSE of 2.59 – reasonably close to what we had obtained on training data..

9. **Summary:** Table 78 summarizes the steps.

Lab assignment 8: KNN for regression

You can find the answers to these questions on page 398.

1. Use the Boston Housing data[28,29] from the file *BostonHousing.csv* to perform a KNN analysis to predict *MEDV* based

[28] D. Harrison and D.L. Rubinfeld. Hedonic prices and the demand for clean air. *J. Environ. Economics & Management*, pages 81–102, 1978

[29] K. Bache and M. Lichman. UCI machine learning repository, 2013. URL `http://archive.ics.uci.edu/ml`

Table 78: Summary of steps for KNN regression on energy efficiency data.

Step no	Description	R command	Remarks
1	Read the data	`ee <- read.csv("energy-efficiency.csv")`	
2	Create dummies	`ee <- dar2ed.dummy(ee, c(6,8))`	The two categorical attributes are in columns 6 and 8.
3	Standardize	`ee <- dar2ed.scale.many(ee, c(1:5, 7))`	Standardized all the predictor attributes – other than the dummies.
4	Create new frame with only relevant attributes – just for convenience	`ee.new <- ee[, c(9, 11:13,` `15:19, 21:26)]`	Gathered the target attribute and the standardized predictors into a new data frame for convenience.

5	Partition	`library(caret)`
		`set.seed(2015)`
		`samp <- createDataPartition(ee$Y1,`
		`p = 0.7, list = FALSE)`
		`train.a <- ee.new[samp, ]`
		`rest <- ee.new[-samp, ]`
		`samp <- createDataPartition(rest$Y1,`
		`p = 0.5, list = FALSE)`
		`train.b <- rest[samp, ]`
		`test <- rest[-samp, ]`
			KNN requires three partitions.

6	Build model for k values between 1 and 10	`library(FNN)`
		`# Try k = 1`
		`res <- knn.reg(train.a[ ,2:15],`
		`train.b[ ,2:15], train.a[ ,1],`
		`1, algorithm="brute")`
		`rmse <- sqrt(mean(`
		`(train.b$Y1-res$pred)^2))`
		`cat("RMSE for k=1: ", rmse)`
		
		`# repeat for other values of k`
		`# Alternately ...`
		`dar2ed.knn.reg.multi(`
		`train.a[ ,2:15], train.b[ ,2:15],`
		`train.a[ ,1], train.b[ ,1],1,10)`
			The second option can be used to try knn for several values of k with one call and see the RMSE for each. We found that k=3 yielded the lowest RMSE

7	Find RMSE on test partition for chosen k	`res <- knn.reg(train.a[ ,2:15],`
		`test[ ,2:15], train.a[ ,1], 3,`
		`algorithm="brute")`
		`rmse <- sqrt(mean(`
		`(test$Y1-res$pred)^2))`
		`cat("RMSE  on test data for k=3: ",`
		`rmse)`	

on the other attributes How does the RMSE compare with what we obtained with Multiple Linear Regression?

2. Use the Auto mpg data from the fila *auto-mpg.csv* to perform a KNN analysis to predict *MEDV* based on the other attributes How does the RMSE compare with what we obtained with Multiple Linear Regression?

Regression Trees

The basic ideas used in *Classification Trees* apply equally well for regression as well. Recall that we easily adapted KNN for regression by changing just the final step – instead of looking at the proportions of the various classes, we just averaged the target attribute. We can do the same thing with regression trees too.

Like classification trees, regression trees can handle numeric, ordinal and categorical attributes and we do not need any special processing.

The tree building and pruning processes remain essentially the same. In classification trees we had used one of two measures of purity of a node – *GINI index* and *Entropy*. Obviously, those metrics do not transfer to the case of continuous values.

What might work as a measure of *purity* or coherence of a collection of continuous values? Clearly, the closer the values are to each other, the purer the collection is. For instance consider the two sets of values (5, 4, 5, 5, 6, 5) and (3, 7, 4, 5, 1, 10). Both sets have the same mean of 5, but the first set has values that are much closer to the mean than the second and can be considered as the *purer* of the two. How can we operationalize this in the form of a single number?

We cannot just add up the difference of each value from the mean since negative and positive values will cancel out. The obvious solution would then be to square the difference of each value from the mean and add up these squares.

The regression tree building process starts with all the cases in a single node – the root node. It then chooses the split that causes the greatest reduction in sum of squared errors across all nodes. It proceeds like this till it has either built the full tree or is unable to split any further because of constraints like *minsplit* or *minbucket* (see the labs on classification trees on pages 161 and 196).

On the tree, each leaf node has a predicted value equal to the mean of the target attribute of the cases in the node.

Subsequently when we are given new cases for prediction, we run them through the tree. Each case will end up at some leaf node. The predicted value for the target attribute for a case is just the predicted value of the corresponding leaf node.

Given the extreme similarity with classification trees, which we have discussed extensively, we can move directly to a brief lab.

Lab 16: Regression Trees

Pre-requisite(s)

✓ You should have read the general introduction to regression models (page 231, quality of regression models (page 231), classification trees (page 155) and the brief introduction to regression trees (page 287) and answered the associated review questions.

✓ You should have completed the lab on classification trees (pages 161 and 196).

Objective

After completing this lab, you will be able to:

✓ Create appropriate partitions for regression trees.

✓ Provide correct inputs to use the *rpart* function for regression.

✓ Interpret the results.

✓ Compute RMS error on the *training* and *test* partitions and determine whether the model is useful.

Overview

We had earlier applied multiple linear regression to the *Boston Housing* data set. Let us see how regression trees perform on that data set. This should make for an interesting comparison.

Since we have processed the *Boston Housing* data set a couple of times already, we do not elaborate on the attributes. You can refer to the page 270 for the attribute descriptions.

Activity steps

1. **Read the data:**

```
> bh <- read.csv("BostonHousing.csv")
```

2. **Create partitions:**

```
> library(caret)
> set.seed(2015)
> sam <- createDataPartition(bh$MEDV,
      p = 0.7, list = FALSE)
> train <- bh[sam, ]
> test <- bh[-sam, ]
```

3. **Build and plot tree on training data:**

```
> library(rpart)
> # using minsplit = 20 and cp = 0
> bh.tree <- rpart(MEDV ~ ., data = train,
      method = "anova",
      control = rpart.control(
      minsplit = 20, cp = 0))
> library(rpart.plot)
> prp(bh.tree, type=2, nn=TRUE,
      fallen.leaves=TRUE, faclen=4, varlen=8, shadow.col="gray")
```

   Figure 138 shows the result – way too big to be useful. Clearly we need to prune this tree!

4. **Prune the tree:** To prune the tree, we need to find the correct *cp* value to use. We first plot the *cptable*.

```
> plotcp(bh.tree)
```

   Figure 139 shows the resulting plot – your plot could be different.
   From Figure 139 we see that the leftmost point below the dashed line corresponds to a tree of size 9 (9 leaf nodes) generated by a *cp* factor of 0.0074.
   In case you find that the x axis label for the point of interest is not visible then resize the width of the graph so as to be able to see that label.
   We can use this to prune the tree:

```
> bh.tree.pruned <- prune(bh.tree,
      0.0074)
```

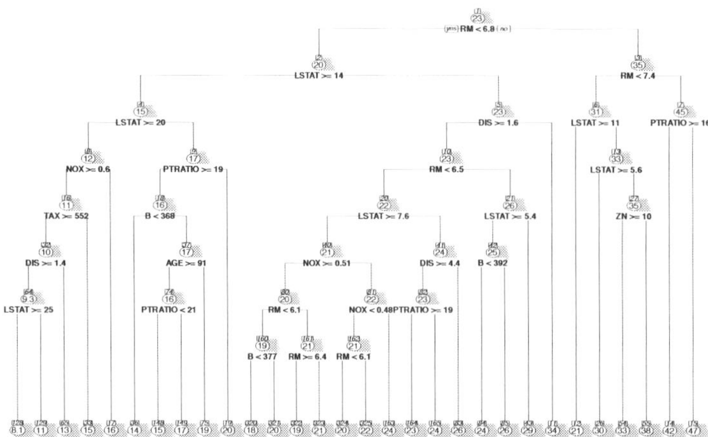

Figure 138: Tree for Boston Housing on training data

```
> prp(bh.tree.pruned, type=2,
      nn=TRUE, fallen.leaves=TRUE, faclen=4, varlen=8, shadow.col="gray")
```

Figure 140 shows the pruned tree.

Let us understand the information in a node:

- **Node number:** The number on the rectangle above the node is the node number. The root has a number of 1. The children of node with number n have node numbers $2n$ and $2n + 1$.
- **Value of node:** The number inside the node represents the (rounded) mean of the target attribute for the cases satisfying the condition for the node. For the root node this will be the overall average across all training cases. You can verify:

  ```
  > mean(train$MEDV)
  ```

  The result of 22.55122 has been rounded to 23. Consider node number 2. This covers all cases with *RM < 6.8*.

  ```
  > mean(train[train$RM < 6.8, "MEDV"])
  ```

  The result of 19.602 has been rounded to 20. Consider node number 3. This covers all cases with *RM >= 6.8*.

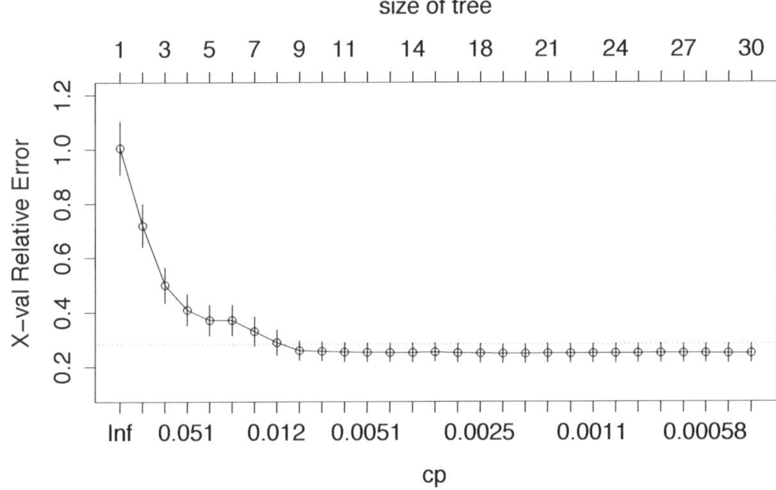

Figure 139: Complexity factor table (cptable) for Boston Housing tree – your plot could be slightly different

```
> mean(train[train$RM >= 6.8, "MEDV"])
```

The result of 35.2 has been rounded to 35.

- **Branching condition:** The condition below a node shows the condition that was used to branch to generate the child nodes from this now. For example, nodes 2 and 3 were generated using the condition *RM < 6.8* on the root node.

Generate the text display of the tree:

```
> bh.tree.pruned
```

Figure 141 shows the textual display of the pruned tree.

Let us understand the information in this representation of the tree. For each node, we see the following information:

- **Node number:** The first item in each row is the node number. For the root it is 1. The indentation in the figure shows parent child relationships. Node n has as its children nodes $2n$ and $2n + 1$
- **The splitting condition used to arrive at that node:** For example, node 2 is reached from its parent (node 1) by applying the condition *RM < 6.797*.
- **Number of cases satisfying the conditions for the node:** For the root, this is all the cases in the training

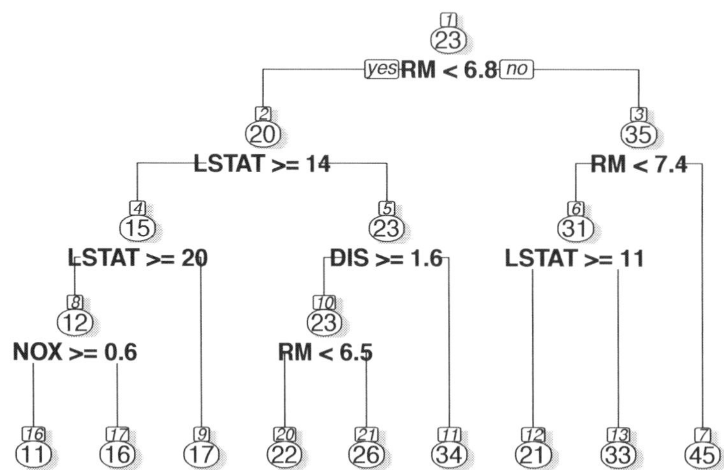

Figure 140: Boston Housing data: pruned tree

partition – or 356. For node 2, this will be the number of cases that satisfy *RM* < *6.797* – 289 cases. We can verify:

```
> nrow(train)     # 356
> nrow(train[train$RM < 6.797,])  # 289
```

- **Deviance:** This is the sum of squared differences from the mean of the target for cases in a node. For the root node this will be the sum of squared deviations of *MEDV* for all the cases in the training partition. Let us verify if the figure of 29818.43 satisfies this explanation:

```
> sum((train$MEDV - mean(train$MEDV))^2 )
```

We get 29818.43 as expected.
Let us check nodes 2 and 3 as well:

```
> # for node 2
> dat <- train[train$RM < 6.797, "MEDV"]
> sum((dat - mean(dat))^2)
> # for node 3
> dat <- train[train$RM >= 6.797, "MEDV"]
> sum((dat - mean(dat))^2)
```

We get 10954.47 for node 2 and 5552.927 for node 3 exactly as shown in the text display of the tree.
Let us see what the first split accomplished. In the root node, the overall deviance was 29818. The sum

```
n= 356

node), split, n, deviance, yval
      * denotes terminal node

 1) root 356 29818.43000 22.55112
   2) RM< 6.797 289 10954.57000 19.60692
     4) LSTAT>=14.395 116  1905.59900 14.61638
       8) LSTAT>=19.645 53   639.48720 11.92075
        16) NOX>=0.603 41   346.28980 10.79756 *
        17) NOX< 0.603 12    64.74917 15.75833 *
       9) LSTAT< 19.645 63   557.00410 16.88413 *
     5) LSTAT< 14.395 173  4222.77100 22.95318
      10) DIS>=1.6009 166  1895.36900 22.50181
        20) RM< 6.543 135  1033.13000 21.61481 *
        21) RM>=6.543 31   293.49100 26.36452 *
      11) DIS< 1.6009 7  1491.55700 33.65714 *
   3) RM>=6.797 67  5552.92700 35.25075
     6) RM< 7.445 46  2115.12600 31.01739
      12) LSTAT>=11.455 7   419.57710 20.75714 *
      13) LSTAT< 11.455 39   826.37440 32.85897 *
     7) RM>=7.445 21   807.63810 44.52381 *
```

Figure 141: Textual output for pruned tree

of the deviances of nodes 2 and 3 is 16506. The split at the root reduced the deviance by about 13,000.

- **Target value:** This is the mean of the target attribute for the cases satisfying the condition for that node. This is the more accurate value underlying the value shown in a node on the graphical tree display.

5. **Find the RMSE on the training and test partitions:**

```
> pred.train <- predict(bh.tree.pruned,
       train)
> rmse.train <- sqrt(mean(
       (train$MEDV - pred.train)^2))
> rmse.train

> pred.test <- predict(bh.tree.pruned,
       test)
> rmse.test <- sqrt(mean(
       (test$MEDV - pred.test)^2))
> rmse.test
```

We get 4.05 and 4.09 respectively. So if an average deviation of 4 from the actual value is acceptable then this model can be used.

Introduction to Data Visualization with ggplot

In the chapter *Exploratory Data Analysis*, we had discussed histograms, boxplots and scatterplots. We saw how these can help us to get a handle on large data sets before we start applying classification or regression methods.

Useful as those plots were, **R** – through the *ggplot2* package – offers to us vastly more elegant and powerful data visualization capabilities. This chapter will get you started on using *ggplot2*. The *ggplot2* package offers us an incredible level of control over almost every aspect of a plot and can quickly get somewhat complicated.

Happily for us, it provides a convenience function called *qplot* to make our job easier for most of our common plotting tasks. This chapter only covers *qplot*.

Single variable plots

We first consider plots of a single attribute on the *BostonHousing* data set[30] that we have looked at in several earlier chapters of this book. For convenience, we repeat the attribute descriptions in Table 79.

[30] K. Bache and M. Lichman. UCI machine learning repository, 2013. URL `http://archive.ics.uci.edu/ml`

We first read the data and load the *ggplot2* package – recall that we had installed it earlier in the lab on **R** packages. We load the package, read the file and then convert the attribute *CHAS* into a factor.

```
> library(ggplot2)
> bh <- read.csv("boston-housing-classification.csv")
> bh$CHAS <- factor(bh$CHAS)
```

In what follows, we will use only the *qplot* function of the *ggplot2* package.

The code below generates the histogram in Figure 142.

Attribute	Description
CRIM	per capita crime rate by town
ZN	proportion of residential land zoned for lots over 25,000 sq.ft.
INDUS	proportion of non-retail business acres per town.
CHAS	Bounds Charles River or not (1 if tract bounds river; 0 otherwise)
NOX	nitric oxides concentration (parts per 10 million)
RM	average number of rooms per dwelling
AGE	proportion of owner-occupied units built prior to 1940
DIS	weighted distances to five Boston employment centres
RAD	index of accessibility to radial highways
TAX	full-value property-tax rate per $10,000
PTRATIO	pupil-teacher ratio by town
B	$1000(Bk - 0.63)^2$ where Bk is the proportion of blacks by town
LSTAT	% lower status of the population
MEDV_CAT	Median value of owner-occupied homes categorized into *High* or *Low*

Table 79: Boston Housing attribute descriptions.

```
> qplot(AGE, data = bh)
```

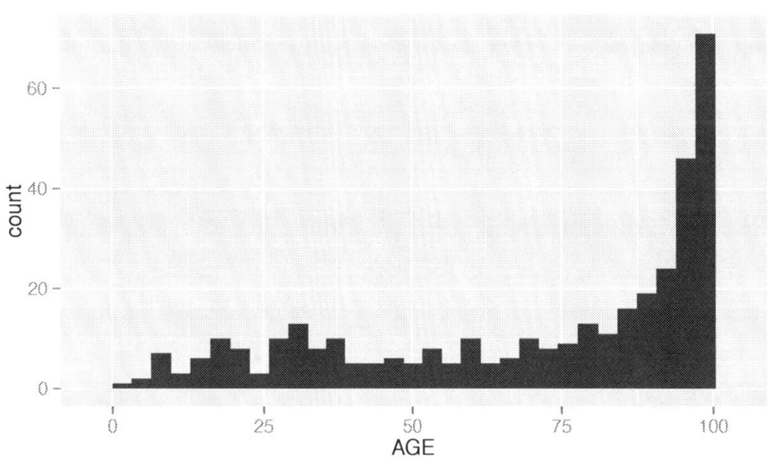

Figure 142: Histogram of AGE generated by *qplot*

When we supply a single numeric attribute to *qplot*, it produces a histogram by default.

In several of the following plots, we use color. Although the plots in the printed version of the book show only gray scales, you will see the colors when you execute these commands on your computer.

We can change the color of the bars:

```
> qplot(AGE, data = bh, fill = I("blue"))
```

You might be wondering why we could not just say *fill = "blue"* instead of *fill = I("blue")*. For now, just hold on to that. You will soon see why.

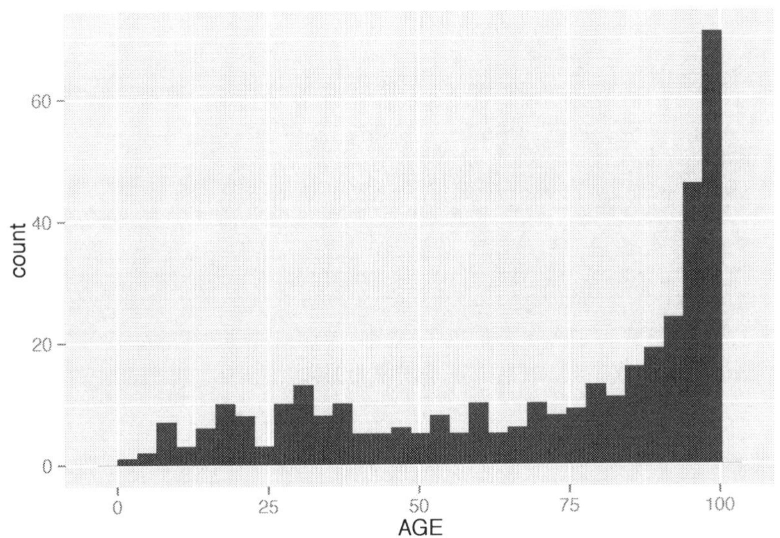

Figure 143: Histogram with a blue fill

If the single attribute that we supply is a factor then we get a bar plot of the count of each value of the factor.

```
> qplot(MEDV_CAT, data = bh,
       fill = I("blue"))
```

Figure 144 shows the result.

We can flip the axes too:

```
qplot(MEDV_CAT, data = bh,
       fill = I("blue")) + coord_flip()
```

Figure 145 shows the result.

As with the base graphics system, we can control various aspects of the plot. We change the default labels below:

```
> qplot(AGE, data = bh,
     xlab = "Proportion built before 1940",
     ylab = "Count",
     main = "Age analysis")
```

Figure 146 shows the output.

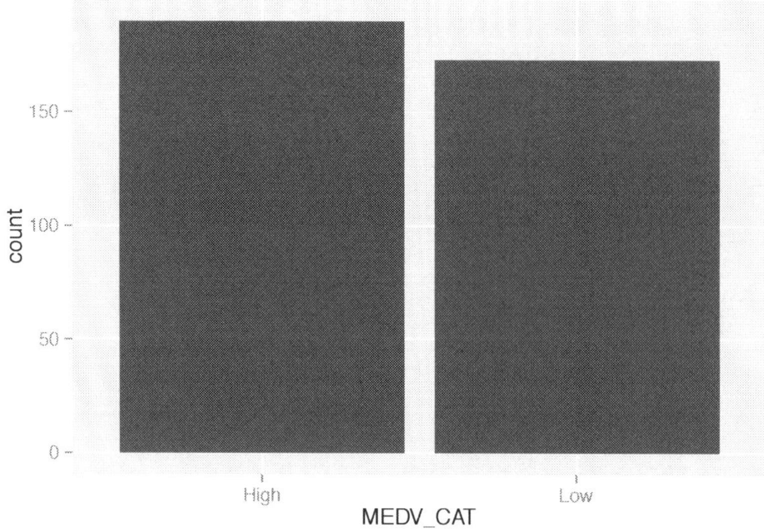

Figure 144: Barplot of a single attribute

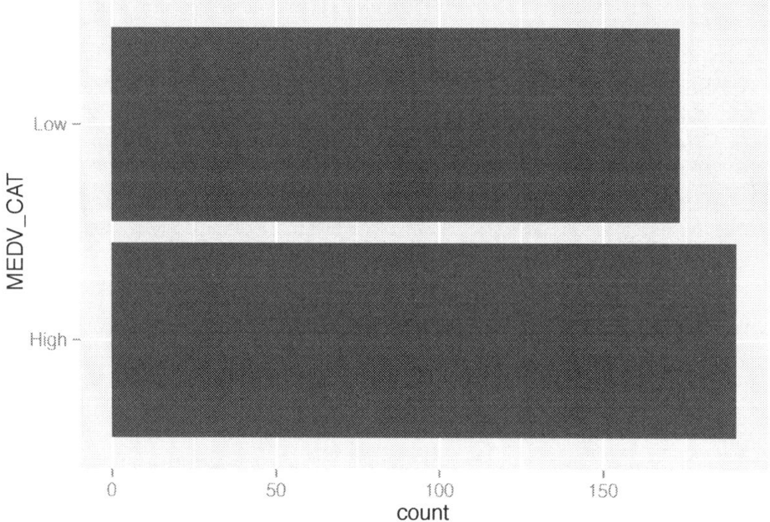

Figure 145: Barplot with axes flipped

Using *qplot*, a histogram is perhaps the most common single variable plot. The *ggplot2* package is designed mainly to display more than one attribute in a single plot – multi-variable plots. Let us turn our attention to these now.

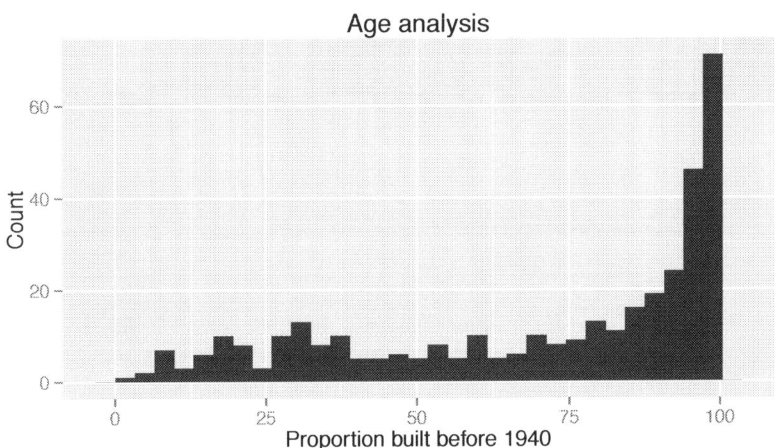

Figure 146: Another histogram of AGE generated by *qplot*

Multi-variable Plots

ggplot really shines when it comes to creating multi-variable plots. When we can include several variables in a plot, we get the ability to tell a story rather than just display data. We can easily present comparisons, correlations and even indicate possible causality.

Let us first add the attribute *MEDV_CAT* to our earlier histogram of *AGE*:

```
> qplot(AGE, data = bh, fill = MEDV_CAT)
```

The *fill* argument tells *qplot* how to fill the bars of the histogram. However, rather than specifying just a single color as we did earlier, we are specifying one of the attributes, *MEDV_CAT* as the fill color. This results in a different color used for the different values of *MEDV_CAT*.

Figure 147 shows the result. We see not just the total number of cases for each bin of the histogram, but also the break up of this between *Low* and *High* values of *MEDV_CAT*.

From the above, you can see how *qplot* is looking to use the *fill* argument to determine the fill color based on some attribute value and hence requires something with multiple values. This is why we had to use *I("blue")* earlier when we had just a single fill color.

We might have expected that neighborhoods with a higher proportion of older homes will tend to have lower median values. This chart lends credence to the expectation.

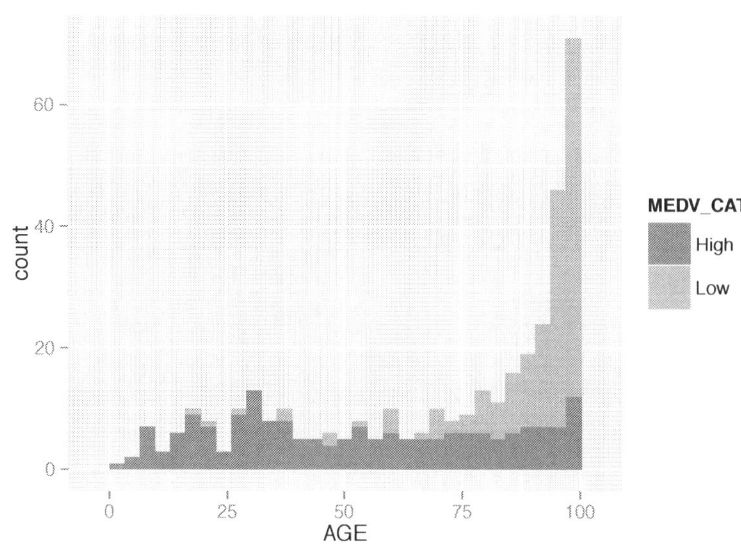

Figure 147: Histogram of *AGE* with *MEDV_CAT* included through *fill*

Let us turn our attention to boxplots. While boating on urban rivers, we often see beautiful large homes on the river banks. We might wonder whether communities that adjoin riverbanks generally have larger homes on average. To check this, we can generate a comparative boxplot of RM against CHAS.

```
> qplot(CHAS, RM, data = bh,
       geom = "boxplot",
       fill = I("lightblue")
```

By default, when we supply two attributes to plot, *qplot* generates a scatterplot. We used the *geom* parameter to indicate that we wanted a boxplot instead. Figure 148 shows the result.

Incidentally, *qplot* does not generate boxplots of just a single attribute. We need to supply two attributes:

When we supply two attributes, the first one appears on the x axis and the other on the y axis. Thus in the context of a boxplot, the first attribute should be a categorical one.

Figure 148 shows us that the median of the average number of rooms is indeed higher for neighborhoods adjoining the river, but not dramatically.

We now turn our attention to the *auto-mpg.csv* data file. The attributes should be self-explanatory.

We first read the data and convert *cylinders* into a factor with

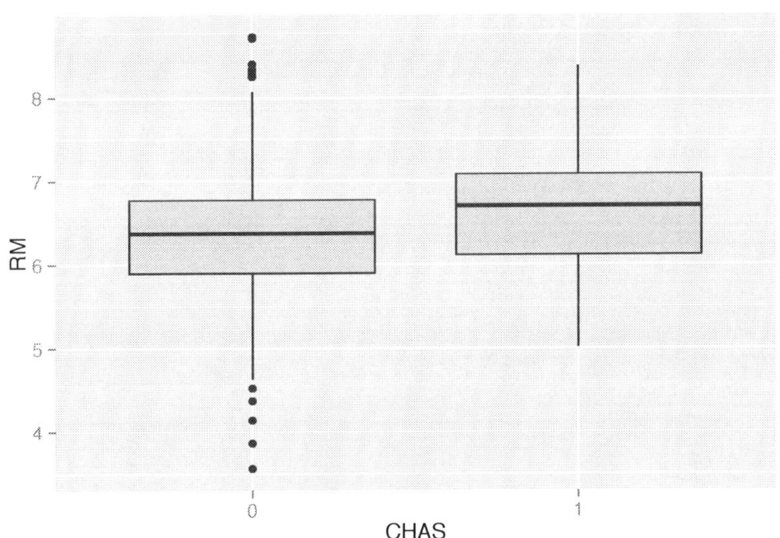

Figure 148: Boxplot of *RM* against *CHAS*

meaningful names:

```
> auto <- read.csv("auto-mpg.csv")
> auto$cylinders <- factor(auto$cylinders,
      levels = c(3,4,5,6,8),
      labels = c("3cyl", "4cyl", "5cyl",
      "6cyl", "8cyl"))
```

Let us see the impact of weight on fuel-efficiency:

```
> qplot(weight, mpg, data = auto)
```

Figure 149 shows the result.

When we supply two attributes, *qplot* generates a scatterplot. As before, the attribute supplied first is plotted on the x axis.

We might suspect that the heavier vehicles also have more cylinders. We can easily add cylinders into this plot as a third dimension – on the two dimensional surface of the paper!

We can make *qplot* color the points based on the number of cylinders:

```
> qplot(weight, mpg, data = auto,
        color = cylinders)
```

Figure 150 shows the outcome. The figure tells us that not only are heavier cars lower in fuel efficiency, but so are cars with more cylinders. We would of course, expect this.

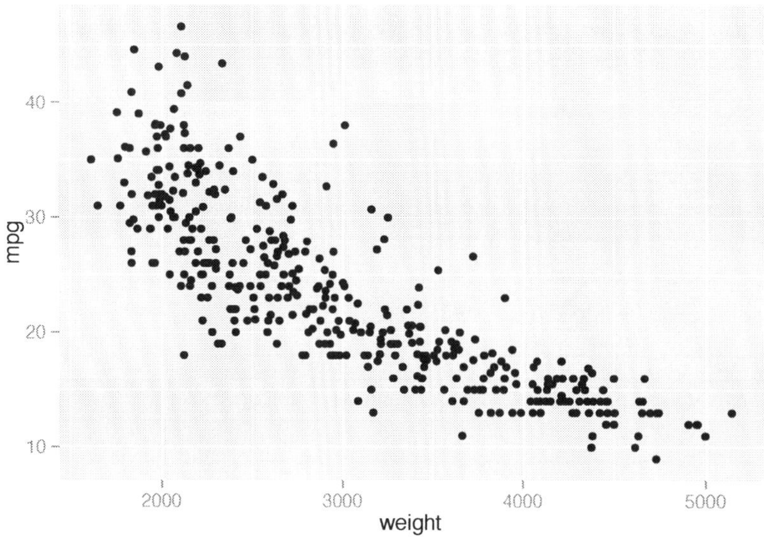

Figure 149: Scatterplot of weight vs mpg

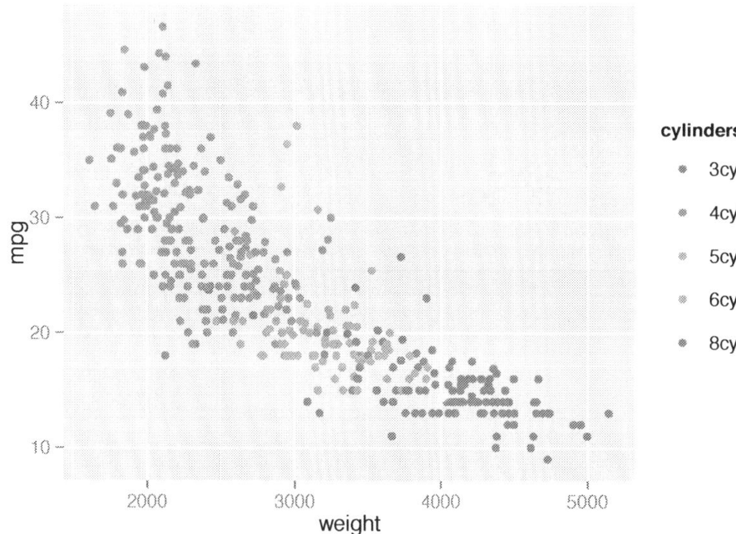

Figure 150: Scatterplot of weight vs mpg with cylinders shown through color

Having shown three dimensions on a two-dimensional surface, can we add yet another one? Indeed, we can. We can make the size of the plotted points show another attribute, say *horsepower*.

```
> qplot(weight, mpg, data = auto,
       color = cylinders,
       size = horsepower)
```

Unlike *cylinders* which is categorical with discrete values, horsepower is a continuous value and we were still able to use it as a new dimension. In fact we can also use a continuous attribute for color as well.

Figure 151 shows the result.

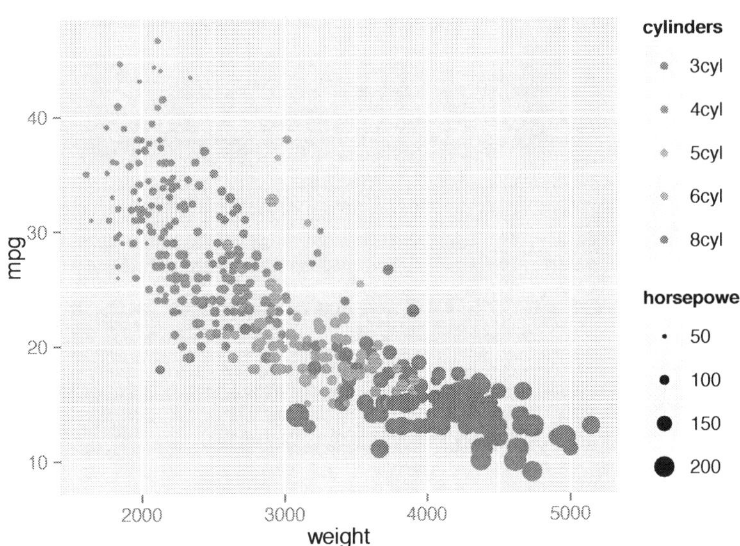

Figure 151: Scatterplot of weight vs mpg with the size of points showing horsepower

We can also add smoothed lines to scatterplots:

```
> qplot(weight, mpg, data = auto,
      color = horsepower,
      geom = c("point", "smooth"))
```

Figure 152 shows the result. The smoothed line is based on *LOWESS* – which we will not go into. The band shows the 95% confidence interval.

We can eliminate the band if we want:

```
> qplot(weight, mpg, data = auto,
      color = horsepower,
      geom = c("point", "smooth"),
      se = FALSE)
```

Instead of the *LOWESS* line, we can get the linear regression line as well:

```
> qplot(weight, mpg, data = auto,
      colour = horsepower,
```

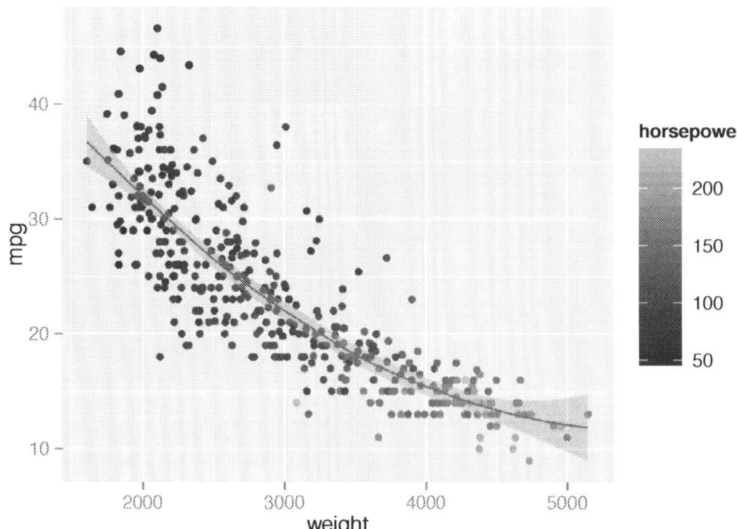

Figure 152: Scatterplot of weight vs mpg with smoothed line

```
    geom = c("point","smooth"),
    method = "lm")
```

Figure 153 shows the result.

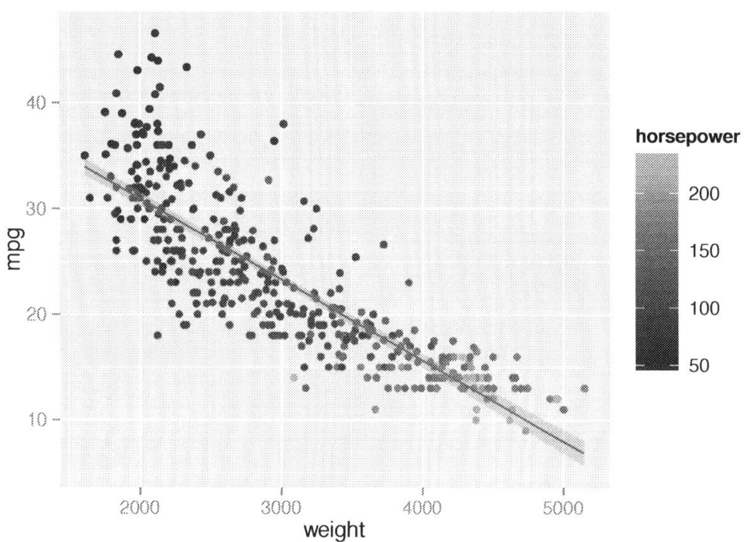

Figure 153: Scatterplot of weight vs mpg with linear regression line

What if we want to see the scatterplot separately for each level of *cylinders*? Even that is easy:

```
> qplot(weight, mpg, data=auto,
```

```
facets= ~cylinders,
geom=c("point", "smooth"))
```

When we use the *facets* parameter, we are asking *qplot* to divide up the data by the factor values of the facet variable and plot the chart separately for each set.

Figure 154 shows the results.

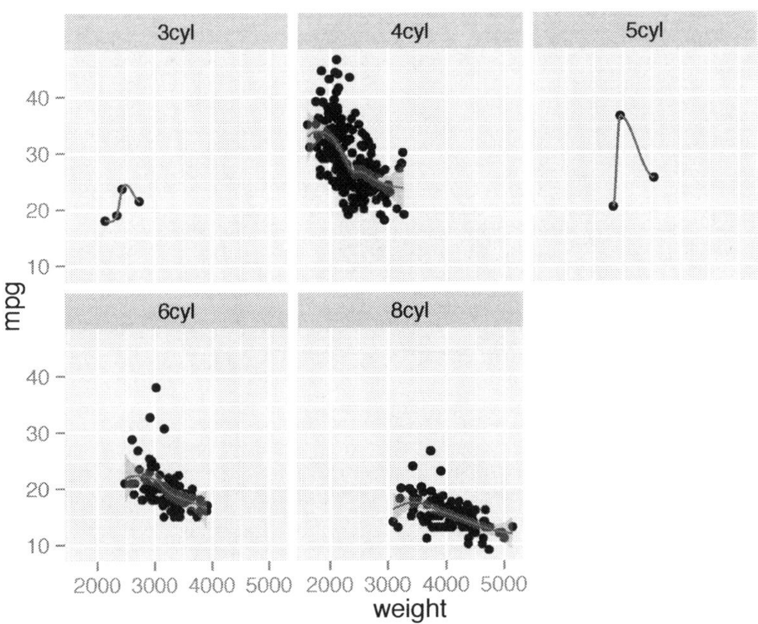

Figure 154: Scatterplot of weight vs mpg for each level of *cylinders*

We can even have two facets! Our data contains just one factor – *cylinders*. Let us create one more based on *horsepower*:

```
> auto$hp_fac <- cut(auto$horsepower,
      breaks =c(quantile(auto$horsepower,
      probs = seq(0, 1, by = 0.33) )),
      labels = c("LowHP", "MediumHP", "HighHP"),
      include.lowest = TRUE)
```

We have now created a new factor attribute called *hp_fac*. We can use this as the second facet:

```
> qplot(weight, mpg, data=auto,
      facets=cylinders~hp_fac, geom=c("point"))
```

Figure 155 shows the result. The expression *cylinders ~ hp_fac* caused the *cylinders* values to occupy the vertical axis of the facet plot. If we had said instead *hp_fac ~ cylinders*, then the orientation of the facets would have been reversed.

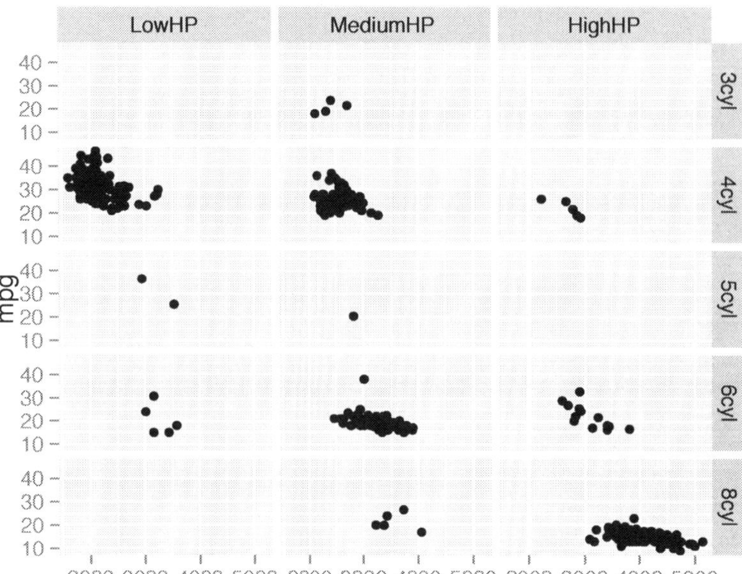

Figure 155: Using two facets

Figure 155 tells us that the negative impact of *weight* on *mpg* is much more pronounced for 4-cylinder LowHP cars than it is for say, 8-cylinder, HighHP cars. If we had a huge amount of data and we were building a predictive regression model for *mpg*, then we could consider splitting the data and building a separate model for cars in each facet.

In this short tour of *qplot*, we have covered several useful features. As we had indicated earlier, rather than creating charts that simply show information, we should aim to provide analytical insights. We can accomplish this by judiciously including several attributes.

Our charts should show comparisons and contrasts. They should also clearly show relationships and indicate possible causality. Even the rudimentary features of *ggplot* that we have discussed in this chapter provide us with ample scope to create effective charts.

Time Series Analysis

Figure 156 shows the price of unleaded gas in the US between 1976 and 2014[31]. It shows time on the horizontal, or x, axis and the gas price on the vertical, or y, axis and helps us to see the big picture of how the gas price has changed over time. The figure represents a *time series*.

[31] US Bureau of Labor Statistics. Price of unleaded gas, April 2014. URL http://download.bls.gov/pub/time.series/ap/ap.data.2.Gasoline

We often see *time series* data – data representing some measurement over time. Other common examples of time series data include consumer prices indexes, daily closing share prices, a medical patient's hourly blood pressure or blood sugar level, company profits, and weather data (like daily or hourly temperature and pressure).

With companies and governments gathering data regularly, and with numerous data capture devices reporting almost continuously, we live amidst a flood of time-series data. Analyzing time-series data can also yield important insights and we will look at a few standard analytical techniques in this chapter.

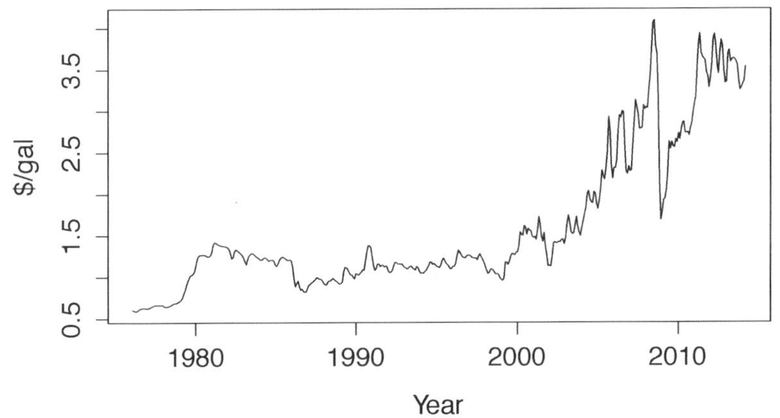

Figure 156: A typical time-series.

Though the price movements in Figure 156 may seem complex and irregular – even capricious – the techniques of *time series analysis* can help us to make use of such data productively.

To understand some of the components of real-life time series data, let us build up from a simplistic and unrealistic time series to a complex realistic one by gradually adding elements.

Fig 157 shows arguably the simplest possible time series – a constant value over time. Why would we consider this time series to be simple? Predictability. Complete lack of surprise. Assuming that nothing in the underlying phenomena changed, we can say with a lot of confidence what the future values of this time series are likely to be – at least in the short run.

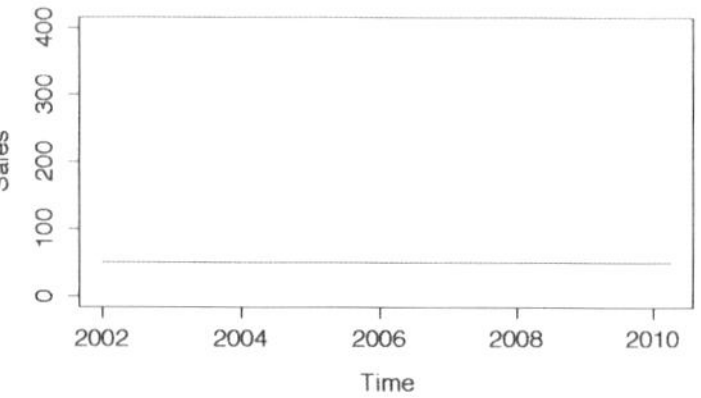

Figure 157: A very simple time-series – constant sales over time.

In real-life scenarios, we seldom study time series that remain constant over time. Interesting ones tend to exhibit variations over time. Businesspeople and economists often obsess over growth – for example, in GDP, profits and earnings per share. Figure 158 shows a hypothetical example with a *linear* growth *trend* over time. We could well have non-linear trends. In fact the trend need not even be just growth or decline. We could see a mix over time – for example, the sales could rise sharply initially and then rise, but at a slowing rate and then plateau off for a long time and then decline as in a typical product-life cycle

Clearly, real-life time series differ from Figures 157 and 158 in a very important sense – real-life time-series are not clean and smooth. They rise and fall many times, seemingly unpredictably, and appear jagged.

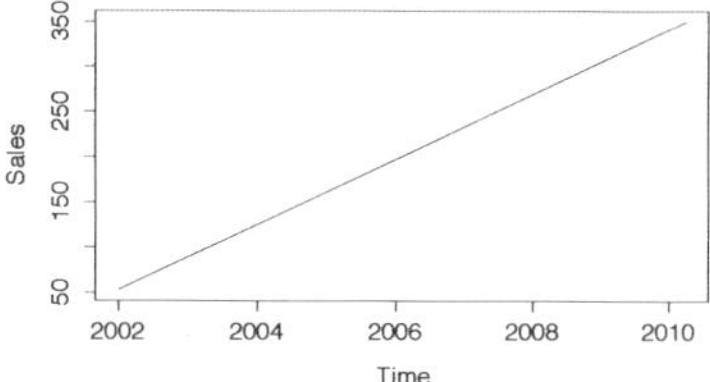

Figure 158: A more interesting time series – sales with a growth trend.

Even a time series that exhibits a plain growth trend will likely have ups and downs as Figure 159 shows. We are now starting to see some elements of realism.

We can see Figure 159 as representing a basic linear growth trend as in Figure 158, coupled with a an irregular element that makes the figure deviate from the underlying trend. Figure 160 shows these fluctuations alone.

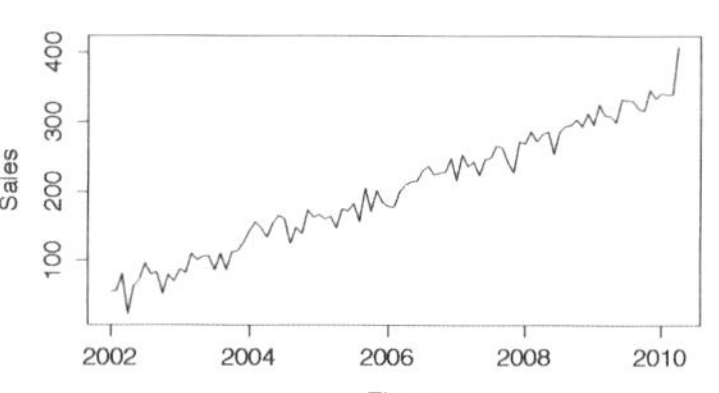

Figure 159: A more realistic time series with irregularities – even though we see an obvious overall growth trend, every single month does not represent growth over the prior month.

We can obtain the sales numbers in Figure 159 for any month by adding the corresponding month's sales from Figures 158 and 160.

For those time periods in which the fluctuation is negative, the sales in Figure 159 fall below the corresponding value on the clean straight line of Figure 158. Likewise, a positive fluctuation value takes the sales above the clean straight line.

When we see a time series that seems to exhibit a general pattern (like growth or decline or a mix) but with some fluctuations as in Figure 159, we can see it as a combination of two other time series – one that shows an underlying smooth pattern, and another that captures the irregular fluctuations from that underlying pattern.

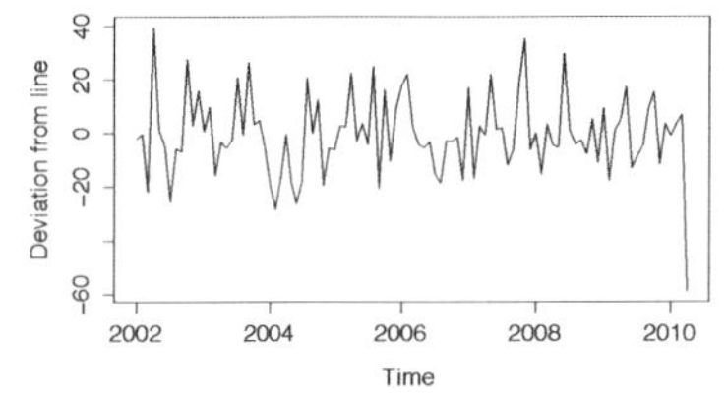

Figure 160: Irregular fluctuation of sales from simple trend. The vastly different scale on the y-axis on this figure makes the fluctuations look big.

Even though the sales in Figure 160 keep rising and falling, we would hardly doubt the overall growth trend. If the real world behaved strictly according to smooth mathematical functions, we might not see irregularities. However, we have to remember that we use mathematics as a tool to represent, understand and predict the real world – and not the other way around!

This brings us to the first important task in time series analysis – given a time series with an irregular pattern, tease out the underlying smooth trend and the irregular fluctuations. That is, we want to *decompose* the observed time-series into two different time series – one to capture the smooth pattern or *trend* and the other to show the *irregular* fluctuations from the smooth trend.

Based on the above discussion, Figure 161 shows how the chart in Figure 159 is literally obtained by adding the data in the charts in Figures 158 and 160.

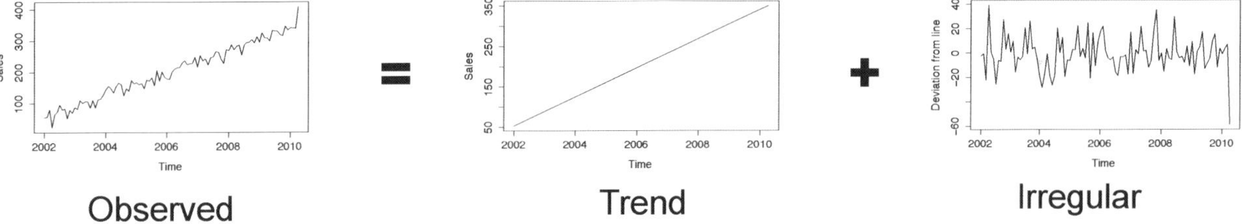

Figure 161: Decomposition of time series into trend and irregular components.

Figure 159 exhibits an obvious trend. Sometimes the trend might be quite subtle and difficult to spot. We need automated techniques to separate the trend from the irregularity.

From the foregoing discussion, we can see that identifying the trend requires us to ignore the effects of the irregular variations. Visually, we can see this as "smoothing" the small disturbances to arrive at the underlying trend.

We can "smooth" time series data by averaging. At the extreme end of simplification, we can average the entire series and use the resulting single value as the "smoothed" value for the whole time span. Table 80 shows the first 10 values from the time series in Figure 159.

Time	Sales
1	51
2	56
3	37
4	101
5	66
6	63
7	45
8	68
9	70
10	107

Table 80: Data extract for smoothing example.

In real life, we would generally not be interested in smoothing time series with a very small number of data points. However we use the 10-element data set in Figure 80 for ease of understanding.

Figure 162 plots the time series from Table 80. It looks extremely jagged compared to the original plot because of the much smaller time frame and the magnified y-axis.

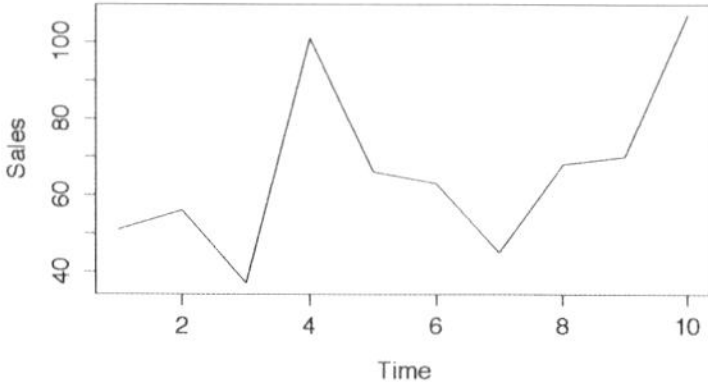

Figure 162: Plot of data from Table 80.

The data from Table 80 averages to 66.4 and Figure 163 shows a smoothed plot based just on this single average – not of much use if we want to capture the underlying trend.

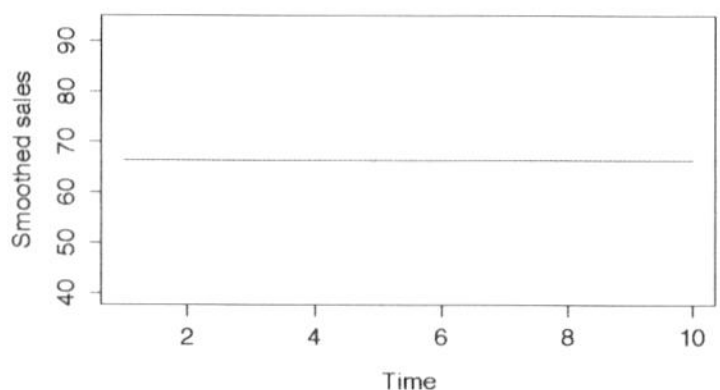

Figure 163: Data from Table 80 smoothed by a single average – not of much use to see the underlying trend.

Instead of averaging the complete data, how about averaging just a few data points around each time instant?

For example, we could average three values at a time and see what that does. To compute the smoothed value for period 2, we will average the original values of periods 1, 2 and 3. For the smoothed value of period 3, we will average the values of periods 2, 3 and 4 and so on. In general, to compute a three-period smoothed value for a period n, we will average the values of periods (n-1), n and (n+1). Of course we cannot compute a smoothed value for period 1 or for period 10 – because computing the smoothed value for period 1 would require the original value for period 0 and our series begins only at period 1. You can reason similarly for the smoothed value for period 10.

In the above, we used the original value from one time period before and one time period after, in addition to the original value of the reference time period while computing the smoothed value. If we took two periods before and two after, we will get a total of five values to average; seven if we took three before and three after. We refer to the number of values we average as the *smoothing horizon*. Clearly it makes sense to use odd numbered *smoothing horizons*.

Figure 164 shows the result of using a smoothing horizon of 3. It looks smoother than Figure 162 and shows the growth trend a little more clearly. As expected, it does not show smoothed values for periods 1 and 10.

		Smoothing horizon		
Period	Original data	3	5	7
1	51			
2	56	48.0		
3	37	64.7	62.2	
4	101	68.0	64.6	59.9
5	66	76.7	62.4	62.3
6	63	58.0	68.6	64.3
7	45	58.7	62.4	74.3
8	68	61.0	70.6	
9	70	81.7		
10	107			

Table 81: Computing smoothed values for various smoothing horizons. For a smoothing period of 3, the smoothed value for each time period is the average of the original value for the time period and one time period before and after. For a smoothing period of 5, we will average two values before and after along with the value for the time period.

We refer to this way of computing the trend in general as the method of *moving averages*.

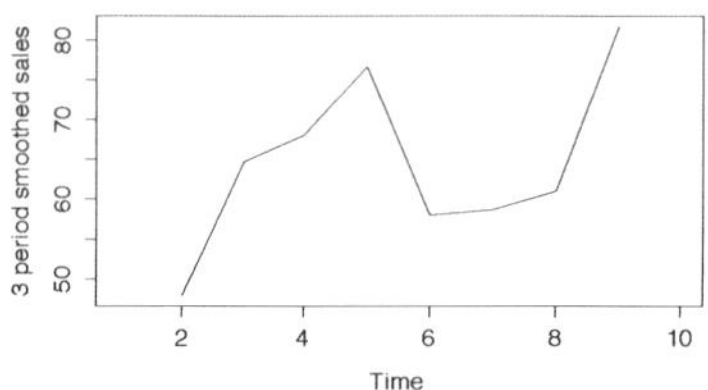

Figure 164: Data from Table 80 smoothed by a three-period average.

To examine the smoothing impact of averaging more values, Figure 165 shows the result of smoothing by averaging 5 and 7 values. However, given that we have just 10 values, these make little sense.

Applying the same idea to the original data in Figure 159 we find the results in Figure 166 for various smoothing horizons. As we increase the smoothing horizon, we get smoother and smoother curves.

What smoothing horizon should we use? We have seen that low values do not smooth out the irregularities well. However, very high values tend to hide some elements of the underlying trend itself. So we need to find a value that is in-between – one that does a good job of smoothing, without losing the underlying trend. By experimenting with several values, we can choose one that seems to work well.

For example, in Figure 166 a horizon of 3 does not smooth out the random variations sufficiently. Values of 5 and 7 do a better job and can be used.

We used a time series that had a linear trend. The smoothing approach works even when the trend is not linear. Figure 167 shows the original and smoothed versions of the US gas price data that we saw at the start of this section.

Figure 168 shows the daily bike rentals[32] by registered users of a bike-sharing service in Washington DC.

[32] Hadi Fanaee-T and Joao Gama. Event labeling combining ensemble detectors and background knowledge. *Progress in Artificial Intelligence*, pages 1–15, 2013. ISSN 2192-6352. DOI: 10.1007/s13748-013-0040-3. URL http://dx.doi.org/10.1007/s13748-013-0040-3

Like the examples we have seen so far, this data also has a trend and an irregular component. However, it also exhibits clear seasonality. Each year we observe a peak during the warmer months and a trough in winter. What else do you see

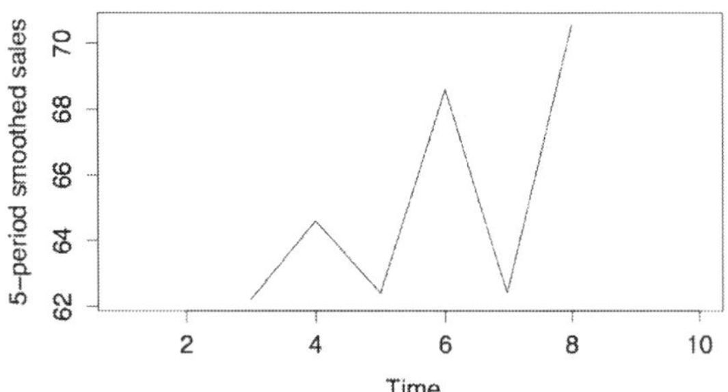

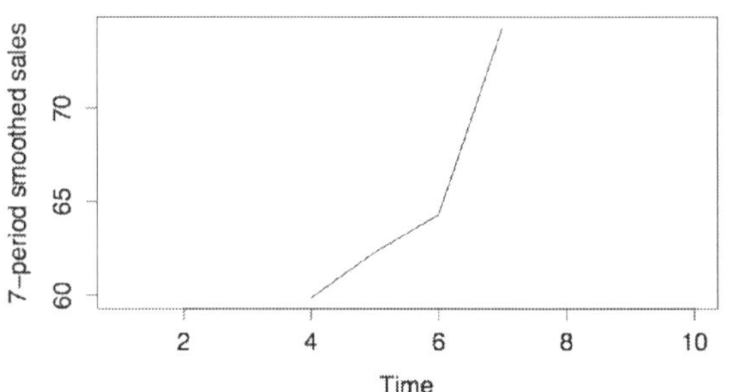

Figure 165: Smoothing by averaging 5 and 7 values respectively.

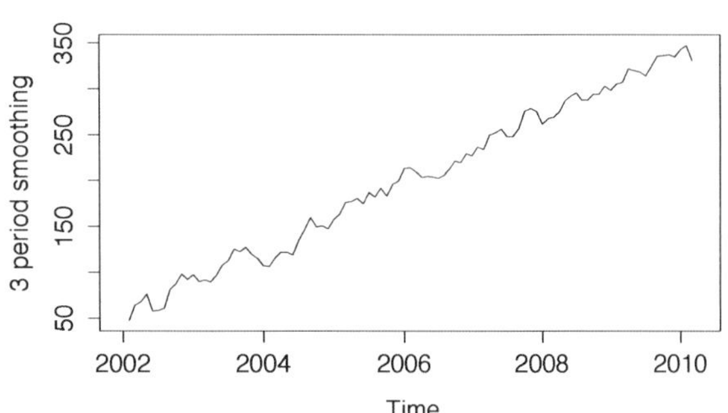

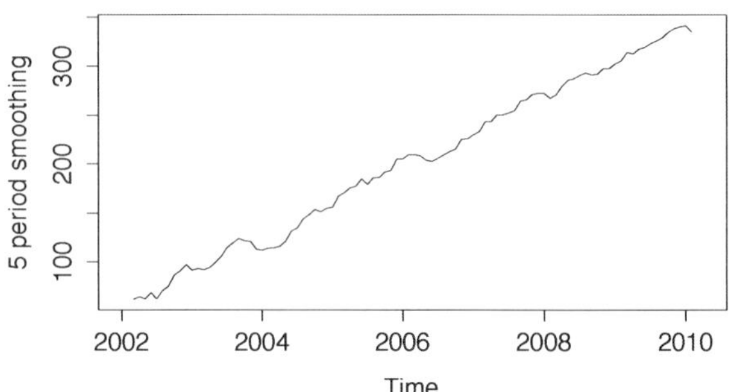

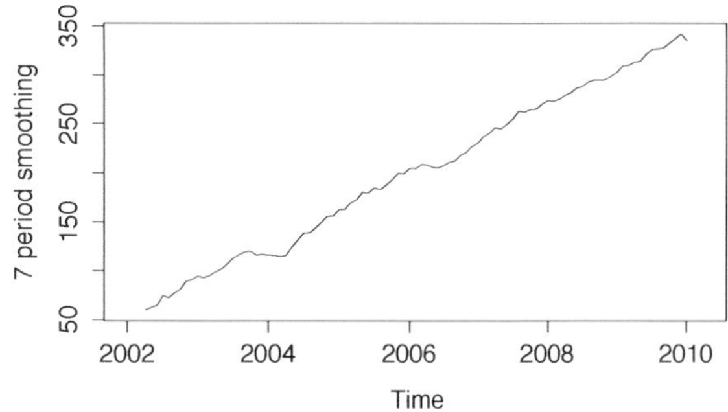

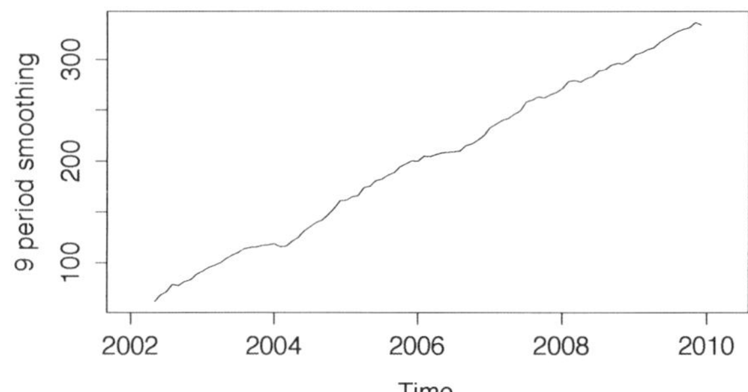

Figure 166: Smoothing on the original data set in Figure 159.

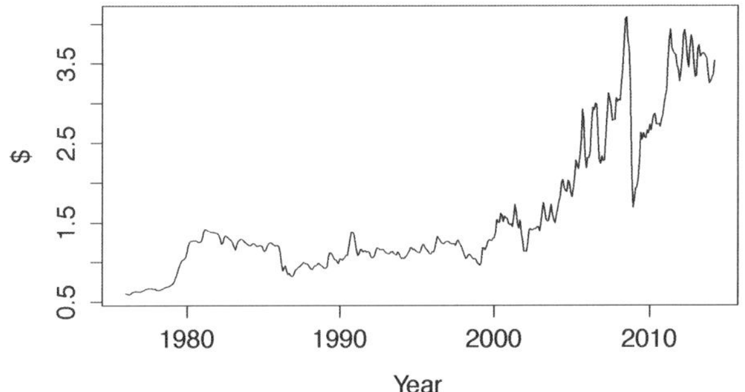

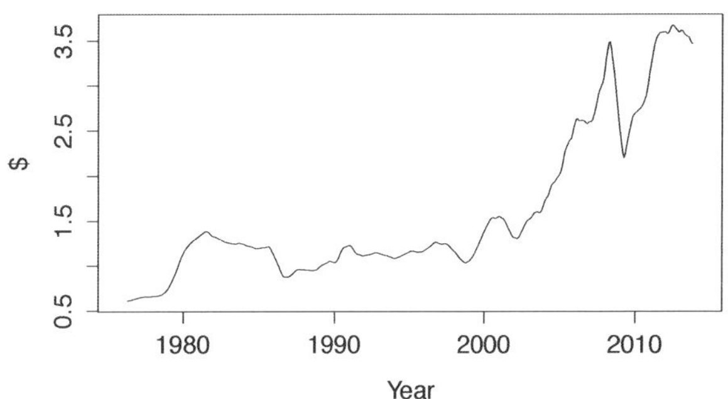

Figure 167: Original and smoothed versions of US gas price.

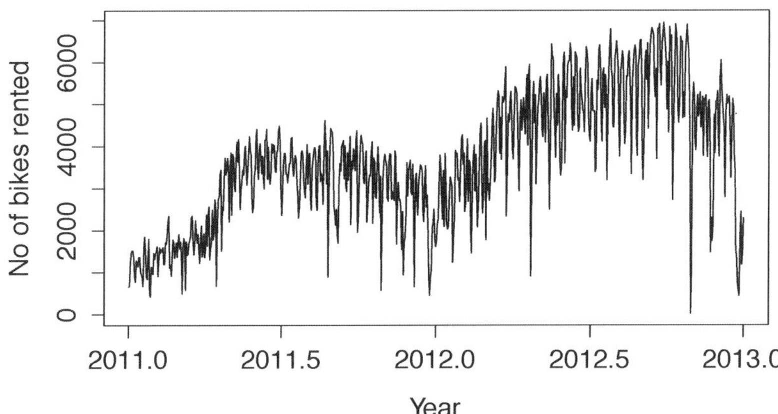

Figure 168: Bike rentals by registered users of a bike-sharing service in Washington DC.

besides seasonality? Disregarding the seasonality, what can we say about the general level of bike rentals over the time period that the chart covers? Does it seem to have stayed steady or increased or decreased or anything else? From 2011 till the third quarter of 2012, we see a rising trend superimposed on the seasonality.

So this time series has three components – trend, seasonality and irregular fluctuations. Just like in the earlier case, we would like to decompose the series into these three elements.

As before, let us build up the pattern from the ground up. Figure 169 shows the monthly number of visitors to a hypothetical museum.

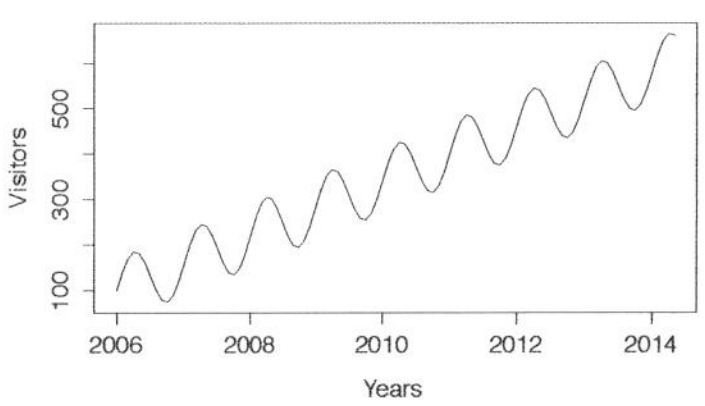

Figure 169: Number of visitors to a museum – an unrealistically smooth series.

We see a clear seasonality with higher numbers of visitors

during the warm months. Despite the regular rise and fall, the museum is seeing a steady growth of visitors over the years.

However, the picture is too smooth to be realistic. Figure 170 shows a somewhat more realistic time series.

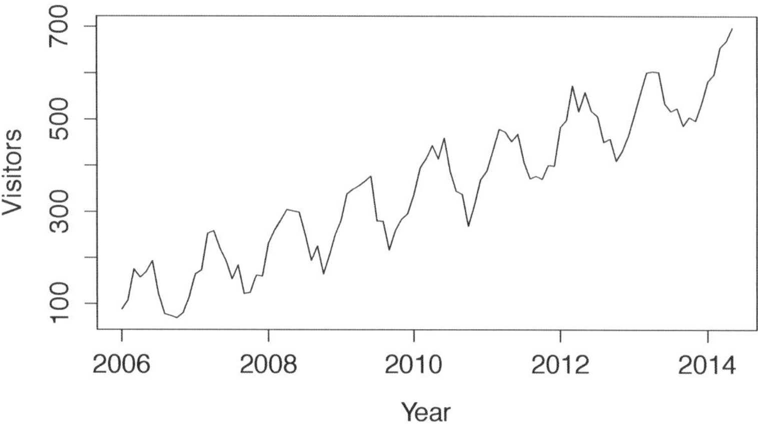

Figure 170: Number of visitors to a museum – a slightly more realistic series.

In Figure 170 we see a trend as before, but also seasonality and irregular fluctuations. We can decompose this into its three components to get Figure 171.

In the examples of decomposition we have considered so far, we identified the individual components – trend, seasonality and irregularity – that when added up yield the observed time series. This is called the *additive model*.

When the seasonal fluctuations are roughly constant over time, as in Figures 159 and 170 we can use the additive model – treat the observed time series as the sum of the components.

Figure 168 shows a case where the seasonal fluctuations seem to be bigger as the general level of rentals rises. This happens when seasonal effects affect the underlying trend by a constant factor. For example, a company could have a base sales level with a growth trend and have seasonal variations with the sales during the year varying between 0.8 and 1.2 times the base sales value. In this case, because the seasonal effects are a multiplicative factor of the sales, their absolute effects are higher at higher sales levels and lower at lower sales effects. For example, at a sales level of 500 units, a seasonal effect of 1.2 produces a sales of 600 units. Whereas the same seasonal effect applied to a base sales level of 700 units would

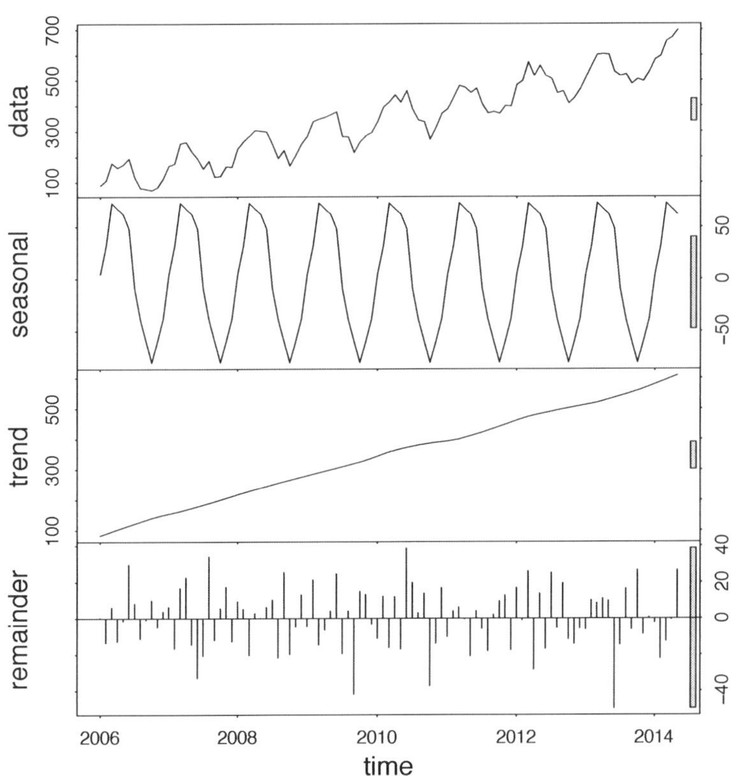

Figure 171: Decomposing a time series with seasonal and trend components. The top chart represents the original time series and the bottom three charts represent the decomposition.

produce a sales of 840 units. This situation represents a *multiplicative model.*

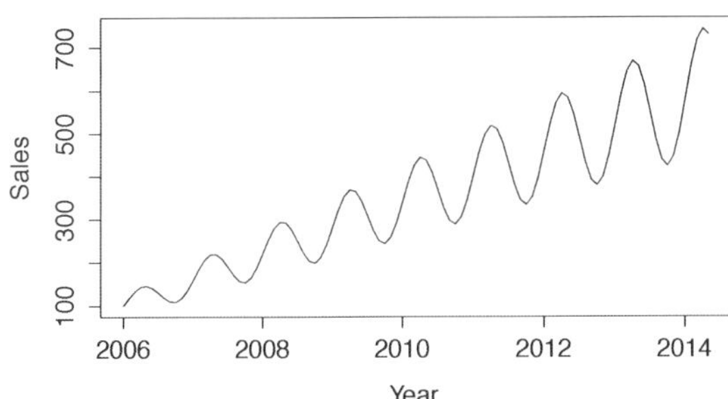

Figure 172: A time series with multiplicative characteristics. Note how the seasonal variation grows as the general sales level rises.

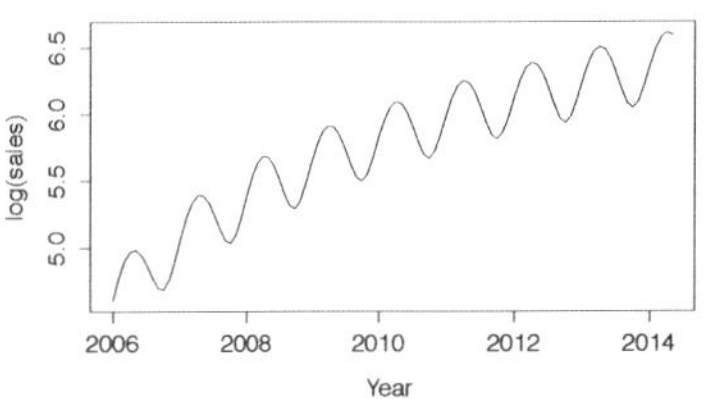

Figure 173: Applying the log function to a multiplicative time series removes the variations in the absolute impact of seasonality and makes it amenable to an additive decomposition.

Figure 172 shows a multiplicative time series with both trend and seasonality. The amplitude of the seasonal variations grows with time.

To decompose multiplicative time series, we can create a

new time series with the logarithm of the original values and then decompose the new series as an additive time series. The logarithm function eliminates the variations in the absolute impact of seasonality. Figure 173 shows a plot of the logarithm of the series in Figure 172. Note how the seasonal impact does not depend on the absolute magnitude anymore – the size of the up and down fluctuations remains more or less constant, enabling the use of the earlier decomposition approach.

Given a time series, we often want to make forecasts. With simple time series, forecasting poses no serious challenges. For example, we can easily extrapolate time series with nearly constant values or those with a clearly visible and almost linear trend. Time series with more complex patterns, pose greater challenges.

Approaches similar to the moving average technique that we discussed earlier perform quite well for forecasting. Moving average helped to smooth out variations and identify the trend. We can use a technique called *exponential smoothing* for forecasting. In computing moving averages, we used the current value and a set of values before and after the current one. While forecasting, we have to take a different approach. When computing a forecast for time period n, we can expect to have the values for all time periods before n, but not the value for n or beyond – if we did, then we would not need to *forecast*!

With moving averages where we wanted just to smooth the curve, we computed a simple average. A simple average might not make as much sense for forecasting because the more recent values generally are more indicative of what is to come and it would make sense to give a higher weights to more recent values. A common forecasting technique called *exponential smoothing* does this by decreasing the weights exponentially for older values.

Time period	Weight
$n-1$	0.5
$n-2$	0.25
$n-3$	0.125
$n-4$	0.0625
$n-5$	0.03125
...	...

Table 82: Example of weights used in exponential smoothing to forecast a value for period n.

Table 82 shows an example of the weights that might be used.

In exponential smoothing for forecasting, analysts use a parameter α, which takes a value between 0 and 1, to determine the weights for various periods. To forecast for time period n, we use the weight $\alpha(1-\alpha)^i$ as the weight for period $n-i$. Choosing a high value for α weights more recent values heavily. Table 83 shows the impact of α on the weights.

Table 85 shows a sample exponential smoothing computation. Simple exponential smoothing like this works well only

period	Weight for $\alpha =$ 0.1	0.3	0.5	0.7
$n-1$	0.1	0.3	0.5	0.7
$n-2$	0.09	0.21	0.25	0.21
$n-3$	0.081	0.147	0.125	0.063
$n-4$	0.0729	0.1029	0.0625	0.0189
$n-5$	0.06561	0.07203	0.03125	0.00567
$n-6$	0.059049	0.050421	0.015625	0.001701

Table 83: Weights for various values of α in exponential smoothing.

time	1	2	3	4	5
value	54	51	53	52	55

Table 84: Sample time series for exponential smoothing.

for time series that do not exhibit any systematic trend or seasonality. In the presence of these conditions, we can use other techniques, notably the Holt-Winter method. We illustrate it in the lab.

time	1	2	3	4	5	6
value	54	51	53	52	55	
weight	0.03125	0.0625	0.125	0.25	0.5	
weight*value	1.6875	3.1875	6.625	13	27.5	
sum(weight*value)/sum(weight)						52

Table 85: Exponential smoothing computation of forecast for time period 6 using the weights in Table 82.

Lab 17: Time series analysis

Pre-requisite(s)

- ✓ You should have read the section on time series analysis (page 307).
- ✓ You should have completed the introduction to **R** data frames lab (page 17).

Objective

After completing this lab, you will be able to:

- ✓ Read time series data into **R** and plot such data.
- ✓ Create **R** time-series objects from time series data.
- ✓ Decompose time series data into seasonal and trend components forecasting.
- ✓ Use the Holt-Winter technique for forecasting.

Overview

In this lab, we will learn to use **R** for working on time series data. Specifically, we will look at creating time series objects, plotting and decomposing time series and using the Holt-Winter forecasting method.

Activity steps

1. **Read data:** Read the data from the file *ts-example.csv*.

   ```
   s <- read.csv("ts-example.csv")
   ```

   The file contains the monthly sales data for a hypothetical company.

2. **Look at the data:** Take a look at the data. You see that it has just a single attribute called *sales*. Explore a little bit by computing a summary, doing a boxplot, histogram and so on, to get a feel for what is in the data frame. With time series data, especially things like stock prices, we often want to explore the propensity of a measurement to change from period to period – its volatility. Financial analysts often look at the volatility of a stock as a measure of its risk. Volatility analysis might not be of importance for all time-series data.

   sales
   summary(s)
   hist(s$sales)
   boxplot(s$sales)

3. **Analyze differences:** If relevant for the time series, we can analyze the period-to-period changes. To compute the period-to-period changes by subtracting the value at period $t-1$ from the value at period t. You can do this with:

   ```
   > d <- diff(s[,1])
   > # In the next command, the letter in quotes is the lowercase L
   > # It signifies that we want a line graph
   > plot(d, type = "l" )
   ```

   Sometimes we would like to analyze the differences. For example we might want to compute the mean and standard deviation of the differences:

   ```
   > mean(d)
   > sd(d)
   ```

Difference between *plot* and *plot.ts*

4. **Plot the time series:** To plot the time series we can use the plot.ts function. We usually plot time series data as line graphs. Try the following commands:

```
> plot(s[,1])  # not pretty
> # Use the plot.ts function to plot a single column of numbers
> # as a decent time series plot. Given a series of numbers,
> # plot.ts plots it as a time series.
> plot.ts(s[,1])
```

Creating *time series* objects

5. **Create a simple time series object:** **R** provides many functions to work with time series data and we have to create specific *time-series* objects to use these functions. *Time series* objects differ from regular data frames that we have used thus far. The following **R** commands give you more insight:

```
> # Use the ts function to create a time series object
> # For convenience, we append a ".ts" to the name to remind
> # us that a variable represents a time series

> s.ts <- ts(s[,1])
>
> # With time series objects, the plot function works fine
> # Do not use the plot.ts function for time-series objects
> plot(s.ts)
> # Look at the x-axis carefully in the resulting chart ...
```

We do not need to use *plot.ts* on time series objects

6. **Creating time-savvy time series objects:** The time series object *s.ts* from the previous step numbers the time periods starting from 1. What if our time series data represents years and the first data point corresponds to 2002 or some such? Try this:

```
> s.ts <- ts(s[,1], start = 2002)
> plot(s.ts)

> # Now the x-axis looks much better. y-axis? Not so much ... therefore ...
> plot(s.ts, ylab="Sales")

> # Now both axes look good
> # We will return to s.ts after a very small detour ...
```

R time series objects understand the concepts of years, months and quarters. Download the file *ts-example-1.csv*. This file contains *monthly* closing stock prices for some stock. The data starts from January of 2002. Load the data and take a look.

The first column contains the date and the second the closing stock price. Try these:

```
> sp <- read.csv("ts-example-1.csv")
> # Create the time series object from the
> # second column of the data frame
> sp.ts <- ts(sp[,2], freq = 12, start = c(2002,1))
> # Use freq=12 for monthly data and use start
> # to specify the starting period c(2002,1)
> # stands for January, 2002

> # Display the data by year and month
> sp.ts
> # Plot the time series object
> plot(sp.ts)     # x-axis looks much better now
```

Let us now examine quarterly data. Download the file *ts-example-2.csv*. It contains just the quarterly closing stock process from the earlier file. Try these:

```
> qsp <- read.csv("ts-example-2.csv")
> qsp.ts <- ts(qsp[,2], freq = 4, start = c(2002,1))
> qsp.ts
> plot(qsp.ts)   # Look again at the x axis
```

Importance of the *freq* parameter

7. **Understand the *freq* parameter:** The parameter *start* plays only a cosmetic role as a label for the data and does not affect any computations. However, *freq* affects *seasonality* computations. *Freq* tells **R** how many secondary time-intervals we have within the primary time interval. For example, if our primary time interval is year and we have monthly data, then we use *freq = 12*. If on the other hand we have quarterly data then we use *freq = 4*. With values of 4 and 12 for *freq*, **R** assumes quarterly and monthly measures respectively and displays them nicely. However we could conceivably have data sets with these frequency values but do not stand for quarters or months. For example, it could be possible that we have data measured once every twelfth of

a second and we want to use *freq* = 12. In these cases, **R** will still assume that these are monthly data and show it as such when we print the data. However, this assumption does not have any impact on the computations.

R uses a default value of 1 for *freq*. If we do not have any secondary measurements – for example, just annual data, then we can use *freq* = 1.

Freq plays an important role in seasonality computations.

Examples of the use of *freq* – pay close attention!

- With monthly data and annual seasonality patterns use *freq* = 12.
- With quarterly data and annual seasonality patterns use *freq* = 4.
- With annual data and 10-year patterns, use *freq* = 10.
- With measurements taken every 10 minutes and patterns repeating hourly, use *freq* = 6 – because we have 6 measurements every hour.
- With measurements taken every 10 minutes and patterns repeating daily, use *freq* = 24*6 – because we have 6 measurements every hour and have 24 hours per day.

The value for *freq* depends on the time period over which we expect seasonal patterns.

8. **Decomposing time series:** When we have time series data with trend, seasonality and irregular components, we could understand the series better by decomposing it. Once we have a time-series object, **R** makes decomposition very easy:

```
> s.ts <- ts(s[,1], start = 2002, freq = 12)
> plot(decompose(s.ts))
```

The function *decompose* does the job and we can plot it directly as above. Alternately, we can store the resulting object in a variable and examine its components:

```
> s.ts <- ts(s[,1], start = 2002, freq = 12)
> s.dec <- decompose(s.ts)
> s.dec$x    # the original time series
> s.dec$seasonal  # seasonal component
> s.dec$trend   # trend component
> s.dec$random        # irregular component
```

9. **Forecasting:** Given a time series object, we can forecast by using the HoltWinters function. This function applies a modified form of exponential smoothing to estimate the base value, trend and seasonality and usually provides excellent short-term forecasts. First let us build the model and see how well it does on the historical data. Of course "forecasting" historical data is not of much use, but it does give us a way of seeing how closely the forecasts matched the actual values. We will soon see how to forecast the future based on the past.

```
> # Create a HoltWinters forecast object and store it in s.ts.hw
> # Recall that we have our original time series object in s.ts
> s.ts.hw <- HoltWinters(s.ts)

> # Now we can plot the result with the plot function
> # We see the actual values and forecast values for the
> # historical data - Black line shows actual or observed data
> # and red shows the forecast
> plot(s.ts.hw)
> # Change colors of the lines if you like
> plot(s.ts.hw, col = "blue", col.predicted = "red")
> # col is for the actual data and
> # col.predicted is for the forecast
```

Figure 174 shows the result of the last command.

By plotting the result of the HoltWinters procedure we were able to compare the original time series with what the method forecasts. We can find the RMS error of the forecast. After all, for each point on the time series, we have an actual value and a forecast value and we can use the deviation to compute the RMSE. The result from the procedure (*s.ts.hw* in our example) can directly give us the sum of squared errors.

```
> s.ts.hw$SSE
```

To compute the RMSE, we need to know the number of data points that the SSE was based on. Remember, exponential smoothing uses a set of previous values and hence it will not have forecasts for the initial periods. The code below first finds the number of points that were forecast and then computes the RMSE. The component *fitted* of the model contains the forecast values.

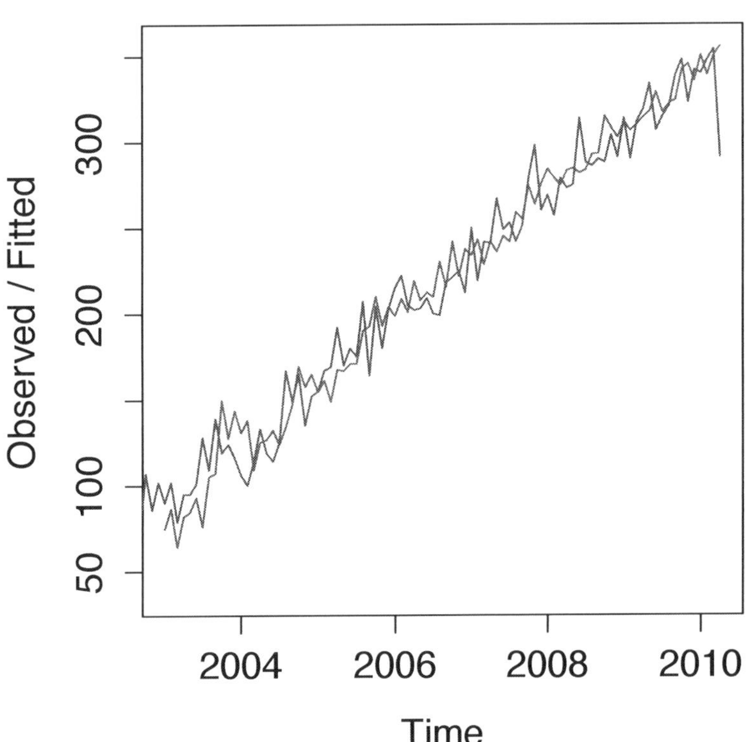

Figure 174: Holt Winters: Actual vs forecast values on historical data. Blue line in your on-screen plot shows the actual.

```
> # Use the nrow function to find the number of forecasts
> n <- nrow(s.ts.hw$fitted)
> rmse <- sqrt(s.ts.hw$SSE/n)
> rmse
```

We find that the RMSE is 18.24 – less than 10% of the mean value of our time series and less than 5% off from the later values. Whether this level of accuracy suffices depends on the context.

If the "forecasts" on the historical values seem reasonable, we can go on to make real forecasts.

```
> # Install the forecast package first
> install.packages("forecast")
> # Load the package
> library(forecast)
```

```
> # Create the forecast object with future values
> # for the next 12 periods. We pass the result of
> # HoltWinters s.ts.hw as an argument. h=12 indicates that
> # we want to forecast for 12 periods.
> s.ts.forecast = forecast.HoltWinters(s.ts.hw, h=12)
> # Now plot the result
> plot.forecast(s.ts.forecast)
```

Figure 175 shows the plot of the HoltWinters forecast.

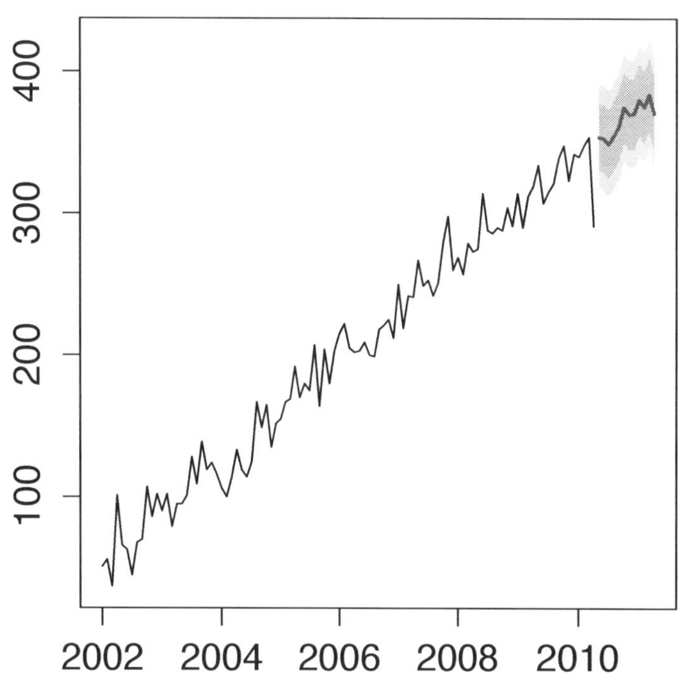

Figure 175: Holt Winters: Future values. The line within the shaded area shows the forecast and the gray bands show the 85% and 95% confidence intervals. See text for details.

The line in the shaded region to the top right shows the forecast. The inner band shows the 85% confidence interval – meaning that we can be 85% sure that the actual value will be in that band. The outer band shows the 95% confidence interval.

Reduction Techniques

In analytics, we often have a huge number of attributes and cases in our data sets – and we see this by and large as good thing. We have the hardware and the software to crunch mountains of data and might sometimes be tempted to just throw raw computing power at problems. Patterns identified from huge data sets usually prove useful and this "throw the kitchen sink" approach can be fruitful.

Often though, we can gain real insights by some initial processing of the data to get at its essence. This might enable us to warp our brains around even very large data sets.

We now look at two different techniques that do quite different things, but serve the purpose of getting to the core of large data sets. The first of these – *cluster analysis* – helps us to condense a huge number of cases into small, comprehensible clusters and the second does the same for the attributes. You can think of the former as simplifying the rows and the latter – *Principal Component Analysis* – as simplifying the columns. We describe one technique for *Cluster Analysis* and provide a very brief intuitive overview of *Principal Component Analysis*.

Cluster Analysis

Look at Figure 176. How would you describe this figure to someone who cannot see it?

One possibility would be to say that we have several diamonds and ovals of various sizes arranged randomly in an approximately rectangular area.

Even if your description did not match mine, you probably came up with some way of grouping the objects into a two or three groups and described the characteristics of each group.

When presented with many items, we instinctively try and reduce the inherent complexity by grouping. In the above task,

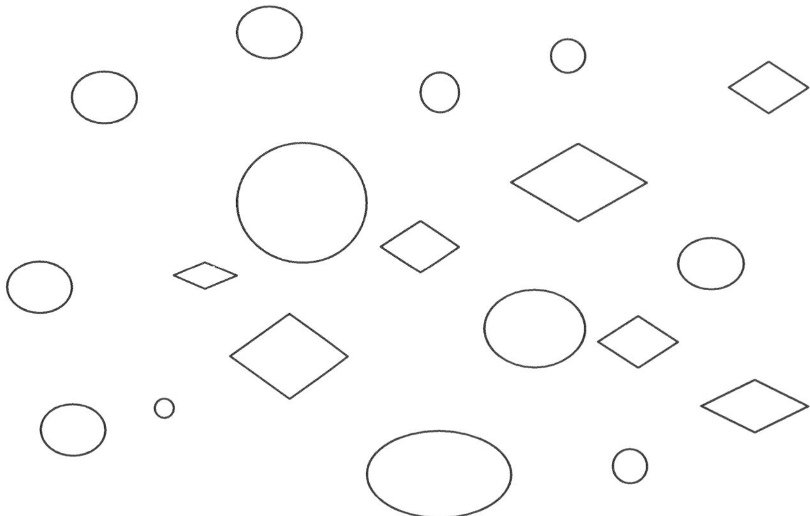

Figure 176: How would you describe this figure to someone who cannot see it?

we could divide the 19 objects into two groups with each object being much more like the other objects in its own group, and different from objects in the other group.

In the previous example, we could have chosen to create two groups or more. We could group the bigger ovals/circles into one group and the smaller ones into another group and do likewise with the diamonds, to get four groups in all.

No matter what scheme we use to group the items, we are looking for each group to be made up of *similar* items. In other words, we seek *coherent* groups.

In analytics, we refer to the process of creating groups of *like* objects as *clustering* and refer to the technique generically as *cluster analysis*. How might cluster analysis be useful in real life?

Organizations deal with numerous distinct entities and often create clusters for convenience. For example, a company might have millions of customers. While each customer is unique, the company might identify a few groups of *similar* customers for various purposes. For example, a company might be able to identify from its millions of customers that about 40% have purchased just one product ever and their total business has amounted to less than $100 per person. On the other hand, 10% of the customers might have made more than 20 purchases and have provided a per-capita business of more than $1,000. For product promotions, credit management and other functions, companies might establish policies based on the broad group to which a customer belongs, rather than separately for each individual customer.

If a politician has to address the concerns of hundreds of thousands of citizens, the task would be very difficult. However, if she is able to identify only 6 fairly homogeneous groups in terms of their concerns, then she can craft messages for the 6 groups instead of addressing the concerns of numerous people separately.

Suppose a company has data on 10,000 customers. The company has created a promotion plan for a new product. The company believes that it will need to customize the details of the promotion based on the attributes of customers; it now faces the daunting task of having to create 10,000 different customizations of the promotion plan. This will take a lot of time effort and money. If, by using cluster analysis, the company is able to identify 5 sufficiently coherent clusters, it can get by with just 5 customized plans. Conceptually, the company would have managed to reduce the 10,000 cases to just five – treating the midpoint of each coherent cluster as representative of the whole cluster.

	age	height
	8.90	53.70
	9.30	55.00
	9.40	53.50
	9.90	52.60
	10.10	53.90
	11.10	51.10
	12.00	66.00
	12.50	68.00
	13.00	70.00
	13.00	68.00
	13.50	70.00
	14.00	72.00
Mean	11.39	61.31

Table 86: Age and height of students.

Quite apart from such considerations, when presented with a large data set, identifying a small number of coherent clusters to which the cases belong can help analysts to understand the data better, before embarking on detailed analysis.

In our earlier discussions of classification and regression, we had the "correct" answers – the values of the target attributes – in the data file. We used the values of the target attributes for *learning*. We accomplished learning by retaining a hold-out data set that we did not use in model development. We then compared the model's predictions on the hold-out data to the known "correct" values of the target attribute. We had referred to this approach as *supervised learning*.

In cluster analysis, we try to find suitable clusters. There is no up-front "correct" clustering that can guide this process. Therefore, cluster analysis, like affinity analysis, represents *unsupervised learning*.

Predictive analytics methods (both classification and regression) use *supervised* learning. Cluster analysis exemplifies *unsupervised* analytics.

Let us make things concrete. Table 86 shows the ages and heights of a set of students (along with the means). Figure 177 shows the same data as a scatterplot (without the attribute means).

From Figure 177, we can see that the data bunches neatly into two groups or clusters of 6 cases each. A clustering tech-

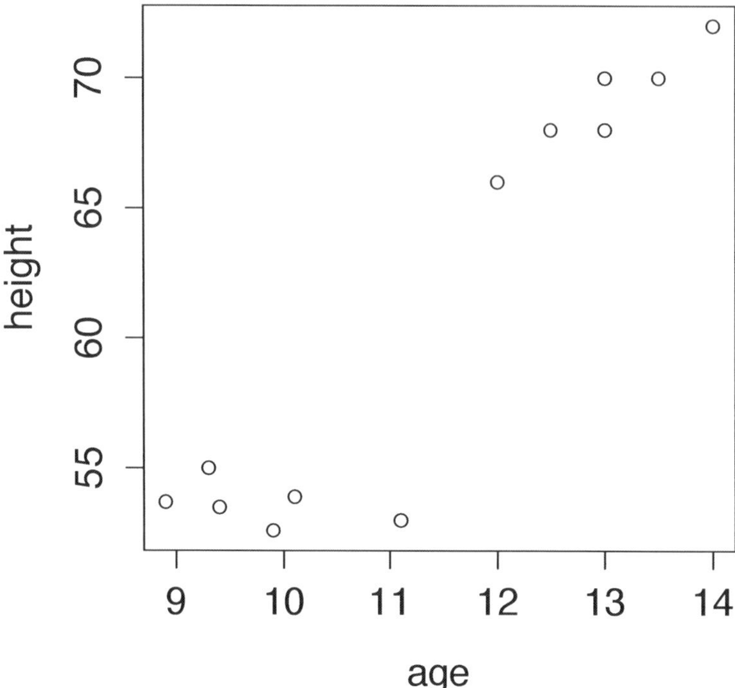

Figure 177: Scatterplot of data in Table 86.

nique will identify these two groups as a good clustering solution for this data. Table 87 shows the data in each of these two clusters as well as the mid-points of the clusters. (In this example, the two clusters happened to be of the same size. In real data sets this will usually not be the case and we might find more than two clusters and they might all differ significantly in size.)

	Cluster 1		Cluster 2	
	age	height	age	height
	8.9	53.7	12.00	66.00
	9.3	55	12.50	68.00
	9.4	53.5	13.00	70.00
	9.9	52.6	13.00	68.00
	10.1	53.9	13.50	70.00
	11.1	53	14.00	72.00
Mean	9.78	53.62	13.00	69.00

Table 87: Two distinct groups in the data from Table 86 and the mean or midpoints of those groups.

Figure 178 depicts visually the two clusters of Table 87. The bottom-left cluster contains the relatively short and young cases, and the other one, the relatively tall and old.

Now that we have two clusters, we can treat the midpoints of the two clusters as being representative of the original data set. In other words, instead of thinking that we have 12 different cases in the data, we can look at it as if we have 6 cases with age 9.78 and height 53.62 and another 6 cases with age 13.00 and height 69.00. Of course this loses some of the richness (variability) from the original data set. However, if we have only lost a little bit of information, but gained a lot by simplifying from 12 different cases to just 2 different cases (with 6 repetitions each), then the analysis would be worthwhile. We can more easily comprehend the data after this process. In other words, we sacrifice some information to gain a lot more in terms of comprehensibility.

Figure 179 shows the same data, but divided into three clusters.

Given a data set, how many clusters should we look for? Data science does not propose any hard and fast rules to determine this. People make subjective decisions based on context. Later in this section we provide concrete guidance on how we might approach this question.

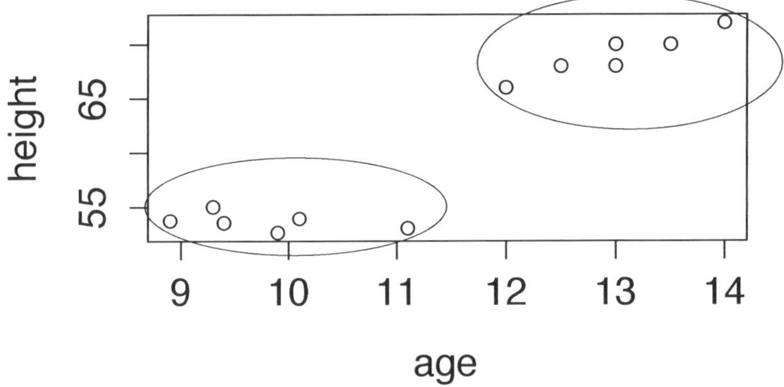

Figure 178: Possible 2-cluster solution for the data in Table 86.

Classification vs. clustering

Have we not already encountered this when we discussed *classification*? After all, in *classification* we discussed a few methods to classify cases based on a set of predictor attributes. If

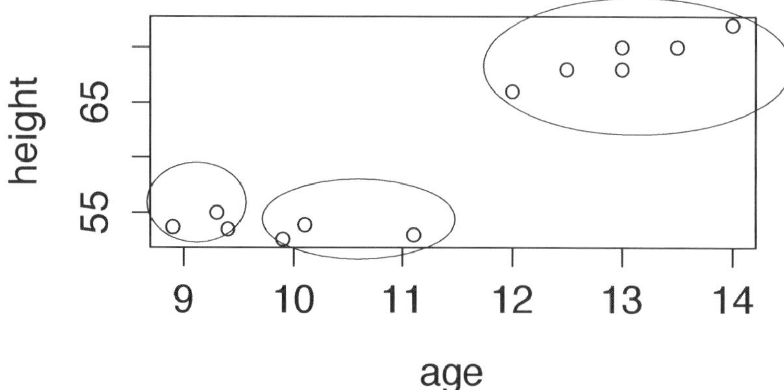

Figure 179: Possible 3-cluster solution for the data in Table 86.

we consider each cluster as a class, then is cluster analysis not doing the same thing?

While *cluster analysis* and *classification* might seem to be similar on the surface, they differ considerably. In *classification* the classes have already been determined up-front – for example *buyer* and *non-buyer* or *fraudulent transaction* and *normal transaction* or *good piece* and *defective piece*. In cluster analysis we do not know up front the number of clusters and the characteristics of each. Cluster analysis helps us find the classes whereas in classification the classes have already been determined.

With the small data set of Table 86 we successfully found two well-separated clusters just visually. With more data and with more than two dimensions, just eyeballing will not help – in fact it might not even be possible – and we need analytical techniques.

Data scientists employ many methods for cluster analysis; we will discuss just one of the common approaches – *k-means clustering*. We will delve into *what* k-means clustering does for us – without getting into the procedural details of *how* it goes about doing this.

Given a large data set, *cluster analysis* seeks to identify a small number of clusters such that the items in each cluster are much more similar to each other than they are to items in other clusters.

What do we mean when we say "items in each cluster are

much more similar to each other than they are to items in other clusters?"

In our discussion of k-nearest neighbors methods, we have already explored a mathematical way of computing similarity – we used euclidean distance there. Clustering methods also use the same approach; they deem cases *close* to each other as being more similar to each other than cases that are more distant from each other. With one, two or three-dimensional data, this translates into identifying groups of points that visually clump together.

Like KNN, most cluster analysis techniques rely on similarity measures and hence requires all attributes to be standardized.

We expect the clustering process to result in *coherent* sets of cases. From this viewpoint, the perfect solution would be have each case in the data as its own cluster because this will yield the best coherence within each cluster. Of course that would also be perfectly useless because we will then end up with as many clusters as there are cases, and our goal of reducing complexity by identifying a much smaller set of coherent cases would remain unfulfilled.

To reduce the number of clusters, we could group individual cases to form larger clusters. As we do this, we will reduce the number of clusters, but also reduce coherence of clusters because we are now lumping together cases with different attribute values into a single cluster. We still gain because the process will result in fewer and fewer clusters that makes the numerous cases easier to understand and manage. Taking this approach to its logical conclusion, we could group all the data into just a single cluster ... but that would not help either, because we completely lose all information about the diversity in the data.

Stdz age	Stdz height
-1.367	-0.931
-1.147	-0.772
-1.093	-0.955
-0.818	-1.065
-0.709	-0.906
-0.160	-1.016
0.334	0.574
0.608	0.818
0.882	1.063
0.882	0.818
1.157	1.063
1.431	1.308

Table 88: Standardized age and height of students from Table 86.

We want to identify a few coherent groups, without getting to either extreme solution of a single cluster or as many clusters as the number of cases.

We need to achieve a trade-off between coherence of the clusters and the number of clusters. We want to avoid too many or too few clusters. For reasons you will appreciate soon, in what follows we will we will talk about the measure of *incoherence* of a cluster rather than *coherence*. Seeking *high coherence* is the same as seeking *low incoherence*.

	Stdz age	Stdz height
	-1.367	-0.931
	-1.147	-0.772
	-1.093	-0.955
	-0.818	-1.065
	-0.709	-0.906
	-0.160	-1.016
Mean	-0.882	-0.941

Table 89: Standardized age and height of students from the first cluster in Table 87.

Ignoring for now the actual data, suppose we have a cluster with more than one case. What would be the ideal data values that represent the minimum incoherence (or maximum coherence) for a cluster? We get a completely coherent cluster when it comprises all identical cases – each case has exactly the same value for every attribute. This represents zero incoherence or maximum possible coherence. Incoherence of a cluster then represents the degree to which its members differ from each other. Can we assign a number to this?

How about just adding up the extent to which the attribute values differ from their respective means? This could work, but the positive and negative differences will cancel out and could make even clusters that have widely differing cases look like they are perfect. To correct for this, we can use the square of the difference.

	Stdz age	**Stdz height**
	0.334	0.574
	0.608	0.818
	0.882	1.063
	0.882	0.818
	1.157	1.063
	1.431	1.308
Mean	0.882	0.941

Table 90: Standardized age and height of students from the second cluster in Table 87

Need a concrete measure of coherence of a cluster

Can you see any other problems? As we have already seen under our discussion of KNN, different attributes would be measured on different scales (age in years, and height in inches for example). The relative magnitudes of the attributes could vary widely and it is possible for attributes with high values to dominate the computations of squared deviations from the mean.

We would therefore need to standardize the values before clustering. Table 88 shows the standardized values corresponding to Table 86. Tables 89 and 90 show the standardized values, along with the attribute means of the cases from the two clusters in Table 87.

How incoherent are the two clusters? Since each cluster has cases that are not identical, neither cluster is perfectly coherent. To compute the extent of incoherence, we can compute the sum of squared deviations from the mean for each attribute – this number is referred to as "within cluster sum of squares" or *within_ss*. Table 91 shows the computation of *within_ss* as 0.9567 for the first cluster from Table 89 and Table 92 shows the shows a *within_ss* value of 1.0815 for the second cluster. Adding these, we get a total *within_ss* of 2.0382.

What does this mean? Is this an improvement over having all the cases in a single cluster?

Using the same approach, if we compute *within_ss* for the complete data set – which is equivalent to having all cases in a single cluster – we get the result as 22 as Table 93 shows. This number – the overall variability in the complete data set – is referred to as the "total sum of squares" or *total_ss*.

Creating two clusters therefore reduced the total *within_ss* from 22 to 2.0382 – a very big reduction indeed. This shows that the original data set had cases that were quite dissimilar to each other and that creating the two clusters did result in two very coherent clusters.

	Stdz age	Stdz height	Sqr dev age	Sqr dev height	Tot sqr dev
	-1.367	-0.931	0.2348	0.0001	0.2349
	-1.147	-0.772	0.0703	0.0286	0.0989
	-1.093	-0.955	0.0442	0.0002	0.0444
	-0.818	-1.065	0.0041	0.0155	0.0196
	-0.709	-0.906	0.0302	0.0012	0.0314
	-0.160	-1.016	0.5218	0.0057	0.5274
Mean	-0.882	-0.941		**Within_ss**	0.9567

Table 91: Computation of *within_ss* or total squared deviation for the cluster in Table 89. For each attribute value, the squared deviation is computed as $(attributevalue - mean)^2$. Within_ss is the sum of the total squared deviations across the rows.

	Stdz age	Stdz height	Sqr dev age	Sqr dev height	Tot sqr dev
	0.334	0.574	0.3010	0.1346	0.4356
	0.608	0.818	0.0752	0.0150	0.0902
	0.882	1.063	0.0000	0.0150	0.0150
	0.882	0.818	0.0000	0.0150	0.0150
	1.157	1.063	0.0752	0.0150	0.0902
	1.431	1.308	0.3010	0.1346	0.4356
Mean	0.882	0.941		**Within_ss**	1.0815

Table 92: Computation of total within_ss for the cluster in Table 90 .

	Stdz age	Stdz height	Sqr dev age	Sqr dev height	Tot sqr dev
1	-1.367	-0.931	1.8685	0.8659	2.734
2	-1.147	-0.772	1.3167	0.5953	1.912
3	-1.093	-0.955	1.1938	0.9120	2.106
4	-0.818	-1.065	0.6697	1.1344	1.804
5	-0.709	-0.906	0.5021	0.8210	1.323
6	-0.160	-1.016	0.0256	1.0326	1.058
7	0.334	0.574	0.1114	0.3293	0.441
8	0.608	0.818	0.3697	0.6698	1.040
9	0.882	1.063	0.7785	1.1300	1.909
10	0.882	0.818	0.7785	0.6698	1.448
11	1.157	1.063	1.3378	1.1300	2.468
12	1.431	1.308	2.0476	1.7099	3.758
Mean	0.000	0.000		**Total_ss**	22.000

Table 93: Computation of *within_ss* for the data seen as a single cluster – since we used all the data, the result is also the *total_ss*.

In this data set, we can visually determine that having two clusters would make eminent sense. In general, how many clusters should we shoot for? To use k-means clustering, we have to specify k – the number of clusters we want. Once we do that, the function will then determine close to the best possible k-cluster solution. We will not go into the actual mechanics of how it assigns individual cases to specific clusters here.

A big question remains – How do we know what value of k to use?

Easy. We try out several values and select a *good* value. What do we mean by a *good* value of k? As we already know, we can only make a subjective judgment. After all we are trying to find a compromise between having too many clusters and too few.

We have a measure of the degree of incoherence of a cluster, or *within_ss* (as Table 91 showed). We can extend that to compute the incoherence value of a set of clusters. That is, if we have a data set, and create three clusters from it, the overall incoherence of this clustering is just the sum of the incoherence values of the three clusters – the *within_ss* values of the clusters.

To subjectively select a good value of k, we first run k-means clustering for various value of k. We can then plot the total of *within_ss* for each value of k. Figure 180 shows an example – the lab activity will show you how to generate this plot.

Figure 180: Plot of total of within_ss across clusters against k.

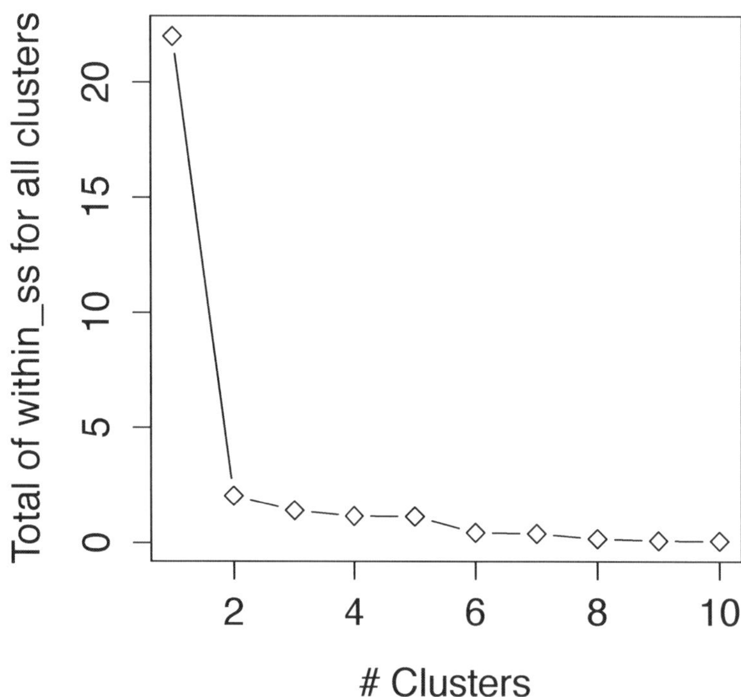

From Figure 180 we see that the total *within_ss* drops as we increase k. We expect this because lower values of k imply larger clusters and lumping more data points into a cluster naturally increases the incoherence or *within_ss*. As we go to the extreme of having each case in its own cluster, we get much more coherent clusters and the total value of *within_ss* drops.

To achieve a good compromise between coherence and number of clusters, we would like to select a value of k where the total incoherence stops its steep drop and starts to taper off. In Figure 180 this would be at k=2. From k=1 to k=2 we see a big drop. After that the drop becomes much more gradual. In this case, we have a very clear choice for k. Sometimes the decision will not be as straightforward and we might have a choice among two or three values.

Figure 180 pertains to the data in Table 86. Using k=2, and running k-means clustering, we get the two clusters in Figure 178 .

The two-cluster solution certainly seems to make sense. Visually we see two distinct groups and the two-cluster solution clearly identifies those two.

Figure 179 shows a 3-cluster solution which also makes sense. However from Figure 180 we see a very small the drop in overall incoherence as measured by the total *within_ss* between k=2 and k=3 and might stick with our k=2 solution. In a real life data set the choice might not be as cut and dried as in this case and we might have to choose between a few k values. We will need to make a subjective selection based on the context of the decision.

We chose the best value of k that we could. But how good is this value in an absolute sense? We can always choose a value for k and obtain k clusters. However our data might be such that no value of k produces *good* clustering. It could be that our data does not have any good clusters at all. The scatterplot of Figure 182 shows an example where we would be hard-pressed to find well-defined clusters. Can we ascribe a number to measure the quality of a clustering?

Let us go back to the standardized data in Table 88 and the two clusters in Tables 89 and 90. Let us represent the cases in each cluster just by the cluster's average characteristics – mean of the standardized age and the mean of the standardized height. We can then think that we have 6 cases with (standardized age, standardized height) as (-0.882, -0.941) and six cases with (0.882, 0.941). We have thus compressed the 12 different cases into just 2 different ones. With these 12 cases we find the total sum of squares is 19.96 . Table 94 shows the computations. This figure of 19.96 represents "between clusters sum of squares" or *between_ss*.

We know that the complete data set of standardized values had a sum of squared variations of 22.

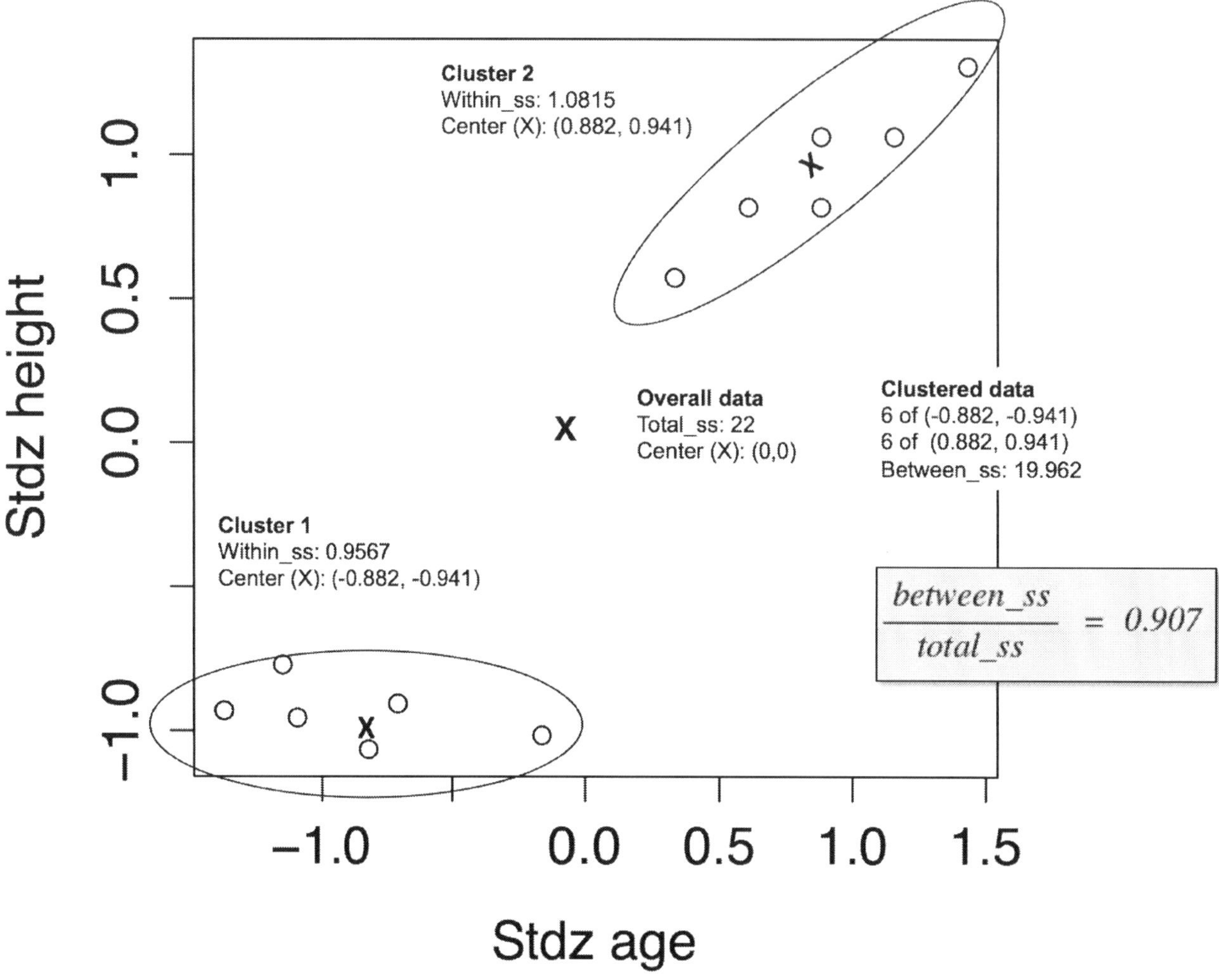

Figure 181: *within_ss*, *total_ss*, *between_ss* and clustering quality.

Table 94: Computation of *between_ss*. We consider each case in a cluster as represented solely by the cluster's mid-point. So we have only two distinct cases with the first six being the midpoint of the first cluster and the next six as the midpoint of the second cluster.

Stdz age	Stdz height	Sqr dev age	Sqr dev height	Tot sqr dev
-0.882	-0.941	0.779	0.885	1.663
-0.882	-0.941	0.779	0.885	1.663
-0.882	-0.941	0.779	0.885	1.663
-0.882	-0.941	0.779	0.885	1.663
-0.882	-0.941	0.779	0.885	1.663
-0.882	-0.941	0.779	0.885	1.663
0.882	0.941	0.779	0.885	1.663
0.882	0.941	0.779	0.885	1.663
0.882	0.941	0.779	0.885	1.663
0.882	0.941	0.779	0.885	1.663
0.882	0.941	0.779	0.885	1.663
0.882	0.941	0.779	0.885	1.663
			Between_ss	19.962

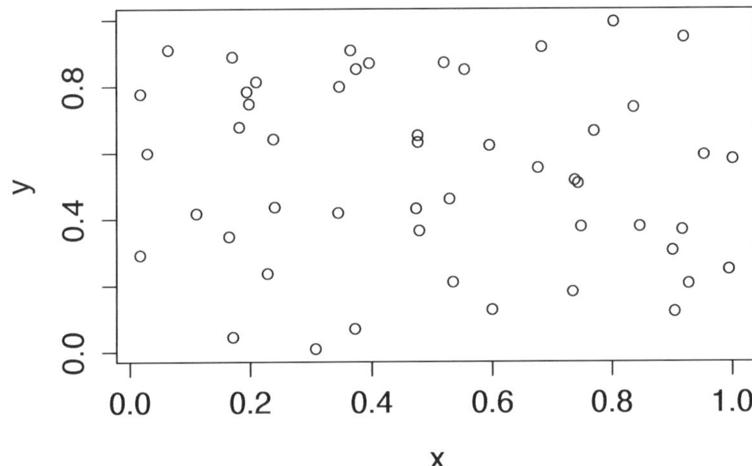

Figure 182: A situation where we cannot find any good clustering because there do not seem to be any well-defined coherent groups.

By treating the data set to be made up of just two kinds of cases represented by the mid-points of the clusters, we see that 19.96 the total variability of 22 in the data still remains. That is, we simplified our view of the data by creating just two clusters, and yet retained more than 90% of the variability.

Figure 181 shows the main ideas pictorially.

The ratio $\frac{between\_ss}{total\_ss}$ is a good measure of the quality of the clustering. We would like a value close to 1.0. Usually, values above 0.7 would be considered as good.

Review 16: Cluster Analysis

You can find the answers to these questions on page 400

1. You are given a data set with 1000 cases and can create any number of clusters from 1 to 1000. Answer the following questions based on this scenario:

   a How many clusters should you create in order for all clusters to have complete coherence?

   b Would you consider the above solution to be useful? Explain.

   c How many clusters should you create if you want to have the highest total value of *within_ss* across all clusters?

d Would you consider the above solution to be useful? Explain.

2. Table 95 shows some hypothetical data about purchases from a company. For various transactions it shows the number of products purchased and the total dollar value of the transaction (in hundreds of dollars). Someone did an analysis and generated the plot that Figure 183 shows. Answer the following questions based on these.

   a Just by examining the table, how many distinct clusters seem to be obviously present in the data?

   b Explain Figure 183 .

3. Someone created two clusters for this data, with the first three cases in the first cluster and the rest in the second cluster. Table 96 shows the standardized data.

   a Compute *total_ss*.

   b Compute *within_ss* for each cluster.

   c Are the above values consistent with what you see in Figure 183? Explain.

   d Compute *between_ss*

   e How much of the variance in the original data does the two cluster solution retain?

num_prods	total_amt
5	10
10	13
6	9
1	40
2	50
2	40

Table 95: Number of products and total purchase value.

num_prods_z	total_amt_z
0.197	-0.929
1.673	-0.765
0.492	-0.983
-0.984	0.710
-0.689	1.256
-0.689	0.710

Table 96: Standardized values of the original data.

Lab 18: Cluster Analysis

Pre-requisite(s)

✓ You should have read the section on cluster analysis (page 325) and answered the associated review questions (page 337).

✓ You should have completed the introduction to **R** data frames lab (page 17).

Objective

After completing this lab, you will be able to:

✓ Select a suitable value for k

✓ Perform k-means clustering

✓ Interpret the results and evaluate the quality of the results

Overview

We will first run kmeans-clustering on the same data set that we used in the description of the method. We will then do the same for a larger, real-life data set.

Figure 183: Plot for review question.

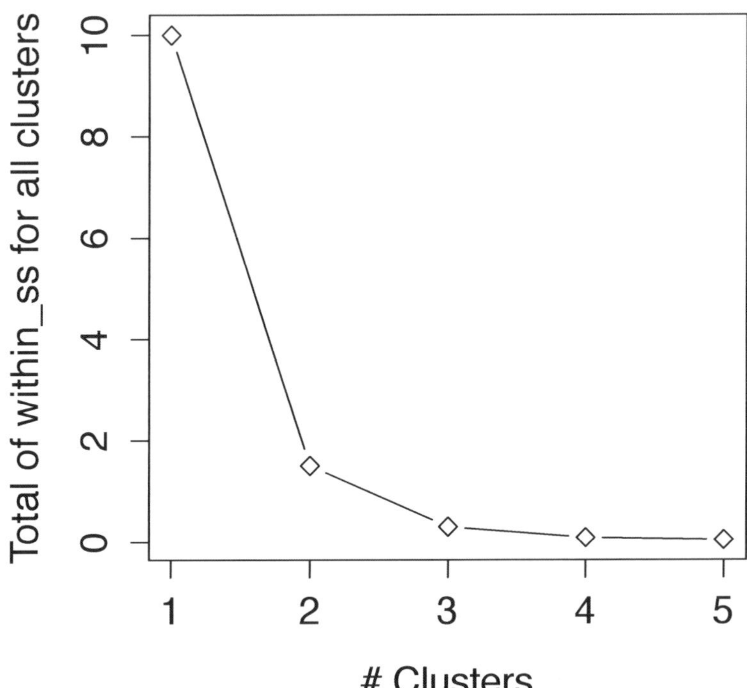

Activity steps

1. **Read the data:** Read the data file *hw-cluster.csv*.

```
> hw <- read.csv("hw-cluster.csv")
```

2. **Run kmeans for a specific k:** We will first learn how to run *kmeans clustering* for a specific value of k. You may – very legitimately – wonder how you are supposed to know the value for k. Hold on to that for a little bit. Once you learn how to run it for a specific value of k and interpret the results, you will be better prepared to proceed to the matter of determining a good value for k.

   As the preceding section discussed, *k-means clustering* is based on distance computations. In the section on *KNN for classification* (page 122) we explained the need to standardize the data in such situations. We will therefore first standardize the data. To standardize both attributes with a single call, we will use the convenience function in the file *dar2ed-scale-many.R*. So first load this file in **RStudio** and then *source* it in.

We first run *kmeans* for k=2.

```
> hw <- dar2ed.scale.many(hw, 1:2)
> fit <- kmeans(hw[ ,3:4], 2)
```

In the above note that we used only the standardized attributes for clustering.

Figure 184 explains the *kmeans* function call.

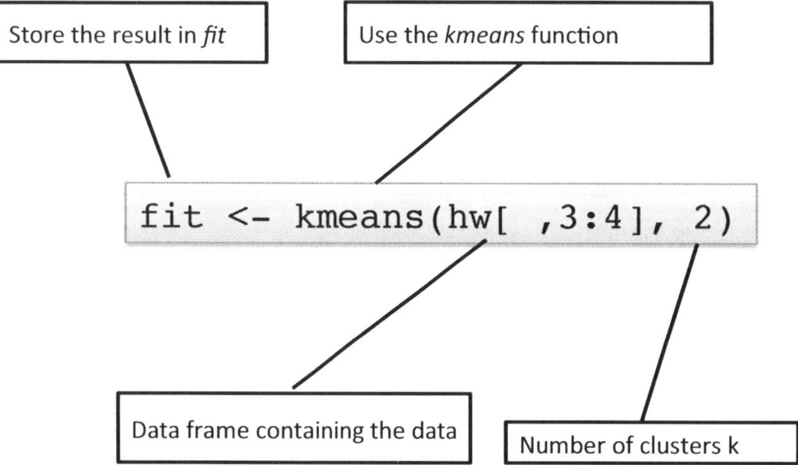

Figure 184: Details of the *kmeans* function call

3. **Explore the results:** Having stored the clustering model in the variable *fit*, let us understand the information in the model.

```
> fit
```

Let us see what the output says:

- **Cluster sizes:** The first line tells us that *kmeans* generated two clusters of sizes 6 and 6. It generated two clusters because we asked it to. Each cluster ended up with 6 cases. In general, cluster sizes need not be equal – it just turned out to be so in this case.
- **Cluster means or centers:** This part represents the mean of the two scaled attributes in each cluster. Thus the mean of *age_z* in the first cluster was 0.8823353 and that for *height_z* was 0.940728.

```
K-means clustering with 2 clusters of sizes 6, 6

Cluster means:
       age_z   height_z
1  0.8823353  0.940728
2 -0.8823353 -0.940728

Clustering vector:
 [1] 2 2 2 2 2 2 1 1 1 1 1 1

Within cluster sum of squares by cluster:
[1] 1.081498 0.956684
 (between_SS / total_SS =  90.7 %)

Available components:

[1] "cluster"      "centers"      "totss"        "withinss"
[5] "tot.withinss" "betweenss"    "size"         "iter"
[9] "ifault"
```

Figure 185: Kmeans output for k=2 on the age-weight data

- **Clustering vector:** This tells us which cluster each case belongs to. It just turned out that the first six cases ended up in the second cluster and the next six ended up in the first cluster. Again, in a general case we would not see such a regular pattern of cluster assignment.
- **Within cluster sum of squares by cluster:** This is the sum of squares for each cluster. This section also shows that the clustering accounts for almost 91% of the overall variability. You see this in the part that says: "(between_SS / total_SS = 90.7 %)"
  This says that the two points that the cluster centers can account for 91% of the variability in all of the 12 cases.
  Any value above 70% is considered very good.
- **Available components:** This segment tells us all the information available in the model. Only some of the information is shown in the default display. We can use the information in this segment to get more information, if needed. For example:

  ```
  > fit$tot.withinss
  > fit$totss
  ```

4. **Now try for other values of k and select k:** You can repeat the above step for several values of k and then choose one that seems to have a low enough value of k and yet explains a lot of the variability. But this would be mind-numbingly boring. So we will automate this as

the next step shows.

5. **Easily determine a good value for k:** We have created a convenience function that automates the process of repeating *kmeans clustering* for several values of k.

   (a) Load the contents of the file *dar2ed-kmeans-plot.R* and *source* it.

   (b) This function in turn uses our earlier convenience function for standardizing. So source in the contents of the file *dar2ed-scale-many.R* as well.

   This convenience function *dar2ed.kmeans.plot* takes care of everything – standardizing the attributes and running *kmeans clustering* for values of from 1 to 10. Since we already standardized the data earlier, we do not want to repeat this process. So let us read the file once again and start afresh. You need to specify the data frame to use and the attributes to use for clustering – we might not want to use all the attributes.

```
> hw <- read.csv("hw-cluster.csv")
> dar2ed.kmeans.plot(hw, 1:2)
```

   Figure 186 shows the resulting plot.

Figure 186: Kmeans plot

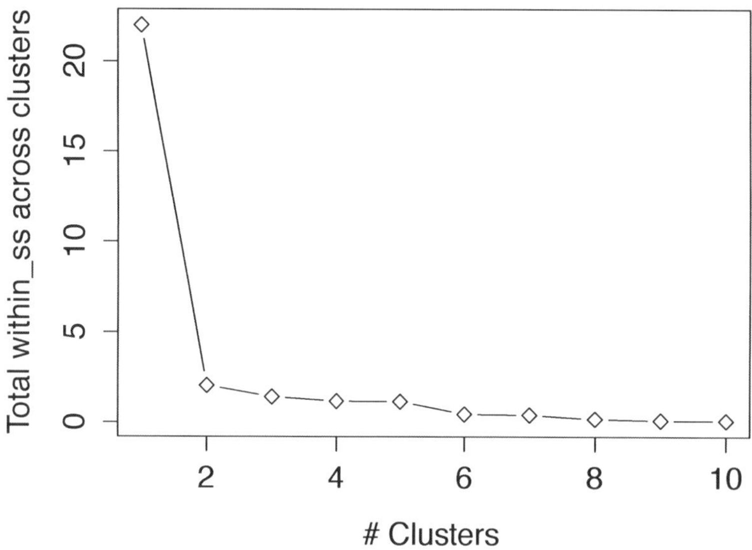

From the plot we see how the total variability reduces as we increase the number of clusters. We want to select a value for k after which the drop in total variability levels off. In this figure, k=2 clearly represents a very good value. After that there is hardly any decrease.

6. **Clarifying the process:** In this lab we first showed you how to run *k-means clustering* for a single value of k and then showed you the way to run it for many values of k with a single command. **This is not what we will do on real data.**

   When we run *kmeans clustering* on real life data, we will reverse the process. We will first use the *dar2ed.kmeans.plot* function to determine a good value for k and then run *k-means clustering* with the chosen value of k.

7. **Run cluster analysis with chosen k:** We need not really do this now ans this is what we did initially in this lab. However, just to show things in the correct sequence, we repeat the step. We chose k=2, and that is what we had tested first! The variable *fit* already contains the model for k=2. Just for clarity here is the code again:

```
> hw <- dar2ed.scale.many(hw, 1:2)
> fit <- kmeans(hw[ ,3:4], 2)
> fit
```

8. **Add cluster information to original data:** In real life we might have performed cluster analysis on a large data set and might want to know the cluster to which each case belongs. We can do that through the command:

```
> hw$cluster = fit$cluster
```

   We added an attribute called *cluster* to store the number of the cluster to which a case was allocated.

9. **Cluster analysis on a bigger data file:** We will use the familiar *auto-mpg.csv* data. We will use the attributes 2 to 7 for this analysis.

   Since we have discussed the steps in detail we show all the code below in two chunks:

```
> auto <- read.csv("auto-mpg.csv")
> dar2ed.kmeans.plot(auto, 2:7)
```

Figure 187 shows the plot.

Figure 187: Plot of k against squared deviations for auto example.

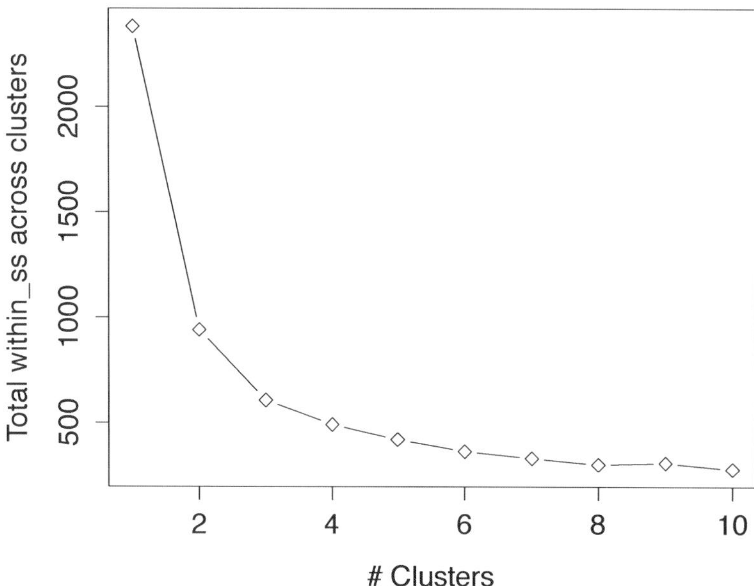

From the plot, it looks like k=3 or k=4 would be good choices. We use k=4 below. We first scale the relevant attributes and use the scaled attributes in the clustering process. The *kmeans* function does not automatically scale the data and so we need to do that explicitly.

```
> auto <- dar2ed.scale.many(auto, 2:7)
> names(auto)
> fit <- kmeans(auto[ , 10:15], 4)
> fit
```

This four cluster solution retains almost 80% of the original variability.

In earlier examples, we used small data sets and we did not find it difficult to *interpret* the clusters. In the height-age example, the two clusters represented younger shorter people and older and taller people.

With larger data sets having more cases and more attributes per case, it will be good if we can characterize each cluster in practical terms – what do the cases in a cluster *represent*?

The midpoints of the clusters from the standardized set can help a lot in this because we can easily see the relative magnitudes. For example, after standardization, each attribute has a mean of 0 and a standard deviation of 1. Thus if we see a value of 1.5 for an attribute, we know that it is among the *high* values because it is 1.5 standard deviations above the mean. If we see a value of 0.97 for an attribute, we know that it is a middling value, and so on.

Let us first add on the clustering information to the main data by:

```
> auto$cluster = fit$cluster
```

Looking at the cluster midpoints, we see the following:

- **Hulk:** The first cluster seems to represent large gas guzzling powerful cars – we might label them as "Hulks".
- **Green:** The second cluster seems to represent highly fuel-efficient, small cars with comparably good performance characteristics. We might label this as "Compact" or even "Green."
- **Salon:** we can see that the cars in the third cluster are well below average in mpg, well above average in number of cylinders, displacement, weight and acceleration and about average in horsepower. Looking at some examples of the cars in this cluster from our data, tells us that this cluster represents large comfortable vehicles – the kind that comfortably retired people might prefer – for example "oldsmobile cutlass salon brougham", "cadillac eldorado" and so on. We could label this cluster as "Salon"
- **Economy:** Arguing in the same vein, the second cluster seems to represent small cars with a somewhat above average mpg and below average in all other characteristics. We could call this "Economy."

Principal Component Analysis

We saw that *Cluster Analysis* helps us to grasp the diversity in a large number of rows of data and to condense their essence into a much smaller number of representative cases.

Principal Component Analysis, or *PCA*, does something analogous for the attributes of a table of data. For example, we might have a data set that has a large number of attributes, say 200. We might be able to use *PCA* to identify a small number, say 10, of *Principal Components* that capture the essence of the data. These components would generally not be original attributes themselves, but each one might be computed based on several of the original attributes.

Since *PCA* allows us to identify a small number of *components* to play the role of a large number of attributes or dimensions, it falls under the category of *dimension reduction* techniques.

We give below a flavor of how *PCA* would be used to reduce the dimensionality of a data set before it is used. (For comprehensibility, we use a small data set for which we would really not need to employ dimension reduction.)

Consider the education data in the file *education.csv*. The file has four numeric attributes. We will assume for now that all of these could act as predictor attributes for some analysis. Our data thus has four dimensions.

If we run the *PCA* algorithm on this data, we might get the results that Figure 188 shows:

```
Importance of components:
                          Comp.1    Comp.2    Comp.3     Comp.4
Standard deviation     1.4451412 1.1233849 0.6838206 0.42657089
Proportion of Variance 0.5221083 0.3154984 0.1169027 0.04549068
Cumulative Proportion  0.5221083 0.8376067 0.9545093 1.00000000
```

Figure 188: Sample PCA output.

The figure shows us that the first component accounts for 52.2% of the variance and the first and second account for almost 84% of the variance. Thus if we were forced to reduce the dimensions from four to two, we could use just the first two components. More typically, we might have data with, say 30, dimensions and find that the first seven components account for 95% of the variance in the data. We would then be able to safely use seven dimensions instead of 30 to build our models.

The output of *PCA* also tells us how each of the original attributes *loads* on the each component – Figure 189 shows the details.

Based on these, *PCA* calculates a *score* on each component for each case of our data. In the current example, if we wanted to use only two of the components, then we would use the

Loadings:				
	Comp.1	Comp.2	Comp.3	Comp.4
urban	-0.563	0.184	0.788	-0.168
income	-0.644		-0.313	0.698
under18	0.207	-0.798	0.416	0.385
expense	-0.475	-0.574	-0.329	-0.580

Figure 189: Sample PCA loadings.

scores on the first two components – in place of the original four attributes – as predictors in an analytics exercise.

Going back to the example with 30 attributes, if we found that the first 7 principal components accounted for 95% of the variation, we will be able to use the computed scores on these 7 components as predictor attributes in a data analytics exercise.

What next?

I hope you have been able to acquire useful analytics skills. Despite the huge amount of ground this book has covered, you have many more exciting topics to learn. Here are a few things you might consider:

- To really apply these new skills, you will need to learn how to **acquire and prepare data for analytics**. In this book we have generally started with ready-made data files and jumped right into processing. However, you will need to perform several important steps to get to this stage. You will benefit a lot by enhancing these skills.
- We have focused a lot on analytics techniques and not as much on exploratory analysis and data visualization as we would have liked. Although we used **R**'s graphic capabilities quite a bit, we did not delve into some of the more powerful features. This is certainly something for you to explore.
- We covered as much of **R** as needed for you to be able to use the analytics techniques we covered. **R** has a lot more to offer than what we have covered; strengthening your skills in **R** would also be very helpful.
- In addition to the techniques that we have covered, you should consider learning about *Random Forests*, *Support Vector Machines*, *Logistic Regression* and *Neural Networks*, among others. Analytics is also rapidly expanding in areas like *Text Mining* and *Social Network Analysis*. These are all areas for you to explore.

Answers

Review 1: Structure of data (page 10)

Answer the following questions based on the data in Table 97.

state	region	urban	income	under18	expense
ME	1	508	3944	325	235
NH	1	564	4578	323	231
VT	1	322	4011	328	270
MA	1	846	5233	305	261
RI	1	871	4780	303	300
CT	1	774	5889	307	317
NY	1	856	5663	301	387
NJ	1	889	5759	310	285
PA	1	715	4894	300	300
OH	2	753	5012	324	221

Table 97: Data for review question

1. How many attributes does this data set have?

   Answer: Six attributes. Recall that the columns of a data set represent the attributes.

2. How many cases or instances does the data set have?

   Answer: Ten. Each row represents an instance or case.

3. Which attributes seem to be categorical ?

   Answer: The first one, *state* clearly is categorical since it is not numeric. The attribute *region*, despite having numeric values, should be treated as categorical as well since the numeric value has no significance and is just a label.

Review 2: Introduction to **RStudio** *(page 17)*

1. What do we gain by setting the *Working Directory*?

   Answer: Without setting it, we would have to enter the *complete path* for any files that we need to use in **R** or **RStudio**. If we set the *Working Directory*, we would need to just specify the file name alone, so long as the file is located in the working directory.

2. In **RStudio**, how do we set the working directory in such a way that this setting takes effect whenever we start **RStudio**?

   Answer: On Widnows: Use the “Tools -> Global options” menu option.

   On Macs: Use the menu option “RStudio -> Preferences”

3. How can we change the working directory setting *temporarily*?

   Answer: On the bottom right hand-pane in **RStudio**, select the “Files” tab and click the “...” button and choose the desired directory. Then use the “Set as working directory” option under the “More” button.

4. How can we find out what the working directory is currently set to?

   Answer: Use the command “getwd()”. Or look in the title bar of the console frame.

Lab assignment 1 Introduction to R data frames (page 34)

From the data files you downloaded, read in *college-perf.csv* into a variable with a name of your choice.

Answer:

```
cperf <- read.csv("college-perf.csv")
```

After this, a variable named *cperf* appears in the *Environment* tab of the top right pane.

Caveat: We have used the name *cperf* for the variable that will hold the data read from the file. If you used a different name then that would appear on the left hand side of your answer. In all of the answers shown below, you should use your variable name in place of *cperf*.

1. How many attributes does the data frame have?

   Answer: 6

   You can find this in one of several ways.

   a Use the command

   `names(cperf)`

   to get the names of all the attrbutes.

b Click on the variable name in the *Environment* tab and display the data. From that you can see the number of columns.

c Use the command

```
ncol(cperf)
```

to find the number of columns in the data frame.

2. How many rows or instances does the file have?

Answer: 4000
You can use the command

```
nrow(cperf)
```

You can also find this if you display the data by typing in the name of your data frame variable. For example, if it is *cperf*:

```
cperf
```

3. What are the names of the attributes?

Answer: SAT, GPA, Projects, Income, Community, Perf (you can see these if you either display the data or use the command:

```
names(cperf)
```

4. Which attributes have numerical values and which one are *factors*?

Answer: Perf is categorical. All others are numeric. When the values of an attribute are strings, it will generally be categorical. Sometimes we have attributes that are just plain strings and not used in any processing.

5. Type the **R** commands for each of the following:

i Display all the data.

Answer:

```
cperf
```

or click on the name of the data frame in the *Environment* tab on the top right.

ii Display the values of all attributes for row 256.

Answer:

```
cperf[256, ]
```

Don't omit the comma – it indicates that we have two subscripts and are leaving the second one blank.

iii Display the values of all attributes for rows 10 to 20.

Answer:

```
cperf[10:20, ]
```

iv Display the values of only the second, third and fourth attributes for all rows – do this using the column positions of the attributes.

Answer:

```
cperf[ ,2:4]
```

Since we want data from contiguous attributes, we have used the colon notation to indicate the range.

You could also say

```
cperf[, c(2,3,4)]
```

but this is more long winded than it needs to be.

v Display the values of only the first and third attributes for all rows – do this using the column positions of the attributes.

Answer:

```
cperf[ ,c(1,3)]
```

We now want information from non-contiguous attributes and hence have to construct the list of columns as a vector using the *c* function.

vi Same as above, except use column names instead of column positions.

Answer:

```
cperf[ ,c("SAT", "Projects")]
```

Since we now want information from non-contiguous attributes we have to construct the list of columns as a vector, but we use the attribute names now. Don't forget the quotes.

vii Display the values of the first and third attributes for rows 200 through 230.

Answer:

```
cperf[200:230, c(1, 3)]
```

viii Display the values of the second and fourth attributes by column positions for rows 2, 3, 10, 15 and 20 only.

Answer:

```
cperf[c(2,3,10,15,20), c(2, 4)]
```

We can use the *c* function to get data on non-contiguous rows as well.

ix Display summary information for all attributes.

Answer:

```
summary(cperf)
```

x Display summary information for *SAT*

Answer:

```
summary(cperf$SAT)
```

We can access a component of a data frame by using the $ notation as above.

The following are also correct:

```
summary(cperf[, 1 ])
summary(cperf[1])
```

xi Convert the attribute *Perf* to be ordinal, with the proper ordering.

Answer:

```
cperf$Perf = ordered(cperf$Perf,
       levels = c("Low", "Medium", "High"))
```

Note that we are using *ordered* instead of just *factor*.

xii Display all the attributes for the cases for which the GPA is 3 or more.

Answer:

```
cperf[cperf$GPA >= 3, ]
```

xiii Compute the value of SAT plus (GPA*100) for each case.

Answer:

```
cperf[,1]+cperf[,2]*100
```

or

```
cperf$SAT + cperf$GPA*100
```

or

```
cperf[,"SAT"] + cperf[,"GPA"]*100
```

xiv What is the name given to the kind of operation in which we operate on a whole set of values in a single command?

Answer: Vector operation

xv Set the value of *Income* to 0 for all cases.

Answer:

```
cperf$Income <- 0
```

or

```
cperf[, 5] <- 0
```

Review 3: Relationships (page 43)

1. To identify fraudulent credit card transactions, credit card companies try to classify each transaction as either normal or as fraudulent. If they record a charge to a credit card and can classify it as potentially fraudulent, then they can immediately alert the card holder by calling to confirm the validity of the charge. What attributes of a transaction might be related to the legitimacy of a transaction – that is, whether it is normal or fraudulent?

   Answer: Based on lots of historical data about normal transactions for a given credit card, a company can establish the merchants, charge amounts, time of day, location and so on which are normal for that card holder. Given the card number of the credit card used in a new transaction along with the amount of the charge, the location and merchant where the card was used and the time when the transaction occurred, the card company could see if this fits the pattern of a normal transaction and alert the card holder if it does not. Here the card company exploits the relationship that the attributes like merchant, location, amount and time of day have to the legitimacy of a transaction. Later in the book, we will look at *classification* methods that can help to build such models.

2. A potential buyer of a new car at a car dealership offers his current used car as a trade-in. The car dealership needs to assess how much the trade-in car will sell for and offer a trade-in value based on the estimated price. What attributes of the trade-in car might be related to its possible sale price?

   Answer: Attributes like the make and model, year of manufacture, condition of the car, installed accessories, number of miles driven, color, horse-power, engine capacity, fuel-type, whether or not the car is a hybrid should all be related to the possible sale price. Later in the book, we will look at *prediction* models for such situations.

Review 4: Important data analytics concepts (page 53)

1. For each of the following items, indicate if the problem is one of *classification* or *Regression*:

   i A text analysis application is to be provided text fragments and it is supposed to identify if the fragment came from the *New York Times* or the *Wall Street Journal.*

   Answer: For each fragment, the task is to identify whether it came from one or the other newspaper. This is a classification task.

   ii An amusement park wants to predict the number of visitors on a particular day based on factors like the expected weather ; weekday or not, summer vacation or not, etc.

   Answer: Since they are trying to predict the number of visitors, this is a regression task. Some of the predictor attributes seem to be categorical, but that does not matter in determining the nature of the task.

   iii A rice farmer wants to build a model to predict the number of tons of rice his land will produce during a specific year.

   Answer: The outcome is a numeric prediction – regression.

   iv Gmail divides the inbox into three tabs *Primary, Social* and *Promotions.* For each mail that it will place in a user's inbox, it needs to determine the appropriate tab.

   Answer: The task is to determine if a given email is social, promotional or a general message – classification

   v A publishing company has two types of books that it publishes – *fiction* and *non-fiction.* The company wants to build a model to predict the sales of each type of publication based historical data on several attributes of its prior publications.

   Answer: Since the task is to predict the sales level – a numeric value – for each type of book, this is a regression task. Don't be misled just because some categories were mentioned. You have to focus on what is being predicted.

2. A credit card company used its historical data to build a model to classify a credit card transaction as *genuine* or *fraudulent*, based on several attributes that would be available at the time a transaction takes place. Of course, for each row of historical data, the company knew if the corresponding

transaction was genuine or fraudulent. The company plans to use this model on every new credit card transaction.

As described in this text, they used data partitioning. They had 100,000 rows in the training partition and 40,000 rows in the test partition.

Without worrying about how they built the model or what is in the model, explain how you might test the quality of the model.

Answer: For each row in the training partition, we can compare the model's prediction and the actual class. This way, we can know the proportion of cases the model got correct.

If this proportion seems acceptable, we can do the same for the test partition – this is data that the model has not seen at all. If the performance on the test partition is also acceptable, we can deploy the model.

Review 5: **R** *Packages (page 59)*

1. What is the name given to a chunk of **R** functionality that we can load and unload as needed?

   Answer: Package

2. List two ways by which we can install packages.

   Answer:

   i Use the function *install.packages* in a command

   ii Use the "Install" button on the *Packages* tab.

3. What two things would you need to do have done before you can use the functionality of a package?

   Answer: Installed and loaded the package

4. What must we already have done before we can load a package?

   Answer: We should have installed it

5. List two ways by which we can load a package.

   Answer:

   i Use the *library* function in a command in the console

   ii Check the package name in the *Packages* tab.

Lab assignment 2 Data Partitioning (page 63)

Show the **R** commands you will use for the following. If a specific package is needed, you should show the **R** command to load it specifically in the step where it is needed.

1. Read the data from the file *college-perf.csv* into an **R** data frame called *cp*. The target attribute is *Perf*. You will use this data frame for questions 2 to 6.

   Answer:

   ```
   cp <- read.csv("college-perf.csv")
   ```

2. Set the seed for the random number generator to 2015.

   Answer:

   ```
   set.seed(2015)
   ```

3. Generate a set of random row numbers from the data frame amounting to 65% of the rows and store the result in a variable called *sel*.

   Answer:

   ```
   library(caret)
   set.seed(2015)
   sel <- createDataPartition(cp$Perf,
          p=0.65, list=FALSE)
   ```

   We used *cp$Perf* because we have been told that it is the target attribute.

   We stored the result in a variable called *sel* as required.

   We set the seed again because loading *caret* seems to somehow upset the random number generator and so we reset it.

4. Create a data frame called *training* that contains the rows of *cp* corresponding to the rows sampled above.

   Answer:

   ```
   training <- cp[sel, ]
   ```

   We used *sel* above because that is the variable with the selected row numbers.

5. Create a data frame called *testing* that contains the remaining rows of *cp*.

   Answer:

```
testing <- cp[-sel, ]
```

6. Write the **R** code to see the total number of rows in *cp*. Then write an **R** expression to total the number of rows in *training* and in *testing*. Should the two match?

   Answer:

   ```
   nrow(cp)    # prints 4000
   nrow(training) + nrow(testing)   # also prints 4000
   ```

   These two should match because we assigned some rows to *training* and the rest to *testing*. So each row of the original is either in one or the other.

7. Read the data from the file *auto-mpg.csv* into a data frame called *auto*. Write all the necessary commands (including loading of packages) to create a training partition with 70% of the rows and a test partition with the rest. Call these two partitions *train* and *test*, respectively. You can assign any name to the other variables you use. As a good practice, always use meaningful names. The target attribute is *mpg*.

   Answer:

   ```
   auto <- read.csv("auto-mpg.csv")
   library(caret)
   set.seed(2015)
   sam <- createDataPartition(auto$mpg,
          p=0.7, list = FALSE)
   train <- auto[sam, ]
   test <- auto[-sam, ]
   ```

   These two should match because we assigned some rows to *training* and the rest to *testing*. So each row of the original is either in one or the other.

Review 6: Affinity Analysis (page 73)

1. Table 98 contains information on a set of emails that a person sent and the recipients for each email. Am email system could use a person's past email recipients to suggest recipients for new emails that the person is in the process of constructing by looking at the recipients already included for the email and suggesting new recipients. Gmail does something like this when it come up with messages like "consider including xxx."

Answer the following questions based on the data in Table 98. Based on the data, we can see that the antecedent and consequent of rules in this situation will be sets of email recipients.

Email no	Recipients
1	John, Ma, Chris, Eduardo, Ram
2	Ram, Eduardo
3	John, Emily, Chris, Ma
4	Ma, Chris, Eduardo
5	Chris, Eduardo

Table 98: Emails and recipients.

a List any two rules that you can infer from the first email's recipients.
Answer: We can make up many rules based on the item set with the five recipients of the first email – these might not necessarily be good rules. We can include any subset of these four people as the antecedent and any other subset made up of the remaining items as the consequent. Some possibilities are:
$\{Ma\} \Rightarrow \{Eduardo\}$
$\{Ma, Eduardo\} \Rightarrow \{Chris\}$
$\{Eduardo, Chris\} \Rightarrow \{John, Ma, Ram\}$
$\{Eduardo\} \Rightarrow \{John, Ma, Ram, Chris\}$
and so on.

b What is the support for item set $\{Ma, Chris\}$?
Answer: The item set $\{Ma, Chris\}$ occurs on three of the five emails and so its support is $3/5$ or 0.6. Remember, the order in which the items are listed bears no significance.

c What is the support for item set $\{John, Eduardo\}$?
Answer: The item set $\{John, Eduardo\}$ occurs in one of the five emails and so its support is $1/5$ or 0.2.

d Which item sets of size 2 have the highest support?
Answer: $\{Ma, Chris\}$ and $\{Eduardo, Chris\}$ both occur in three of the five emails for a support of 0.6.

e What is the confidence for rule $\{Chris, Ma\} \Rightarrow \{Eduardo\}$?
Answer: $\{Chris, Ma\}$ occurs in three emails. In two of them $\{Eduardo\}$ also occurs and so the confidence is $2/3$ or 0.67.

f What is the confidence for rule $\{Chris\} \Rightarrow \{Eduardo, Ma\}$?
Answer: $\{Chris\}$ occurs in four emails. In two of them $\{Eduardo, Ma\}$ also occur and so the confidence is $2/4$ or 0.5.

g Why are the confidence levels different for the above two even though exactly the same items are involved in both?

Answer: Although the same item sets appear in the antecedent and consequent combined, the antecedent differs and so the denominators in the two differ while the numerator remains the same. Hence we get different values for confidence.

h What is the lift for rule $\{Chris\} \Rightarrow \{Eduardo\}$?

Answer: $\{Eduardo\}$ occurs in four emails out of the five, for a support of 0.8. In three of the four emails where $\{Chris\}$ occurs, $\{Eduardo\}$ also occurs, for a confidence of 0.75. Thus the lift is 0.75/0.8 It is below 1.0.

i What is the lift for rule $\{Ma, Chris\} \Rightarrow \{Eduardo\}$?

Answer: We have already found that $\{Eduardo\}$ has a support of 0.8. Among the three cases where $\{Ma, Chris\}$ appears, $\{Eduardo\}$ appears in two for a confidence of 0.67. The lift therefore is 0.67/0.8, again less than 1.

j Which rule with $\{Ma\}$ as the consequent and having exactly a single item in its antecedent has the maximum lift?

Answer: $\{Ma\}$ has a support of 0.6 (three of the five cases). If we look at each of the other people with whom Ma appears, we see that Ma appears whenever $John$ appears. Thus $\{John\} \Rightarrow \{Ma\}$ has a confidence of 1.00 and therefore a lift of 1.00/0.6 = 1.67. None of the other rules with Ma as the consequent has a higher lift.

2. Suppose we have a rule $\{A\} \Rightarrow \{B\}$ that has a confidence of close to 1. This would mean that whenever A occurs, B is also almost certain to occur. Under what conditions might this fact alone not be a very good indicator that these two items are closely associated?

   Answer: A high confidence alone does not show solid association. If an item set or item has a very high support, then every rule in which it is a consequence will also tend to have high confidence because it will tend to occur with almost all item sets – coincidental association Without a high lift, a high confidence is not of much significance.

3. Under what conditions might a rule with a very high lift still not be a useful?

   Answer: A rule with a high lift surely shows a strong association between the antecedent and consequent item sets. However, such a rule might not be very useful if the support is very low because of its relative rarity. It would not occur often enough to be of practical use. In other words, we will not find many opportunities to put this rule into use.

4. Suppose we have a rule with support of 1.0, what would its confidence be? What about lift?

   Answer: For a rule to have a support of 1.00 the items making up its it antecedent and consequent item sets will have to appear in each and every case, let us say 1000 cases. Therefore we can also infer that the antecedent item set occurs 1000 times and so does the consequent item set and so the confidence is 1.00 as well. Therefore the lift will also be 1.00.

5. Which of the following statements **are** possible in the context of the three measure of the quality of rules?

   a A rule with confidence of 0.8, support of 0.3 and lift of 1.5
   b A rule with confidence of 1.5, support of 0.3 and lift of 1.5
   c A rule with confidence of 0.8, support of 1.3 and lift of 0.75
   d A rule with confidence of 1.2, support of 1.3 and lift of 1.0

   Answer: Only the first alternative is feasible because only lift can have a value greater than 1. The other two have to be between 0 and 1.

Lab assignment 3: Affinity Analysis (page 79)

Let us suppose that a school wants to make its on-line course registration system more student-friendly. To do this, the school wants to augment the registration system with course recommendations for students. When a student registers for a particular course, the school wants its system to suggest other courses to the student, based on historical information about sets of courses that students took. The data file *student-courses.csv* contains information on courses that students took. The file contains 4247 rows of data with each row containing a student id and a course number. The data represents the sets of courses taken by 1645 distinct students. An extract of the data appears below in Table 99.

If a student has taken several courses, then several rows of data occur for that student. For example, student 4 has taken 6 courses whereas student 5 has taken just one course. You can see the similarity of this data with the market basket data that we looked at in the lab on Affinity Analysis. The student id here is like the transaction id earlier and the course number is like the item.

1. Load the data into **R**.

   Answer: Use a command like the following (of course, your variable name might be different from *regdata*):

student_id	course_no
4	FI201
4	LA321
4	LA325
4	MG501
4	MK601
4	EC408
5	MK605
6	IT701
7	AC103
7	LA301
7	EC402
8	AC104
8	FI201
8	MG501
8	QA812
8	EC408
...	...

Table 99: Course registration information.

```
regdata <- read.csv("student-courses.csv")
```

2. Perform an affinity analysis using the settings $support = 0.02$ and $confidence = 0.3$.

   Answer: Assuming that the variable *regdata* holds the data, and we want to store the results in a variable called *res*, we can use the command:

```
library(arules)
binary <- as(split(regdata[,2], regdata[,1]),
       "transactions")

res <- apriori(binary,
       parameter=list(support=0.02,
       confidence = 0.3))
```

3. How many rules did the system generate with the above values for support and confidence?

   Answer: 40

4. Sort the display by descending order of *lift*.

   Answer: Use the command:

```
inspect(sort(res, by="lift"))
```

5. Look at the first rule. What are the values of *support, confidence* and *lift* for the rule?

   Answer: The output says the following:

   lhs rhs support confidence lift 1 AC113 => AC102 0.02249240 0.9736842 41.069501

   From the above we can get the needed answers.

6. Use one or more of the above measures to find out the following without going back to the original data: Of the total of 1645 students, approximately how many took all the courses involved in the first rule displayed?

   Answer: The support for the rule is 0.02249240. We are told that there are 1645 students – which means that we have 1645 transactions. The concerned item set occurs in 0.02249240 of the 1645 transactions. 1645 * 0.02249240 = 37.

7. Infer, without actually going back to the data file, how many students took the courses appearing in the antecedent of the first rule displayed.

   Answer: This one is tricky. We know that 37 students took both the courses. We also know that the confidence of the rule is 0.9736842. This means that of all the people who took the antecedent, say x,0.9736842 of them took the consequent and that figure is 37. Therefore $0.9736842x = 37$ and hence $x = 38$.

8. If a student has taken AC104 and you had to recommend just one course for this student, which one would that be? Why?

   Answer: Of all the rules that have just AC104 in the antecedent, rule 21 has the highest values for all measures. Thus we can recommend QA812.

9. If a student has taken AC104 and FI201 during the current registration session and your system had to recommend just one course to this student, which course would that be? Why?

   Answer: Rules 7 and 13 from the list apply, but rule 7 in the list, we should recommend QA 812.

10. As above, but if you could recommend two courses what would those two be?

    Answer: Now we can use both rules 7 and 13 and hence recommend QA812 and MK601.

11. We see that the lift for even the last rule is 3.84 – very high. What might you do to get even more rules?

    Answer: We can generate more rules because our parameter settings could have eliminated some promising ones. To increase the number of rules, we can set a lower cutoff value for *support* or *confidence* or both and try again.

Review 7: Classification (page 116)

For each of the following tasks which the concerned entities will carry out based on historical data, indicate if the task involves *classification* or *regression*.

1. An on-line store wants to calculate the possible rating that a specific customer might assign to a product and decide whether or not to present the product to the customer.

   Answer: Prediction – because the store wants to calculate a specific number.

2. A company wants to mark each of its current customers as one who is likely to switch to a competing product or not, and base some promotions on this determination.

   Answer: Classification – because the company simply wants to categorize each customer as likely to switch or not.

3. A credit card company looks at every card transaction and wants to label it as fraudulent or not.

   Answer: Classification – because the company wants to categorize each transaction as fraudulent or not.

4. A store wants to find out how many units of a specific product will sell during a certain time period.

   Answer: Regression – because the store watts to predict *the number of units* of a product it will sell – predict a numeric value.

5. A bank is planning to invite some of its existing clients for a dinner event to promote a new financial product. It therefore wants to look at each current client predict if they will adopt the product. They plan to invite customers who seem likely to adopt the product.

   Answer: Classification – because the bank simply wants to categorize each customer as likely to adopt the new product or not.

Review 8: KNN for Classification (page 132)

Table 100 shows fictitious data on some people's age, family income and the type of smart phone they own.

Table 101 shows the original and standardized values of the 10 cases in the Training.A partition.

Table 102 shows the original and standardized values of 4 cases in the Training.B partition.

Age	Family_income	Phone_type
14	50,000	iPhone
17	80,000	Android
23	70,000	Android
30	100,000	Android
40	120,000	iPhone
60	200,000	Other
16	40000	iPhone
13	48,000	iPhone
17	80,000	Android
22	71,000	Android
29	100000	Other
41	120000	iPhone
60	210000	Other
16	42000	iPhone

Table 100: Table for KNN review question.

No	Age	Family_income	Phone_type	Age_z	Family_income_z
1	14	50000	iPhone	-0.895	-0.842
2	17	80000	Android	-0.709	-0.281
3	23	70000	Android	-0.337	-0.468
4	30	100000	Android	0.098	0.092
5	40	120000	iPhone	0.718	0.466
6	60	200000	Other	1.959	1.960
7	16	40000	iPhone	-0.771	-1.029
8	13	48000	iPhone	-0.957	-0.879
9	17	80000	Android	-0.709	-0.281
10	22	71000	Android	-0.399	-0.450

Table 101: Training.A partition for KNN review question

No	Age	Family_income	Phone_type	Age_z	Family_income_z
1	29	100000	Other	0.035	0.092
2	41	120000	iPhone	0.780	0.466
3	60	210000	Other	1.959	2.146
4	16	42000	iPhone	-0.771	-0.991

Table 102: Training.B partition for KNN review question

1. Use Excel (or anything else) to calculate the **three** nearest neighbors in the Training.A data set for the second row of the Training.B data set.

   Answer: Table 103 shows the squared distances of each Training.A case from the second Training.B case. From the table we see that Training.A cases 3, 4 and 5 are the three nearest neighbors to Training.B case 2.

Trg.A case no	Sqr dist from case 2
1	4.517
2	2.776
3	2.120
4	0.606
5	0.004
6	3.623
7	4.640
8	4.828
9	2.776
10	2.228

Table 103: Squared distances.

2. Based on the above calculations, how would you classify the item on the second row of the validation data set? Don't confuse this with what the table already shows; your classification might be the same, or could be different.

   Answer: From table 103 we see that two of the three nearest neighbors own Android phones. So we will classify this case as Android – and our classification would be incorrect!

Lab assignment 4: KNN for classification (page 146)

The file "academic.csv" contains historical data that a professor maintained about her students. The file contains the score that students obtained on the first test of one of her courses and the student's attendance record till the first test. The file also has information on the overall performance of each student classified as *Acceptable* or *Not-acceptable*.

The professor wants to see if she can build a model to predict how students will perform based on the score in the first test and their attendance record. She wants to use this information to spot potential poor performers and counsel then in advance to enhance their chances of success.

1. Load the data now into a data frame called *students*.

   Answer:

   ```
   students <- read.csv("academic.csv")
   ```

2. List the data in the **R** data frame *students* that you created in the previous step.

   Answer:

   ```
   students
   ```

3. What is the target attribute?

   Answer: *perf* – because we are building a model to predict a student's overall performance based on the score in the first test and their attendance record.

4. What are the predictor attributes?

   Answer: *score* and *attendance*

5. Take a look at the data. What are the maximum and minimum values of the two predictor attributes?

   Answer: *score* – max = 25, min = 13 *attendance* – max = 1, min = 0.4

6. What additional processing do you need to do to the data so that you can use KNN?

   Answer: Because KNN relies on distance computations, we need to standardize or scale the predictor attributes.

7. Store the standardized values of the two predictor attributes in two new attributes in the same data frame.

   Answer:

```
students$score_z <- scale(students$score)
students$attendance_z <-
         scale(students$attendance)
# Alternately, we can "source" in
# the convenience function dar2ed.scale.many
# from the file dar2ed-scale-many.R and:
students <- dar2ed.scale.many(students, c(1,2))
```

8. What do you need to do next to set up for KNN analysis?

   Answer: Partition the data

9. Create three partitions with a 70-15-15 breakup (remember to set the seed to 2015 if you want to match your answers to those given in the book).

   Answer:

```
library(caret)
set.seed(2015)
samp <- createDataPartition(students$perf,
       p = 0.7, list = FALSE)
# Create the train.a partition
train.a <- students[samp, ]
# Store the rest of the data in a new
# variable called rest
rest <- students[-samp, ]
# We need to sample half of the rest
# into the second partition train1
samp <- createDataPartition(rest$perf,
       p = 0.5, list = FALSE)
train.b <- rest[samp, ]
test <- rest[-samp, ]
```

10. Run KNN for k=1, 3 and 5. For each one, generate the classification-confusion matrix.

    Answer:

```
train.b$pred.1 <- knn(train.a[,4:5],
       train.b[, 4:5], train.a[ ,3], 1)
tab.1 <- table(train.b$perf, train.b$pred.1,
       dnn = c("Actual", "Predicted"))
tab.1

train.b$pred.3 <- knn(train.a[,4:5],
       train.b[, 4:5], train.a[ ,3], 3)
```

```
tab.3 <- table(train.b$perf, train.b$pred.3,
       dnn = c("Actual", "Predicted"))
tab.3

train.b$pred.5 <- knn(train.a[,4:5],
       train.b[, 4:5], train.a[ ,3], 5)
tab.5 <- table(train.b$perf, train.b$pred.5,
       dnn = c("Actual", "Predicted"))
tab.5
```

Figure 190 shows the classification-confusion matrices (error matrices) for k=1, k=3 and k=5.

k = 1

```
                Predicted
Actual           Acceptable Not-acceptable
  Acceptable              4              3
  Not-acceptable          1              4
```

k = 3

```
                Predicted
Actual           Acceptable Not-acceptable
  Acceptable              6              1
  Not-acceptable          2              3
```

k = 5

```
                Predicted
Actual           Acceptable Not-acceptable
  Acceptable              6              1
  Not-acceptable          2              3
```

Figure 190: Classification-confusion matrices for k=1, k=3 and k=5.

11. Based on the classification-confusion matrices you obtained, select a value for k to use.

    Answer: Based on the overall performance, k=3 and k=5 classify 9 of the 12 cases correctly whereas k=1 gets 8 correct. Note that k=1 performs better on the *Non acceptable* cases and k=3 and 5 perform better on the *Acceptable* cases. Since we have no information on which one would be preferred, we will go with the overall performance and choose k=3. There is no point in choosing k=5 as the performance is the same as for k=3, but more computation would be involved.

12. Use the chosen value of k and generate the classification-confusion matrix for the test partition. Did it turn out to be better or worse than the performance on the training data?

    Answer:

```
test$pred.3 <- knn(train.a[,4:5],
       test[, 4:5], train.a[ ,3], 3)
test.tab.3 <- table(test$perf, test$pred.3,
       dnn = c("Actual", "Predicted"))
test.tab.3
```

Figure 191 shows the result.

```
                Predicted
Actual           Acceptable Not-acceptable
  Acceptable              3              3
  Not-acceptable          0              4
```

Figure 191: Classification-confusion matrix for the test partition on k=3

13. Without the use of data analytics, what would have been your error rate? Does the KNN approach provide any lift? If so, how much?

    Answer: The summary of *students$perf* reveals that there are 45 *Acceptable* and 31 *Non-acceptable* cases. Without the model we would have classified all cases as *Acceptable* for a performance of 45/76 or 59%; the error rate would be 41%.

With the model, based on the test partition, the correctness rate is 7 out of 10 or 70%.

The model does provide a lift of 70/59 = 1.186.

Review 9: Attribute conversion (page 151)

1. **Categorical to numeric:**Let us suppose that a data file has 5 attributes and two of these are categorical. One of the categorical attributes has three possible values and the other has four. If someone adds just the correct number of dummy attributes to the data file while retaining the original attributes as well, how many attributes will the data have overall after the addition of dummies?

   Answer: For each categorical attribute the data-miner should add dummy attributes totaling one less than the number of different values. Thus the first categorical attribute will add two dummy attributes and the second will add three for a total of five new attributes. The data will thus have 10 attributes after the process.

2. **Numeric to categorical:** Suppose a data file has information on many stores of a grocery chain. The file contains a numeric attribute *return_on_investment*. A data analyst wants to apply a classification technique to this file to be able to classify stores as *High_ROI* or *Low_ROI* and wants to convert this numerical attribute to categorical. Assuming that the data file has many rows of data, how might the data analyst proceed?

   Answer: The data analyst can approach this in many ways. One would be to find a cutoff value for *ROI* and classify every store having a value at or above the cutoff as *High_ROI* and the rest as *Low_ROI*.

   However, since we are told that there is no dearth of data, the data analyst could break the data into three levels based on the *ROI* and drop the middle. She can then categorize the top bracket as *High_ROI* and the bottom one as *Low_ROI*. This way, there will be sharp distinction between the two levels with much less scope for ambiguity.

Review 10: Classification Trees-1 (page 159)

Look at the classification tree in figure 60. The tree is based on historical data about some students' performance in the first test of a course, their attendance record until the first test and their overall performance at the end of the course as *Acceptable* or *Not-acceptable* – these have been shortened in the tree diagram.

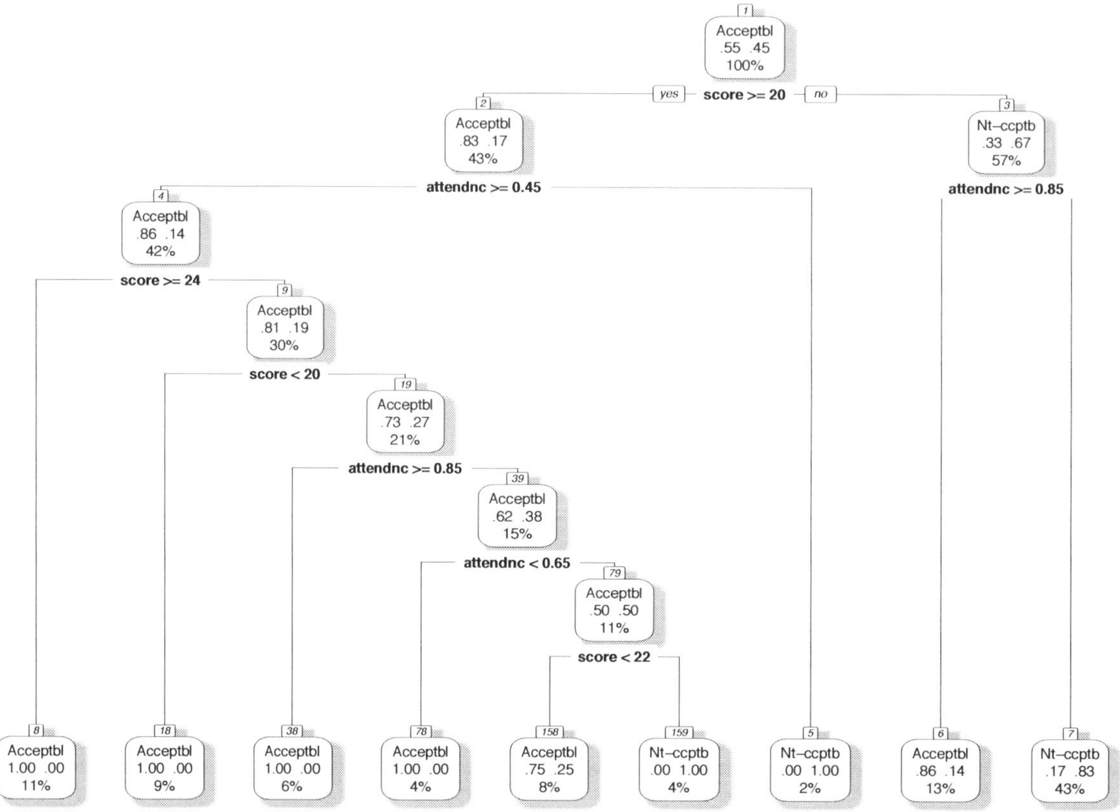

Figure 192: Classification tree for review questions

The tree in Figure 192 looks slightly different from the one we saw in Figure 59. Each interior node of the tree in Figure 59 showed the count of cases of each class satisfying the condition for the node. The tree in Figure 192 shows the proportion of cases of each class in the node, labels each node based on the majority class and also shows (at the bottom of the node) the overall percentage of cases satisfying the conditions for the node. Each node also has a node number and we refer to those numbers in the questions below. Despite these differences, the two figures contain the same kind of information. Use the tree in Figure 192 to answer the following questions:

1. How many leaf nodes does the tree have?

Answer: 9 – these are the nodes at the very bottom. They are leaf nodes because we cannot branch any further from any of those nodes.

2. Look at the node numbered 2. What conditions do the cases in that node satisfy?

   Answer: Starting at the root, to reach node 2, we have to go to the left – which means that the condition under the root is true. Thus cases in node 2 have score >= 20.

3. What proportion of the overall cases satisfy the condition for node 2?

   Answer: 43% – the percentage at the bottom tells us this. Note that for the root, this figure is 100% – as we would expect.

4. What proportion of the cases satisfying the condition for node 2 had *not-acceptable* performance?

   Answer: Although each node mentions the proportions of each case in the node, we cannot immediately figure out which number corresponds to which class. For example, in the root node, we see 0.55 and 0.45, but to which class does 0.55 correspond? The answer lies in the classification for a node at the top of the node. The root node is classified as *acceptable* and therefore that class should have a majority. There we can infer that 0.55 corresponds to *acceptable*. In each node therefore, the first number corresponds to the proportion of *acceptable*. Using this, we can now say that in node 2, the proportion of *not-acceptable* is 0.17.

5. Using this tree for classification, how would you classify someone who had a score of 18 and an attendance of 0.95? Which leaf node did you end up at?

   Answer: Starting at the root, we see that the condition is score >= 20. Our case does not satisfy this condition and so we take the *no* branch and arrive at node 3. With an attendance of 0.95, being greater than the node condition 0.85, we take the *yes* branch and arrive at the leaf node 6 – and classify the case as *acceptable*.

6. Using this tree for classification, how would you classify someone with a score of 21 and attendance of 0.43? Which leaf node did you end up at?

   Answer: Arguing as above, we will take the *yes* branch from the root and the *no* branch from node 2 to reach node 5 – *not-acceptable*.

7. Did this tree classify every case correctly? How did you find out?

Answer: No, it did not. If it had classified every case correctly, every leaf node would be pure and the proportions in each leaf node would have been (1.0, 0) or (0, 1.0). As things stand, many leaf nodes have cases of both types and they have been classified based on the majority class.

8. Under what conditions would it be impossible to find a perfect tree – that is, a tree which can classify every case correctly?

   Answer: If two or more cases had exactly the same value for every predictor attribute, but differed in their actual classification, then we could never get a perfect tree because all of these nodes will always end up at the same leaf node no matter what tree we construct. Thus some of them have to be misclassified.

Review: Lab Classification Trees 1 (page 174)

Review questions : Answer the following general questions on classification trees

a In some tree diagram for a classification problem, you see a node numbered 10. What numbers will its two child nodes have?

Answer: 20 and 21 – because the child nodes of a node numbered n will always be $2n$ and $2n + 1$.

b If a tree has 25 splits, how many leaf nodes will it have? Draw a few small trees and you will see a pattern – you just have to draw trees in which you have one root node and each node can have zero, one or two child nodes. Your trees do not need to have any other details like branching conditions to answer this question.

Answer: Each time you split a node, you increase the number of leaf nodes by 1. For example, when you have just the root node, you have one leaf node (the root itself). When you split it, you have two leaf nodes – the root is no longer a leaf node and only the two new nodes are leaf nodes. Reasoning this way, after n splits we will have $n + 1$ leaf nodes. Thus with 25 splits, we will have 26 leaf nodes.

c If a tree has 30 leaf nodes, how many splits were made? The logic of the previous answer should help you to answer this.

Answer: Reasoning as above, we get 29 splits.

d Assuming that in a particular situation, we have two classes for the target attribute (like *Luxury/ Non-luxury* or *Buyer/Non-buyer*), and we are able to obtain a *perfect* tree. In this case, what would you expect the proportions of the two classes to be in the leaf nodes?

Answer: With a perfect tree, every leaf node will have all cases of one class. Thus the proportions will be $(1, 0)$ or $(0, 1)$.

e Same as above, but we have three classes. What would be the proportions of the three classes in the leaf node?

Answer: Reasoning as above, the proportions will be $(1,0,0)$ or $(0,1,0)$ or $(0,0,1)$.

f In the problem that we took for this lab we were able to get a perfect classification tree – every leaf node had only cases of one class. Can you change any one of the data rows (cases) in such a way that it would be impossible to get a perfect tree?

Answer: If at least two rows or cases in the data have exactly the same values for the predictor attributes, but have different values for the target attribute then we can never get a perfect tree. For example, the first case $(89000, 1, Luxury)$ ends up at node 4 of the tree and is correctly classified as *Luxury*. Suppose we had another case with values $(89000, 1, Non - Luxury)$ then no matter what the tree is, both cases will have to end up at the same leaf node and thus the leaf node will have at least one case of each type and thus the tree cannot be perfect.

Review questions – Luxury car problem : Use the information in the tree diagram (Figure 193) and the textual output (Figure 194) to answer the following questions:

a How would this tree classify a case with income 70,000 and family size 1? Which leaf node with the case end up at?

Answer: Starting at the root, we go left to node 2 (because income is greater than 49,000) and left again to the leaf node 4 (because family size is less than 2.5), and stop. Thus the tree will classify the case as *Luxury*.

b Why is node 3 is marked as *Non-Luxury*?

Answer: The majority class there is *Non-Luxury* – 89% of the cases in fact.

c What conditions does a case have to satisfy to reach node 5?

Answer: Just following the path from the root and checking the conditions tells us: Income >= 49,000 and family size >= 3.5.

d Of the 24 cases in total, how many meet the conditions for node 5?

Answer: We can see the text display for the node and see that 6 cases meet the conditions. Alternately, the tree tells us that 25% of the cases meet the conditions and taking 25% of 24 gets us to the same place.

e What conditions does a case have to satisfy to reach node 11? State it as simply as you can.

Answer: Going simply by the conditions we get: income >= 49,000 and family size >= 3.5 and income >= 92,000. Since

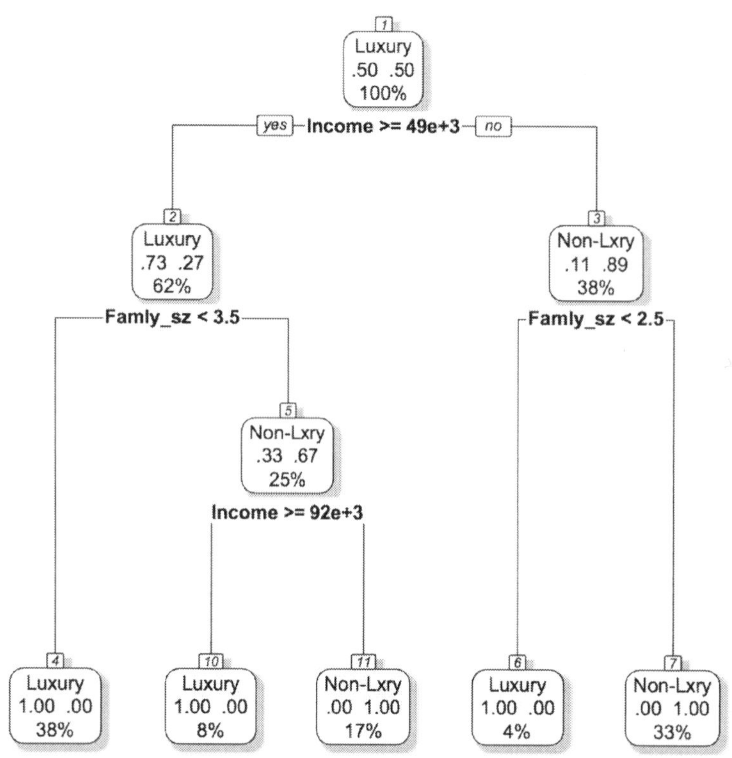

Figure 193: Complete tree for car ownership classification problem.

```
node), split, n, loss, yval, (yprob)
      * denotes terminal node

 1) root 24 12 Luxury (0.5000000 0.5000000)
   2) Income>=49350 15  4 Luxury (0.7333333 0.2666667)
     4) Family_size< 3.5 9  0 Luxury (1.0000000 0.0000000) *
     5) Family_size>=3.5 6  2 Non-Luxury (0.3333333 0.6666667)
      10) Income>=91600 2  0 Luxury (1.0000000 0.0000000) *
      11) Income< 91600 4  0 Non-Luxury (0.0000000 1.0000000) *
   3) Income< 49350 9  1 Non-Luxury (0.1111111 0.8888889)
     6) Family_size< 2.5 1  0 Luxury (1.0000000 0.0000000) *
     7) Family_size>=2.5 8  0 Non-Luxury (0.0000000 1.0000000) *
```

Figure 194: Basic text output from *rpart* for classification for car ownership example.

income has to be greater than or equal to 49,000 and 92,000, the latter condition holds. So we can simplify it to: income >-92,000 and family size >= 3.5.

f Use the text output to find how many cases do not belong to the majority case in nodes 2 and 5.

Answer: If we look at the text display and also the description of what each line says, we can see that 4 cases in node 2 and 2 cases in node 5 do not meet the conditions for the respective nodes.

Review 12: Naïve Bayes (page 220)

Assume that the table below shows the high school GPA, SAT score and the first semester performance in college for a set of students. All data are categorical.

Row no.	GPA	SAT	Performance
1	High	Medium	Medium
2	High	Medium	High
3	Low	High	High
4	Low	Medium	Low
5	Low	Low	Low
6	Medium	Medium	Medium
7	High	Medium	Medium
8	High	Medium	High

Calculate the following:

1. $P(Performance = High)$

   Answer: Of the 8 cases (rows), 3 have High performance (rows 2, 3 and 8). So the probability is 3/8.

2. $P(GPA = Low)$

   Answer: Of the 8 cases, 3 have Low GPA (rows 3, 4 and 5) and so the probability is 3/8.

3. $P(SAT = Medium)$

   Answer: Of the 8 cases, 6 have Medium SAT (rows 1, 2, 4, 6, 7 and 8). So the probability is 6/8 or 3/4.

4. $P(GPA = High|Performance = High)$

   Answer: We now have a condition – that Performance is High. So we should consider only those rows. There are 3 such rows (2, 3 and 8). Of these rows, 2 have High GPA as well (rows 2 and 8). Thus the probability is 2/3.

5. $P(SAT = Low|Performance = Low)$

   Answer: We have 2 cases with Low Performance (rows 4 and 5). Of these, SAT is Low in one (row 5) and so the probability is 1/2.

Lab assignment 5: Naïve Bayes (page 228)

Load the file "car-classification.csv" into **R**. Take a look at the data. It has input information about *price, maint, doors, persons, boot* and *safety*. The variable *acceptability* gives the level of acceptability of a car with specific values for these input attributes. We would like to build a classification model to classify new cases for their acceptability. All attributes, even though shown as numbers are actually categorical. Before starting your work, convert all attributes to categorical (factors).

Load the data with the command (the data frame name can be anything):

```
c <- read.csv("car-classification.csv")
```

1. What is the target attribute?

   Answer: *acceptability*: because we want to classify the level of acceptability of various cars, given the values of the other attributes.

2. How many rows does your data frame have?

   Answer: 1728: We can use the command *nrow(c)* to find this.

3. All attributes other than *acceptability* have numeric values and **R** will treat them as such by default. Recall that *Naïve Bayes* requires all of the attributes to be categorical. Convert all attributes other than *acceptability* to factors.

   Answer:

   ```
   c$price <- factor(c$price)
   c$maint <- factor(c$maint)
   c$doors <- factor(c$doors)
   c$persons <- factor(c$persons)
   c$boot <- factor(c$boot)
   c$safety <- factor(c$safety)
   ```

4. Partition the data into two partitions (70-30) as needed for Naïve Bayes.

   Answer:

   ```
   library(caret)
   set.seed(2015)
   sam <- createDataPartition(c$acceptability,
          p=0.7, list = FALSE)
   train <- c[sam, ]
   test <- c[-sam, ]
   ```

5. Build a Naive Bayes model based on the data in the training partition.

   Answer:

```
library(e1071)
c.nb <- naiveBayes(acceptability ~ ., data = train)
```

We used "acceptability ~." to specify the model because we want to use all other attributes than the target as the predictors. *train* contains our training data.

6. From the model created – what is the a-priori probability of *acc*?

   Answer: To print the model, just use the name of the model as a command. In my case that is *c.nb*.

   Looking in the "A-priori probabilities" section we see the value to be 0.22213047

7. Which value of *acceptability* has the highest a-priori probability ?

   Answer: Looking in the "A-priori probabilities" section we see that *unacc* has the highest value, 0.69942197.

8. Look at the conditional probabilities for *safety*. Explain what the three elements on the first row mean. What conditional probabilities do they represent?

   Answer: The first row is:

	1	2	3
acc	0.000000	0.4535316	0.5464684

   This says:

   P(safety=1|acceptability=acc) = 0.00

   P(safety=2|acceptability=acc) = 0.4535316

   P(safety=3|acceptability=acc) = 0.5464684

9. What do you see that is common to every single row of every conditional probability matrix generated by the model? Why is this so?

   Answer: They all add up to 1.0. This is because they represent all the conditional probabilities for a specific denominator. For example, looking at the first row for the conditional probabilities for *safety*, we see from the previous answer that all the conditional probabilities have the same condition – *acceptability=acc*. The only possible values for safety are 1, 2 and 3 and thus the cases for these three values will cover all cases for *acceptability=acc*. Thus the three numbers on the row showing their conditional probabilities must add up to 1.

10. What is the name of the **R** function you use to classify new cases?

    Answer: *predict*

11. Use the model to classify the cases in the training and test partitions and store the results in a new variable in the respective partitions. Generate the error matrix for each partition.

    Answer:

```
pred.train <- predict(c.nb, train)
tab.train <- table(train$acceptability, pred.train,
       dnn = c("Actual", "Predicted"))
tab.train

pred.test <- predict(c.nb, test)
tab.test <- table(test$acceptability, pred.test,
       dnn = c("Actual", "Predicted"))
tab.test
```

Figure 195 shows the result for the training partition.

Figure 196 shows the result for the test partition.

Actual \ Predicted	acc	good	unacc	vgood
acc	198	7	64	0
good	34	14	0	1
unacc	35	2	810	0
vgood	19	2	0	25

Figure 195: Error matrix on training partition for car acceptability data.

Actual \ Predicted	acc	good	unacc	vgood
acc	77	4	34	0
good	12	7	0	1
unacc	14	0	349	0
vgood	11	0	0	8

Figure 196: Error matrix on test partition for car acceptability data.

12. Based on the error matrix of the training partition, what proportion of acceptable cars (*acc*) were classified as acceptable (*acc*)?

    Answer: Looking at row 1 of the error matrix on the training partition, we see that there were 269 *acc* cars. Of these the model classified 198 as *acc* for a proportion of 198/269, or 0.736.

    Another way to get this would be to print the proportions on the matrix using the prop.table function:

    ```
    prop.table(tab.train)
    ```

    This generates the row-wise proportions (since we used 1 as the second argument) for the tab.train table and we get the same answer from that as well.

13. Based on the error matrix of the test partition, what proportion of acceptable cars (*acc*) were classified as acceptable (*acc*)?

    Answer: Looking at row 1 of the error matrix on the validation partition, we see that there were 120 *acc* cars. Of these the model classified 77 as *acc* for a proportion of 77/120, or 0.6695.

    Another way to get this would be to print the proportions on the matrix using the prop.table function:

    ```
    prop.table(tab.test)
    ```

    This generates the row-wise proportions (since we used 1 as the second argument) for the tab_t table and we get the same answer from that as well.

14. What was the overall percentage of errors on the training partition?

    Answer: We can find this by adding up all the misclassifications and finding the proportion they constitute of the cases in the training partition.

    The training partition has 1211 cases. Of these only the elements in the main diagonal represent correct classifications.

These add up to 198+14+810+25 = 1047. So the proportion of correct classifications is 0.8646 or 86.46%. The error rate therefore is 13.54%.

Another way would be to print the overall proportions and get the answers from there. We can use the command: prop.table(tab.train) and then add up the numbers along the main diagonal to get the correctness rate.

15. What was the overall percentage of errors on the test partition?

    Answer: Using a similar approach, we find the correctness rate to be: 85.3% and the error rate to be 14.7%.

16. What lift does data mining provide in this case based on overall error rate?

    Answer: Using the a-priori probabilities, we would classify every case as belonging to the majority class or as *unacc*. We would then have a correctness rate of 69.94%.

    On the test partition, data mining gives us a correctness rate of 85.3% for a lift of 85.3/69.94, or 1.22.

Review 13: Simple Linear Regression (page 245)

Table 104. shows a portion of a large data set that contains the annual restaurant expenses of families and their annual income per member (annual income divided by number of family members). We would like to build a simple linear regression model to predict the annual restaurant expense for future cases knowing only the annual income per member for a family.

rest_exp	income_pm
500	20000
600	30000
510	15000
520	25000
650	35000
...	...

Table 104: Per member family income and family annual restaurant expenses.

Answer the following questions based on Table 104.

1. Using the column headings as attribute names, what is the target attribute?

   Answer: Since we want to predict the annual restaurant expense, *rest_exp* will be the target attribute.

2. What is the predictor attribute?

Answer: Since we want to use the annual per-member income to predict the annual restaurant expense, *income_pm* will be the predictor attribute.

3. Which of the following represent correct forms of simple linear regression models for the problem (with the Greek letters representing the regression coefficients or constants). Select **all** applicable options. As is conventional, we have used the "hat" notation to indicate the predicted value for an attribute.

   a. $\widehat{income\_pm} = \beta_0 + \beta_1\, rest\_exp$
   b. $\widehat{rest\_exp} = \beta_0 + \beta_1\, income\_pm$
   c. $\widehat{rest\_exp} = \beta_0 + \beta_1\, income\_pm + \epsilon$
   d. $\widehat{rest\_exp} = \beta_0 + \beta_1\, income\_pm^2$
   e. $income\_pm = \alpha_0 + \alpha_1\, rest\_exp + \epsilon$
   f. $\widehat{rest\_exp} = \delta_0 + \delta_1\, income\_pm$
   g. $rest\_exp = \beta_0 + \beta_1\, income\_pm$

   Answer: The target attribute *rest_exp* has to appear on the left hand side and *income_pm* has to appear on the right hand side. The regression model calculates a predicted value for the target attribute; therefore we have to use the notation for the *predicted* value of the target attribute – with the "hat" on top. This leaves only b, c, d and f as possible choices. We can rule out c because the regression model that we will use to make predictions should not have the error term ϵ. We can rule out d because the expression is not *linear* (it is *quadratic* because *income_pm* has been raised to the second power). Both b and f represent correct choices – the actual names used for the intercept and the slope are immaterial. Using β_0 and β_1 is conventional, but we can use any names we want and option f uses δ_0 and δ_1 .

4. Let us assume that we have built a simple linear regression model for the above situation and find the intercept to be 366 and the regression coefficient for the predictor attribute to be 0.0076.

   a. What would the predicted annual restaurant expense be for a family with zero annual income per member?
      Answer: Plugging in the values in the proper regression equation, we compute 366+0.0076*0 to get 366 as the answer.
   b. If the annual income per member increases, would the predicted annual restaurant expense increase or decrease?
      Answer: Since the slope of the regression equation is positive, the predicted annual restaurant expense will increase.

c. If the annual income per member increases by $10,000, by how much would the predicted annual restaurant expense change?

Answer: From the regression equation, we can see that the predicted annual restaurant expense will increase by 10000*0.0076, or $76.

d. Given a family with an annual per-member income of $200,000, what would the family's predicted annual restaurant expense be?

Answer: 366+ 200000*0.0076, or $1886.

e. Let us suppose that a family has an annual per-member income of $12,000 and an annual restaurant expense of $850. What is the error (or, more correctly, *residual*) for this case based on our regression model?

Answer: The regression equation will predict the expense as 366 + 12000*0.0076, or $457.2. The actual expense is $850 and therefore the residual is $850 - 457.2$ or 392.8.

5. The regression coefficients mentioned in Question 4 were actually arrived at using only the first six rows of Table 104 Answer the following based on the data in Table 104 and the slope and intercept mentioned in Question 4.

a. Compute TSS (total sum of squares), SSE (sum of squared errors) and SSR (sum of squares regression).

Answer: The mean of the annual restaurant expense is the average of the values: 556.

To calculate TSS: For each row we take the difference of *rest_exp* from 556 and square it. We then add all of these to get 17,320. (For your reference, the squared deviation for the first row is 56*56, or 3136.)

To calculate SSE: For each row, we take the difference between the expense that the regression model predicts and the actual expense, and square this difference. We then add all these to get 2880. (For your reference, the prediction for the first row is 366 + 20000*0.0076, or 518. The difference from the actual value is therefore 18 and the square of this is 324.)

To calculate SSR: For each row we take the difference between the prediction and the mean and square this. We then add up the values for all rows and get 14440. (For your reference, we already know from the prior answer that the prediction for the first row is 518. Therefore the difference from the mean of 556 is 38 whose square is 1444.)

b. Do the numbers add up?

Answer: They do, indeed. We know from prior discussion that the equation TSS = SSR + SSE should hold, and it does.

c. How much of the variation in the target attribute does the regression explain?

Answer: 14440/17320 or 0.834 or 83.4%.

Lab assignment 6: Simple Linear Regression (page 256)

Load the data from the file *auto-mpg.csv* into an **R** variable called *auto*. The file contains information about various cars made between 1970 and 1982. The file contains 398 rows of data. Below is an extract of the first 10 rows to give you an idea of the data.

No	mpg	cylinders	displacement	horsepower	weight	acceleration	model_year	car_name
1	28	4	140	90	2264	15.5	71	chevrolet vega
2	19	3	70	97	2330	13.5	72	mazda rx2 coupe
3	36	4	107	75	2205	14.5	82	honda accord
4	28	4	97	92	2288	17	72	datsun 510 (sw)
5	21	6	199	90	2648	15	70	amc gremlin
6	23	4	115	95	2694	15	75	audi 100ls
7	15.5	8	304	120	3962	13.9	76	amc matador
8	32.9	4	119	100	2615	14.8	81	datsun 200sx
9	16	6	250	105	3897	18.5	75	chevroelt chevelle
10	13	8	318	150	3755	14	76	dodge d100
...	...	...	...	...	...	...	...	...

1. Summarize the data set. What is the mean of mpg?

   Answer:

```
# Load the data
auto <- read.csv("auto-mpg.csv")

# model_year should not be treated as a
# numeric attribute - convert it
auto$model_year <- factor(auto$model_year)
# Summarize
summary(auto)
```

2. What is the median value of mpg?

   Answer: From the output we see that it is 23.00

3. Which value is higher – mean or median? What does this indicate in terms of the skewness of the attribute values? What plots could you use to verify your answer?

   Answer: Mean is higher – Mean:23.51; Median 23.00. This means that the distribution is skewed to the right. We can verify this by plotting a histogram or the density.

4. Draw a histogram of mpg.

   Answer:

```
hist(auto$mpg)
```

   See Figure 197

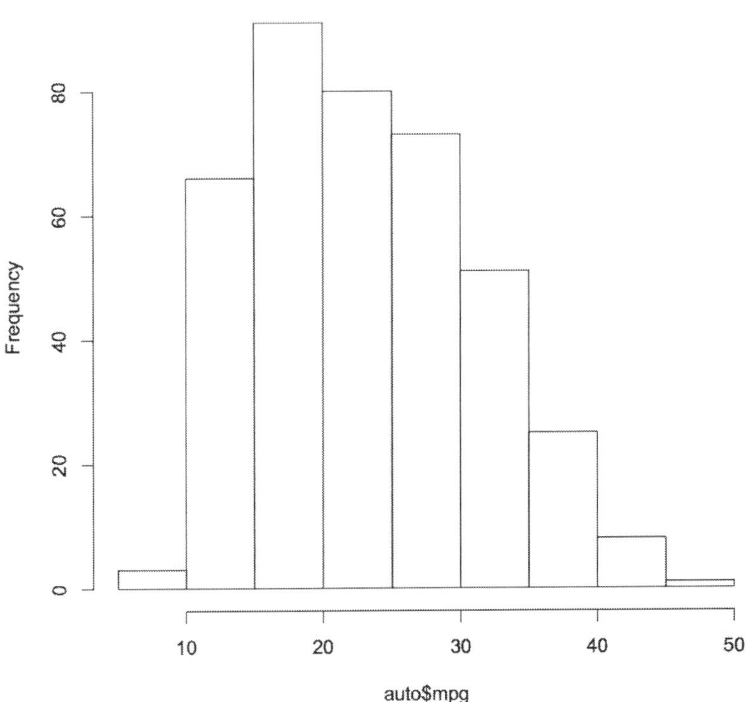

Figure 197: Histogram of auto mpg.

5. Draw a density plot of mpg.

   Answer:

```
plot(density(auto$mpg))
```

   See Figure 198

6. Looking at the histogram and at the mean and median of mpg, can you explain the relative magnitudes of the mean and the median – that is, what about the histogram would lead us to believe that one would be higher than the other?

   Answer: The histogram shows a slight right skew – which is consistent with the mean being higher than the median.

7. Draw a scatterplot matrix of all the relevant numeric attributes.

   Answer: We leave out the column *No*. We have already converted *model_year* into a factor.

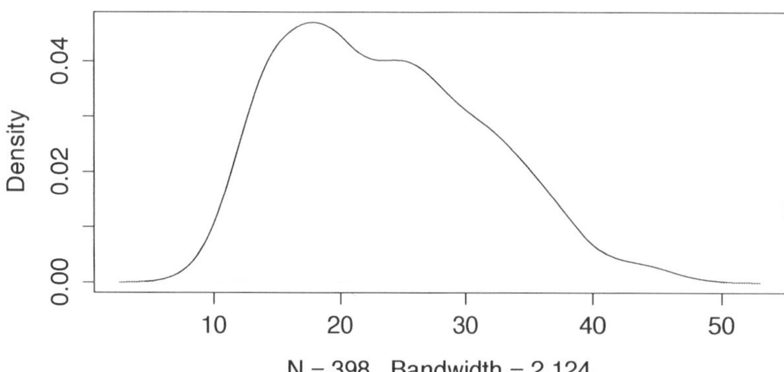

Figure 198: Density plot of auto mpg.

```
pairs(~mpg+cylinders+displacement+
       horsepower+ weight+acceleration, data=auto)
```

See Figure 199

8. Based on the scatterplot matrix, which two attributes seem to be most strongly linearly correlated?

   Answer: It is a toss-up between (*weight*, *horsepower*) and *displacement*, *horsepower*. The points on these two plots line up closest to a straight line. If we want to find out exactly which pair has greater linear relationship, we can compute the correlation coefficients. Some others line up nicely along a curve – but we are looking here for a strong linear correlations and hence lining up well along a curve does not count.

9. Based on the scatterplot matrix, which two attributes seem to be most weakly correlated?

   Answer: *acceleration* and *mpg* because the scatterplot is widely distributed.

10. Produce a scatterplot of the two attributes *mpg* and *displacement* with *displacement* on the x axis and *mpg* on the y axis.

    Answer:

```
# We can do this in one of two ways
# Using the plot function, we specify first the
# attribute for the x axis and then the
# one for the y axis
plot(auto$displacement, auto$mpg)
# Alternately, we can specify what is to
# be plotted in terms of a formula expression.
# The plot function then places the
```

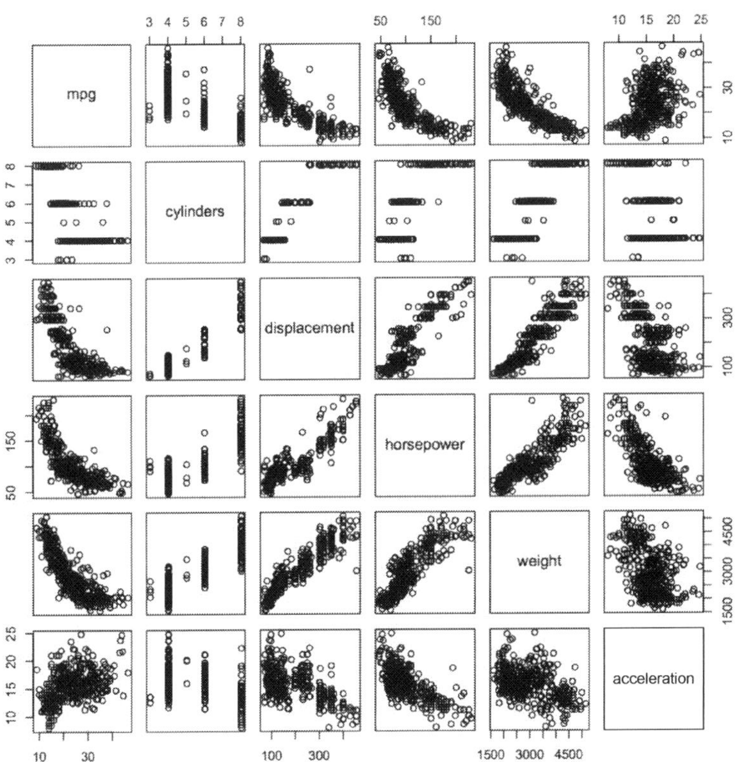

Figure 199: Scatterplot of auto attributes.

```
# target attribute on the y axis
plot(auto$mpg ~ auto$displacement)
# Even better would be
plot(mpg ~ displacement, data = auto)
```

11. Partition the data and store the result in a variable called *adat*.

    Answer:

```
library(caret)
set.seed(2015)
sam <- createDataPartition(auto$mpg,
     p=0.7, list = FALSE)
train <- auto[sam, ]
test <- auto[-sam, ]
```

12. Build a linear regression model with *mpg* as the target and *displacement* as the predictor. Answer the following questions based on the regression model.

    Answer: Use the following command to build the model:

```
auto.mod <- lm(mpg ~ displacement, data = train)
```

Then type the following command to see the details of the model:

```
summary(auto.mod)
```

Figure 200 shows the results.

```
Call:
lm(formula = mpg ~ displacement, data = train)

Residuals:
     Min       1Q   Median       3Q      Max 
-12.6096  -2.9107  -0.4873   2.5541  18.6451 

Coefficients:
              Estimate Std. Error t value Pr(>|t|)    
(Intercept)  34.712873   0.565209   61.42   <2e-16 ***
displacement -0.058618   0.002581  -22.71   <2e-16 ***
---
Signif. codes:  0 '***' 0.001 '**' 0.01 '*' 0.05 '.' 0.1 ' ' 1

Residual standard error: 4.488 on 278 degrees of freedom
Multiple R-squared:  0.6497,	Adjusted R-squared:  0.6484 
F-statistic: 515.6 on 1 and 278 DF,  p-value: < 2.2e-16
```

Figure 200: Simple linear regression output for auto-mpg data.

(a) For your model, what is the value of the intercept β_0 ?
Answer: 34.712873: We see this from near the middle of the regression output.

(b) For your model, what is the value of the coefficient β_1 of the attribute *displacement*?
Answer: -0.058618 : We see this also from near the middle of the output.

(c) For your model, what is the value of the slope?
Answer: -0.058618 : For simple linear regression, the slope is the same as the coefficient of the predictor attribute.

(d) What is the regression equation as per the model?
Answer: $\hat{mpg} = 34.712873 - 0.058618\, displacement$
Note the "hat" sign on top of *mpg* to denote that it is the predicted value that the model calculates.

(e) For your model, does the predicted value for *mpg* increase or decrease as the *displacement* increases?
Answer: In the regression model, *displacement* has a negative coefficient. Therefore as it increases, $\hat{mpg}$ decreases.

(f) By how much does the predicted *mpg* change for every unit change in *horsepower*?
Answer: The predicted *mpg*, $\hat{mpg}$ decreases by 0.058618 for each unit change in *horsepower*.

(g) Given a car with a *displacement* value of 220, what would your model predict its *mpg* to be?

Answer: Plugging in the values into the regression model, we get $34.712873 - 0.058618 * 220$, or 21.817.

(h) What is the RMSE on the training partition?

Answer: From the regression output we see that the RMSE (Residual standard error) is 4.488.

(i) What does this mean in terms of the data and the model?

Answer: This means that on the average, we can expect a predicted value to be off by 4.488 from the actual value.

(j) What proportion of the variability in *mpg* does the model explain?

Answer: From the regression output we can get this from the Adjusted r-squared value: 0.6484. This is the proportion of the variation that the model explains.

(k) Are the intercept and the slope statistically significant?

Answer: From the regression output, we see that they are both at the "***" level. So they are extremely significant.

(l) Compute and store the model predictions on the test partition in an attribute called *fitted*.

Answer: Use the following command to add the predictions to the model:

```
pred.test <- predict(auto.mod, test)
```

(m) What is the mpg of the car on the tenth test row? What is the model's prediction for this car?

Answer: You can use the following command to display the actual mpg and the fitted values (or model predictions) for all test cases:

```
# Use one of the following two
# to get the actual mpg
test[10, "mpg"]
test$mpg[10]

# use the following for the prediction
pred.test[10]
```

We see that the actual value was 32 and the fitted value is 26.79941.

(n) What is the RMSE on the test partition?

Answer:

```
rmse <- sqrt(mean(
          (test$mpg-pred.test)^2))
rmse
```

We see this to be 5.032225. This compares reasonably well with the performance on the training partition.

Review 14: Multiple Linear Regression (page 261)

Table 105. shows a portion of a large data set that contains information about many homes. For each home you can see number of rooms, the floor area, the age of the home in months and the price.

We would like to build a multiple linear regression model to predict the price for future cases when given only the number of rooms, the floor area and the age of the home in months.

rooms	area	age	price
3	1200	50	200000
4	1400	60	220000
3	1100	60	205000
4	1500	60	220000
4	1800	50	300000
4	1600	70	268000
3	1500	70	210000
4	1200	70	230000
5	2000	60	250000
5	1800	50	290000
5	2100	65	310000
5	2200	75	300000
4	1700	80	220000
3	1300	70	190000
3	1200	20	220000
5	2400	20	350000
5	2300	40	300000

Table 105: Extract from data about attributes of several homes.

Answer the following questions based on Table 105.

1. Using the column headings as attribute names, what is the target attribute?

   Answer: Since we aim to build a model to predict *price*, that will be the target attribute.

2. What attributes should serve as predictors?

   Answer: We want to predict the price based on the other attributes and so *rooms*, *age* and *area* will be the predictor attributes.

3. Which of the following represent correct forms of multiple linear regression models for the problem? Following convention, the Greek letters represent the regression coefficients or constants and the "hat" notation denotes the predicted value for an attribute . Select **all** applicable options.

a. $\hat{price} = \beta_0 + \beta_1\, rooms + \beta_2\, area + \beta_3\, age$
b. $\hat{rooms} = \beta_0 + \beta_1\, price + \beta_2\, area + \beta_3\, age$
c. $\hat{price} = \beta_0 + \beta_1\, rooms + \beta_2\, area + \beta_3\, age + \epsilon$
d. $\hat{price} = \beta_0 + \beta_1\, rooms + \beta_2\, area^2 + \beta_3\, age$
e. $\hat{price} = \alpha_0 + \alpha_1\, rooms + \alpha_2\, area + \alpha_3\, age$
f. $price = \beta_0 + \beta_1\, rooms + \beta_2\, area + \beta_3\, age$

Answer: In a correct regression expression, we have the predicted value of the target attribute on the left and a linear expression, comprising an intercept and the predictor attributes on the right.

- The regression equation finds only a *predicted* value. Therefore the attribute name on the left hand side of the equation should have a "hat" on it. This rules out choice f.
- In a regression equation, *the target attribute appears on the left.* Given that *price* is our target attribute, we can rule out choice b.
- The regression equation *should not have an error term* in it. The error term appears only if we show the actual and not the predicted value on the left. This rules out choice c.
- Since we are doing *linear* regression, we can rule out any choice that has a non-linear expression This removes choice d, a quadratic expression.
- The remaining two represent correct choices. The use of the Greek letter beta is merely conventional and we can use any other symbol and therefore choice e is still correct even though it uses alphas.

4. Let us assume that we have built a multiple linear regression model for the above situation and obtained the following results: $\beta_0 = 105756.6$, $\beta_1 = 19054.8$,, $\beta_2 = 62.85$ and $\beta_3 = -627.01$ (the beta values correspond to the left to right order in which the attributes are listed in Table 105

   a. What would the predicted annual price be for a 45 month old home having 3 rooms, measuring 1350 sq. ft?
   Answer: The regression equation is $\hat{price} = \beta_0 + \beta_1\, rooms + \beta_2\, area + \beta_3\, age$. Plugging in the values for the predictors, we get the predicted value as 219553.
   b. What could be a logical explanation for the signs of β_1, β_2 and β_3?
   Answer: We would expect the price of a house to be higher if the number of rooms is higher or if the area is higher. Therefore it makes sense that these two coefficients are positive. On the other hand, the older a house is, the lower a price that we will expect for it, other things being similar. Therefore the negative coefficient for age also makes sense.

c. Based on the regression coefficients mentioned above, what is the error (or, more correctly, *residual*) for the house on the first row?

Answer: Plugging in the predictor attributes into the regression equation, we get a predicted price of 206991. The actual price is shown as 200000. Therefore the residual – $(actual - predicted)$ – is 6991.

5. The regression coefficients mentioned in Question 4 were actually arrived at using only the data in Table 105. Answer the following based on the data in Table 105 and the regression coefficients mentioned in Question 4.

a. Compute TSS (total sum of squares), SSE (sum of squared errors) and SSR (sum of squares regression).

Answer: Table 106 shows the computations.

$price$	$\hat{price}$	$(price - \hat{price})^2$	$(mean - \hat{price})^2$	$(mean - price)^2$
200000	206991	48867090	2020563315	2697885813
220000	232345	152403963	384002293.8	1020238754
205000	194435	111610773	3306914327	2203474048
220000	238630	347084352	177182094.6	1020238754
300000	263755	1313678278	139573514.8	2309650519
268000	238645	861710154	176785649.5	257885813
210000	213305	10925008	1492730951	1759062284
230000	213505	272081726	1477331974	481415224.9
250000	289110	1529592100	1381521443	3768166.09
290000	282810	51694662	952890439.9	1448474048
310000	292260	314709374	1625603499	3370826990
300000	292275	59677943	1626805220	2309650519
220000	238660	348195600	176389648.4	1020238754
190000	200735	115246666	2622041785	3836709343
220000	225801	33649281	683319282	1020238754
350000	339330	113840364	7636876389	9615532872
300000	320505	420463227	4701025323	2309650519
251941		**6105430561**	**30581557149**	**36684941176**
mean		**SSE**	**SSR**	**TSS**

Table 106: Computation of TSS, SSR and SSE.

b. Do the numbers add up?

Answer: We should have TSS = SSR+SSE. But there is a slight discrepancy due to rounding errors when rounding the regression coefficients to two decimal places.

c. How much of the variation in the target attribute does the regression explain? Using the expression $MultipleR^2 = \frac{SSR}{TSS}$, we get 0.8336 as the answer. This means that the regression explains nearly 84% of the variation in the observed prices.

d. What is the RMSE in this example and what does it say about the predictions that this model makes? If the average home price is $250,000, what is the average percentage error that we can expect on the model's predictions?

Answer: We know that the RMSE is the average residual per case. We already know the total of the squared residuals –

SSE – from the previous answer as 6105430561. We can divide this by the number of cases (17) and then find the square root. That is:

$$RMSE = \sqrt{\frac{SSE}{n}}$$

This comes out to be 18951.
This means that, on the average we can expect the model's prediction to be off by around $19,000. If the average home price is $250,000, then the average percentage error will be around 7.6%.

Lab Assignment 7: Multiple Linear Regression (page 271)

Load the data from the file auto-mpg.csv into **R**. The file contains information about various cars made between 1970 and 1982. Although the data are old, we can easily comprehend it and it provides good practice. The file contains 398 rows of data. Table 107 shows the first 10 rows to give you an idea of the data. We want to build a model to predict the fuel efficiency as measured by the *mpg*.

Table 107: Sample of *auto-mpg* data.

No	mpg	cylinders	displacement	horsepower	weight	acceleration	model_year	car_name
1	28	4	140	90	2264	15.5	71	chevrolet vega
2	19	3	70	97	2330	13.5	72	mazda rx2 coupe
3	36	4	107	75	2205	14.5	82	honda accord
4	28	4	97	92	2288	17	72	datsun 510 (sw)
5	21	6	199	90	2648	15	70	amc gremlin
6	23	4	115	95	2694	15	75	audi 100ls
7	15.5	8	304	120	3962	13.9	76	amc matador
8	32.9	4	119	100	2615	14.8	81	datsun 200sx
9	16	6	250	105	3897	18.5	75	chevroelt chevelle
10	13	8	318	150	3755	14	76	dodge d100
...	...	...	...	...	...	...	...	...

Answer: Load the data with the command:

```
auto <- read.csv("auto-mpg.csv")
```

a We want to use all attributes other than *No*, and *car_name* as predictors. Which attributes can be used as is and which ones would need dummies? Do what is needed for these.

Answer: The attribute *cylinders* has numeric values and is perhaps well correlated with fuel-efficiency – more cylinders implies higher gas consumption and hence lower *mpg*. Still, it is possible that the attribute might not be on a proper ratio-scale. We could treat it as categorical and would need dummies for this. Although *model_year* has numeric values, we should treat that also as categorical because the numeric value has no mathematical significance. Recall however that the *lm* function takes care of creating dummies – provided it knows which attributes are categorical. For this we need to convert them to *factors*:

```
auto$cylinders <- factor(auto$cylinders)
auto$model_year <- factor(auto$model_year)
```

b Create a new data frame with just the target and the predictors we will use.

Answer: We have been asked to use all attributes other than *No* and *car_name*.

```
anew <- auto[ , -c(1,9)]
names(anew)
```

c Partition the data and run a linear regression to predict *mpg* in terms of the remaining attributes. Based on the output, what is the approximate RMSE? What does this mean in terms of the model's predictions on the average for the training partition?

Answer: Now that we have all the data we need in our new data frame *anew*, we will partition it and then build and evaluate the model:

```
# Partition
library(caret)
set.seed(2015)
sam <- createDataPartition(anew$mpg, p = 0.7, list = FALSE)
train <- anew[sam, ]
test <- anew[-sam, ]

# Build and view model on training data
auto.lm <- lm(mpg ~ ., data = train)
summary(auto.lm)
```

From the output we see that "Residual standard error" is 2.856. This can be used as the RMSE. It means that on the average the model's predictions on the training partition will be off by around 2.9 mpg – pretty good.

d What percentage of the variation in the target attribute does the regression explain (use the adjusted R-squared value)?

Answer: The "Adjusted R-squared: " value is 0.8576. This means that the regression is able to account for almost 86% of the variation in the target attribute – very good.

e Which coefficients are significant at the 95% level?

Answer: From the output we see that the attributes *displacement*, *acceleration* and *horsepower* are not significant at the 95% level.

We do see that some of the dummy attributes for each factor are not significant, but since some of them are, we just have to treat both *cylinders* and *model_year* as being significant.

f Build a linear regression model with only the statistically significant attributes (at the 95% level) from the previous model. This will involve typing out the predictor attributes explicitly. What percentage of the variation in the target attribute does the new model explain (use the adjusted R-squared value)? What is the RMS Error on the training partition?

Answer: Since we now know the attributes that are significant, we can build a new regression model with those as predictors.

```
auto.lm.1 <- lm(mpg ~ cylinders
    + weight + model_year,
    data = train)
summary(auto.lm.1)
```

We see that the adjusted r-squared now is 0.8562 – marginally worse than before. The RMS Error now is 2.87 – again marginally worse. We did not lose much by eliminating attributes, We got a significantly simpler model at a minuscule cost in terms of performance.

g What is the RMS Error of the new model on the test partition? How does it compare with the RMS Error on the training partition?

Answer:

```
pred.test <- predict(auto.lm.1, test)
rmse <- sqrt(mean(
    (test$mpg-pred.test)^2))
rmse
```

We see that the RMSE on test is 3.39 – as compared with 2.856 on the training partition.

Review 15: KNN for regression (page 278)

A person collected data on many high school students . The data included *height, weight* and the *distance* that each student was able to throw a baseball. Using this data, the researcher is in the process of building a model to predict the distance that a high school student can throw a baseball, knowing only the student's height and weight. Table 108 shows the Training.A partition. For this assignment, we need only the target attribute *distance* and therefore we do not show the values of the other attributes in the table.

Training.A partition			
Case no	height	weight	distance
1	...	...	100
2	...	...	150
3	...	...	175
4	...	...	130
5	...	...	180
6	...	...	108
7	...	...	140
8	...	...	130
9	...	...	170
10	...	...	160

Table 108: Training.A partition: Distance some students threw a baseball.

Table 109 shows the Training.B partition and the three nearest neighbors (with the first being the nearest) in the Training partition.A to each case of the Training.B partition. You can assume that we also have a Test partition that we have not shown here.

Training.B partition				Neighbors in Trg.A		
Case no	height	weight	distance	1st	2nd	3rd
1	...	...	130	1	3	5
2	...	...	170	9	5	3
3	...	...	130	8	4	2
4	...	...	165	10	5	9
5	...	...	140	4	2	8

Table 109: Training.B partition and three nearest neighbors: Distance some students threw a baseball.

Answer the following questions based on the information in Tables 108 and 109.

a For k values of 1, 2 and 3 calculate the predicted distance thrown for the five cases of the Training.B partition and compute the RMSE for each k value.

Answer: Table 110 shows the predicted distances. For each case we can calculate the predicted distance by averaging the distances for the k nearest Training.A neighbors. For example, for case 1 and k=1, we see that the nearest Training.A neighbor is 1 and thus the predicted distance will be the distance in the first training case, which is 100. For case 1 and k=2, the two nearest training neighbors are 1 and 3 and we thus average the distances of the first and third training cases to get 137.5.

Table 111 shows the squared errors and the RMSE values. To compute the RMS errors for a specific value of k, we need to

Training.B case	Predicted distance		
	k=1	k=2	k=3
1	100.0	137.5	151.7
2	170.0	175.0	175.0
3	130.0	130.0	136.7
4	160.0	170.0	170.0
5	130.0	140.0	136.7

Table 110: Baseball throw question: Predicted distances.

find the sum of the squared errors for each case for that value of k and then find the square root. For example, in Table 111, the error for case 1, k=1 is the difference of the predicted distance of 100 and the actual distance 130, or 30. The squared error is thus 30*30, or 900. The other squared errors have been arrived at analogously. To compute the RMSE for k=1, we first add up all the squared errors and then compute the average, which comes out as 1025/5 or 205. The square root of 205 is 14.32.

Training.B case	distance	k=1		k=2		k=3	
		predicted dist	sqr err	predicted dist	sqr err	predicted dist	sqr err
1	130	100.0	900.00	137.5	56.25	151.7	469.44
2	170	170.0	0.00	175.0	25.00	175.0	25.00
3	130	130.0	0.00	130.0	0.00	136.7	44.44
4	165	160.0	25.00	170.0	25.00	170.0	25.00
5	140	130.0	100.00	140.0	0.00	136.7	11.11
		RMSE	14.32		4.61		10.72

Table 111: Baseball throw: RMSE calculations.

b Assuming that you planned to consider only these k values, which one would you prefer? Why?

Answer: We will generally choose the k with the lowest RMSE providing that its RMSE is acceptable. In our case, we get the lowest RMSE as 4.61 for k=2. If we feel that this is sufficiently accurate, we can choose k=2.

c Having chosen your preferred k as above, what would you need to do to check whether the model is ready for use in predicting for new cases?

Answer: Once we have chosen a k based on building the model using the data from the Training.A and Training.B partitions, we will need to ensure that the model works acceptably on the hold-out data in the Test partition as well by computing the RMSE for the chosen k value on the test partition. We can use the model for future cases only if it performs adequately on the test partition too.

Lab assignment 8: KNN for regression (page 285)

1. Use the Boston Housing data[33] [34] to perform a KNN analysis to predict *MEDV* based on the other attributes How does the RMSE compare with what we obtained with Multiple Linear Regression?

[33] D. Harrison and D.L. Rubinfeld. Hedonic prices and the demand for clean air. *J. Environ. Economics & Management*, pages 81–102, 1978

[34] K. Bache and M. Lichman. UCI machine learning repository, 2013. URL http://archive.ics.uci.edu/ml

a **Read the file:**

```
bh <- read.csv("BostonHousing.csv")
names(bh)
```

b **Standardize the data:** Source in the code from the file *dar2ed-scale-many.R* and then:

```
bh <- dar2ed.scale.many(bh, c(1:13))
names(bh)
bh.new <- bh[, 14:27]
```

c **Partition:**

```
library(caret)
set.seed(2015)
samp <- createDataPartition(bh.new$MEDV,
       p = 0.7, list = FALSE)
# Create the train.a partition
train.a <- bh.new[samp, ]
# Store the rest of the data in a
# new variable called rest
rest <- bh.new[-samp, ]
# We need to sample half of the
# rest into the second partition train.b
samp <- createDataPartition(rest$MEDV,
       p = 0.5, list = FALSE)
train.b <- rest[samp, ]
test <- rest[-samp, ]
# verify
nrow(bh)
nrow(train.a) + nrow(train.b) + nrow(test)
```

d **Build knn model:** First source in the functions from the file *dar2ed-knn-reg-functions.R*. Then:

```
library(FNN)
dar2ed.knn.reg.multi(train.a[ ,2:14],
       train.b[ ,2:14], train.a[ ,1], train.b[ ,1],1,10)
```

k=2 gives the lowest RMSE of 3.196.

e **Compute RMSE on test partition:**

```
res <- knn.reg(train.a[ ,2:14], test[ ,2:14],
        train.a[ ,1], 2, algorithm="brute")
rmse <- sqrt(mean((test$MEDV-res$pred)^2))
cat("RMSE  on test data for k=2: ", rmse)
```

We get an RMSE of 3.676 on the test partition – pretty close to that on the training data.

2. Use the Auto mpg data from the file *auto-mpg.csv* to perform a KNN analysis to predict *MEDV* based on the other attributes How does the RMSE compare with what we obtained with Multiple Linear Regression?

   a **Load the necessary packages:**

   ```
   library(FNN)
   ```

   b **Read the data:**

   ```
   auto <- read.csv("auto-mpg.csv")
   ```

   c **Create dummies for *cylinders* and *model_year*:**

   ```
   auto <- dar2ed.dummy(auto, c(3,8))
   ```

   d **Standardize predictors:**

   ```
   auto <- dar2ed.scale.many(auto, 4:7)
   ```

   e **Create new data frame and partition:**

   ```
   auto.new <- auto[ , c(2, 10:13,
          15:26, 28:31)]
   library(caret)
   set.seed(2015)
   samp <- createDataPartition(auto.new$mpg,
          p = 0.7, list = FALSE)
   # Create the train.a partition
   train.a <- auto.new[samp, ]
   # Store the rest of the data in a
   # new variable called rest
   rest <- auto.new[-samp, ]
   # We need to sample half of the
   # rest into the second partition
   samp <- createDataPartition(rest$mpg,
          p = 0.5, list = FALSE)
   train.b <- rest[samp, ]
   test <- rest[-samp, ]
   nrow(auto.new)
   nrow(train.a) + nrow(train.b) + nrow(test)
   ```

   f **Build knn model:** Source in the file *dar2ed-knn-reg-functions.R*

   ```
   library(FNN)
   dar2ed.knn.reg.multi(train.a[ ,2:21],
          train.b[ ,2:21], train.a[ ,1], train.b[ ,1],1,10)
   ```

   We get a minimum RMS error of 3.09 for k=4.

   g **Compute RMSE on test partition:**

   ```
   res <- knn.reg(train.a[ ,2:21],
          test[ ,2:21], train.a[ ,1], 4, algorithm="brute")
   rmse <- sqrt(mean(
   ```

```
        (test$mpg-res$pred)^2))
cat("RMSE  on test data for k=4: ",
        rmse)
```

On the test partition the RMSE is 3.622. Using multiple linear regression, we had got an RMSE of 3.38 on the holdout data.

Review 16: Cluster analysis (page 337)

1. You are given a data set with 1000 cases and can create any number of clusters from 1 to 1000. Answer the following questions based on this scenario:
   a How many clusters should you create in order for all clusters to have complete coherence?

   Answer: 1000. For maximum coherence, each case would be in its own cluster – unless we have cases which have identical values for every attribute, in which case, they can be combined into a cluster.

   b Would you consider the above solution to be useful? Explain.

   Answer: No. In cluster analysis, we look to describe the data in a small number of coherent clusters. Having as many clusters as the original number of cases does not achieve anything.

   c How many clusters should you create if you want to have the highest total value of *within_ss* across all clusters?

   Answer: One cluster with all the data cases. This will have all the variability in the complete data set. As we start creating smaller clusters, we reduce the total value of *within_ss* because each cluster will be a bit more coherent.

   d Would you consider the above solution to be useful? Explain.

   Answer: No. Having just one cluster with all the data would not help, because we want to identify a small number of coherent groups.

2. Table 112 shows some hypothetical data about purchases from a company. For various transactions it shows the number of products purchased and the total dollar value of the transaction (in hundreds of dollars). Someone did an analysis and generated the plot that Figure 201 shows. Answer the following questions based on these.
   a Just by examining the table, how many distinct clusters seem to be obviously present in the data?

   Answer: Two clusters. Three cases with moderate values for the two attributes and three cases with low values for num_prods and high values for total_amt. A scatterplot will show this clearly.

num_prods	total_amt
5	10
10	13
6	9
1	40
2	50
2	40

Table 112: Number of products and total purchase value.

b Explain Figure 201.

Answer: The figure shows a plot of the sum of the *within_ss* values of all clusters against the number of clusters. We see a big drop from 1 cluster to 2. After that we see only a very gradual drop as we increase the number of clusters.

3. Someone created two clusters for this data, with the first three cases in the first cluster and the rest in the second cluster. Table 113 shows the standardized data.

a Compute *total_ss*.

Answer: *total_ss* is the sum of squared deviations in the original data. Since the data has been standardized, the mean is be 0 for each attribute. Thus the sum of squared deviations is just the sum of the squared values of the standardized attributes from Table 113. This comes out to 10.

b Compute *within_ss* for each cluster.

Answer: *within_ss* is the total of squared deviations from the mean for each cluster. Table 114 shows the computations for the first cluster. You can work this out for the second cluster. The values of *within_ss* come out as 1.247 and 0.257.

num_prods_z	total_amt_z
0.197	-0.929
1.673	-0.765
0.492	-0.983
-0.984	0.710
-0.689	1.256
-0.689	0.710

Table 113: Standardized values of the original data.

Table 114: Computation of *within_ss*for review.

	Cluster 1				
	stdz_num_prods	stdz tot_amt	sqr dev num_prods	sqr dev tot_amt	Total sqr dev
	0.197	-0.929	0.349	0.001	0.350
	1.673	-0.765	0.785	0.016	0.801
	0.492	-0.983	0.087	0.008	0.095
Mean	0.787	-0.892		Within_ss	1.247

c Are the above values consistent with what you see in Figure 201? Explain.

Answer: The sum of *within_ss* is 1.504. From what we can see in Figure 201, this is the value of the y axis for two clusters (k=2). So the two are consistent.

d Compute *between_ss*

Answer: See next answer.

e How much of the variance in the original data does the two cluster solution retain?

Answer: We need to compute $\frac{between\_ss}{total\_ss}$.

From the answer to an earlier question, we already know *total_ss* to be 10.

To compute *between_ss*, we have to assume that the data is made up of just the mid-points of each cluster. That is 3 cases with (0.787, -0.892) and three with (-0.787, 0.892). We then need to compute the squared deviations for this data set. Table 115 shows the details. We see that *between_ss* is 8.496. Thus we see that the clustering retains about 85% of the variation in the original data.

Table 115: Computation of *between_ss* for review question.

stdz_num_prods	stdz tot_amt	sq dev num_prods	sqr dev tot_amt	tot sq dev
0.787	-0.892	0.620	0.796	1.416
0.787	-0.892	0.620	0.796	1.416
0.787	-0.892	0.620	0.796	1.416
-0.787	0.892	0.620	0.796	1.416
-0.787	0.892	0.620	0.796	1.416
-0.787	0.892	0.620	0.796	1.416
			Between_ss	8.496

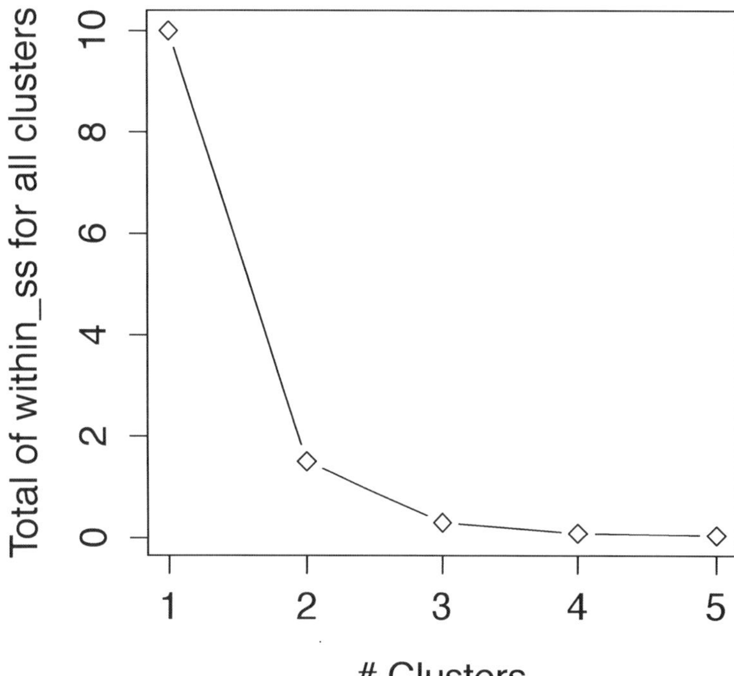

Figure 201: Plot for review question.

Bibliography

Rakesh Agrawal, Tomasz Imieliński, and Arun Swami. Mining association rules between sets of items in large databases. In *Proceedings of the 1993 ACM SIGMOD International Conference on Management of Data*, SIGMOD '93, pages 207–216, New York, NY, USA, 1993. ACM. ISBN 0-89791-592-5. DOI: 10.1145/170035.170072. URL http://doi.acm.org/10.1145/170035.170072.

K. Bache and M. Lichman. UCI machine learning repository, 2013. URL http://archive.ics.uci.edu/ml.

World Bank. Motor vehicles (per 1,000 people), July 2013. URL http://data.worldbank.org/indicator/IS.VEH.NVEH.P3.

M Bohanec and V Rajkovic. Expert system shell for decision making. *Sistemica*, pages 145–147, 1990.

Hadi Fanaee-T and Joao Gama. Event labeling combining ensemble detectors and background knowledge. *Progress in Artificial Intelligence*, pages 1–15, 2013. ISSN 2192-6352. DOI: 10.1007/s13748-013-0040-3. URL http://dx.doi.org/10.1007/s13748-013-0040-3.

Gartner Group. IT glossary, 2013. URL http://www.gartner.com/it-glossary/data-mining/.

D. Harrison and D.L. Rubinfeld. Hedonic prices and the demand for clean air. *J. Environ. Economics & Management*, pages 81–102, 1978.

G. Linoff and M. Berry. *Data Mining Techniques: For Marketing, Sales, and Customer Relationship Management*. IT Pro. Wiley, 2011. ISBN 9781118087459.

D. MacMillan. Netflix, AT&T are real winners of Netflix Prize, September 2009. URL http://www.businessweek.com/the_thread/techbeat/archives/2009/09/netflix_att_are.html.

US Bureau of Labor Statistics. Price of unleaded gas, April 2014. URL http://download.bls.gov/pub/time.series/ap/ap.data.2.Gasoline.

J Ross Quinlan. Combining instance-based and model-based learning. In *ICML*, page 236, 1993.

P. J. Rouseeuw and A. M. Leroy. *Robust regression and outlier detection*. Wiley, 1987.

G. Shmueli, N.R. Patel, and P.C. Bruce. *Data Mining for Business Intelligence: Concepts, Techniques, and Applications in Microsoft Office Excel with XLMiner (Second edition)*. John Wiley and Sons., Hoboken, NJ, USA, 2010. ISBN 0470526823.

P. Tan, M. Steinbach, and V. Kumar. *Introduction to Data Mining, (First Edition)*. Addison-Wesley Longman Publishing Co., Inc., Boston, MA, USA, 2005. ISBN 0321321367.

Athanasios Tsanas and Angeliki Xifara. Accurate quantitative estimation of energy performance of residential buildings using statistical machine learning tools. *Energy and Buildings*, pages 560–567, 2012.

P. Warden. *Data source handbook: A guide to public data*. O'Reilly Media, January 2011.

Wikipedia. Bayes' theorem, February 2014a. URL http://en.wikipedia.org/wiki/Bayes'_theorem.

Wikipedia. Pearson product-moment correlation coefficient, January 2014b. URL http://en.wikipedia.org/wiki/Pearson_product-moment_correlation_coefficient.

Wikipedia. Anscombe's quartet, August 2015. URL https://en.wikipedia.org/wiki/Anscombe%27s_quartet.

Graham J. Williams. *Data Mining with Rattle and R: The art of excavating data for knowledge discovery*. Use R! Springer, 2011. URL http://www.amazon.com/gp/product/1441998896/ref=as_li_qf_sp_asin_tl?ie=UTF8&tag=togaware-20&linkCode=as2&camp=217145&creative=399373&creativeASIN=1441998896.

Made in the USA
Lexington, KY
20 April 2016